T0304301

NETWORKS, TRUST AND SOCIAL CAPITAL

Networks, Trust and Social Capital
Theoretical and Empirical Investigations from Europe

Edited by
SOKRATIS M. KONIORDOS
University of Crete

LONDON AND NEW YORK

First published 2005 by Ashgate Publishing

2 Park Square, Milton Park, Abingdon, Oxon OX14 4RN
711 Third Avenue, New York, NY 10017, USA

Routledge is an imprint of the Taylor & Francis Group, an informa business

First issued in paperback 2016

British Library Cataloguing in Publication Data
Networks, trust and social capital : theoretical and
    empirical investigations from Europe
    1. Economics - Sociological aspects - Congresses 2. Social
    capital (Sociology) - Europe - Congresses 3. Social networks
    - Europe - Congresses 4. Trust - Europe - Congresses
    I. Koniordos, Sokratis M.
    306.3

Library of Congress Cataloging-in-Publication Data
Networks, trust and social capital : theoretical and empirical investigations from
Europe / [edited] by Sokratis M. Koniordos.
        p. cm.
    Papers from the Economic Sociology Research Network of the European Sociological
Association which met at the Helsinki conference held in late August and early
September 2001.
    Includes bibliographical references and indexes.
    ISBN 0-7546-3636-4
    1. Economics--Sociological aspects--Congresses. 2. Sociology--Economic aspects--
Congresses. 3. Social capital (Sociology)--Europe--Congresses. 4. Social networks--
Europe--Congresses. 5. Trust--Europe--Congresses. I. Koniordos, Sokratis M.

    HM548.N485 2004
    306.3--dc22

                                                        2004017828

ISBN 978-0-7546-3636-6 (hbk)
ISBN 978-1-138-26632-2 (pbk)
Transfered to Digital Printing in 2012

Contents

PART A: THEORETICAL INVESTIGATIONS

PART B: INVESTIGATIONS OF EMBEDDEDNESS

List of Figures

List of Tables

List of Contributors

Filippo Barbera	Assistant Professor, Department of Social Sciences, University of Turin.
Christian W. Haerpfer	Professor, Director, Centre for Strategic Development, Institute for Advanced Studies, Vienna and Research Professor, School of Slavonic and East European Studies, University of Glasgow.
Søren Jagd	Associate Professor, Department of Social Sciences, Roskilde University.
Béla Janky	Assistant Professor, Department of Sociology and Communication, Budapest University of Technology and Economics.
Sokratis M. Koniordos	Assistant Professor, Department of Sociology, University of Crete.
Anne Kovalainen	Professor, Department of Management and Organisation, Turku School of Economics and Business Administration.
György Lengyel	Professor, Department of Sociology and Social Policy, University of Economic Sciences and Public Administration, Budapest.
Rafael Marques	Assistant Professor, Centre for Research on Economic Sociology and the Sociology of Organizations, Institute of Economics and Business Administration, Technical University of Lisbon.
Enrica Morlicchio	Associate Professor, Faculty of Sociology, University of Naples, Federico II.
João Peixoto	Assistant Professor, Institute of Economics and Business Administration, Technical University of Lisbon and Research Centre on Economic Sociology and the Sociology of Organisations, Lisbon.

Vadim Radaev   Professor, The State University, Higher School of Economics, Moscow.

Martin Raiser   PhD, Chief Economist, European Bank for Reconstruction and Development (EBRD), London.

Jochen Tholen   PhD, Senior Research Fellow, Institute for Labour and the Economy, University of Bremen.

Claire Wallace   Professor, Institute for Advanced Studies, Vienna and University of Derby.

PART A
THEORETICAL INVESTIGATIONS

Chapter 1

Introduction

Sokratis M. Koniordos

Issues pertaining to networks, trust and social capital have, in one way or another, always been part of sociology's concerns and baggage, although trust and especially social capital were not necessarily clearly identified and used as such from the outset. Still, the notions, their specific if variable conceptualisations, their usage and interconnectedness, are singularly pertinent to contemporary sociology. Indeed, during the last fifteen or so years there has been a proliferation of interest in sociology in the social-capital *cum* trust *cum* networks nexus. Moreover, there has been a trickle-down effect, so that other social science, such as political science, economics, development studies, geography, and in particular social policy, also research and debate these themes.

Possibly the most comprehensive of these notions is that of *social capital*. Social capital directs attention to sociability, to reciprocity and the trust that unfolds within both formal and informal sets of social relations, and is a situational and relational concept. For present purpose it may be provisionally defined as the ability to safeguard benefits through participation in social networks and other social structures, for instance the family (Portes 1988: 8).

While social capital had an earlier undeveloped career (explicitly employed in the 1920 by L. H. Hanifan and much later by the economist G. Loury), there has been new interest in it over the last few years. The idea of social capital rooted itself in the sociological literature after P. Bourdieu had discussed it in the context of educational reproduction and as a form of capital that is convertible to other capital forms (1994 [1980]; 2001 [1985]). In J. S. Coleman's subsequent treatment the concept pertains to micro-level processes (1988; 1990), and it is now often perceived as a suitable candidate for constructing a Mertonian 'middle-range' theory. However, it was after the political scientist R. Putnam (1993a; 1993b; 2000; 2002), who followed a Tocquevillean strand of civic-mindedness, had extended the notion from its individual or collective agency level of analysis to that of communities, regions and even whole countries, that its visibility increased dramatically and its use multiplied rapidly.

According to Putnam, 'social capital ... refers to features of social organisations, such as trust, norms and networks that can improve the efficiency of society by facilitating coordinated actions' (1993a, p. 167). This definition has been employed as the basis for a series of empirical research projects that give priority to individual participation. Criticism of the Putnamian social capital (which

Haerpfer, Wallace and Raiser, in this volume, designate as 'formal' social capital) has since been forthcoming. Criticism of the notion of social capital also touched on the variants of Bourdieu and of Coleman, which have equally been disputed. Is social capital just a metaphor then? Is it an oxymoron? Is it related to the properties of 'real' (i.e. economic) capital and if so, is it expended, replenished and in what way? Is it defined in an unsatisfactory or even circular way? Can it be confounded with trust? Is it quantifiable? A. Portes and his associates (Portes 1998; 2000; Portes and Sensenbrenner 1996; Portes and Landolt 1996; Portes and Mooney 2002), Durlauf (1999; 2002), B. Fine (2001), B. Fine and F. Green (2002), P. Loizos (2002), N. Lin (2001), Woodcock (1998) and several other authors have commented on the issue how to define social capital, on its theoretical standing, on the social scope of the concept, on the appropriate level of generality to which it applies, and on other methodological and analytical difficulties and concerns associated with it.

The proliferation in the use of social capital by a variety of social-science disciplines (Mohan and Mohan 2002; Healy 2001; Fernandez, Castilla and Moore 2000; Fukuyama 1995), by social medicine and social epidemiology (Lindstöm 2003; Cambell, Williams and Gilden), and its diagnosed relevance for social policy (Barbera in this volume), socio-economic development (Trigilia 2001) and modernisation (Inglehart 1997), has added complexity to the meaning and usage of social capital. The notion has acquired an interdisciplinary character (Bertolini and Bravo 2001; Castle 2002) of an extent seldom encountered in the social sciences and has been employed implicitly and increasingly explicitly in the 1990s and the 2000s as a theoretical matrix. Social capital now forms the starting point, the basic premise that is developed in accordance with a farther and more specific definition.

Nevertheless, there have been attempts to synthesis, which are of particular relevance for the on-going debate on how to measure social capital (Onyx and Bullen 1998), how to do so comparatively (Debertin 1998; Foley and Edwards 1998) and internationally (Narayan and Cassidy 2001), which raises the important issue of cultural specificity (Tsujinaka 2002; Robinson 1997) and of the antecedent bias in comparative exercises (Davies 2001; Healy 2002).

The situation is somewhat better with the other two key notions. Thus, *trust* can minimally be seen as reliance (Jones 2001), and social *networks* refer to individuals linked to each other by social relations (see Marshal, 1998, pp. 446-47, also Castells 1997), although there is debate and differentiation over these terms too.

Indeed, trust in its particular senses (e.g. as individual trust, as generalised trust, as 'encapsulated interest' (Hardin 2002)) is understood ideal-typically as a bonding element for primary-type group members – as the 'glue' in the bond. Also, it is understood as a bridge between external social networks, supporting and aiding their interrelationship – in other words it operates as a 'lubricant' of social relations. In either case, it 'can improve the efficiency of society by facilitating coordinated action', according to R. Putnam (1993a, p. 167). It is in this sense that it is claimed that there is a causal link between a high degree of trust, an increase in civicness and participation, and an enhancement in socio-economic development. This claim is put forward despite some serious questioning of the validity of such a causal link – exactly the same concern has been voiced regarding specific conceptualisations of social capital of the same provenance (e.g. by A. Portes). That such critiques are not answered satisfactorily while the trend to adopt and employ the formulation remains largely intact, requires an explanation. Is it a case of Festinger's cognitive dissonance, or does it signify something like a Kuhnian paradigm of institutionalisation?

In any event, empirical data collected on such ground and their policy implications may be prone to political-ideological manoeuvring. A relevant dubious example are that of the pertinent sections on social capital and trust of the *European Social Survey*,[1] and some of the alarmist claims that have been made by certain media invoking them (as was the case in Greece in late 2003), but also by academics too (see Norris and Davis, 2003). Since, the danger appears to be real enough, it is worth considering.

Trust may also be analysed in relation to the concreteness of social relations in a social formation. So, it is seen as more personal in less differentiated social environments that are confronted with real dangers, and as more institutional in modern and more differentiated ones, facing risks.

Networks are much less of a contentious terrain than the other two key notions. Nevertheless, there is a degree of divergence in the focus of studies on networks. For instance, while 'personalised exchange among many agents' may encompass the idea of a network (Rauch and Hamilton 2001), at a more general level networks are understood as visualisations of association that aim at mapping social relations and eliciting social structures and their properties (see Scott 2001). Accordingly social networks have been applied as analytical devices, but also more descriptively as ways of organising relations among agents (Powell and Smith-Doerr 1994, 368), and this is being done in increasingly complex as well as interesting ways (see for instance, Burt 1995; 2000; 2001; Wasserman and Faust 1998; Wellman and Berkowitz 1997).

Within economic sociology social networks have been utilised widely in studies as varied thematically as is business and work organisations, processes of innovation, markets and in particular labour markets, entrepreneurship, inter-firm relations, socio-economic development and in eliciting the role of social capital and trust for economic purposes. The level of analysis has not been unitary either. Consequently, it may assume diverse forms such as that at the level of the individual actor around which the network revolves (actor centrality) (Stokman 2001), that of the networks' structure (systemic), or that concerned with the flows within social networks.

Of course, the task here is *not* to arrive at a singular 'true' or 'proper' definition or conceptualisation or use of the notions of 'social capital', 'trust' or 'social networks'. Such an essentialist objective is beyond our scope, even though one cannot forego all criticism, especially if non-circular conceptualisations are to be advanced. However, the chief interest here is on how these key notions are

---

[1] The complete *European Social Survey* data base, which has specific and most interesting information about the issues discussed in this volume, is accessible at http://ess.nsd.uib.no/ .

employed to aid our understanding of specific situations and problematics. Indeed, this is the rationale for bringing together eleven studies that explore a set of diverse topics, but which are nevertheless linked by the utilisation of the key notions of networks, trust, and social capital.

The papers in this volume originate mostly from the Economic Sociology Research Network of the European Sociological Association, of which it is an integral part, that met at the Helsinki conference, in late August/early September 2001. This is one aspect of the European character referred to in the book's subtitle; the other is that, to my knowledge, it forms the first attempt to discuss some of the prime concerns of economic sociology from an uncertain but emerging European viewpoint.

The volume is organised in three parts for purposes of thematic unity. PART A, entitled 'Theoretical Investigations', contains the studies of *Rafael Marques, Søren Jagd* and *Anne Kovalainen*. The authors present more theoretically oriented papers which explore reciprocity, trust and social capital, the relation of social capital to gender, and the network dimension and cultural aspects of the contemporary 'spirit' of capitalism.

Rafael Marques in *From* Charis *to* Antidosis: *The Reciprocity Thesis Revisited*, takes up the notion of reciprocity as carrying a strongly moral meaning that furthers the continuation of social interaction within small-scale social settings and networks. Reciprocity as an idea and practice is to be found in all cultures, permeating several spheres of social interaction and appearing to be trans-historical. As the author notes, it forms part of the ethical bedrock of societies, and is certainly a cultural universal. Marques hold that reciprocity forms a quintessential dimension of social interaction which, although related to trust, it is not identical with it.

Reciprocity is closely interconnected with social capital. It is a very important but not absolutely necessary element in Portes' (1998) conceptualisation of social capital, although its presence is not necessary for benefits to flow to specific individuals, i.e. those identified as free- riders. In fact, free-riding is nothing other than the absence of reciprocity, so that a particular individual may profit from her/his participation in a network or group without reciprocally contributing in return. Although free-riding may be deemed a rational way for an individual actor concerned with maximising profit, it is a problem when seen from the viewpoint of the network or group as it erodes group cohesion and so the continued generation of social capital. Actually, in the Putnam (1993) conception of social capital, a low level of reciprocity (which operates as the functional equivalent of trust) and/or a high degree of free-riding practices directly and adversely affects the social capital of a region, territory or country. However, for Marques reciprocity is an analytically distinct category that should not be conflated with trust; it may even be empirically distinct, as in when, in the absence of trust, reciprocity functions in the place of trust. The operation of reciprocity involves networks of actors and it is often, but not necessarily, present in materialisations of social capital.

Marques essay advances the creation of an intermediate theory of reciprocity which he believes will facilitate the sociological study of both economic transactions and social exchange.

The overall aim in *Søren Jagd's* paper, *The 'Network Ethic' and the New Spirit of Capitalism in French Sociology of Capitalism*, is to give due attention to the importance of the ideals, beliefs and values of actors in networks, in an attempt to redress the undertheorizing in network analysis. To this end he extensively presents and discusses of Boltanski and Chiapello's (B&C) contribution to the analysis of the cultural aspects of networks. Jagd focuses on the basic model developed by B&C that involves an interplay between various forms of capitalism, on criticism of them that is perceived as indispensable for the continuing survival of capitalism, and on what is designated as the spirit of capitalism. The latter entails a number of portrayals and shared justifications associated with the capitalist order that support its modes of action and dispositions. The spirit of capitalism is thus transformed into a dynamic concept that is applicable to the analysis and interpretation of shifts and adaptations in the forms of capitalism in relation to social change.

Jagd is particularly interested in the critical analysis of what B&C designate as the emergent spirit of 'network capitalism'. Seen as a response to criticism of Fordist capitalist organisation, this new spirit of capitalism has been in the making for the last thirty or so years. It involves a new form of justification, the 'Project World', which also recognises autonomy on the basis of self-knowledge and personal fulfilment. Jagd compares this new spirit of networked capitalism to earlier structural and process-oriented network-perspectives. His purpose in doing so is to find whether the B&C cultural perspective may direct network research into unexplored aspects of modern business organisations.

Anne Kovalainen in her essay *Social Capital, Trust and Dependency* is concerned with the relation, or lack of it, of social capital to gender. Notwithstanding the fact that social capital and its constituent elements are not loaded with the more established and, one could add, solid sociological theoretical categories such as class or power (to which fact one may attribute its plasticity and the great popularity), social capital in the various conceptualisations also fails to incorporate the gender dimension. The question is why this is so, especially given that at the empirical level, social capital and trust in their operation are intrinsically far from gender-blind (as in the case she cites of the Finnish welfare-state reorganisation).

Kovalainen scrutinises key social-capital authors for bringing out the reasons behind the neglect of the gender dimension in their conceptualisations of it. Bourdieu is largely absolved of the charge of ignoring gender because of his overall, sketchy, if path-breaking conceptualisation of social capital. However, Putnam, whose definition of social capital meets the author's approval, is insensitive to gender, while Coleman comes in for a heavier critique. Coleman's formulation, which resembles that of neo-classical economics which is characterised by an inherent a-social orientation, is in line with his rational-choice approach. The agent appears as an atomised male who is largely detached from social ties. More concretely, for Coleman social capital is generated within social structures and especially that of the family, which is stamped by its normative environment; the family itself is generalised in its traditional and more patriarchal form. This means that there are gender-biased assumptions in operation to which social-capital theorists are not sensitised. The implication is that the contextual and gender element inherent in the family is not recognised as such and remains absent; the same is true about the problematics in use with respect to civil society. This, according to Kovalainen, is the root cause for the neglect of gender in this rather more open and flexible notion of social capital as well as in the conceptualisation of trust.

PART B contains several 'Investigations of Embeddedness'. It consists of essays by *João Peixoto, Filippo Barbera, Enrica Morlicchio*, and *Sokratis M. Koniordos*. The essays are attempts to relate their respective empirical material to the idea of social embeddedness, and to show how and where this embeddedness is rooted and, while upholding the embeddedness idea, to indicate some of its possible limitations.

In his paper titled *The Social Foundations of Labour Markets: Foreign Immigration in Portugal*, João Peixoto explores the social foundations of labour markets to show that they do not act strictly by themselves, but are activated by powerful social ties. Drawing on labour immigration into Portugal he shows that social networks actively facilitate specific immigration patterns, and argues that these patterns cannot be reduced to *mere* historical experience or geographic proximity, nor dire economic necessity. He contends that the migratory flows are also propped by exposure to contemporary life-styles and symbolisation, and that these, (as they have a meaning effect) are important for understanding the phenomenon. Peixoto purports to demonstrate how at the heart of the migrant experience lies social embeddedness in networks of intimate social relationships, and specific social practices rooted in society and the meaning this gives them.

Peixoto's focus is on two kinds of network. The one is informal social networks, in which personal ties create channels of information, the framework for decisions, and the conditions for social support and integration that frame the actual migration flows. He considers the role of trust involved in migration processes and argues that personal trust, deeply conditions migration decisions. The second kind are formal social networks that support migration, i.e. trafficking and smuggling, although they disrupt the traditional logic of migration.

Peixoto also examines the migration of a highly skilled segment of the labour force, that of professionals who go to work abroad either independently or within the framework of the upper-tier internal labour market of transnational corporations. He demonstrates that the role of labour markets in migratory flows cannot be explained in only economic terms, but must be coupled with the action of social networks and trust.

Filippo Barbera's essay *Social Networks, Collective Action and Public Policy: The Embeddedness Idea Reconsidered* argues in favour of the idea that social capital, which he considers a key ingredient for development, may be promoted at the local level by deliberate State policies; that the generation of social capital may be purposefully planned by the State. If this is indeed so, this should lead to a partial reconsideration of the Granovetter argument of social embeddedness, since the informal web of networked social relations (as the independent variable) may cause particular effects, i.e. particular kinds of economic activity.

The author warns that for a public policy to have an impact on the creation of social capital it is imperative to avoid conflating it with the social-embeddedness idea; the latter is much wider than the former. It is also necessary to draw a clear distinction between social capital and trust.

To explore the relationship between social capital and public policies, Barbera focuses on the Italian experience of industrial districts and the attempts made there to overcome their crisis. His paper shows that empirically it is possible to generate or stimulate social capital through particular kinds of formal contracts and financial incentives, that are managed from a central institution in a power relationship with peripheral institutions. A theoretical consequence of this setting is that it overturns the perspective of embeddedness: social networks do not explain economic transactions; it is rather that formal contracts and economic exchange become a possible source of social relations.

Enrica Morlicchio in *The Insignificance of Weak Social Ties and the Uselessness of Strong Ones (With Two Case Histories of Low-income Families in Naples)* subscribes to the view that social capital is a general concept as well as an ambivalent one that is made concrete in specific acts and social situation. It therefore can assume contradictory shapes. Accordingly, she opts for a selective use of the social capital notion and focuses on how it operates at the micro-level, the aim being to ascertain its role in a social context of endemic poverty. To do so Morlicchio explores by means of the biographical method two low-class families in the area of Naples that are steeped in intragenerational unemployment and poverty.

Morlicchio takes up Granovetter's thesis on strong and weak ties to argue that its usefulness lies in recognising the importance of the social context for deciphering the relationship between information and choice in a specific context. A social context, such as the one she investigates in the Naples cases may offer little or no opportunity to cultivate either strong or weak ties effective for developing a variety of social capital which actors can draw on in their search for a job or a better job. In other words, in this social setting, the whole exercise of cultivating one's social capital may be structurally blocked, although someone may be capable as the next person to develop relationships, in particular family and other ties. But given the particular context in which they are enmeshed, such primary level networks do not suffice for effectively assisting shifts from poverty into a stable job, as Morlicchio's Naples cases demonstrate.

In his essay *Informal Support Networks in the Making of Small Independent Businesses: Beyond 'Strong' and 'Weak' Ties? Sokratis M. Koniordos* investigates the specific role of informal support networks which working-class agents rely on in their attempt to establish themselves as independent business proprietors in a specific country of the semi-periphery, i.e. Greece. This is a process seen to be analogous to that of obtaining a job that pays wages.

Since the pattern of support provided through these ego-centred appears to have remained over time, more in-depth analysis focuses on the type of the support offered. Utilising the Granovetter metaphor of strong and weak ties, it emerges that both these features are present in the networks in question and, again, both are necessary for realising the objective of setting up an independent workshop. But the social capital these networks are instrumental in mobilising does not suffice for the project of creating a job for oneself by becoming independent. The paper argues that the decisive factor in achieving the objective of independence is the actors' personal agency, which is as much the outcome of personal determination as of socialisation within a specific context and opportunities structure. Indeed, when personal agency is channelled into setting up an independent business and not elsewhere, this must be accounted for. Accordingly it is suggested that the notion of social embeddedness and the institutions in which it is rooted need to be identified specifically and concretely if they are to retain their hermeneutic vigour.

PART C is concerned with 'Investigations of Eastern European Capitalism', and consists of the papers by *Vadim Radaev, György Lengyel* and *Béla Janky, Jochen Tholen,* and *Christian Haerpfer, Claire Wallace* and *Martin Raiser.*

Vadim Radaev in *Informal Institutional Arrangements and Tax Evasion in the Russian Economy* explores the links between formal rules and informal practices in the Russian economy. The emergence of efficient formal rules is usually seen as a consequence of the formalisation of habitual and informal practices developed spontaneously by economic agents, so that new formal rules luck viability if they are not embedded in the norms and practices of everyday life. However, the situation in transition economies where the regulatory framework has been a recent (hierarchical) introduction is such that the new entrepreneurs are not particularly loyal to the formal rules by which they are supposed to abide and which are officially supposed to organise the capitalist *modus operandi* – they do not trust in the existing institutional arrangements.

Radaev recons that the problem lies with the structure of formal economic rules and the way they are introduced into the economy. A spiral of multiple arguments and interpretations between economic agents and officials eventually leads to legitimate practices of rule informalisation. Radaev uses this term to refer to a continuous transformation of institutions when informal ones and built-in informal relationships largely replace formal rules. In a sense this process is the reverse of the norm in earlier capitalist economies. Nonetheless, the set of processes involved seem to embed formal rules in institutional dynamics and on-going social practices. Drawing on empirical material from Russia with regard to tax avoidance and tax evasion, Radaev examines the consequent elements of informalisation by looking at several instances in the development of company compliance with formal rules.

György Lengyel and *Béla Janky* in their paper *Security, Trust, and Cultural Resources: Hungarian Manufacturing Enterprises in the Post-socialist Transformation* investigate in the transition economy of Hungary the impact of material, cultural and social resources on security as perceived in a business environment. They hypothesise that that strong social ties 'tend to reduce uncertainty in business transactions if managers are worse off in terms of material and cultural resources'. Accordingly, they concentrate on the correlation between material and cultural resources, forms of trust based on solidarity and interest, as well as the perception of insecurity among the Hungarian manufacturing firms they have sampled.

Contrary to Lengyel and Janky's initial hypotheses, their research findings indicate that it is the extent of a firm's market width that plays a significant role in perceptions of security. Overall, cultural resources proved more important than material resources. It also emerges that it is not special but general knowledge that is more convertible and contributes to a higher level of security, and that solidarity-based trust too (unlike general trust) is important for security. In addition, the authors emphasise that the picture is too complex to allow one to postulate unidirectional causality.

Jochen Tholen in his *Young Entrepreneurs in the New Market Economies: Cultural and Social Capital as a Basis for Economic Capital* reports on research in several counties of Eastern Europe with regard to the conditions in which entrepreneuring activity unfolds and its distinctive features. In a context of political instability and rapid change, several contrasting patterns were discerned among the counties studied.

Tholen introduces a typology of self-employed entrepreneuring youths of, on the one hand, the 'westernised' young entrepreneur, and on the other the post-Soviet young self-employed. The youths he researched operate in conditions of relative scarcity of material capital. Accordingly, it is very interesting to see how they utilise their education (obtained in State institutions), i.e. their cultural capital, as well as what support they can muster by using their social capital for the purpose of creating economic capital – a process the author describes in some detail.

The study of *Social Capital and Economic Performance in Post-Communist Societies*, is the theme developed by *Christian Haerpfer, Claire Wallace* and *Martin Raiser*. Their paper analyses the impact of social capital on the economic performance of several Eastern European countries. The authors discuss different theories of social capital (often invoked to explain their lagging behind when compared with Western counties), but caution about the validity of the explanations offered for the observed patterns and differences. This leads them to introduce their distinction between formal and informal social capital; they argue only the former can produce non-ambiguous proposals.

The discussion in the paper focuses on evidence from a number of huge samples, with a very cautious reporting on their findings. The authors point out the difficulties in identifying the direction of causality with a degree of accuracy. They note that 'differences in trust among anonymous individuals are not a good explanation for variation in economic performance of the transition countries', while they note that civic participation and trust in public institutions correlate positively with economic performance.

From this position I would like to thank, Byron Kaldis, Anastasia Liapi, Nikos Mouzelis, John Scott and Ellen Sutton for their help and support as well as Claire Annals, Jacqui Cornish, Carolyn Court and Mary Savigar from Ashgate.

One last word: I warmly thank the contributing authors for their papers, and for their patience while this volume was put together. They are absolved of all the shortcomings of this book although they retain, of course, responsibility for their own contributions.

References

Bertolini, S. and Bravo, G. (2001), 'Social Capital: A multidimensional concept', *Euresco Conference*, 'Social Capital: Interdisciplinary perspectives', University of Exeter, 15-20 September 2001.

Bourdieu, P. (1994), 'Social Capital: Preliminary notes', in N. Panagiotopoulos (ed.), *P. Bourdieu: Sociological Texts*, Athens, Delfini, pp. 91-95 (in Greek).

Bourdieu, P. (2001), 'Forms of Capital', in M. Granovetter and R. Swedberg (eds), *The Sociology of Economic Life*, second edition, Boulder, Westview, pp. 96-111.

Burt, R. S. (1995), *Structural Holes: The Social Construction of Competition.* Cambridge, Mass., Harvard University Press.

Burt, R. S. (2000), 'The Network Structure of Social Capital', in R. I. Sutton and B. M. Staw (eds), *Research in Organizational Behavior*, vol. 22, Greenwich, CT., JAI Press, pp. 1-93.

Burt, R. S. (2001), 'Structural Holes versus Network Closure as Social Capital', in N. Lin, K. Cook and R. S. Burt (eds), *Social Capital: Theory and research*, New York, Aldine de Gruyter, pp.31-56.

Campell, C., Williams, B. and Gilden, D. (2002), 'Is Social Capital a Useful Conceptual Tool for Exploring Community Level Influences on HIV Infection? An Explanatory Vase Study from South Africa', *Aids Care*, 14 (1), pp. 41-54.

Castells, M. (1997), *The Information Age: Economy, Society and Culture*, three volumes, Oxford, Blackwell.

Castle, E. N. (2002), 'Social Capital: An interdisciplinary concept', *Rural Sociology*, 67(3), pp. 331-349.

Coleman, J. S. (1988), 'Social Capital in the Creation of Human Capital', *American Journal of Sociology*, 94, Supplement, pp. S95-S120.

Coleman, J. S. (1990), *Foundations of Social Theory*, Cambridge, Mass, Harvard University Press.

Davies, A. (2001), 'But we knew that already! – A study into the relationship between social capital and volunteerism', Conference paper, Anne Davies, Home Start, Sheffield.

Debertin, D. L. (1998), 'A Comparison of Social Capital in Rural and Urban Settings', (mimeograph).

Durlauf, S. N. (1999), 'The Case 'Against' Social Capital' (mimeograph).

Durlauf, S.N. (2002), 'On the Empirics of Social Capital', *The Economic Journal*, 112 (483), pp. 459-79.

Fernandez, R. M., Castilla, E. J., and Moore, P. (2000), 'Social Capital at Work: Networks and employment at a phone center', *American Journal of Sociology*, 105(5), pp. 1288-1356.

Fine, B. (2001), *Social Capital versus Social Theory: Political economy and social science at the turn of the millennium*, London, Routledge.

Fine, B. and Green, F. (2002), 'Economics, Social Capital and the Colonization of the Social Sciences', in S. Baron, J. Field and T. Schuller (eds), *op.cit.*, pp. 78-93.

Foley, M. and Edwards, B. (1998), 'Beyond Tocqueville: Civil Society and Social Capital in Comparative Perspectives', *American Behavioral Scientist*, 41(6).

Fukuyama, F. (1995), *Trust: The social virtues and the creation of prosperity*, New York: The Free Press.

Hardin, R. (2002), *Trust and Trustworthiness*, New York, Russell Sage Foundation.

Healy, T. (2001), 'Networks and Social Norms can be Good for Business: The role of social capital in organisations', *Euresco Conference*, 'Social Capital: Interdisciplinary perspectives', University of Exeter, 15-20 September 2001.

Healy, T. (2002), 'Measurement of Social Capital at International Level', *OECD-ONS International Conference on Social Capital: The challenge of international measurement* – paper 2, London, September 25-27.

Inglehart, R. (1997), *Modernization and Postmodernization: Cultural, economic and political change in 43 societies*, Princeton, Princeton University Press.

Jones, K. (2001), 'Trust: Philosophical aspects', in *The International Encyclopedia of the Social and the Behavioral Sciences*, pp. 15917-22.

Levi, M. (2001), 'Trust: Sociology of', in *The International Encyclopedia of the Social and the Behavioral Sciences*, pp. 15922-26.

Lin, N. (2001), 'Building a Network Theory of Social Capital', in N. Lin, K. Cook and R. S. Burt (eds), *op.cit.*, pp. 3-29.

Lindstöm, Martin (2003), 'Social Capital and the Miniatirization of Community Among Daily and Intermittent Smokers: A population-based study', *Preventative Medicine*, 36 (2), pp. 177-184.

Loizos, P. (2002), 'Are Refugees Social Capitalists?', in S. Baron, J. Field and T. Schuller (eds), *op.cit.*, pp. 124-41.

Marshall, G. (1998), *Dictionary of Sociology*, Oxford, Oxford University Press.

Mohan, G. and Mohan, J. (2002), 'Placing Social Capital', *Progress in Human Geography*, 26(2), pp. 191-210.

Narayan, D. and Cassidy, M. F. (2001), 'A Dimensional Approach to Measuring Social Capital: Development and validation of a social capital inventory', *Current Sociology*, 49(2), pp. 59-102.

Norris, P and Davis, J. (2003), 'A Continental Divide? Social Capital in the US and Europe', http://naticent02.uuhost.uk.uu.net .

Onyx, J. and Bullen, P. (2000), 'Measuring Social Capital in Five Communities in New South Wales', *Journal of Applied Behavioral Science*, 36(1), pp. 23-42.

Portes, A. (1998), 'Social Capital: Its origins and applications in modern sociology', *Annual Review of Sociology*, 24, pp. 1-24.

Portes, A. (2000), 'The Two Meanings of Social Capital', *Sociological Forum*, 15, pp. 1-12.

Portes, A. and Landolt, P. (1996), 'Unresolved Mysteries: The Tocqueville Files II: The downside of social capital', *The American Prospect*, 7 (26), May 1-June 1.

Portes, A. and Mooney, M. (2002), 'Social Capital and Community Development', in M. F. Guillén, R. Collins, P. England and M. Meyer (eds), *The New Economic Sociology: Developments in an emerging field*, New York, Russell Sage Foundation, pp. 303-29.

Portes, A. and Sensenbrenner, J. (1996), 'Embeddedness and Immigration: Notes on the social determinants of economic action', *American Journal of Sociology*, 98(6) pp. 1320-1350.

Powell, W. W. and Smith-Doerr, L. (1994), 'Networks and Economic Life', in N. J. Smelser and R. Swedber (eds)(1994), *The Handbook of Economic Sociology*, Princeton/New York, Princeton University Press/Russell Sage Foundation, pp. 368-402.

Putnam, R. D. (1993b), 'The Prosperous Community: Social capital and public life', *The American Prospect*, 4 (13), March 21.

Putnam, R. D. (2000), *Bowling Alone: The collapse and revival of American community*, New York: Touchstone.

Putnam, R. D. (2002), 'Proposed Questions for CPS Supplement on Social Capital', Annex in L. Hudson and C. Chapman, 'The Measurement of Social Capital in the United States', Paper for the *OECD-ONS International Conference on Social Capital: The challenge of international measurement*, London, 25-27 September, pp. 12-14.

Putnam, R. D., with Leonardi, R. and Nanetti, R. Y. (1993a), *Making Democracy Work: Civic traditions in modern Italy*, Princeton University Press, Princeton, NJ.

Rauch, J. E. and Hamilton, G. G. (2001), 'Networks and Markets: Concepts for bridging disciplines', in J. E. Rauch and A. Castella (eds), *Networks and Markets*, New York, Russell Sage Foundation, pp. 1-29.

Robinson, D. (ed.) (1997), *Social Capital and Policy Development*, Institute of Policy Studies, Wellington, New Zealand.

Scott, J. (2001), *Social Network Analysis: A handbook*, second edition, London, Sage.

Stokman, F. N. (2001), 'Networks: Social', in *The International Encyclopedia of the Social and the Behavioral Sciences*, pp.10509-14.

Trigilia, C. (2001), 'Social Capital and Local Development', *European Journal of Social Theory*, 4(4).

Tsujinaka, Y. (2002), 'The Cultural Dimension in Measuring Social Capital: Perspectives from Japan', *OECD-ONS International Conference on Social Capital: The challenge of international measurement* – paper 5, London, September 25-27.

Wasserman S. and Faust K. (1998), *Social Network Analysis: Methods and applications*, Cambridge, Cambridge University Press.

Wellman, B. and Berkowitz, S. D. (eds)(1997), *Social Structures: A network approach*, JAI Press, Greenwich, CT.

Woolcock, M. (1998), 'Social Capital and Economic Development: Towards a theoretical synthesis and policy framework', *Theory and Society*, 27(2), pp. 151-208.

Chapter 2

From *Charis* to *Antidosis*: The Reciprocity Thesis Revisited[*]

Rafael Marques

Introduction

Sociological thought has devoted some attention to the reciprocity concept, but has failed to present a comprehensive description and identification of the phenomenon. This paper can be seen as an initial tentative approach to devising a middle-range theory of reciprocity. Reciprocity theory can offer some valuable contributions to Economic Sociology, especially with regard to the study of economic transactions and social exchange mechanisms (*antidosis*). In order to do so, the concept of reciprocity should cease to be seen as a mere substitute for cooperation and virtue or, as the Greek epinician poets put it, as a form of *charis*. Reciprocity is a powerful social mechanism capable of explaining some paradoxical features of social life that defy common sense or assertions taken to be true by economists and sociologists. Exchange contexts, where trustful relations are nuclear, may be regarded as very suitable starting blocks for the study of reciprocity and confirm the validity of the hypothetical statements launched in this paper.

The Constellation of Reciprocity

As a social practice, reciprocity can be considered as the moral memory of mankind. Reciprocity expresses what societies, communities and even small groups define as the appropriate ways and means to react to someone's moves, be it in terms of offences or sympathy. Reciprocity is a civility mode that averts widespread bloodshed, by containing conflict within well-defined social groups,

[*] A first version of this paper was presented at the Fifth Conference of the European Sociological Association (ESA), Economic Sociology Research Network, University of Helsinki, Finland, 28th August – 1st September 2001. A second version was presented at a conference on the Ethics of Social Policy at the University of Bath in June 2002. I thank the participants of both conferences and several colleagues for their very useful comments. The errors and shortcomings are the exclusive responsibility of the author.

even at the cost of high levels of violence inside these groups. Reciprocity is sufficiently disseminated across the globe to be taken as a cultural universal. It is almost impossible to find a society or a religion without formal references to it. The Rg Veda,[1] the Mahabaratha,[2] the Bible, the Koran,[3] the Edda[4] are all good examples of the pervasive nature of reciprocity in different cultures and in different times.

All societies define their particular ways of dealing with reciprocity. *Xenia* (Reece, 1993),[5] *antidosis*,[6] liturgies[7] and *charis* (Maclachlan 1993),[8] in classical Greece, evergetism (Veyne, 1976) in ancient Rome, the *lex tallionis* in the Jewish world, the ill-omens passed on by gift-giving in India (Raheja 1988), *guanxi* in China (Yan 1996; Yang 1994), *giri* and *gimou* in Japan (Lebra 1976), *blat* in Russia (Ledeneva 1998),[9] Mensur duelling in XIXth century Germany (McAleer 1994), thaumaturgic actions by the French and English kings until the 1800s (Bloch 1983), agonistic competition in sport, the *kula*-ring in the Trobriand Islands, the *potlatch* among the *Kwakiutl* are all excellent examples of the durable character of reciprocity and constitute a vivid testimony of its plasticity and capacity to adapt. Reciprocity survives in completely different social settings and under the most severe economic conditions. But reciprocity is not an archaism or an

---

[1] The Rg Veda is a very appropriate way to start a discussion on reciprocity. Many authors who studied the concept (including several experimental economists) begin their papers with a short citation from the Hindu text: 'The first to offer a gift, I consider him to be the king of men'.

[2] The Mahabharata, the great Hindu epic specifies with much clarity the five reasons that justify gift giving (duty, self-interest, fear, love and piety). At the same time, it offers us a hint as to the appropriate moments and occasions in which to give, while not ignoring the polite ways to give, in considering the roles of giver and receiver. Marcel Mauss was deeply influenced by the Mahabharata, and we can find important echoes of the epic in the *Essai sur le Don*. To him, *the* Mahabharata expresses a gigantic potlatchian process (Mauss 1988, p. 160). Mauss, mindful of Mahabharata's Book XIII, cleverly discovers that reciprocity relates not only to the stringent rules regulating the acceptance or refusal of gifts (following conventions of etiquette), but also to the ambiguity of bestowing gifts, equating to the possibility that the gift may rapidly turn into poison. An exchange of favours can easily become an exchange of bad omens or retaliatory moves.

[3] The Bible and the Koran are full of fine examples of positive and negative reciprocity. A close comparison of the more 'retaliatory' Old Testament and the more 'sympathetic' would certainly shed some light on the ebbing and flowing of the reciprocity issue across cultures.

[4] The Edda is certainly one of the most perfect examples of the canonical way to address negative reciprocity.

[5] Hospitality.

[6] Exchange.

[7] Performance of public duties by wealthy citizens.

[8] Grace.

[9] *Guanxi*, *giri* and *blat* are all expressions of the same social practice: a favor exchange situated at the frontier between what is considered appropriate and what is regarded as socially unacceptable.

anthropological curiosity; its roots go deep and we can certainly find its seeds in today's societies.

Reciprocity can also be seen as a civilizing mechanism, operating as a refining device that averts hot-tempered reactions. Those who give must wait for the reaction of their counterparts before they can repeat the act. Those who receive must wait and think before they can return the favour with the right counter-gift. By establishing a rule of alternance between gift and counter-gift (no one gives twice in a row) and by imposing a time lag between these two movements, reciprocity proves to be an excellent example of a social process of refinement and sophistication. The time lag can be seen as a clever way to create social distance, thus helping to avoid hot-tempered reactions.

Despite the centrality of the concept in social theory, we have to recognize that most of the contributions put forward by sociologists and anthropologists are extremely narrow-minded, constituting an impoverished interpretation of the reciprocity phenomenon. Reciprocity is generally regarded as a social device that fosters cooperation, promotes solidarity and guarantees social order. In other words reciprocity is an easy, elegant way to solve the so-called Hobbesian problem (how can we achieve social order with selfish and rational social actors that only want to advance their positions and maximize their utilities?). Following the major statements of this conception, reciprocity can be considered as a non-contractual device that promotes high levels of cooperation in non-market economies.

However, reciprocity cannot be reduced to a simple form of cooperation and solidarity based on a series of gift-giving practices. Contrary to some authors' expectations, reciprocity is not entirely destroyed by market forces and its role is not reduced to an archaic exchange mode. Reciprocity coexists with markets even in the most advanced economies of today. A closer look at different forms and manifestations of the phenomenon reveals that reciprocity is much more than a mere form of exchange (as it was defined by Karl Polanyi) or a clever way of promoting solidarity in traditional communities. There is another obvious dimension in reciprocity that we cannot forget: retaliation, competition and agonism. Reciprocity involves two different dimensions: cooperation embedded in symbiotic and asymmetrical relations; competition among peers subject to a rule of emulation whereby the status distinction and social prestige are the consequence of the prodigality shown by the relevant social actors. At the same time, we should bear in mind the fact that gift giving creates debts and social obligations that can cause resentment and discomfort. Quite literally there is always some sort of 'poison in the gift', an element emphasized by Benveniste (1969a, 1969b), in his analysis of the Indo-European vocabulary, and clearly shown by Gloria Godwin Raheja (1988) in her anthropological studies on India.

In many different areas reciprocity is currently presented as some sort of magical solution to the problems posed by the globalisation process, the market crisis or the impasses facing the new social order. Several programs that invoke reciprocity as their ideological framework have been developed over the last 30 years. Some, like the M.A.U.S.S. (Mouvement anti-utilitariste pour les sciences sociales) propose reciprocity as the basis for a new economy; others, like the economist and philosopher Serge-Christophe Kolm (1984) advance the idea that reciprocity can be the foundation of a new/good economy capable of fulfilling the ideals of the French Revolution, by emphasizing the most widely neglected element of the ideology of 1789: fraternity. Others, such as Gibbard (1990) or Becker (1990), go as far as to consider that reciprocity is the most promising prospect to edify a new ethical pattern. Amitai Etzioni (1988, 1991, 1993) and his communitarians, together with Robert Bellah and his associates (1985, 1992) indicate that reciprocity can be an interesting basis for recovering the traditional communitarian values to be adapted to a new social context.

But recently the reciprocity project has become more than a simple area of discussion for academics. Some visionaries in Canada, France or Germany have tried to use the idea of reciprocity as a real opportunity to develop a freer and more just economic system, capable of combating poverty and social exclusion. The Anglo-Saxon promoters of the LETS (Local Exchange Trading Systems), together with the German-speaking defenders of the *Tauschring* and the French orientated supporters of the SEL (Systèmes d'Échange Local) elect reciprocity as the pillar of their endeavour, considering reciprocity to be the only viable basis upon which to erect alternative communities outside the global world. The SEL, the LETS or the Tauschring are interesting essays of allowing the reciprocity argument to leave the academia and enter the real world.

Many authors, however, refuse the idea that reciprocity is limited to some sort of reserve space, a protected enclave, a peaceful haven or an alternative community for all who have been deserted by today's societies. Titmuss (1997) in a book originally published in 1970, used a model of indirect reciprocity to prove that gift giving is simultaneously safer, more efficient and morally more sound than the market when it comes to supplying the hospitals' blood banks. At the time it was published, Titmuss's book was seen as a warning against blood bank contamination by the Hepatitis B virus. Thirty years later it is the spectre of the HIV virus that makes Titmuss's exposition so vivid. The arguments used by Titmuss (in a famous discussion that was closely monitored by prominent economists, such as Arrow and Solow) were specifically designed to prove that the market would entirely crowd-out the altruism of the gift, thus causing a quality decline in the blood supply.

This debate is still very much alive, especially in the areas of organ procurement. Following Titmuss, Thorne (1998a, 1998b, 2000) claims that the introduction of market mechanisms in the organ procurement area would actually reduce the supply of organs available for transplants, on account of crowding-out effects. Those willing to donate their organs would refuse to sell them and see them turned into commodities. The only solution possible is to rely on incentives and exhortation to attract more donors. The arguments of Thorne have been consistently challenged by authors who favour the market solution to the organ shortage (Addams III *et al.* 1999; Barnett and Kaserman 1992, 1995, 2000).

The economic value created by reciprocity has been a major source of discussion among economists in the past ten years, especially since Waldfogel (1993, 1996, 1998) published his articles on the deadweight loss of Christmas. After conducting some experiments, Waldfogel asserted that the cost of the

Christmas gifts to the givers exceeded by far the subjective value attributed to them by the recipients, meaning that a direct transfer of money would be more efficient for all. Opposition mounted and several studies (*cf.* List and Shogren 1998; Solnick and Hemenway 1996, 1998) have tried to prove Waldfogel wrong. According to his critics, Waldfogel failed to understand both the social pleasure associated with giving and receiving, and the importance of social bonds established by the gift. Estimating the cost of a gift is only one part of the equation, but probably not the decisive one.

Reciprocity's inner dynamic cannot be reduced to a simple exchange or to a straightforward mechanism of give and take. As Marcel Mauss claimed in his famous *Essai sur le Don*, reciprocity defines a type of transaction that can best be described as a total social phenomenon, involving all the sectors and forms of social life. The potential of the concept of reciprocity can also be shown by the fact that we cannot limit its scope to balanced social relationships. This is the kind of error that most authors seem to fall into, without even noticing it. Reciprocity, like power (defined here in the sense of Simmel or Crozier as an asymmetrical, reciprocal and changeable social relationship) is always a social relationship that bears the remarkable trait of often being a paroxysmic, sumptuous practice that can never be limited to a perfectly well-balanced relationship. Only rarely can we find, in the realms of reciprocity, the just measure or the fixation of a balanced perspective. What best describes the dynamic of reciprocity is the practice of power and status games. Anyway, we can easily define two main types of reciprocity: one based on gifts, bequests, exchange of favours, aid, charity, philanthropy or, in a single word, altruism (positive reciprocity); and another, based on revenge, threat, menace, violence and spirals of mimetic desire (Girard 1972; Lacourse 1987), that can be defined as negative reciprocity. In the light of this consideration and mindful of the sumptuous character of this type of relationship, we have a clear sign that reciprocity is an important emotion management device (Elias 1987, 1989, 1993; Scheff 1990).

Reciprocity is what we could call, using a French expression, *un mot valise*, in that it contains too many simultaneous meanings. Each author seems to have a particular view of reciprocity that is quite incompatible with that of his fellow researchers. As it is a *portmanteau word*, reciprocity is a very dangerous concept to be used as the building block of a new sub field of research. In saying that we are clearly acknowledging that the use of reciprocity as a central concept in Sociology or Social Policy can be more a source of problems than a productive asset. In fact, reciprocity is used in such a loose way that we can easily find it associated with trust, cooperation, solidarity, friendship, altruism, etc. Usually these types of concepts, that are prone to successive adjacencies, are not the best solution when it comes to building a theory that can score high in terms of explanation, description and prediction. And yet, reciprocity seems to be one of the most promising concepts when it comes to granting a sound methodological basis to Sociology or to Social Policy.

A Brief History of the Reciprocity Concept

Although its coinage is difficult to establish, we know that the word reciprocity entered the vocabulary of the social sciences mainly through the efforts of several anthropologists, namely Thurnwald, Malinowski and Mauss. We can obviously consider that Mauss (1998) in his *Essai sur le Don* is the true founder of the modern concept of reciprocity.[10] His canonical model of reciprocity is based on the idea of a triple obligation: to give, to receive and to render (almost certainly inspired by the three Charites/Graces myth). If the references to Thalia, Aglaea and Euphrosyne give us a clear picture of what reciprocity seems to be (expressing beauty, grace, elegance and poetry – the *charis*), we have to admit that this classical definition does not pay full respect to the wealth of the concept and does not take into account some of the more important levels of the phenomenon. Although Mauss's analysis became the starting point for every author interested in discussing reciprocity, a sense of uneasiness was always felt by all dealing with the issue of the mechanism involved in the obligation to return a gift. The particular solution found by Mauss – the *hau* – was never taken to be a very serious one. Some went as far as to say that Mauss was completely mystified by the Maori, Ranapiri's description of the hau. Ironically, the fruitful reciprocity thesis was probably based on an error of interpretation.

Howard Becker (1956) was so convinced of the importance of the reciprocity concept that he coined the term *homo reciprocus*. This type of approach is symptomatic of the uneasiness of sociologists towards the concept of *homo œconomicus* proposed by mainstream economics. Each sociologist tried to present his own particular and general term that could provide a valuable option to the dominating view on the human subject. Thus, in a way, the idea of reciprocity becomes a sort of alternative to the views that consider the human being as a rational, selfish individual, always ready to defect and to choose the best way to

---

[10] We should not forget that there are as many interpretations of Mauss as there are authors who read it. Each one tends to read the *Essai* in a quite one-sided way. Levi Strauss defined one of the most important lines of research by underlining the structural elements of Mauss's work and seeing reciprocity as a prototypical form of exchange, comparing it to the incest taboo, in the sense that both concepts deal with the dividing line between nature and culture. More recently, Annette Weiner (1992) and Maurice Godelier (1996) presented what they claim to be an entirely new perspective on reciprocity. Based on a new analysis of the data collected by Malinowski on the subject of the *kula ring* and with a direct observation of the Polynesian societies that were the starting point for the definition of reciprocity, both authors presented what seems to be a Copernician revolution. Their thesis is very simply a reversal of the canonical perspective that places emphasis on the act of giving. For them, the most important issue is that the act of giving is performed to avoid losing those goods and objects that are considered to be the expression of the identity of the group. Their thesis is known as the paradox of keeping while giving and is intended to be a return to the original message of Mauss, liberating it from the misinterpretations of Strauss. Furthermore, this new framework of analysis enables us to take into account a forgotten dimension: women's contribution to the circulation ring.

further his own objectives and achieve his particular pleasures. Having said that, we are implicitly recognizing that the concept of reciprocity was to become a very poetic, romantic view on the human being, fostering an image of altruism and self-sacrifice, as opposed to opportunism. This is a view of reciprocity as poor as the one presented by those who consider it as a traditional mechanism only suited to describe the practices of archaic societies. At the same time, we have a further problem. If the concept of *homo œconomicus* is obviously anchored in the domains of rationality (which facilitates the formalisation of scientific models), we have yet to find the corresponding link, when it comes to the analysis of *homo reciprocus*. The difficulty lies in the fact that reciprocity is far from being a linear concept. We cannot define reciprocity through the filter of altruism, as is commonly done by many social scientists, because reciprocity is, at the same time reason and emotion; morality and power; nature and culture. The wealth of the concept and its huge potential are derived from this simple fact.

In 1960, Alvin Gouldner presented a first major synthesis in which he tried to offer some insight into the possibility of building a theory of reciprocity. Unfortunately, this project was never fully developed and the promises made at the time remain unfulfilled. From then on, countless authors, particularly anthropologists, have devoted the best of their efforts to proving the usefulness of the concept. The concept seems to be more appropriate to the study of East Asian societies than to the description of the western world. The Japanese practices of *giri* and *gimou*, the Chinese *guanxi* or the Indian practices of transferring bad omens with the gifts are all clear expressions of the validity of the concept outside the western world. In the West, reciprocity was mainly regarded as the last relic of some ancestral practices and a useful approach to the study of traditional societies.

Reciprocity is a boundary concept. As it lies on the frontier between opposing worlds, contrasting schools of thought can activate reciprocity simultaneously without losing its illuminating potential. Functionalists and Methodological Individualists; Marxists and Conservatives; Communitarians and Liberals have all, in some particular way, used this concept and applied it to their particular needs. This incongruous capacity for semantic multiplication turns reciprocity into an odd concept. Far from the traditional dichotomies received from our classical sociological schools, reciprocity is, above all, a bridge or a linking pin between contrasting and opposing views.

Reciprocity is used independent of the particular research agendas or theories that we decide to adopt. The plasticity shown by this concept is one of its major assets, a fact that can be confirmed by the use made by authors that are concerned with trust, community and the non-contractual bases of society (Etzioni, 1988 1993; Etzioni and Lawrence 1991; Burgenmeier 1994), but also by authors that defend that social life can be best described by rational choices (Schelling 1980, 1986; Coleman 1990). With the help of reciprocity schemes it is possible to build a scenario in which the altruistic behavior and the moral action occur without the presence of a rigid constraint or without an oppressive socialisation.

During the eighties and the nineties several efforts have been made to bring back the concept of reciprocity to the limelight of social theory. Seaford's (1994) used it to describe the Greek world of Odysseus and the tragic models of Euripides, Sophocles and Aeschylus; Lawrence Becker's (1990) systematic construction of a moral system based on deontic virtues and the contributions of the M.A.U.S.S. journal (1990, 1993, 1994; Nicolas 1996) show us the huge potential for explanation that reciprocity can contribute to the social sciences in general and to Economic Sociology in particular. The concept has also been used to serve many and sometimes contradictory objectives. Lewis Hyde made it a piece of his argument against the commodification of art. Girard (1972) considered it to be a basis of the perverse mimetic process that fosters violence and channels it to convenient scapegoats. Derrida entered the discussion (1992, 1995) with two polemic works questioning the possibility of a pure gift (without reciprocation).

The last few years have witnessed a renewed interest by economists and sociologists in the reciprocity theme, specially from the perspective of exchange theory (Blau, Emerson, Cook), but also around the themes of cooperation (Axelrod 1984; Macesich 1994), order and justice (Sugden 1986), collective action and agency theory (Bendor and Mookherjee 1985; Frey 1997), risk sharing (Coate and Ravallion 1993), altruism (Spicker 1988; Solow 1994), obligation mechanisms (Swaney 1990), trust (Allat and Yeandle 1992), negotiation and commitment (Richardson, 1987), emotional strategies (Frank, 1988), or sacrifices (Arnoux *et al.* 1993). At the same time the rediscovery of Polanyi's works (1957, 1983), reintroduces the question of reciprocity at the core of Economics discussions. This new direction taken by several economists regarding reciprocity not only departs from the more traditional views on the subject (almost exclusively cantered on the discussion of international treaties, trade negotiations, bilateral agreements, competition regulation mechanisms and insurance systems), but also tends to converge into an area where the contributions of sociology, political science, and cognitive psychology share common ground.

Antidosis or the Exchange Side of Reciprocity

Traditionally, that is, until the 1980s, reciprocity was narrowly conceived by economists as nothing more than a practice of mutual favours and protectionism between two countries, a practice that constituted a major obstacle to the general practice of free trade around the world. However, since the beginning of the 1980s several experiments in game theory, specially the development of new games like ultimatum, dictator, gift giving, moonlighting or trust made is possible for a new field of research to emerge. Experimental Economics replaced International Trade Theory as the main producer of studies on reciprocity inside the Economics field.

The definitions of reciprocity advanced by experimental economists, during the last three decades, reveal some important traits that should be addressed by our middle-range theory of reciprocity. Marking an important departure from the so-called standard or neo-classical model, experimental economists use the concept of reciprocity as a cornerstone for the enlightenment of actions and behaviours that do not seem to fit the usual explanations given by the rationality modelling of economic and social exchange. Awkward situations such as preferring less to more or incurring in important costs with the sole purpose of retaliating are difficult to reconcile with the standard model, but are easily explained by the reciprocity thesis. In this section, we shall try to synthesize the contributions made by experimental economists by means of a meta-analysis of over 200 papers published from the early 1980s until 2001 (Marques 2001). Although, among experimental economists, important internal differences exist between authors and schools of thought, it is possible to find a coherent project, reduced to a set of simple, verifiable theoretical propositions. Ultimatum (Bolton and Zwick 1995; Gale *et al.* 1995; Güth *et al.* 1992), dictator (Ben-Ner and Putterman 1998; Bohnet and Frey 1999; Bolton *et al.* 1998), trust (Bolle 1998; Burnham *et al.* 2000) or moonlighting (Abbink *et al.* 2000) games are clever devices that can be used to illustrate some of the more relevant aspects of the reciprocity thesis. Despite their obvious shortcomings, they will be used in support of our own thesis.

All reciprocity definitions used by experimental economists emphasize the idea of cost (*cf.* Rabin 1993). This means that reciprocation of an action either involves costs or sub-optimal gains, whether it be in terms of positive reciprocity (rewarding those who acted nicely), or in terms of retaliation (punishing those who defect). To reciprocate is to agree to earn less than would possible if we were to use a *homo œconomicus* motivation only. The rationale behind this kind of behavior does not result from an optimising or maximizing orientation but from a strong attachment to an equity rule (*cf.* Bolton and Ockenfels 2000; Charness and Haruvy 1999; Kolm 2000). In this type of modelling, equity solely means a relevant comparison of contributions given and results achieved by social actors who see themselves as exposed to the same circumstances as their peers.

A strong attachment to an equity rules signifies both low levels of tolerance to unequal distributions among peers subjected to the same events and a willingness to do anything within their reach to correct the inequity. Costs and equity are the first building blocks on the pillar of the reciprocity theory of exchange. Falk, Gächter and Kovács (1999, p. 4) give us a paradigmatic proof of this kind of reasoning, claiming that reciprocity is a conditional and non-strategic willingness to reward friendly acts and to punish the unfriendly ones, irrespective of the costs involved. It is worth noticing that the choice of rewards and retaliations is filtered by the actor's perceptions of the others' intentions, and the intensity of the reaction is proportional to the existing bond (friendship, indifference or enmity) that characterize the relationship (*cf.* Falk and Fischbacher 1999, p. 3). Evaluation of the intentional nature of an action is much more decisive in negative reciprocity contexts than in positive reciprocity situations (*cf.* Charness and Haruvy 1999, p. 5; Falk, Fehr and Fischbacher 1999). The punishment of perceived intentional nastiness seems to be consistently stronger than the reward of perceived intentional sympathy. Anyway, this evaluation is always subject to the dominant social frames, the alternative available behaviours and general considerations concerning equity norms.

Bowles and Gintis (1998c, p. 5) also underline the central issue of cost and equity, but move a little closer to the sociological tradition, namely Marxism and

Network Analysis. For them it is important to emphasize the structural and normative dimensions of reciprocity, a concept defined as a natural propensity for cooperation with those who obey the same social norms and for punishment of those who systematically violate them, even at a cost. The costs and the perception of equity are shaped by the prevalent social norms embedded in each society. The inclusion of social patterns and moral frames in the reciprocity model makes it possible to reconcile agency and structure, strategy and norm abiding behavior, by subjecting them to the same theoretical endeavour. Equity defines a local relational frame that can only explain reciprocal relations established among peers facing similar situations and produce useful comparisons among themselves. These comparisons result from the calculation of a ratio involving contributions made by ego (and alter) and results obtained by ego (and alter). The comparisons are not based on absolute results but on relative data, which justify the fact that an asymmetric distribution can be interpreted as fair, especially if the less well-off concede legitimacy to the inequality or if they recognize the existence of property rights granting privilege to those who earn more (*cf.* Fahr and Irlenbusch 2000).

The norm of equity results from the social situation structure in which the social actors are embedded and not from a particular human nature orientation. The norm of equity presupposes a power relationship among social actors, according to a model that implies that those who are momentarily in disadvantage have the capacity to retaliate in such a way as to guarantee an alignment of interests and a more or less egalitarian distribution. Reciprocity offers local solutions to social problems, ignoring the general law and not taking into account the principles of justice. Based on equity and reversible asymmetry models, reciprocity is a powerful operator that reduces transaction costs and realigns divergent interests, especially in agency contexts (Fehr *et al.* 1998; Kirchler *et al.* 1996). Reciprocity tends to reinforce the existing social linkages or to recover the lost or threatened ones, without the need to appeal to external protection mechanisms or to entirely specified legal frames.

Reciprocity is established inside long chains of events dominated by the alternance of moves between the social actors involved in the process. These actors present a vivid memory of past events and act under a social logic by which every one of them respond to the previous move according to their own perception and evaluation of others' reactions. The expectation system is embedded in the reciprocity model. At the same time, experimental economists do agree that reciprocity is a universal social practice,[11] not bounded by archaic transaction spaces, that involves a constant conversion flux between commodities and gifts, whenever the legal framework is limited, unspecified or absent. Reciprocity is facilitated whenever we face non-existent, weak or doubtful legal frames, and is always problematic when it is impossible to identify the author of an action, and when it is difficult to assign the responsibility for a particular course of action. Reciprocity is directly related to the legal void and inversely related to anonymity

---

[11] Ultimatum games conducted across the globe (Cameron, 1999; Okada and Riedl 1999; Slonim and Roth 1998) clearly show the veracity of this assertion.

and uncertainty. Reciprocity tends to be an efficiency mechanism aligning divergent and incompatible interests, whenever there is a chance of retaliating and punishing those who deviate from the agreements established in formal or tacit contracts. Reciprocity accelerates social relations thanks to the presence of a mechanism that intensifies the emotions and generates conspicuous and paroxysmic reactions.

All social practices dominated by reciprocity define a minimalist normative framework that guarantees a spontaneous order dominated by a state of equilibrium at the extremes: whether it is total cooperation or total retaliation. Reciprocity is a minimalist solution that can be considered as an embryonary form for more sophisticated social relations. Reciprocity power is derived from its ability to act as a form of dissuasion for cheating in contracts and free riding in collective action agreements. This dissuasive power results from the internal dynamic of each relation and not from external sanctioning mechanisms. Reciprocity avoids the total specification of contracts, thus economizing on transaction costs. Reciprocity is an implicit mechanism that binds social actors to their agreements. In agency contexts, characterized by the difficulty of aligning divergent interests, reciprocity offers a series of endogenous mechanisms that assure that contracts are binding. In order to assure that, reciprocity solely uses its internal dynamic that fosters rewards and punishments, without the need to specify contracts or to appeal to arbitrage forces. Social reputation engenders trust and trust promotes cooperation and fosters transactions. Social ordering induced by reciprocity is a by-product of threshold (or critical mass) behaviours (*cf.* Granovetter 1978) but is not a consequence of automatic adjustments or invisible hand mechanisms.

Although many experimental economists usually conceive altruism as the main cause for reciprocity,[12] we think that this explanation is flawed on two accounts. Firstly, to explain reciprocity through the lenses of altruism does not pass our Sorokin's razor test because it is always impossible to know the exact motivations of the relevant social actors.[13] At this stage of theorizing we do not have the requisite methodological instruments to presuppose the motivational frame that leads an actor to decide on a particular course of action. At the same time we cannot establish an unproblematic relation between an amicable action and altruism. Secondly, altruism cannot be considered a decisive element in the construction of a general theory of reciprocity because it can only offer explanations for one of the tails of the distribution of social action. It can justify the reasons that lead someone to give more than is expected by the standard economic

---

[12] This is particularly true when we consider the authors who analyze reciprocity as an evolutionary mechanism (*cf.* De Vos and Zeggelink 1994, 1997). These authors are deeply influenced by the idea of reciprocal altruism developed in biological context by Trivers (1971) and Alexander (1979).
[13] The idea that sociology cannot devote itself to philosophical discussions that lead to dead-ends, as they are constitutionally undecidable is attributed to the Russian-born sociologist, Pitirim Sorokin. Following in his footsteps, we consider that to debate actor's motivations is useless.

model, but cannot enlighten the retaliatory behavior that is so common when we study reciprocity.

Abandoning altruism as the sole explanation of reciprocity forces us to present a more complex theoretical approach to the phenomenon. We consider that reciprocity constantly involves three distinct dimensions: behavioural, structural and social survival (the latter divided into two areas: aristocratic and symbiotic). The behavioural dimension of reciprocity is activated by a norm of equity. The structural aspect is defined by chains of sequential interactions, dominated by mimicry, competitive emulation and the long memories of the relevant social encounters. The aristocratic dynamic tends to transform social relations among peers into a search for social distinction and difference. A paroxysmic and conspicuous dimension characterizes this type of reciprocity relationship because they are built within social frames dominated by agonistic settings where the presentation of the self is decisive and where any signs of weakness can cause loss of face or threat to ones status. Giving something of equal worth can only represent an inability to reciprocate or a refusal to understand what a gift is all about. This statement is valid both to cycles of offence-retaliation and to spirals of gift and counter gift. The symbiotic relationship transforms reciprocity into an encounter between unequals that can only survive in social terms thanks to the other with whom they establish a relationship of mutual dependency. The aristocratic side of reciprocity is a clear change factor, but the symbiotic expression is a blocking mechanism for change.

Reciprocity is a robust, evolutionary stable social relation (*cf.* Bergstrom and Stark 1993; Bester and Güth 1994; Guttman 2000; Prisbrey 1993). The robustness of reciprocity does not emanate from its perfection, but from its sub-optimality. Although, reciprocity is a sub-optimal relational solution for every social actor (considered individually), it assumes the dimension of *second-best* as a social practice. If we consider divergent interests among the members of a population, reciprocity can be considered as an interesting equilibrium point. Reciprocity is evolutionarily stable because it makes it possible to develop long-term cooperation and solidarity within a particular society if certain important conditions are met: behavioural learning; undefined time spans; repeated and constant interactions; capacity to retaliate against deviant actions (appealing to the creation of dependency and control mechanisms). These four conditions are crucial to the development of reciprocal relations. Without behavioural learning, social actors cannot adjust their actions, and their expectations to other actors' moves. Exploitation and dependency would be the outcome of this particular situation. Undefined time spans are mandatory because if a social actor knows the exact moment when the relation will end s/he has a powerful incentive to defect or cheat the other, without expecting any kind of retaliation. Repeated and constant interactions are the *sine qua non* condition for the existence of reciprocity. The alternate moves between social actors engender the necessary debts that promote reciprocity. As for retaliation, we have to consider that it is a powerful mechanism assuring compliance and convergence of practices. Without it, it would be almost impossible to keep reciprocity alive.

These four elements should constantly be in the mind of experimental game designers, since they define the true tests of reciprocity. All the games designed to test reciprocity should present the following characteristics: players with memory of past actions; sequential chains of events; possibility of rewarding and retaliating against previous moves by other players; ignorance of the timing of the last play; possibility of constructing images of other players and developing a valuable knowledge of their actions; consideration of agency situations but without the exclusion of relations between peers;[14] presence of structural and normative frames capable of replicating well-known, relevant social phenomena. Unfortunately, most of the games used in experimental economics to test reciprocity fail to follow these instructions. Retaliatory moves seldom occur;[15] memories are rarely considered; reciprocity between peers is uncommon; image and reputation are more often used in simulation than in real life experiments.

The experimental design of a major part of these games cannot constitute a true test for reciprocity, as it does not enable a true interaction between the participants to emerge and develop. A one-shot game is always a poor candidate to test reciprocity and all the games that preclude any chance of developing reputations cannot fully evaluate reciprocity. The experiences based on two movements (player A makes a proposal and player B responds to the proposal) are not true tests of reciprocity. We need at least three plays (the threshold of acceptance) to establish a valid test of reciprocity. The sole use of financial assets as reward-promising devices also limits the scope of the experiments as true tests of reciprocity.

Reciprocity finds a favourable niche in low social volume contexts, dominated by a strong inter-individual knowledge among the participants. Reciprocity is mainly established in small-scale social settings, which are modelled by a succession of repeated interactions. Whenever the practice of reciprocity is not dominant inside a particular society, we tend to see it as associated with social enclaves constituting a place of refuge, operating as an escape and protection mechanism before the mercantile world. Reciprocity is also based on a system of permanent debts that involve the setting up of time lags between gift and retribution. This system produces a clear-cut separation between 'us' and 'them', nurturing parochial social relations (sometimes xenophobic) under the general rule of never to forget and never to forgive.[16]

---

[14] The games developed by experimental economists tend to test only the asymmetrical relations mirroring agency problems involving a principal (who makes a proposal) and an agent (that chooses his degree of effort). Experimental economists fail to test the symmetrical relations established among peers.

[15] These games have an impoverished conception of retaliation. Negative reciprocation is only considered as a way of achieving conformity and alignment of interests between social actors with divergent objectives.

[16] Experimental economists tend to consider that reciprocity is an important way of curving opportunism and social parasitism as it fosters continuous social relations and establishes distrust towards foreigners. This situation can obviously solve collective action dilemmas or agency problems but at the cost of parochialism. The parochial dimension of reciprocity can be reduced by an opening gift from the newcomer who, thanks to that, can achieve a trustful

Reciprocity is, thus, fostered by social settings where is easy to establish an alternating and sequential principle of gifts and counter gifts. Reciprocity requires that the time lag between gift and retribution be understood not as a refusal of the social link but as a refining mechanism. Reciprocity is neither a fixed strategy nor a pre-designed mental program. Reciprocity implies a capacity to discriminate social actors and relevant social situations within a framework where the types of response result solely from the chains of events. The response given in $t+2$ is always caused by the events in $t+1$. The strategic dimension (resulting from rationality and expectation games) is not totally absent from the reciprocity phenomena, but is always dominated by memorial logic. The continuity and prevalence of reciprocal behavior inside a particular society is derived from the critical mass of reciprocators found therein.

At the core of reciprocity theory we can find the *homo reciprocans* figure (*cf.* Bowles and Gintis 1998b; Bowles *et al.* 1997; Fehr and Gächter 1998). This theoretical construction can be considered a viable alternative to both *homo œconomicus* and *homo sociologicus* because, as opposed to them, it does not obey a monist behavioural explanation (be it rationality, or norms). The *homo reciprocans* acts in accordance with the social context and the frames considered relevant in each situation. At the same time, the *homo reciprocans* figure cannot be defined either by strategy or obedience to cultural patterns (even if s/he does not ignore any of them), but her/his course of action can be explained by the interaction patterns s/he establishes with the relevant partners. The reaction levels experienced by the *homo reciprocans* result from a triple dimension: the expectation systems created by previous interactions; the perception (and anticipation) of plausible reactions answering their previous moves; the institutional framework that defines and encompasses the social action. Reciprocity harmonizes memory (the major factor), strategic anticipation (ancillary factor) and the normative space.

Reciprocity as a Functional Substitute for Trust

Reciprocity is strongly associated with trust and social capital. Trust and reciprocity are a self-generating energy that reduces the levels of social litigation; fostering contacts and promoting social arrangements that circumvent the transaction costs that permeate contracts. At this level, we tend to emphasize their positive aspects, forgetting that when reciprocity is mobilized as a proxy for trust, it is also capable of nurturing parochialism, nepotism, corruption and bribery (the so-called downside of trust). A trustful society is a rich society capable of investing its resources in social activities that advance the quality and the living prospects of its citizens. A correct assessment of the dynamics of trust can be an invaluable tool to

---

reputation. Reciprocity involves discriminating social actors with the capacity to identify the others with whom they establish a social relation. The established interaction, the type of transaction, the intensity of response, and the feeding of sequential chains of events vary under the influence of experience, learning and reputation of the relevant others.

promote economic growth and social development. Being a close substitute for institutional confidence and interpersonal trust embedded in economic activities and social relations, reciprocity can assume a prominent role in societies on the verge of social crises or threatened by legal voids. This is probably the reason why the studies of reciprocity and trust are so prevalent in the so-called economies of transition.[17] Reciprocity must be considered as an asset capable of improving the relationship between citizens and government institutions, encouraging cooperation among organisations, nurturing collective action programs, developing more conscious social policies and promoting solidarity among social actors.

To study reciprocity in close connection with trust, social capital and social networks is a difficult task, because it involves attributing coherence to a fragmented realm, offering several avenues of research. If we discard the classical presentation of the topic in moral philosophy, it is safe to say that classical sociological thought ranging from Tönnies, Durkheim, Weber or Simmel to Parsons has ushered in a new look into trust. And yet, despite the centrality of the subject, and the availability of new, important studies conducted by prominent sociologists and philosophers (Barber 1983; Bernoux and Servet 1997; Gambetta 1989a; Granovetter 1985; Lewis and Weigert 1985; Luhmann 1979, 1989; M.A.U.S.S. 1994; Misztal 1996; Seligman 1997; Sztompka 1999; Thuderoz, Mangematin, Harrison 1999), the concept remains under theorized. It is fair to say that, up to the 1980s, trust was a silent partner in social theory. Most of the studies published during the last 20 years present trust as a complement to other important social domains like solidarity and cooperation (Bassi 2000); social and cultural capital (Pendenza 2000); social networks (Lorenz 1989); political action (Dunn 1989); economic and organisational dynamics (Kramer and Tyler 1996; Lazaric and Lorenz 1998; Dasgupta 1989); patrons and clients (Eisenstadt and Roniger 1984); social order (Gellner 1989); labour markets (Granovetter 1974); evolutionary theory (Bateson 1989) or criminal organizations (Gambetta 1989b, 1992). Some go as far as to claim that trust is the major force behind the economic success (or failure) of a particular country (Fukuyama 1996). Trust can also be conceptualised as a moral device capable of economizing transaction costs and contracts (Landa 1994).

The existence of trust corresponds to the idea of having a minimalist way of organizing social life. Trusting your partner equates to simplifying social relations (Good 1989) and is a way of guaranteeing social order without explicit coercion mechanisms. By the same token, selfish and altruistic actors can converge in similar

---

[17] Trust has become an explicit way of conceptualizing the new forms of integration in transition economies. The economic transition of the Eastern European economies after 1989 can easily be seen as one of the major causes for the recovery of interest in studying trust. The books written by Sztompka (1999), Seligman (1997) and Misztal (1996) are clear indicators of this hypothesis. To think about trust as 'a form of social integration is equivalent to the idea of considering that today's societies are on the verge of important, devastating crises, requiring new forms of cohesion capable of revamping civic participation, fostering solidarity and developing the sense of community.

lines of behaviour, despite their very different motivational frameworks. Trust can be both an indicator of archaism and tradition and a strong modernizing and rationalization factor. This face of trust is highly convergent with our presentation of reciprocity, which makes our concept an excellent proxy for the study of trust. Recent texts, discussing the centrality of *guanxi* in China (Ang *et al.* 1999; Bian 1997; Kiong and Kee 1998), or *blat* in Russia (Ledeneva 1998; Lovell *et al.* 2000) have proved that trust can be simultaneously the basis of an economy supported by the 3F factor (family, friends and firms) and a source of corruption, bribery, nepotism and favour exchange. Trust is a shadowy presence behind most of the entrepreneurial ethnic enclave debates (Hart 1989; Portes 1995), and is also used as an important causal mechanism to explain the convergences and divergences of organizational structures around the world, namely the business groups (Hamilton and Biggart 1988).

If trust and reciprocity act as exchange facilitators, we must consider that distrust is at the root of the contractual sophistication defining today's societies. Distrust is a source of refinement and a civilizing trigger that seemingly reconciles rationality and tradition. The crises of trust, lead social actors in search of clever, sophisticated contractual arrangements capable of shielding them from the nastiness of their partners. This search for protection is self-generating, conducting communities and societies to further levels of refinement and contractual complexity. The litigation potential increases with this contractual sophistication, thus creating new needs for reciprocity and trust. This is the reason behind the mounting pressure to grant renewed importance to the study of trust and reciprocity in today's societies. Trust is a powerful rational asset embedded in tradition and social values (Hollis 1998). The concepts of risk and reflexive modernity have also placed the concept of trust on the agenda of contemporary Sociology. Civil society theoreticians (namely Seligman) conceptualise trust in order to explain political life in contemporary societies, assuming that trust can easily reconcile freedom, equality and civic responsibility.

Although reciprocity is clearly a cultural universal, we can easily spot major differences in the expression of the phenomenon among countries experiencing diversified economic environments, facing particular polities or living peculiar cultures. The differences between particular reciprocity arrangements (*cf.* Alston 1989), such as the Russian *blat*, the Chinese *guanxi*, the Japanese *giri* or the Korean *inhwa* reflect the historical experiences of these nation-states and can only be perceived if we pay close attention to the cultural and political axis of these societies.[18] At the same time, an understanding of these particular devices used to shape and regulate both informal relations and the formal structuring of political and economic activities can be a precious instrument to predict the critical paths of development chosen by these four countries. Reciprocity is an invaluable social mechanism to explain how the micro interactions can be converted into

---

[18] Although not discussed in this paper, *inhwa* can be considered as the functional equivalent of *guanxi, blat,* and *giri* for the Korean society.

macrostructures both at the level of industrial organization and the formation of business groups, and in the areas of political affinities.

A close look at reciprocity makes it easier to understand why the Japanese organizational structure (namely the *zaibatsu* of the pre-war period and the *keiretsu* of modern times) is regulated by a complex arrangement involving a regulatory state, powerful elites and an almost non-existent foreign capital. It also sheds some light on the reasons that produced the South-Korean *chaebol* (modelled by an interventionist state, and weak elites) or the Chinese *Jituanqiye* (shaped by closely knit relations among families). The study of *blat* is an important way to understand the peculiarities of the soviet transition, especially when it comes to comprehending how a practice of favour exchange became the basis of a new economy of corruption, bribery and nepotism.

Blat is a reciprocity type of social relation developed in Russia. It was central to the definition of daily activities during the Soviet era, especially during the Brezhnev consulate. Uncertainty, rationing and scarcity in a poorly monetarized society are the main causes of *blat*. People try to obtain the goods and services they need through the activation of social networks and informal contacts. Procurement of scarce goods is not only central to physical survival, but is also nuclear to social enhancement and status achievement. *Blat* is both a product and a producer of informal networks of help and favour exchange, supplying the goods that are unobtainable in the market or by activating the formal links of the economic system. Paradoxically, by supplying what is rarely available, *blat* contributes to the stabilization of a totalitarian, repressive society, acting as a safety valve that mitigates protest, freezes revolt and stabilizes the perception of social asymmetries.

Blat is a tacit relationship developed thanks to *savoir-faire* rules and polite behavior. *Blat* is a mixed type of transaction, oscillating between the gift and the market and between the alienable and the inalienable. Two intangibles (social actors' reputations and durable, trustful relations), and three major assets (information, knowledge and contacts) define the *blat* exchange mode. The key to the understanding of the inner dynamic of the *blat* model of exchange is the existence of an asymmetric valuation system. This asymmetry signifies that the provider of a good X underrates the value of what s/he is offering whilst the receiver overrates its value. When we face non-monetarized economies or economies with doubtful equivalences, asymmetrical relational valuations are the main reason for exchange clearing. The equity of the relationship results from the fact that those who have or control a good do not want it as much as they want another to which they have no access, but can be obtained either by a direct exchange or by triangulation or indirect reciprocity.

The moral and legal condemnation of *blat* does not destroy the practice, but make it a more or less underground activity. Its survival is probably due to the social consensus regarding the existence of an enemy that must be beaten – the state. Fighting an omnipotent state is a way of enchanting a disenchanted world, thus providing a living objective to alienated citizens. The small victories obtained at the state's expense are sufficient rewards within an economy of scarcity. However, it is important to underline that the climate of solidarity and cooperation traditionally fostered by *blat* has almost entirely disappeared with the economic transition. The economic monetarization of the Russian society paved the way to corruption and bribery. The social brokers (trust negotiators) and the *blatmeisters* who controlled access to significant economic areas took advantage of the position they occupied, thus promoting their own interests. Some of the more relevant brokers of the past were left in the doldrums, because they controlled access to areas that have become almost entirely irrelevant in an economy that is no longer dominated by the rationing spectre.

The Japanese experience of reciprocity tends to reinforce the collective dimension of society, limiting the role of the social actor to a face management behavior, by which s/he tries to avoid the creation of obligations and social burdens. Reciprocity of harmony and avoidance seems to be an adequate label to describe the particular Japanese sensibility expressed in the terms *giri*, *gimou* or *on*. On the other hand, the Russian *blat* puts an enormous emphasis on the role of individuals and the place they occupy in relevant social networks. The *blatmeister* thrives in situations of scarcity and rationing by cultivating the right contacts and establishing useful networks of influence and exchange. In a non-monetarized economy, social relations are frequently mediated and defined by social brokers, responsible for the reciprocity of contacts. These brokers actively scour the sources for the important goods and services that will eventually be traded for the assets in demand. In China, the practice of *guanxi* is a clear indication of the pervasive nature of reciprocity over time and attests to its transformation from a traditional mechanism of solidarity into a clever way of doing business. Reciprocity is embedded in social structures and can transform itself according to the needs and requirements of the new situations faced by social actors.

Some westerners, fascinated by *guanxi*, go as far as to claim that knowledge of this Chinese practice is a must to do business with Chinese companies or managers. Considering that *guanxi* is present whenever we are faced with Chinese entrepreneurs across the globe, there are huge profits to be gained for those who know how to cash in on them. The horizontal exchange of favours that characterizes the *guanxi* can easily become the foot in the door that enables one to do business in apparently hostile environments. In some devious way, an almost natural practice (reciprocity) becomes one of the most intelligent strategies to develop economic activities.

The *Homo Reciprocans* at Work

The concept of reciprocity we use in this paper and the closely associated idea of the *homo reciprocans* are not only scientific devices designed to produce good results but are also instruments able to enlighten us as to some projects of social reform. To express this idea more clearly, we shall provide a brief example taken from the classical world. As we are fully aware, to ensure the compliance of citizens when it comes to paying taxes is always a very difficult task. This is as true today as it was in the past. At the time of the Solon reformation, the Greeks developed a particularly artful system to ensure that their richest citizens agreed to pay taxes or perform what was to become known as liturgies.[19] The particular device used (which gave rise to some bitter remarks by Isocrates and Demosthenes) was called *antidosis* (a concept that can be literally translated as exchange).

Let us try to imagine a situation in which we have two particularly rich Athenians: Licurgus and Pericles (fictitious names, obviously), and let us assume for the sake of argument that Licurgus' property is slightly more valuable than the property of his fellow citizen. Bearing this situation in mind, we shall try to determine what will happen should Pericles be chosen to perform a liturgy and Licurgus remain free of that burden. The obvious reaction of Pericles will be surprise, shortly followed by bitterness, anger and a sense of being treated unfairly. As we all know, the principles of justice can be quite simple and easily accepted by all. This is because they are general and blind to the particular interests of every one. But these principles always fall short when it comes to what the social actor regards as a violation of the equity norms, that is, when someone compares the ratio of her/his contributions to the outcome for her/him, and compares it with the same ratio in a peer.

Before a dramatic situation, Pericles is not without means to defend his position. At this precise moment, feeling that he was ill-treated by the Athenian tax system, Pericles will activate his *antidosis* prerogative. This prerogative simply states that each and every taxed citizen who feels he is paying more taxes than any other citizen owning what he considers to be a more valuable property can rightly claim that his entire estate be exchanged for that of the less heavily taxed citizen (or tax-free). As may be easily seen, the device is both simple and powerful. By promoting a policy of *antidosis*, the state puts the burden of control in the hands of every citizen. The fairness of the system is assured by the reciprocal control that everyone applies to each other. The jealousy and envy expressed by the citizens become a sort of virtuous behavior that spares the state the cost of enforcing the law by resorting to more repressive means. As far as we know the system seems to have worked quite well and the prerogative was scarcely used. But, as the more curious reader will notice, there is obviously a catch in the process. The catch is simply the logical consequence of a social mechanism that was built around the idea of reciprocity. As we stated in the opening pages of this paper, there is an inner dimension in the practice of reciprocity that always leads us in the direction of excess, paroxysm, and conspicuous behaviours. The same applies to the *antidosis* rule. Let us, for a while, imagine that the citizens of the city are law abiding and show a strong unwillingness to establish any sort of collusion to cheat the state. At the same time, all of them want to be treated fairly and to gain more than they have. In these conditions, the practice of the *antidosis* can easily become a game of paroxysm in which everyone wants to pay more than s/he is forced to do in order to activate her/his prerogative of exchange. The final state of this game of reciprocity (or, as René Girard would put it, mimetic process) could be a rich state

---

[19] The richest citizens were chosen to perform a task that would favor the entire community and would give power to the state.

with just a handful of rich, taxable citizens. This is a sort of potlatchian outcome of a very clever device.

Final Remarks: A Sensitising Concept and Eleven Theoretical Statements

To conclude, and in order to further clarify our view on the subject of reciprocity, we shall propose a tentative definition of the concept. It must be considered as a sensitising concept or the first approach to a very complex realm of social life. Reciprocity is a particular type of interaction dominated by asymmetry, memory, obligation and a sense of debt in which every move by a social actor engenders an adequate response by another actor, thus establishing a long-lasting temporal chain of events, and alternate moves. This not only mobilizes the original actors who began the relation but also their relatives, friends and acquaintances. Reciprocity is a universal social relationship across space and time based on the building-up of a system of permanent debts and duties created by past relationships in which saving face and enhancement of personal status are the main objectives.

Reciprocity is dominated by the desire to balance the relationship. But, in order to do so and keep the social relationship alive it needs to create debts. The social mechanism that assures the maintenance of duties and debts (the two *d*s) is formed by two simple rules: never forget and never forgive (the two *f*s). This simple social logic leads the relations to states of paroxysm and excess (the potlatchian nature of reciprocity). This excess may be revealed by spirals of conspicuous gifts, or by spirals of revenge. Reciprocity is an aristocratic practice that manifests itself in terms of never returning without a time lag between the bestowing of the gift and of the counter gift (creating distance), and never returning precisely what was received (a practice of social sophistication, clearly demonstrated by Norbert Elias (1987 1989, 1992, 1993) in his analysis of the civilizing process).

Reciprocity establishes symmetrical relations between peers that generate competing mechanisms, conspicuous activities, and status-enhancing practices that undermine the social order and introduce change to the social system. Reciprocity establishes asymmetrical and symbiotic relations between unequals that tend to stabilize the social order. Reciprocity is a social-creating mechanism that is the prototypical device for systems of value and justice. It creates the rules of equivalence and the rules of just measure that will eventually materialize in written laws and regulations that will bind the citizens of today's societies.

This brief definition leads us to a corpus of theoretical statements that constitute the basis of a middle-range theory of reciprocity.

(1) *Reciprocity is a very simple and parsimonious instrument that passes Ockham's razor test.* Reciprocity is a memorial rule that does not create a moral burden on social actors. It simply involves following the rules of the *do ut des* and *tit for tat*. As it is simple, the rule is easily understand by all social actors, regardless of their preferences, tastes and needs. The expectation system developed by reciprocity allows easy predictions and avoids surprises. As a parsimonious

instrument, reciprocity does not need any ancillary concepts to become a source of enlightenment and to explain why social actors choose and decide. Reciprocity actions are based on a sequence of events in which we find a rotation in the roles of giving and receiving. On the normative side, reciprocity is a minimalist solution capable of defining a peaceful entente between social actors, since it proclaims that an aggressive move is only possible as retaliation. A reciprocator never hurts her/his partner in her/his first move.

(2) *Reciprocity is a powerful construction that explains both retaliation and gifts embedded in social transactions.* The power of this particular type of explanation results from the fact that the same social rule can be applied to explain retaliation and gift giving. Memory preservation, status enhancement mechanisms, face management strategies, obligation to repay all debts, obligation to keep a lag between gift and retribution are simultaneously causes and logical steps towards retaliation and gift giving. The aristocratic ethos of reciprocity enables counter gifts to easily be turned into retaliation and retaliation into counter gifts. In a reciprocity chain, the second mover is always a prisoner or a hostage of the first mover. Those who give or offend are apparently the only free actors in the process, but following the counter gift or the retaliation, their liberty is gone forever. That is why we can consider that reciprocity is very similar to tragedy. The social actor's liberty in choosing the way s/he acts does not conflict with the fact that the final outcome of the play is a foregone conclusion. The reciprocity system generates easy expectations that frame the decisions and the strategic moves taken by social actors.

(3) *Reciprocity avoids the pitfalls caused by the consideration of motivation systems (Sorokin's razor argument).* By using the reciprocity framework we can easily discard any considerations regarding the motivations and intentions of social actors. We consider that the use of motivation as a cornerstone of a social theory leads us to spurious and undesirable debates, because it is impossible to define altruism or selfishness as the basis for a reciprocal behavior. We can never be sure about the real motivations that lead an actor to choose a particular course of action. If an external observer (a relational demon or an impartial Smithian spectator) proves s/he is unable to evaluate the true motivations of a particular actor and if reliance on the self-presentation of social actors is naturally misleading, then avoidance of the discussion seems to be the wisest decision, mainly at this stage of theorizing. Furthermore, acceptance of the self-image of actors, implies a triumph for hypocrisy, as most social actors would love to present themselves as altruistic and sympathetic toward the others. The reciprocity theory is only concerned with actions and tries to explain the social logic behind every player's move. Reciprocity theory bases its conclusions on the *homo reciprocans* figure, someone who we know acts according a particular chain of events, but whose motivations we know nothing about. The discarding of motivations can easily be undertaken whenever we know that actors (motivated differently) converge with regard to their course of action. Knowledge of the fact that selfish and unselfish actors are pushed in the same direction when framed by the same context lies beyond the motivation nexus.

(4) *Reciprocity explains the reasons why trust systems like the Russian blat, the Chinese guanxi or the Japanese giri evolved in different ways*. Reciprocity can be considered as a functional equivalent of trust in societies with non-existent, feeble or threatened law systems. Reciprocity offers an easy way out of the social order and collective action dilemmas by activating informal ways of dealing with uncertainty and risk. Although reciprocity is a cultural universal, expression of it varies considerably. Reciprocity can become a form of horizontal exchange of favours, offering opportunities to obtain goods and services that are sorely needed, whenever society is plagued by scarcity and rationing within the framework of a totalitarian state (*blat*). Reciprocity may be a form of vertical payment of favours that confirms a certain allegiance to the powerful, in exchange for security (as in the case of Mafia-type rings). Reciprocity can be an important part of a gigantic system of face management in which people give in order to cultivate important relations that may be used when the need arises (*guanxi*). Reciprocity can result in a form of avoiding the burden of recognition and gratitude by not imposing a gift on the other even when the other seems to be in need (*giri*). The pervasive character of reciprocity and debt in all social systems should not delude us. Every society has its own particular ways of activating the reciprocity rules, depending on structural characteristics, power relations, cultural frames, economic situation and the orientation of social actors. A comparative study of reciprocity across cultures requires that we know the history of the societies compared, the nature of their social hierarchies and the dominant cultural and structural traits that frame social actor's moves, strategies and decisions.

(5) *Reciprocity offers a value theory that can be used to avoid the spurious distinction between gifts and commodities, by explaining the conversion mechanisms that transform one into another*. Economic Anthropology has made considerable efforts to build-up a value theory adjustable to the theories of value constructed by classical, Marxist and neo-classical economists (*cf.* Gregory 1982, 1997). Reciprocity is not an archaic way of conducting exchange, limited to traditional societies and it is not bartering. Reciprocity is a particular form of exchanging goods and services, subject to a blend of liberty and obligation. It establishes long-lasting social interactions that are dominated by a mutual recognition of debt. Reciprocity Theory defines a value system that is not based on classical or neo-classical criteria, and refuses the universal validity of both labour and marginal theories of value. The valuation system of reciprocity is not based on a particular exchange regime, but on the type of social relations established among social actors. The value given to a good depends on the type, intensity and quality of social relations established by actors and the memories and genealogical value people invest in it. A good is not alienable or inalienable according to its nature and cannot be defined as commodity or gift according to a canonical solving formula. Gifts can become commodities, re-entering the market, whenever the quality of the relation declines. At the same time, a commodity can become an inalienable gift when the relationship established by two social actors becomes intimate and strong attachments have emerged. Market and reciprocity are not irreconcilable

categories, but logical extremes of a distribution. Reciprocity Theory claims that the discovery of the conversion mechanisms that regulate the transition between gifts and commodities is as crucial for Value Theory as the explanation of the conversion logic between social, cultural and economic capitals is for Economic Sociology.

(6) *Reciprocity makes it clear why we need lags between gifts and retributions (whether it be it in terms of positive gifts and bequests, or in terms of revenge and retaliation).* Reciprocity is an aristocratic practice always oriented towards social etiquette and face management activities. Since debt is a constitutional variable of this kind of social relationship, we must recognize that the immediate payments of a debt or the failure to postpone retribution are tantamount to a refusal of the social bond. Repayments of a debt without a lag or producing a counter-gift to be delivered immediately are simple ways of denying the importance and relevance of the other. Reciprocity is a social interaction in which the self and the other are formed by the same process – the direct exchange of goods, services, linguistic signs, emotional expressions, etc. Social encounters are profoundly dependent on a clever management of the reciprocity lag. The reciprocity lag is a civilizational construct that signifies a pause for maturation, a mourning moment to accept a dramatic change, a refining preparation. But it can also be an emotional accelerator, increasing the intensity of the experiences felt and developing expectation systems capable of aligning divergent interests. Without a time lag, social relations would become more common and vulgar, and lose their aura of sophistication. If an offended party immediately reacts to the striking of a glove in his face, he will never be able to settle the dispute in a civilized manner. The possibilities of reactivating the relationship will be lost forever. Dueling is not bravado or quarrelling; it implies following social rules, even when these rules contravene the general law. By the same token, an actor who insists on repaying the received gift immediately is signalling that s/he does not understand the social rules of politeness, thus condemning herself/himself to social ostracism.

(7) *Reciprocity gives us a hint as to the reasons why apparently fragile or irrational behavior (like preferring less to more) is justifiable and, sometimes, evolutionarily stable.* Reciprocity systems discard justice arrangements, based on a universal mode of settling disputes and refuses rationality as the sole criterion to reach decisions. Reciprocity offers equity and a mix of emotion, expectation systems and rationality as the major causes for action in social exchange systems. A social actor oriented towards equity is someone who compares her/his results with those obtained by other social actors that s/he considers to be her/his peers. The relevant comparisons result from the simple calculation of the ratio effort-commitment/results obtained. Each and every time a social actor facing someone s/he considers an equal is confronted with a violation of the equity rule, s/he will act in such a way as to reduce the gap to zero even if, in order to achieve the desired result, s/he has to surrender some important gains (precisely what happens in some ultimatum games). Retaliation is justifiable not because social actors are

moved by atavism, but because they have very good reasons to signal their unwillingness to be exploited. Experiments do confirm that actors are more prone to react in face of equity violations than to act when a principle of justice is threatened. Foregoing some potential gains is justifiable if the actor is avoiding being taken as a sucker. The possibility of activating a retaliatory move (negative reciprocity) makes it easy to reconcile divergent interests, because it will lead to clearer expectations.

(8) *Reciprocity makes it clear why a pure gift leads to economic stagnation and parochial social systems.* Many different sources have more or less explicitly proved that pure, perfect gifts are incompatible with economic development and universal orientation patterns. Inspired by O. Henry's 'Gift of the Magi', by the LETS experiments, by the deuteronomic prohibition of usury, by the counsels given by Rousseau to the Polish and by the deontic moral theories of today, we can easily conclude that reciprocity systems entirely dominated by gift-giving develop an untouchable boundary between an interior world, defined as perfect and full of virtue, and an external world, entirely dominated by sinful behavior. The only way to preserve a perfect way of life is to isolate the perfect community from a disenchanted world and avoid any possibility of growth. Growth and contacts are anathema to the pure gift-giving communities. These communities develop a brick wall morality to deal with the outside world and an altar morality to deal with the rest of the community. Growth and exchange will disrupt these communities in such a way, that there is no other chance to survive but to close the community to the outside world. Thus, perfection and purity lead to parochialism and, sometimes, to xenophobia, whereas reciprocity conducts society to open grounds shaped by interaction and contacts. The advantages of reciprocity can be compared to the well-known theses of the *doux-commerce.* The perfection of the pure gift can only be achieved in the arena of small communities, which are entirely dominated by strong ideological cement or by kin-like relationships. On the other hand, reciprocity can be the foundation of more cosmopolitan relations.

(9) *Reciprocity is a powerful instrument to explain the sumptuous and paroxysmic nature of the social relations established between peers.* The relationship established between actors who see themselves as peers is one of competition, rivalry and the fight for status. Every time a social actor faces a peer, s/he wants to derive some advantage and prove herself/himself to be better than her/his competitor. The way to achieve this result depends on her/his capacity to give more, to retaliate more or to assert herself/himself before the peer audience. This move will be followed by other moves by her/his rivals and the final outcome of this particular social mechanism will be a sumptuous, paroxysmic type of exchange. The rivals who enter a reciprocal exchange cycle tend to exhaust themselves, both energetically and financially. Thus, the reciprocal relationship between peers tends to change the existent social order and produce new opportunities for those who have never had a chance to further their own positions. The depletion of accumulated revenues by the conspicuous consumers; the physical exhaustion of

the duellists and the absolute poverty of the *potlatch* participants are good examples of the extraordinary capacity of social regeneration offered by competition systems among peers. By destroying their wealth, the old members of the elite pave the way for the rise of new members, even if the social structure is not entirely changed.

(10) *Reciprocity clarifies the reasons that lead to the stability of rigid social hierarchies dominated by symbiotic relationships.* In symbiotic relations, social actors have a strong incentive to maintain the *status quo*, and preserve the existent social order, since the privileged ones acquire status, prestige, revenues and power from the gifts received by the social inferiors, in exchange for protection and help in case of need. The social inferiors tend to accept their situation because they receive the goods and services that they value most, namely security. The key to the continuity of this kind of symbiotic relationship lies in the fact that the two classes have different valuation systems regarding the same good. When a good is considered unimportant by a class, which can actually provide it, and, at the same time, that very good is highly considered by a class which has no access to it, we are creating a social system in which asymmetrical exchange not only assures the continuity of the established relations, but guarantees significant advantages to both classes. The dominant value system defines an asymmetrical valuation of goods and services by the classes that participate in the exchange. If, to that, we add powerful ideological mechanisms that provide legitimacy to the social superiors, it is easy to explain the prevalence and continuity of this kind of social arrangement. Feudalism, paternalism and Mafia-like arrangements are good examples of this type of social relationship. However, we should consider that agency relations are also an important source of information on this subject. The relationship between a principal and an agent is stabilized by the presence of an exchange in which both actors have something to gain by accepting the contract rules (formal or informal).

(11) *Reciprocity can only be generalized by triangulation or indirect relationships. Reciprocity is usually understood as the product of face-to-face relations.* However we cannot overlook the indirect dimension of reciprocity if we are to understand its potential for generalization. Indirect reciprocity means that those who give or bequest something to a second figure receive a counter gift from a third party to whom they have given nothing. This is the only way to avoid the paroxysmic, sumptuous dimension of direct reciprocity, because it prevents *potlatch* and status enhancement practices among dyads. The game it engenders is both stable and robust and has the potential to be generalized in archaic (the *kula* ring) or modern societies (the blood gift). Indirect reciprocity is conducted by a discriminating *homo reciprocans* who acts in accordance with the relevant frames s/he faces. Acting upon frames makes it easy to understand why the *homo reciprocans* thesis escapes the pitfalls of the under and over socialized conceptions of men. Indirect reciprocity can be seen as a clever response to the dilemmas of parochialism and autarchy usually associated with pure or perfect gifts. The parochial demons can only be destroyed if we accept the transition from relations based on social dyads to

relations shaped by triangulation and large networks which do not necessarily involve mutual knowledge among participants. The gift of blood is the paradigm of indirect reciprocity, corresponding to the viability of a gift project within low emotional societies. Contrary to direct reciprocity, which is constantly nourished by trust, reputation and monitoring, indirect reciprocity exists and prospers because the relations are established anonymously. The link between people is established by the constant flow of goods and services. A third party who acts as a social broker or an exchange facilitator usually assures this flow. The social mediators assume a crucial role in the development of indirect reciprocity schemes. As we know, direct reciprocity leads to excess and highly emotional relations, generating either a potlatchian gift festival or a retaliatory frenzy. In 'hot' societies dominated by direct reciprocity, social actors need to recognize the other, mobilizing total identification mechanisms. In the mercantile context, indirect reciprocity is a product of partial identification systems. This means that the other with whom someone interacts is not a simple statistical figure or a totally anonymous person, even if the interaction is not of the face-to-face type. Each and every time reciprocity plays the part of a functional equivalent of trust, social actors intervening as social brokers are responsible for the build-up of triangular relations and social networks. In doing so, they help to develop an indirect reciprocity scheme capable of generalization. Widespread reciprocity obeys a simple rule: give and give repeatedly. This generalizing rule is at the root of many alternative communities that elect reciprocity as its founding principle. These communities are entirely molded by widespread debt mechanisms that prohibit all forms of bilateral debt clearing. A personal debt can only be paid within a network, by giving a good or granting a service to someone that was not our original creditor. The lesson to be learned from these experiences is that we must generalize debt and avoid bilateral payments if we want to construct virtue and avoid mimetic desires and paroxysm.

References

Abbink, K., Irlenbusch, B. and Renner, E. (2000), 'The Moonlighting Game: An experimental study on reciprocity and retribution', *Journal of Economic Behavior and Organization*, 42, pp. 265-277.

Alexander, R. D. (1979), *The Biology of Moral Systems*, New York, Aldine de Gruyter.

Allat, P. and Yeandle, S. (1992), *Youth Unemployment and the Family: Voices of disordered times*, London/New York, Routledge.

Alston, J. P. (1989), 'Wa, Guanxi, and Inhwa: Managerial principles in Japan, China and Korea', Working Paper, *American Sociological Association*.

Ang, S., Tan, M. L. and Bian, Y. (1999), 'Does Trust Mediate the Relationship Between Guanxi and Performance of Business Ventures in China?', Working Paper, *American Sociological Association*.

Arnoux, R., Dawson, R. and O'Connor, M. (1993), 'The Logics of Death and Sacrifice in the Resource Management Law Reforms of Aotearoa/New Zealand', *Journal of Economic Issues*, 28 (4), pp. 1059-96.

Axelrod, R. (1984), *The Evolution of Cooperation*, New York, Basic Books.

Barber, B. (1983), *The Logic and Limits of Trust*, New Brunswick, Rutgers University Press.

Barnett, A.H. and Kaserman, D. L. (1992), 'The Shortage of Organs for Transplantation: Exploring the alternatives', *Issues in Law and Medicine*, 9(2), pp. 117-37.

Barnett, A. H. and Kaserman, D. L. (1995), 'Comment on "The Shortage in Market-Inalienable Human Organs": Faulty analysis of a failed policy', *American Journal of Economics and Sociology*, 59(2), pp. 335-49.

Barnett, A. H. and Kaserman, D. L. (2000), 'The "Rush to Transplant" and Organ Shortages', *Economic Inquiry*, 33, July, pp. 506-15.

Bassi, A. (2000), *Dono e Fiducia: Le Forme della Solidarietà nelle Società Complesse*, Rome, Edizioni Lavoro.

Bateson, P. (1989), 'L'Evoluzione Biologica della Cooperazione e della Fiducia', in D. Gambetta (ed.), *Le Strategie della Fiducia: Indagini sulla razionalità della cooperazione*, Turin, Einaudi, pp. 19-39.

Becker, H. (1956), *Man in Reciprocity: Introductory lectures on culture, society & personality*, New York, Frederick Praeger.

Becker, L. C. (1990), *Reciprocity*, Chicago, The University of Chicago Press.

Bellah, R., *et al.* (1985), *Habits of the Heart: Individualism and commitment in American life*, Berkeley, University of California Press.

Bellah, R., *et al.* (1992), *The Good Society*, New York, Vintage Books.

Bendor, J. and Mookherjee, D. (1985), 'Institutional Structure and the Logic of Ongoing Collective Action', *Stanford Graduate School of Business Research Paper* No 845, October.

Ben-Ner, A. and Putterman, L. (1998), 'Reciprocity in a Two Part Dictator Game', paper presented at the panel *Economics, Values, and Organization*, Chicago, American Economic Association, mimeo.

Benveniste, É. (1969a), *Le Vocabulaire des Institutions Indo-Européenes: 1- économie, parenté, société*, Paris, Minuit.

Benveniste, É. (1969b), *Le Vocabulaire des Institutions Indo-Européenes: 2- pouvoir, droit, religion*, Paris, Minuit.

Bergstrom, T. and Stark, O. (1993), 'How Altruism Can Prevail in Evolutionary Environments', *American Economic Review*, 83, pp. 149-55.

Bernoux, P. and Servet, J-M. (1997), *La Construction Sociale de la Confiance*, Paris, Montchrestien.

Bian, Y. (1997), 'Bringing Strong Ties Back in: Indirect ties, network bridges and job searches in China', *American Sociological Review*, 62 (3), pp. 366-85.

Bloch, M. (1983), *Les Rois Thaumaturges: Étude sur le caractère surnaturel attribué a la puissance royale particulièrement en France et en Angleterre*, Paris, Gallimard.

Bohnet, I. and Frey, B. (1999), 'The Sound of Silence in Prisoner's Dilemma and Dictator Games', *Journal of Economic Behavior & Organization*, 89 (1), pp 335-39.

Bolle, F. (1998), 'Rewarding Trust: An experimental analysis', *Theory and Decision*, 45, pp. 83-98.

Bolton, G. and Ockenfels, A. (2000), 'ERC - A Theory of Equity, Reciprocity, and Competition', *American Economic Review*, 90 (1), pp. 166-94.

Bolton, G. and Zwick, R. (1995), 'Anonymity Versus Punishment in Ultimatum Bargaining', *Games and Economic Behavior*, 10 (1), pp. 95-121.

Bolton, G., Katok, E. and Zwick, R. (1998), 'Dictator Game Giving: Rules of Fairness versus Acts of Kindness', *International Journal of Game Theory*, 27, pp. 269-99.

Bowles, S. (1998), 'Endogenous Preferences: The Cultural Consequences of Markets and Other Economic Institutions', *Journal of Economic Literature*, 36, pp. 75-111.

Bowles, S. and Gintis, H. (1997), 'The Moral Economy of Communities: Structured populations and the evolution of pro-social norms', Amherst, *University of Massachusetts*, mimeo.

Bowles, S. and Gintis, H. (1998a), 'How Communities Govern: The structural basis of pro-social norms', in Ben-Ner and Putterman (eds), *Economics, Values, and Organization*, New York, Cambridge University Press.

Bowles, S. and Gintis, H. (1998b), 'Is Equality Passé? *Homo Reciprocans* and the Future of Egalitarian Politics', Amherst, University of Massachusetts, mimeo.

Bowles, S. and Gintis, H. (1998c), 'Mutual Monitoring in Teams: The Effects of Residual Clemency and Reciprocity', Amherst, University of Massachusetts, mimeo.

Bowles, S. and Gintis, H. (1998d), 'The Evolution of Strong Reciprocity', Amherst, University of Massachusetts, mimeo.

Bowles, S. and Gintis, H. (2000), 'Optimal Parochialism: The dynamics of trust and exclusion in networks', Amherst, University of Massachusetts, mimeo

Bowles, S., Boyd, R., Fehr, E. and Gintis, H. (1997), '*Homo Reciprocans*: A research initiative on the origins, dimensions, and policy implications of reciprocal fairness', Amherst, University of Massachusetts, mimeo.

Boyd, R. and Richerson, P. J. (1989), 'The Evolution of Indirect Reciprocity', *Social Networks*, 11, pp. 213-36.

Burgenmeier, B. (1994), *La Socio-Économie*, Paris, Economica.

Burnham, T., McCabe, K. and Smith, V. F. (2000), 'Friend-or-Foe Intentionality Priming in an Extensive Form Trust Game', *Journal of Economic Behavior and Organization*, 43, pp. 57-73.

Cameron, L. (1999), 'Raising the Stakes in the Ultimatum Game: Experimental evidence from Indonesia', *Economic Inquiry*, 37 (1), pp. 47-59.

Charness, G. and Haruvy, E. (1999), 'Altruism, Equity, and Reciprocity in a Gift-Exchange Experiment: An encompassing approach', Berkeley, University of California, mimeo.

Coate, S. and Ravallion, M. (1993), 'Reciprocity Without Commitment: Characterization and performance of informal insurance arrangements', *Journal of Development Economics*, 40, pp. 1-24.

Coleman, J. (1990), *Foundations of Social Theory*, Cambridge, MA, Harvard University Press.

Dasgupta, P. (1989), 'La Fiducia come Bene Economico', in D. Gambetta (ed.), *op cit.*, pp. 63-93.

De Vos, H. and Zeggelink, E. P. H. (1994), 'The Emergence of Reciprocal Altruism and Group Living: An object-oriented simulation model of human social evolution', *Social Science Information*, 33, pp. 433-51.

De Vos, H. and Zeggelink, E. P. H. (1997), 'Reciprocal Altruism in Human Social Evolution: The viability of reciprocal altruism with preference for "old-helping partners"', *Evolution and Human-Behavior*, 18, pp. 261-78.

Derrida, J. (1992), *Given Time I: Counterfeit money*, Chicago, The University of Chicago Press.

Derrida, J. (1995), *The Gift of Death*, Chicago, The University of Chicago Press.

Dunn, J. (1989), 'Fiducia e Agire Politico', in D. Gambetta (ed.), *op cit.*, pp. 95-121.

Eisenstadt, S. N. and Roniger, L. (1984), *Patrons, Clients and Friends*, Cambridge, Cambridge University Press.

Elias, N. (1987), *A Sociedade de Corte*, Lisboa, Estampa.

Elias, N. (1989), *O Processo Civilizacional*, 2 vols., Lisboa, Dom Quixote.

Elias, N. (1992), *A Busca da Excitação*, Lisboa, Difel.

Elias, N. (1993), *Mozart: Sociologia de um Génio*, Porto, Edições Asa.

Etzioni, A. (1988), *The Moral Dimension: Toward a new economics*, New York, The Free Press.

Etzioni, A. (1991), 'Socio-Economics: A Building Challenge', in A. Etzioni and P. R. Lawrence (eds), *Socio-Economics: Toward a new synthesis*, Armonk, M. E. Sharpe.

Etzioni, A. (1993), *The Spirit of Community: The reinvention of American society*, New York, Touchstone - Simon & Schuster.

Etzioni, A. and Lawrence, P.R. (1991), *Socio-Economics: Toward a new synthesis*, Armonk, M. E. Sharpe Inc.

Fahr, R. and Irlenbusch, B. (2000), 'Fairness as a Constraint on Trust in Reciprocity: Earned property rights in a reciprocal exchange experiment', *Economics Letters*, 66, pp. 275-82.

Falk, A. and Fischbacher, U. (1999), 'A Theory of Reciprocity', Working Paper No. 6, *Institute for Empirical Research in Economics*, Zurich, University of Zurich.

Falk, A., Fehr, F. and Fischbacher, U. (1999), 'On the Nature of Fair Behavior', Working Paper, Zurich, University of Zurich.

Falk, A., Gächter, S. and Kovács, J. (1999), 'Intrinsic Motivation and Extrinsic Incentives in a Repeated Game with Incomplete Contracts', *Journal of Economic Psychology*, 20, pp. 251-84.

Fehr, F. and Gächter, S. (1998), 'Reciprocity and Economics: The Economic Implications of *Homo Reciprocans*', *European Economic Review*, 42, pp. 845-59.

Fehr, F., Kirchler, E., Weichbold, A. and Gächter, S. (1998), 'When Social Norms Overpower Competition: Gift exchange in experimental labour markets', *Journal of Labour Economics*, 16 (2), pp. 324-51.

Frank, R. (1988), *Passions within Reason: The strategic role of the emotions*, New York, W.W. Norton.

Frey, B. (1997), *Not Just For the Money - An Economic Theory of Personal Motivation*, Cheltenham, Edward Elgar Publishing.

Fukuyama, F. (1996), *Confiança: Valores sociais e criação de prosperidade*, Lisboa, Gradiva.

Gale, J., Binmore, K. and Samuelson, L. (1995), 'Learning to Be Imperfect: The ultimatum game' *Games and Economic Behavior*, 8, pp. 56-90.

Gambetta, D. (1989a), *Le Strategie della Fiducia: Indagini sulla razionalità della cooperazione*, Turin, Einaudi.

Gambetta, D. (1989b), 'Mafia: I Costi della Sfiducia', in D. Gambetta (ed.), *op cit.*, pp. 203-226.

Gambetta, D. (1992), *La Mafia Siciliana: Un'Industria della protezione privata*, Turin, Einaudi.

Gellner E. (1989), 'Fiducia, Coesione e Ordine Sociale', in D. Gambetta (ed.), *op cit.*, pp. 183-201.

Gibbard, Al. (1990), *Wise Choices, Apt Feelings: A theory of normative judgment*, Cambridge, MA, Harvard University Press.

Gintis, H. (2000), 'Strong Reciprocity and Human Sociality', Amherst, University of Massachusetts, mimeo.

Girard, R. (1972), *La Violence et Le sacré*, Paris, Grasset.

Godbout, J.T. (1992), *L'Esprit du Don*, Paris, Éditions La Découverte.

Godbout, J.T. (2000), *Le Don, La Dette et L'Identité*, Paris, Éditions La Découverte/M.A.U.S.S.

Godelier, M. (1996), *l'Énigme du Don*, Paris, Fayard.

Good, D. (1989), 'Individui, Relazioni Interpersonali e Fiducia' in D. Gambetta (ed.), *op cit.*, pp. 41-62.

Gouldner, A. W. (1960), 'The Norm of Reciprocity', *American Sociological Review*, 25 (2), pp. 161-78.

Granovetter, M. (1974), *Getting A Job: A study of contact and careers*, Cambridge, MA, Harvard University Press.

Granovetter, M. (1978), 'Threshold Models of Collective Behavior', *American Journal of Sociology*, 83 (6), pp. 1420-43.

Granovetter, M. (1985), 'Economic Action and Social Structure: The problem of embeddedness', *American Journal of Sociology*, 91 (3), pp. 481-510.

Gregory, C. A. (1982), *Gifts and Commodities*, London/New York, Academic Press.

Gregory, C. A. (1997), *Savage Money: The anthropology and politics of commodity exchange*, Amsterdam, Harwood Academic Publishers.

Güth, W., Schmittberger, R. and Schwarze, B. (1982), 'An Experimental Analysis of Ultimatum Bargaining', *Journal of Economic Behavior and Organization*, 3, pp. 367-88.

Guttman, J. M. (2000), 'On the Evolutionary Stability of Preferences for Reciprocity', *European Journal of Political Economy*, 16, pp. 31-50.

Hamilton, G. and Biggart, N. W. (1988), 'Market, Culture, and Authority: A comparative analysis of management and organization in the Far East', *American Journal of Sociology*, Vol. 94, Supplement, pp. S52-S94.

Hart, K. (1989), 'Parentela, Contrato e Fiducia: l'Organizzazione economica degli immigrati nei bassifondi di una città Africana', in Diego Gambetta (ed.), *op cit.*, pp. 227-49.

Hollis, M. (1998), *Trust Within Reason*, Cambridge, Cambridge University Press.

Hyde, L. (1983), *The Gift: Imagination and the Erotic Life of Property*, New York, Vintage Books.

Kiong, T. C. and Kee, Y. P. (1998), 'Guanxi Bases, Xinyong and Chinese Business Networks', *British Journal of Sociology*, 49 (1), pp. 75-96.

Kirchler, E., Fehr, E. and Evans, R. (1996), 'Social Exchange in the Labour Market: Reciprocity and trust versus egoistic money maximization', *Journal of Economic Psychology*, 17, pp. 313-41.

Kolm, S.-C. (1984), *La Bonne Économie, La Réciprocité Générale*, Paris, PUF.

Kolm, S.-C. (2000), 'Introduction: The economics of reciprocity, giving and altruism', in L.A. Gérard-Varet, S.-C. Kolm and J. M. Ythier (eds), *The Economics of Reciprocity, Giving and Altruism*, London, Macmillan Press, pp. 1-44.

Kramer, R.M. and Tyler, T.R. (eds) (1996) *Trust in Organizations: Frontiers of theory and research*, Thousand Oaks, Sage.

Lacourse, J. (1987), 'Réciprocité Positive et Réciprocité Negative: de Marcel Mauss à René Girard', *Cahiers Internationaux de Sociologie*, 34, N° 83, Juillet/Décembre, pp. 291-305.

Landa, J. T. (1994), *Trust, Ethnicity, and Identity: Beyond the new institutional economics of ethnic trading networks, contract law, and gift-exchange*, Ann Arbor, The University of Michigan Press.

Lazaric, N. and Lorenz, E. (eds)(1998), *Trust and Economic Learning*, Cheltenham, Edward Elgar.

Lebra, T. S. (1976), *Japanese Patterns of Behavior*, Honolulu, University of Hawaii Press.

Lebra, T. S. and Lebra, W. P. (eds) (1986), *Japanese Culture and Behavior: Selected readings*, Honolulul, University of Hawaii Press.

Ledeneva, A.V. (1998), *Russia's Economy of Favours: Blat, networking and informal exchange*, Cambridge, Cambridge University Press.

Lewis, J. D. and Weigert, A. (1985), 'Trust as a Social Reality', *Social Forces*, 63, pp. 967-85.

List, J. A. and Shogren, J. F. (1998), 'The Deadweight Loss of Christmas: Comment', *American Economic Review*, 88 (5), 1350-55.

Lorenz, E.H. (1989), 'Né Amici Né Estranei: Reti Informali di Subappalto nell'Industria Francese', in D. Gambetta (ed.), *op cit.*, pp. 251-72.

Lovell, S., Ledeneva, A. and Rogachevskii, A. (2000), *Bribery and Blat in Russia: Negotiating reciprocity from the Middle Ages to the 1990s*, London, Macmillan.

Luhmann, N. (1979), *Trust and Power*, New York, John Wiley.

Luhmann, N. (1989), 'Familiarità, Confidare e Fiducia: Problemi e Alternative', in D. Gambetta (ed.), *op cit.*, pp. 123-40.

M.A.U.S.S. (1990), *La Socio-Économie. Une Nouvelle Discipline?*, Revue, 9, Paris, La Découverte.

M.A.U.S.S. (1993), *Ce que Donner Veut Dire*, Revue, 1er semestre, Paris, La Découverte.

M.A.U.S.S. (1994), *A Qui se Fier? Confiance, Interaction et Théorie des Jeux*, Paris, Éditions La Découverte.

Macesich, G. (1994), *Successor States and Cooperation Theory: A model for Eastern Europe*, Westport, Greenwood/Praeger.

Maclachlan, B. (1993), *The Age of Grace: Charis in early Greek poetry*, Princeton, Princeton University Press.

Marques, R. (2001), 'Economia Experimental e Reciprocidade: Uma meta-análise', Lisboa, Socius Working Papers, 2/2001.

Mauss, M. (1988), *Ensaio sobre a Dádiva*, Lisboa, Edições 70.

McAleer, K. (1994), *Dueling: The cult of honor in fin-de-siècle Germany*, Princeton, Princeton University Press.

Misztal, B.A. (1996), *Trust in Modern Societies*, Cambridge, Polity Press.

Nelson, B. (1969), *The Idea of Usury: From tribal brotherhood to universal otherhood*, 2nd edition, Chicago, The University of Chicago Press.

Nicolas, G. (1996), *Du Don Rituel au Sacrifice Suprême*, Paris, Éditions La Découverte/ M.A.U.S.S.

Okada, A. and Riedl, A. (1999), 'When Culture Does Not Matter: Experimental evidence from coalition formation ultimatum games in Austria and Japan', mimeo.

Pendenza, M. (2000), *Cooperazione, Fiducia e Capitale Sociale: Elementi per una teoria del mutamento sociale*, Naples, Liguori Editore.

Polanyi, K. (1957), *Trade and Markets in the Early Empires*, New York, Free Press.

Polanyi, K. (1983), *La Grande Transformation: Aux origines politiques et économiques de notre temps*, Paris, Gallimard.

Portes, A. (1995), 'Economic Sociology and the Sociology of Immigration: A conceptual overview', in A. Portes (ed.), *The Economic Sociology of Immigration: Essays on networks, ethnicity, and entrepreneurship*, New York, Russell Sage Foundation, pp. 1-43.

Prisbrey, J. (1993), 'Bounded Rationality, Evolutionary Model for Behavior in Two Person Reciprocity Games', Universitat Pompeu Fabra, mimeo.

Rabin, M. (1993), 'Incorporating Fairness into Game Theory and Economics', *American Economic Review*, 83, pp. 1281-302.

Raheja, G. G. (1988), *The Poison in the Gift: Ritual, prestation and the dominant caste in a North Indian village*, Chicago/London, The University of Chicago Press.

Reece, S. (1993), *The Stranger's Welcome: Oral theory and the aesthetics of the Homeric hospitality scene*, Ann Arbor, The University of Michigan Press.

Richardson, J. D. (1987), 'International Coordination of Trade Policy', National Bureau of Economic Research, Working Paper 2293, June.

Sahlins, M. (1972), *Stone Age Economics*, Chicago, Aldine.

Scheff, T. J. (1990), *Microsociology: Discourse, emotion, and social structure*, Chicago, The University of Chicago Press.

Schelling, T. C. (1980), *La Tyrannie des Petites Décisions*, Paris, PUF.

Schelling, T. C. (1986), *Stratégie du Conflit*, Paris, PUF.

Seaford, R. (1994), *Reciprocity and Ritual: Homer and tragedy in the developing city-state*, Oxford, Clarendon Press.

Seligman, A. (1997), *The Problem of Trust*, Princeton, Princeton University Press.

Slonim, R. and Roth, A. (1998), 'Learning in High Stakes Ultimatum Games: An experiment in the Slovak republic', *Econometrica*, 66 (3), pp. 569-96.

Solnick, S. J. and Hemenway, D. (1996), '"The Deadweight Loss of Christmas": Comment', *American Economic Review*, Vol. 86 (5), pp. 1299-305.

Solnick, S. J. and Hemenway, D. (1998), '"The Deadweight Loss of Christmas": Reply', *American Economic Review*, 88 (5), pp. 1356-57.

Solow, J. L. (1994), 'Paternalistic Preferences, Interpersonal Transfers and Reciprocity', *Southern Economic Journal*, 61 (2), pp. 379-86.

Spicker, P. (1988), *Principles of Social Welfare: An introduction to thinking about the welfare state*, London, Routledge.

Sugden, R. (1986), *The Evolution of Rights, Cooperation and Welfare*, Oxford, Basil Blackwell.

Swaney, J. A. (1990), 'Common Property, Reciprocity and Community', *Journal of Economic Issues*, 24 (2), pp. 451-62.

Sztompka, P. (1999), *Trust: A sociological theory*, Cambridge, Cambridge University Press.

Thuderoz, C., Mangematin, V. and Harrisson, D. (eds) (1999), *La Confiance: Approches économiques et sociologiques*, Levallois-Perre, Gaëtan Morin Éditeur.

Titmuss, R. M. (1997), *The Gift Relationship: From human blood to social policy*, Original Edition with New Chapters edited by Ann Oakley and John Ashton, London, LSE Books.

Trivers, R. (1971), 'The Evolution of Reciprocal Altruism', *Quarterly Review of Biology*, 46, pp. 35-57.

Veyne, P. (1976), *Le Pain et le Cirque: Sociologie historique d'un pluralisme politique*, Seuil, Paris.

Waldfogel, J. (1993), 'The Deadweight Loss of Christmas', *American Economic Review*, 83 (5), pp. 1328-36.

Waldfogel, J. (1996), 'The Deadweight Loss of Christmas: Peply', *American Economic Review*, 86 (5), pp. 1306-08.

Waldfogel, J. (1998), 'The Deadweight Loss of Christmas: Peply', *American Economic Review*, 86 (5), pp. 1358-59.

Weiner, A.B. (1992), *Inalienable Possessions: The paradox of keeping while giving*, Berkeley/Los Angeles, University of California Press.

Yan, Y. (1996), *The Flow of Gifts: Reciprocity and networks in a Chinese village*, Stanford, Stanford University Press.

Yang, M. M.-H. (1994), *Gifts, Favours and Banquets: The art of social relationships in China*, Ithaca, NY, Cornell University Press.

Chapter 3

The 'Network Ethic' and the New Spirit of Capitalism in French Sociology of Capitalism

Søren Jagd

Introduction

The concept of a network has increasingly been applied in efforts to understand recent changes in society at large (Castells 1996, 2000), business enterprises (Podolny and Page 1998; DiMaggio 2001), and markets (Podolny 2001; White 2001). The research concerning networks has been very impressive and its results most interesting, nevertheless, some limitations remain. Importantly, most of network research has, as in the tradition of social network theory, focused on structural aspects of networks leaving the cultural aspects of networks inadequately analysed. As pointed out by Emirbayer and Goodwin, network analysis 'has inadequately theorized the causal role of ideals, beliefs, and values of the actors that strive to realize them, as a result it has neglected the cultural and symbolic moment in the very determination of social action' (Emirbayer and Goodwin 1994, p. 1446).

This chapter attempts to take a small step toward giving due attention to the importance of ideals, beliefs and values of actors in networks. The specific aim of the chapter is a critical discussion of a recent French contribution to the analysis of the cultural aspects of networks namely Boltanski and Chiapello's book *Le nouvel esprit du capitalisme* (Boltanski and Chiapello 1999).[1] Boltanski and Chiapello analyse the complex dynamics of the emergence of a 'new spirit of capitalism'.

The contribution is quite impressive in a number of ways. Here I will only point to two major reasons for examining this work in greater detail. Firstly, Boltanski and Chiapello propose an interesting ideal type model of the form of justification related to the new 'spirit of capitalism'. This ideal type model of the new aspect of capitalism may serve to generate an important reference for understanding recent

---

[1] The book has generated considerable attention both in France and abroad. This had led to further comments by Boltanski and Chiapello stressing their main arguments (Boltanski and Chiapello 2000a, 2000b, 2001a, 2001b, 2001c, 2002; Chiapello and Fairclough 2002).

changes in capitalism. Secondly, Boltanski and Chiapello take a critical perspective on the emergent model of 'network capitalism' and its accompanying spirit by applying the theoretical framework of 'worlds of justification' developed earlier by Boltanski and Thévenot (Boltanski and Thévenot 1991).

My aim in this chapter is to present the most important aspects of Boltanski and Chiapello's analysis of the emergent spirit of 'network capitalism', and to explore how this perspective can help to us to understand the cultural aspects of the network society. First, I present the basic model developed by Boltanski and Chiapello to understand the interplay between capitalism, its criticism, and the spirit of capitalism. Second, I present the analysis of the changes in management discourse from the 1960s to the early 1990s. This analysis points to a change in the spirit of capitalism during the last thirty years. Third, I present a description of the emerging new forms of justification linked to the network perspective, the 'Project World'. This new form of justification, still under construction, forms, according to Boltanski and Chiapello, the basic point of reference for the development of the spirit of network capitalism. Fourth, I discuss the problems of justice in network forms of organisations as discussed by Boltanski and Chiapello. Last, I discuss how this framework could be used as a step toward understanding the forms of justification in new organisational forms such as project- and team-based organisations.

The General Framework for Analysing the Evolution of Capitalism

Boltanski and Chiapello start out by outlining a dynamic model of the evolution of capitalism stressing three elements: 1) capitalist activity and its organisational models, 2) criticism of capitalist activity, and 3) the spirit of capitalism, namely the justification of capitalist activity. Boltanski and Chiapello's aim is to 'clarify the relations between capitalism and its criticism' (Boltanski and Chiapello 1999, p. 36) to interpret the phenomena that have affected the ideological sphere[2] during the last decades. The concept of the spirit of capitalism is brought in to investigate the interplay of the two central concepts: capitalism and the criticism of capitalism. Here I only discuss the way Boltanski and Chiapello articulate the concept of the spirit of capitalism and how they apply this concept for the empirical analysis of the new spirit of capitalism.

Capitalism is, following Max Weber, described as being based on a 'search for an unlimited accumulation of capital by peaceful means' (Boltanski and Chiapello 1999, p. 37). The concept of 'the spirit of capitalism' is defined by Boltanski and

---

[2] Boltanski and Chiapello intends to propose a non-reductionist theoretical framework 'to understand the modification of ideologies associated with economic activities' where ideology is seen as 'an assembling of shared beliefs, inscribed into institutions, made commitment to in actions and thereby anchored in reality' (Boltanski and Chiapello 1999, p. 35).

Chiapello as the 'ideology that justifies the involvement with capitalism' (Boltanski and Chiapello 1999, p. 42). The general perspective is 'the idea that actors need strong moral reasons to join themselves with capitalism' (Boltanski and Chiapello 1999, p. 44). There may, according to Boltanski and Chiapello, be two types of reasons for involving yourself in capitalist activities. First, individual justifications motivating personal involvement in capitalist activity. Second, general justifications demonstrating how involvement in capitalist activity is serving the common good. Weber's position was that capitalism had less need of moral justification once it was institutionalised as a social system. In contrast, Boltanski and Chiapello stress the continuing importance of the justification of capitalist activity, making the spirit of capitalism an important element in explaining the development of capitalism.

> The question of moral justification of capitalism is not only of historical importance to understand its origins. ... It is also of an extreme importance in Western countries like France where the population is integrated into a capitalist cosmos to a degree never seen before. In effect, the systematic constraints on actors do not suffice, in themselves, to cause their engagement. The constraints have to be internalised and justified. ... If capitalism has not only survived ... but has not stopped extending its influence it is also because it has been able to find support in a certain number of representations – capable of guiding action – and shared justifications that holds it an acceptable and desirable order, the only possible order, or the best of possible orders (Boltanski and Chiapello 1999, p. 45).

The spirit of capitalism is thus the assembly of representations and shared justifications associated with the capitalist order supporting the modes of action and the dispositions coherent with it. Boltanski and Chiapello then transform the spirit of capitalism into a more dynamic concept. An interesting problem then becomes to describe variations in the spirit of capitalism.

According to Boltanski and Chiapello the spirit of capitalism has to present a satisfying answer to three crucial questions in relation to the development of capitalist accumulation (Boltanski and Chiapello 1999, p. 53-54):

- How may the engagement in the process of capitalist accumulation be a *source of enthusiasm* for those that do not necessarily benefit from the realised profit?
- To what extent can those who involve themselves in the capitalist cosmos expect a *minimal security* for themselves and their children?
- How can one justify, in terms of a *common good*, the participation in the capitalist enterprise and defend, in face of accusations of injustice, the way it is managed?

To secure recruitment to capitalist activities, the spirit of capitalism has presented different combinations of enthusiasm, security and the search for a common good.

Two spirits of capitalism have, according to Boltanski and Chiapello, been presented earlier. The first was the spirit of *entrepreneurial capitalism* embodied in the bourgeois entrepreneur. The capitalist adventure was linked to the process of personal liberation in two ways. In relation to space, because of new means of communication, and in relation to tradition through the possibilities to find wage labour in the cities. The promise of security was found in a combination of rationalist economic values, such as saving, rational management, accounting and planning, and traditional domestic values, such as the family, tradition, and patriarchal relations with employees. Justification in relation to a common good was not so much found in economic liberalism as in the belief in progress, in the future, in science, in technology, and in the benefits from industry.

The second spirit of capitalism was the spirit of *organisational capitalism* linked to the rise of the large business enterprise at its peak between the 1930s and the 1960s. The salaried managing director (and managers) striving for continuously growing companies embodied the powerful actors that were able to change the world. Security was found in the belief in rationality, long-term planning, and 'gigantism'. The large enterprises constituted a protecting milieu for career, future employment and social security.

Boltanski and Chiapello applies the theoretical developed earlier by Boltanski and Thévenot in *De la Justification* (Boltanski and Thévenot 1991).[3] In this work, Boltanski and Thévenot describe six major forms of justification and present an ideal type framework describing the basic dimensions of these 'worlds of justification' (*citées*)[4] as presented below on Table 3.1.

The world of inspiration is based on St. Augustine's *City of God*. Worth rests upon the attainment of a state of grace independent of the recognition by others. The expressions of grace are diverse: holiness, creativity, artistic sensibility etc. Valuable objects in this world are products expressing the genius of the producer. The market value or the functionality of a piece of art is not important in this world. What counts is the extent to which it expresses the creativity and the genius of the artist.

In the *domestic world* peoples' worth depends on 'a hierarchy of trust based on a chain of personal dependencies' and the link between beings is based upon 'a generalisation of kinship and is based on face-to-face relationships and on the respect for tradition' (Boltanski and Thévenot 1999, p. 370). Education and adjustment to authorities are important qualities. Typical objects in this world are visiting cards, gifts, houses, and titles.

The *civic world* is based on Rousseau's *Contral Social*. Worthy are those exclusively concerned with the general interest. The peculiar aspect stressed by the civic world is 'to lay stress on beings who are not individual beings but collective

---

[3] Boltanski and Thévenot have more recently presented and discussed this framework in English at several occasions: (Boltanski and Thévenot 1999, 2000; Lamont and Thévenot 2000; Thévenot 2001a, 2001b, 2002).
[4] Boltanski and Thévenot use the word 'cité' to describe a coherent form of justice. I use the concept 'world' to describe the coherent mental construction of a specific form of justice.

ones' (Boltanski and Thévenot 1999). Individuals are only relevant and worthy in so far as they belong to a group or as the representatives of a collective person. Important in this world are federations, public communities, representatives or delegates. Relevant objects may be immaterial, such as rules, codes, procedures, or material, such as ballot boxes.

The *world of opinion* is based on Hobbes' *Leviathan*. Worth in this world is the result of other people's opinion and measurement of worth depends on conventional signs of public esteem. Worthy people are the famous, the recognised, the successful, or the convincing such as stars, opinion leaders, journalists. Important objects in this world may be trademarks, newspapers, book etc.

Table 3.1 Worlds of justification

	INSPIRED	DOMESTIC	CIVIC	OPINION	MARKET	INDUSTRIAL
Mode of evaluation (worth)	Grace, non-conformity, creativity	Esteem, reputation	Collective interest	Renown	Price	Productivity efficiency
Format of relevant information	Emotional	Oral, exemplary, anecdotal	Formal, official	Semiotic	Monetary	Measurable criteria, statistics
Elementary relation	Passion	Trust	Solidarity	Recognition	Exchange	Functional link
Human qualification	Creativity, ingenuity	Authority	Equality	Celebrity	Desire, purchasing power	Professional competency and expertise

Source: Boltanski and Thévenot 1999, p. 368.

The *market world* is based on the first chapters of Adam Smith's *Wealth of Nations* and is concerned with the construction of a harmonious polity on the market. Boltanski and Thévenot stress that the market world should not be mixed up with the sphere of economic relations. Instead, Boltanski and Thévenot want to show 'that economic actions are based on, at least, two main forms of coordination, one by the market, the other by an industrial order, each of them being the support of a different reality test' (Boltanski and Thévenot 1999, p. 372). Important people are buyers and sellers. Their main qualities are to 'be opportunistic in spotting and seizing the opportunities of the market, to be unhampered by any personal link and to be emotionally under control' (Boltanski and Thévenot 1999, p. 372).

The *industrial world* is concerned with the production of material goods. Worth is based on efficiency and can be measured according to specific criteria. Important people are the experts and their quality is measured as their ability to control the production of goods. They are said to be worthy when they are efficient, productive and so forth. Important objects are tools, methods, criteria, plans, figures, and graphs. Harmonious relationships are organised, functional, standardised.

Boltanski and Thévenot advance the hypothesis 'that the same people have, on the same day and in the same social space, to use different devices for assessment, including the reference to different types of worth, when they shift from one situation to another' (Boltanski and Thévenot 1999, p. 369). In this perspective it is necessary for actors to come to some sort of common agreement of which of the possible worlds of justification should be applied to evaluate their past, present, or planned actions.

Boltanski and Chiapello argue that the first and the second spirit of capitalism draw in different ways on these orders of worth. The first spirit of capitalism, family capitalism, found its justification in a compromise between the Domestic and the Market world. The second spirit of capitalism, organisational capitalism, found its justification in a compromise between the Industrial and the Civic world.

The Forms of Justification in the Third Spirit of Capitalism

Boltanski and Chiapello's basic hypothesis is that during the last thirty years, an important change in the spirit of capitalism has taken place leading to the emergence of a third spirit of capitalism, the spirit of 'network capitalism'. To analyse this transformation from the second to the third spirit of capitalism Boltanski and Chiapello undertake a comparison[5] of two sets of management texts from the 1960s and from the 1990s. The aim is to demonstrate how the ideological traits of the second spirit of capitalism have been criticised and gradually have led to the elaboration of a new general representation of the enterprise and the economy. While the description of the six general forms of justification in Western societies was based on 'manuals' found in political philosophical literature it has

---

[5] The comparative analysis involved several steps. First, a classic analysis of the two sets of texts was made to extract the general themes of the texts, the representations they give of the forms inherited from the past, and the solutions they propose of the problems they find. Second, the hypothesis developed in the first step was checked using qualitative software counting the number of references to the different worlds of justification in the two sets of texts. Third, the texts have been ordered according to the primary and the secondary references to a world of justification.

not been possible to find a 'manual' for the justification of network capitalism. The empirical reference was, instead, found in management literature.

Boltanski and Chiapello analyse the evolution of management discourse from the 1960s to the 1990s by focussing on three questions: 1) which questions and problems do the authors pose?, 2) how do they reject the present situation?, and 3) which responses and solutions are advanced to remedy these problems?

In the 1960s, authors were, first and foremost, preoccupied with problems concerning the motivation of managers. The most important problem was the strong dissatisfaction of managers related to the management of still larger enterprises. The managers were not satisfied with the role they were given. First, they were restricted to playing the role of technical experts. Second, they were restricted to playing a mediating role in the hierarchy sending orders downward and informing higher levels of problems raised at lower levels. They were aspiring to have decision-making power, to be autonomous, to understand strategic decisions, to be informed of the economic situation of the enterprise. These problems are related to the rise of managers as a new social group accompanying the growth of companies. The managers in the 1960s had the feeling of incarnating modernity but being confined by a mode of management and structures that have characterised earlier forms of paternalistic enterprises.

The texts of the 1960s criticise, explicitly or implicitly, the earlier model of 'family capitalism'. The models and forms of management that served as points of criticism were, in diverse ways, based on the domestic logic. Management based on 'personal judgement' was rejected as an open door to nepotism and advancement based on seniority only. Seniority was seen as rewarding fidelity – the value par excellence of the domestic world – and not as rewarding efficiency.

In the management literature, the proposed solutions to these problems were decentralisation of large enterprises, 'meritocracy', and management by objectives. The texts of the 1960s had, essentially, the aim of imposing these new modes of management. Especially management by objectives had the potentiality to give managers the autonomy they were aspiring to. Each manager had greater autonomy, though it was constrained by the objectives given. The manager was only judged in relation to their realisation of objectives. Organisational control was thereby safeguarded, the autonomy of managers was extended, and the enterprises could profit from a well-motivated staff. Management by objectives also had the advantage of offering an objective and a more just criterion to measure performance and to take decisions concerning careers. Advancement was accorded to those who had met their objectives, and not based on 'unjust' subjective criteria.

The discourse of the 1990s was a continuation of the movement concerning the autonomy of managers and the softening of bureaucracies through decentralisation. The problem of the motivation of managers that preoccupied the authors in the 1960s was extended, in the 1990s, to the problem of motivating all employees. On the other hand, different questions were raised concerning the growing awareness of the pressure of competition and the demands of clients. The texts from the 1990s reject large hierarchical and planned organisations. Hierarchy is rejected to the extent that it is based on domination. Formal planning is rejected as being too rigid.

To remedy these problems, the authors of the 1990s, proposed instruments based on a few key ideas: 'lean' enterprises working in complex networks, organised in teams or by projects, oriented toward satisfaction of the client, and a general mobilisation of workers through the visions of their leaders.

The solution proposed by the management literature in the 1990s is found in the metaphor of the network. The network metaphor is mobilised in all sorts of contexts: autonomous working teams organised in network relations with partners internal and external to the enterprise, development of partnership relations based on trust (strategic alliances), distance working, and enterprise networks in industrial districts.

To promote these new organisational forms the authors criticises certain aspects of contemporary organisations that are judged obsolete in relation to efficiency and to acceptable human relations. While the organisation in the 1960s was seen to expand the separation between the private world and professional relations at work, the authors of the 1990s searched to reintegrate these spheres. The project is then to abolish important parts of the old enterprise model by, on the one side, de-legitimating hierarchy, formal planning, formal authority, Taylorism, the statute of leaders and life-long carriers, and on the other side, reintroducing criteria linked to personality and proper personal relations.

The history of management may, according to Boltanski and Chiapello, be seen as a permanent sophistication of the means to manage the internal and external relations of the enterprise. Taylor and Fayol pointed to employees as the principal focus of control. With business strategy, the focus extends to markets and competitors. Marketing further extended this focus to distribution and customers. Purchase management to control of suppliers. Public relations extended the aim to control the press and political organisations. This leads to the question of which modalities of control are brought forward by neo-management. As before the question of control is seen as central. One of the key problems becomes that of controlling the 'liberated enterprise' based on self-organised teams, working in networks. The solution is that employees internalise control mechanisms. This explains the focus on culture and values and the visions of leaders. Self-controlled individuals should voluntarily exercise control on themselves.

An important aspect of this self-control is internalisation of the conditions of competition through the focus on the customer as expressed in the perspective that 'the customer is the king'. This dogma offers two advantages. First, it orients self-control in a direction favourable to profit, and second, it transfers part of the control exercised in the hierarchy in the 1960s to the client.

With the decline of hierarchical control, the theme of trust becomes important. Trust is a sign that the situation is under control in the sense that you only make agreements with people who do not abuse the trust, who are predictable and do what they say they will. To develop trustful relations you must yourself be worthy of trust. Trust is then another name for self-control. In a schematic way, the most marked traits of the evolution of management in the last 30 years is the passage from control to self-control, and the externalisation of control costs earlier assumed by the organisation to employees and customers.

Based on this analysis of the management literature, it is possible to distinguish the spirit of capitalism in the two collections of texts. In the texts of the 1960s, the attractive dimension of capitalist management was decentralisation and autonomy of leaders. In relation to society, it is argued that the new form of management makes the enterprises more efficient and thereby leads to economic and social progress. Security was, in the 1960s, linked to the assurance of careers in the large organisations and the expansion of the role of the State to take care of other aspects of risks such as unemployment.

In the 1990s, the principal attraction of capitalist activity was the possibilities of liberation from outmoded forms of organisation. Creativity and flexibility are the new key words. A second, seducing, dimension of neo-management is the possibility to develop personally. The new model proposes a 'real autonomy' founded in self-knowledge and personal fulfilment.

In the 1960s, it was believed that everyone should be rewarded according to their efficiency and their results. In the 1990s, the valuable people were those able to work with different sorts of people, those who are open and flexible in relation to change of projects and who are continuously able to adapt in new circumstances. The proper way to reward these mediators in networks may still be imprecise and unclear due to the fact that a new form of justice is emerging that may not have developed its proper instruments yet.

To validate the classic analysis of the two sets of texts Boltanski and Chiapello add an analysis with the help of qualitative software.[6] The importance of the new world of justice, the Project World, in recent management literature is further validated by an analysis of the total number of references made to the different worlds of justification, or 'logics', in the two groups of texts.

The presence of a world of justification is measured as the relative share of all references to this world of justification. This analysis should, of course, be taken more as an indication of the change in the spirit of capitalism than a full description of this change. A full description would demand the analysis of other types of material, among others of the values of both managers and employees. Nevertheless, this analysis can give us an important indication of the current change. The data[7] show, first of all, that the industrial logic is the dominating point

---

[6] The concepts in the two sets of texts were coded and the total number of occurrences counted. In both sets of texts the most important concept was 'enterprise'. In the texts from 1960s the following ten most important concepts were: manager (cadre), subordinates, leaders (dirigeants), management, work, chef, cadre, organisation, authority, and objectives. In the 1990s the following ten most important concepts were: work, organisation, network, team, project, leaders (dirigeants), customer-supplier, subordinates, manager and management.

[7] The relative share of references was in the 1960s (in per cent): Industrial logic 47, Domestic logic 14, Market logic 13, Civic logic 9, network logic 8, Inspirational logic 5 and Opinion logic 3. In the 1990s the relative share was (in per cent): Industrial logic 32,

of reference in both periods. Its dominance was weakened relatively speaking with the share of all references falling from 47 to 32 per cent. The second most important logic in the 1960s was the domestic one, with 14 per cent in the 1960s, while in the 1990s it was the network logic with 26 per cent. The market logic occupies the third place (13-14 per cent) in both periods.

Boltanski and Chiapello maintain that this empirical analysis supports the hypothesis of a transformation in the forms of justification that has taken place in the management literature. According to Boltanski and Chiapello, we are now witnessing the emergence of a new spirit of capitalism linked to the rise of *network capitalism*. It is not found possible to describe this world alone with reference to the six worlds of justification described earlier by Boltanski and Thévenot. Boltanski and Chiapello's make a first attempt to analyse the 'residual' of this new spirit of capitalism by modelling a seventh world of justification, the Project world, using the architecture of political 'cités' described earlier by Boltanski and Thévenot (Boltanski and Thévenot 1991).

The 'Network Ethic' – The Architecture of the 'Project World'

As described above the key elements of the second spirit of capitalism have, according to Boltanski and Chiapello, gradually been questioned, transformed, and replaced. The processes have lead to the need for a new general representation of the economic world to make the new 'rules of the game' explicit. The network concept is found to link the different elements of this emergent form of organisation. Multiple networks are seen as linking diverse groups operating at social, professional, geographical and cultural distances. New maxims are gradually constituted in the process of establishing a new system of values. These maxims assist judgements, help to discriminate adequate behaviour from inadequate, to price the qualities and the attitudes which before was not properly identified, and to legitimise new power positions.

The network concept is not in itself found able to codify the new emerging form of justification because it does not properly specify the constraints on the network. Boltanski and Chiapello have chosen to name this new form of justification the Project World because projects are the occasion and the pretext of the connective actions leading to the development of networks. From this perspective, an enterprise is organised around a multitude of projects associating various people of whom some may participate in several projects. The nature of these projects is to have a start and an end, projects are continued, changed, restructured according to the priorities and needs. By analogy, it is possible to speak of a social structure based on projects or a general organisation of society based on projects. The Project World specifies constraints on a 'network world' not to extend the network in ways and in directions that are not justifiable in relation to the specific projects.

Network logic 26, Market logic 14, Domestic logic 9, Inspirational logic 9, Civic logic 5, and Opinion logic 5.

The ideal typical architecture of the project world is analysed using the dimensions presented in *De la justification* (Boltanski and Thévenot 1991). In the Project World, the central figure is the mediator who forms networks. From this perspective, the mediation is a value in itself and in the conceptual scheme applied. All actors may take the role as mediator when they make relations and contribute to develop networks.

Activities related to network constitution is not assumed to be a new phenomenon. Boltanski and Chiapello nevertheless argues that:

> ... we have had to wait until the last third of the 20th century to see the activity of the mediator, the art of weaving and utilising the diverse links, as an autonomous activity detached from other activities, identified and valued in itself. This process constitutes in our view a new aspect worthy of attention (Boltanski and Chiapello 1999, p. 162).

What is new is that the activity related to network formation is identified and valued as an important aspect of human action and not only the network formation in itself.

The basic features of the Project World are described by using the framework developed earlier by Boltanski and Thévenot (Boltanski and Thévenot 1991). The description of the architecture of the Project World is organised around three key dimensions:

- A *principle of equivalence* specifying how to organise things and people and how to make judgements according to their quality as being 'great' or 'small'.
- A *form of justice* applied in the 'World' concerning the conditions to be met to secure that the hierarchy of states established is transformed into a justifiable order.
- The foundation of the World in a *definition of nature,* both in relation to the nature of society and to human nature.

The key concepts specifying the general architecture of worlds of justification are in small capitals while the concepts specifying the Project World are in *italics*.

The first dimension (see Table 3.2), the principle of equivalence, specifies the criteria applied to judge people and actions as well as the most important types of subjects and objects in this specific world. The COMMON GENERAL PRINCIPLE is the criteria applied in the judgement of actions, things and people. In the Project World the criteria applied to order the greatness of people and things is *relational activity*. While in the Industrial World the important activity is paid work, the important activity in the project world is activity oriented toward *generating projects* or to be *integrated into projects* generated by other actors. The activity par excellence is to be *inserted in networks* and to explore them. Life is viewed as a succession of projects oriented to different aspects: family, affections, education, artistic, religious, political, charity, etc. What is important is to be active, always to have something in preparation, not to be without projects, or to be without ideas. It is precisely because the project is a transitory form that it is well adjusted to a network world. The succession of projects leads to the *multiplying of connections* leading to development of the network. The extension of the network is the manifestation of life and the end of extension is likened to death.

The NATURAL RELATIONS BETWEEN BEINGS specify the verbs attached to beings in a world of justice. In a network world, the natural preoccupation is the desire *to be connected* to others, to *enter in relation*, to *establish links*, to *avoid being isolated*. To be successful you have to *trust* others, *be trustful, communicate, discuss, adjust to others*, and *co-operate* in a common project.

Knowing how to be committed in a project, 'savoir s'egager', is a marker of the STATE OF GRANDEUR. To be engaged you have to *mobilise enthusiasm, establish trust*, be *available, reactive* and *mobile*. The great is *adaptable, flexible, polyvalent*, and *employable*. The great takes the initiative and takes the risks making new and potentially rich contacts. The great is not limited by rigid plans hindering interesting connections. He knows the good sources of information and knows how to optimise the most limited resource, his time, choosing his relations, avoiding to be linked to people occupying positions too close who only leads to redundant information (Burt 1992). In the Project World, the importance of social capital and information capital is correlated. To find the important connections the information should be integrated in a local universe. The useful representations are local, singular, circumstantial, linked to a personal experience. The great is not only able to identify connections, but also to establish links as durable as necessary. This call for the ability to attract attention and sympathy from others, to make them interested. The great is also capable of *engaging others*, to inspire *trust*, charisma, and vision. The leader is not a head of a hierarchy, but an integrator, a facilitator. In such a context, everyone is able to develop their employability, both technical competences and capacities to work in teams. The enhancement of individual *employability* is the return given to the individual from the enterprise.

As opposed to the great, THE SMALL in this world is people who are *not committed* to a project, or those who are *rigid* and incapable to change projects. The non-committed are people not able to create trust. The fundamental rule is reciprocity. The small is also people who are not able to communicate with other actors, the *intolerant* and actors incapable of making compromises. It is the *rigidity*, in contrast to flexibility, that constitutes the most important deficiency in this World.

The REPERTOIRE OF SUBJECTS specifies the most important subjects in the Project World. If everyone is capable of entering into relations and to be integrated in a network some realise this potentiality in an exemplary way. These are *mediators, project leaders*, and *coaches*. Other important subjects may be *clients, suppliers*, and *subcontractors* when they enter into partnership relations.

The REPERTOIRE OF OBJECTS specifies the important objects in the Project World. The important objects are instruments and means of connection,[8] technical

---

[8] Boltanski and Chiapello uses the word *dispotifs* to describe both that personal may be disposed to relate to others as well as the devices and mechanisms of relevance to relational activities.

objects applied in communication, most importantly *information technology*, as well as means linked to interpersonal relations such as *informal relations, trust relations, alliances, subcontractors, enterprise network, projects* etc.

The second dimension of the architecture of the Project World is the form of justice found in this World. The first dimension is THE REPORT OF GREATNESS specifying the nature of relations between the great and small and how the big may contribute to the common good. The relation between big and small is found to be just when the big, in exchange of the trust they have received from the small, attempt to *increase the employability* of the small by *enhancing their capacity* to be integrated into a new project when actual projects stop. Instead of a classical contract what is needed is a feeling of commitment, which helps the individual to preserve and advance his employability. First of all, the great have to *redistribute* the limited goods that they have access to, most importantly information and the links to networks. Furthermore, the great should inspire others by their dynamism.

The FORMULA OF INVESTMENT is a condition of equilibrium in a world of justice linking the access to the state of greatness to a sacrifice to establish a proper balance between benefits and sacrifices. The access to the state of greatness demands that all have the capacity to engage in a new project, to be *mobile*. The demand of *lightness* supposes abandoning stability, to be firmly rooted, to have local attachment, and to have the security of long-term links. Knowing that time is limited it is important to use time efficiently by establishing relations with different types of people and of groups instead of resting in the same old circles. The great is also light in the sense that he is liberated from his own passions and values. He is open for differences and he is not critical if only to defend *tolerance* and difference. Following the same principle of eliminating everything that may limit mobility the great is also light in the way that he is not attached to property. The connectionist being is not captured by institutions with all the sorts of obligations they may imply. This is the reason why he prefers to renounce official power instead of the form of power in the network. He prefers autonomy to security. He also renounces to exercise any sort of domination linked to hierarchical positions. His authority only depends on his competences not on his position in any hierarchy. The most important sacrifice of the network mediator is then to give up a distinctive personality. He becomes a chameleon.

In case of disagreement, there is need of an appropriate test to establish the state of greatness of a person. In this world, THE TEST is *the passage from one project to another*. In this process, all are evaluated, positively for those who have augmented their reputation during the project, and negatively for those who have not been able to maintain or develop relations. When the test is linked to the passage from one project to another the Project World becomes more just the shorter, the more multiple and the more changing the projects are, leading to a multiplication of tests.

The MODE OF EXPRESSION OF JUDGEMENT specifies the way judgement is commonly seen in the specific world of justice. In the Project World those who are appreciated are the people' other wants *to know, to meat, to contact* or *to work with*. Those from whom there is nothing to be expected are *ignored*. One of the particular traits of the Project World is the way the non-worthy is treated. Those not found to be worthy loose their visibility, and in a certain sense, also their existence in relation to the logic of this world. Existence in itself is a relational attribute in the sense that all exists more or less in relation to the number and value of the connections they have to others. This is the reason why such a world does not have other sanctions than the *rejection* or *exclusion* that leads to disaffiliation by pushing them toward the limits of the network where the links are fewer and less valuable.

The third dimension of the Project World is the definition of nature. The DIGNITY OF PEOPLE concerns this dimension in each world. In the Project World, all actors can access superior states because all have the possibility to relate to others. The *desire to connect* is a fundamental property of human nature. In this anthropology, the need to be committed is universal and is the reason why all can be attached to a network and increase their employability. The functioning of the network satisfies, in other words, the human characteristic to be free and to be committed at the same time.

All worlds of justification suppose the designation of a FIGURE OF HARMONY. In the Project World the most natural form is *the network*. It is described as a universal order.

The last problem addressed is the question of whether the Project World constitutes a specific form and not an unstable compromise between other existing worlds. To illuminate this question, Boltanski and Chiapello compare the distinguishing features of the Project World with the six other worlds described in *De la justification* (Boltanski and Thévenot 1991).

The Project World has some common features with the *Inspirational World* such as the importance accorded to creativity, innovation, and the singularity of human beings. However, this similarity is found to be quite superficial. In the Inspirational World, the people are creative when they are separated from other beings. In the Project World, creativity is a function of the number and the quality of relations to other human beings.

In relation to the *Market World* several points of difference can be found. Although models of network relations are increasingly applied in microeconomic theory to model the relational aspects of market exchange it is argued that it is possible to distinguish the specific traits of a Project World in relation to the ideal model of the market. First, time is conceptualised differently in these two worlds. While the market transactions are punctual and ignore time, the network perspective supposes the establishment of relatively durable relations. Second, the aspect of transparency is different. While markets suppose transparency to secure formation of prices, networks are only gradually made transparent. No one has access to all the information floating in networks. This points to a particularly vulnerable aspect of networks. In the case that someone for strategic reasons hides information from other network members, the network is in danger of breaking up. The third aspect that highlights the difference between the Market World and the Project World is the different perspectives taken on personal relations between actors. While markets are based on anonymous actors where personal relations are

Table 3.2 The architecture of the project world

Principles of equivalence	Common general principle	*The relational activity, the projects, the extension of network, proliferation of ties*
	Natural relation between individuals	*The connection* To connect, to communicate, to co-ordinate, to adjust to others, to trust
	State of the 'great'	*Committed, engaging, mobile* Enthusiastic, involved, flexible, adaptable, polyvalent, evolutionary, employable, autonomous, unlimited, know engaging others, listening, tolerant, giving employability
	State of the 'small'	*Uncommitted* Unadaptable, not trustworthy, authoritarian, Unenthusiastic, rigid, intolerant, immobile, local, deep-rooted, wrapped up, preferring security
	The disgraceful	*Closing of the network* Corruption, privileges, mafias
	Repertoire of subjects	*Mediator, project leader* Coach, expert, supplier, innovator
	Repertoire of objects	*All instruments of connection* Information technologies, informal relations, trust relations, partnerships, agreements, alliances, subcontracting, enterprise network, network enterprise, projects
Forms of justice	Report of greatness	*Redistribution of connections* To make contact, redistribute information, attach to networks, give employability
	Formula of investment	*Adaptability* Lightness, flexibility, tolerance
	Model test	*The end of a project* and the start on another
	Mode of expression of judgment	*To be asked to participate* Attach, participate, talk to, to avoid, to keep out of, ignore, exclude
	Criteria of evidence	*Participation*
Definition of nature	Dignity	*The need to relate*
	Figure of harmony	*The network*

Source: Boltanski and Chiapello 1999, pp. 161-238.

distant and reduced to a minimum, networks suppose a capacity to establish and stabilise interdependent relations and trust in the long run. The effects of thrust are the possibility to exchange goods and services which cannot be specified exactly in contracts, the possibility to exchange fine grained information, and the possibility to limit the search for short term and purely egoistic gains. A fourth aspect concerns the qualification of products. While the product in the Market World is detached from personal or external standards, in a connectionist world the products are not clearly identified and detached from people. The product is then qualified according to the specific relation between buyers and sellers. These specific characteristics of a connectionist world are from the market perspective frictions in the harmonious competition of a market world. This point leads Boltanski and Chiapello to question the interpretations of recent changes as a simple reinforcing of economic liberalism. In several cases, successful action in a Project World is only loosely coupled to market tests. In their view, the market while not necessarily affecting the reputation of their leaders may sanction enterprises and their projects negatively.

Apparently, there may be important common traits between a Project World and the *World of Opinion*. The extension of relations in a connectionist work is profitable to the extent that they lead to the improvement of the reputation of the actors involved. An important difference is that the transparency supposed in the *World of Opinion*, as discussed above, is absent in the Project World.

There seems to be important common traits between the *Domestic World* and the Project World. In both cases personal relations, face-to-face interaction and trust are important. Nevertheless, there are several dimensions in which these two worlds are opposed. In the Domestic World, personal relations are more or less predefined according to the qualities attached to people and their place in the hierarchy. In the Project World, personal relations are not prescribed. Everyone searches to establish relations to other beings of his own choice. In contrast to the stability observed in the domestic world one of the important prerequisites of greatness it the Project World is the mobility of people in the search for interesting relations.

The Project World is found, in many ways, to be in opposition to the *Industrial World* that was an especially important element in the second spirit of capitalism. In the Industrial World, people are measured in relation to their functions and the posts they occupy in the organisational structure. In a connectionist world people are measured according to their flexibility and their capacity to adapt and to learn, a more important aspect than their technical expertise. The personal elements, communicative qualities, the openness toward other count more than the effectiveness to meat predefined objectives.

This description of the new emerging world of justification, the Project World, is probably the most elaborated description of the form of justification and the values related to network forms of organisations. Richard Sennet's (Sennett 1998) description of the 'corrosion of character' in modern flexible capitalism may have struck some of the same points but gives a more partial picture of the new set of values that are part of flexible capitalism.

Manuel Castells' (Castells 1996; Castells 2000; Castells 2000) impressive analysis of the 'network society' attempts to describe the values through the concept of the 'spirit of informationalism'. The ideal typical description of the network society is based on several elements (Castells 2000, p. 210-215): business networks, technological tools, global competition, and the state. Castells elaborated on the question of what may be the 'cultural glue' that brings these elements together? Castells seems not to find a clear-cut answer. He argues that the 'spirit of informationalism' is not a new culture because 'the diversity of networks reject such a unifying 'network culture'. Nor is it a set of institutions' (Castells 2000, p. 214). According to Castells' answer it is 'a multi-faceted, virtual culture, ... The 'spirit of informationalism' is the culture of 'creative destruction' accelerated to the speed of the opto-electronic circuits that process its signals (Castells 2000, p. 214-215). Though Castells' analysis may be impressive and interesting it is seriously flawed by a technological determinism that does not take account of changes in the orientation of actors. Castells gives a good description of the 'network society', but he does not establish an ideal typical description of the new form of capitalism.

As remarked by several critics (Piore 2000; Freyssenet 2001; Hatchuel 2001) the analysis of the actual compromises between the Project World and pre-existant forms of justice in actual organisations are less developed. Boltanski and Chiapello admits this limitation of their analysis but argues (Boltanski and Chiapello 2000) that their choice was to construct the pure ideal type of the Project World. It is found premature to conceive the compromises with other worlds of justice that haven't yet been stabilised and institutionalised.

With regard to the ideal typical model of the Project World Boltanski and Chiapello argue that our understanding of this world of justification still is in the process of being established. We may still not have adequate knowledge of the tensions inherent in this world and of the proper ways of solving these tensions. We now turn to Boltanski and Chiapello's attempt to point out some of the tensions and problems that may be in the form of justification in the Project World.

The Project World and New Social Criticism

Boltanski and Chiapello elaborate on the problems and the criticism that can be directed toward the project world as an emerging world of justification. They argue that a major reason why recent criticism has proved inadequate is that it fails to refer to this new form of justification when referring to recent changes in the capitalist system.

According to Boltanski and Chiapello, network logic may lead to a new form of opportunism, different from that in the Market World. To distinguish the opportunist from the actor that contributes to the common good (who is called a *network maker* (*mailleur*)) the opportunist is called a *networker* (*faiseur*). Only the network maker acts in a proper way to attain the 'state of greatness'. The actions of the networker only aim at his own profit while the actions of a network maker are profitable for all, for the common good. In depicting the strategic actions of a networker, Boltanski and Chiapello draw on Ronald Burt's work on 'structural holes' (Burt 1992). One of the points taken from Burt is that the networker profits from the inequalities among actors regarding their institutional stability and loyalty.

Following the same critical line toward networks Boltanski and Chiapello elaborates on the new form of exploitation found in the Project World. The flexibility and mobility of the 'great' is only possible because others are immobile. The exploitation in a Project World takes the form of putting limits of the mobility of the weakest. This may take the form of the privation of the links to networks and the possibilities to make new links or to explore existing links to others. Exploitation then takes the form of exclusion.

To avoid opportunism and exploitation in a Project World it is, according to Boltanski and Chiapello, necessary to establish relevant mechanisms of justice that are able to confront actions with the relevant tests. Boltanski and Chiapello examine mechanisms that may make the tests clearer and 'harder'. Therefore the tests should, at the same time, preserve the flexibility of networks and secure a better protection of actors, especially the weakest actors. The propositions are intended to open the possibility for all to be mobile and flexible, but organising this mobility in a way that improves the equality among actors. Three sorts of mechanisms are discussed: 1) mechanisms intended to facilitate internal transparency of projects, 2) mechanisms intended to secure more just principles for rewards in networks, and 3) mechanisms intended to give all equal possibility to be mobile and flexible.

The sign of the formation of a new world of justification is the development of tests and mechanisms specific to this world. In that sense, the 'Project World' is still in the process of being constituted. That is why Boltanski and Chiapello point to the urgency of vigilant criticism to put sufficient pressure on the construction of justice in the Project World. Although the new spirit of capitalism has already incorporated an important part of the 'artist critic'[9] deployed since the 1960s, which pointed to the need of liberation, autonomy and authenticity, there is an urgent need for the artistic critique to pose the questions of liberation and authenticity again. The renewed project of liberation could, according to Boltanski and Chiapello, point to the problems of the demand for mobility as an incontestable value. The value of mobility and the capacity to establish new relations conflicts with the constitution of identities in relation to pre-constituted collectives such as nations, social classes and families. The liberty to choose stability and fidelity may be less and less assured. This calls for the constitution of temporal spaces larger than the individual project or for giving people the means to survive between engagements in different projects.

---

[9] Boltanski and Chiapello distinguish between to major types of criticism raised of capitalism: social criticism pointing first of all at problems of inequality and exploitation, and artist criticism pointing to problems concerning liberation, autonomy and authenticity.

This brief summary of Boltanski and Chiapello's views concerning the problems inherent in the Project World may point to a possible constructive role for the social sciences in the development of new organisational forms. The social sciences may contribute by pointing out what the major problems are and may contribute to finding effective mechanisms to solve some of these problems. This points to the urgent need for social scientists to look at network forms of organisations from a critical perspective. This has also been argued recently by others working on network forms of organisation (Podolny and Page 1998; Uzzi 1996).

Toward a Theory of the Evolution of Capitalism

Boltanski and Chiapello also propose a general model of changes in capitalism. The model is not intended to be a fully developed theory, but only to present the history of these changes during the last thirty years, and do so in a way that opens up the possibility for generalisation.

According to this, 'axiomatic' capitalism needs a 'spirit', a moral dimension, to involve the people who are necessary for production and management. The spirit of capitalism is a solution to problems created by the insatiability inherent in capitalism. To survive, capitalism has to stimulate and to limit its insatiability at the same time. The spirit of capitalism may be seen as a solution to this problem, because it activates the insatiability in the form of excitation and liberation, incorporating the moral demands that are made in relation to some common good. It is then clear that the spirit of capitalism cannot be seen as an ideology, in the sense of an illusion without any effect on the world.

Capitalism has a tendency to continuously change. Drawing on Hirschman (Hirschman 1970) Boltanski and Chiapello elaborated on the role of criticism in the process of capitalist change. An important factor in this change in capitalism is 'economic criticism' in the form of competition (exit) that leads to permanent 'creative destruction' to use Schumpeter's expression. The principal operator of creation and transformation of the spirit of capitalism is oral criticism (voice). If critique in the form of voice is not the principal agent of change in capitalism it has a central role in the construction of the different forms of the capitalist spirit that have accompanied capitalism in different periods. Under certain circumstances criticisms may even in themselves be a factor of change in capitalism, and not only of a change in its spirit.

According to Boltanski and Chiapello, it is important to avoid the two extreme interpretations of changes in capitalism: on the one hand as strategies elaborated and organised by an omnipotent actor, and on the other as unconscious processes without reflexivity. Competition may stimulate a diffusion of changes. However, it is necessary to reflect on what seems to have been profitable and to generalise successful local methods. In the beginning of a phase of change, the success of change agents may, even to themselves, be relatively mysterious. Nevertheless, to the extent that these changes are successful, an intuition of what seems to have been the cause of the success is gradually formed in the consciousness of the actors. A growing number of actors may then turn to new ways of organising production and market relations.

The new ways of organising need to legitimate themselves against criticism. In this process it is especially helpful that criticism of capitalism demonstrates a plurality of voices, which at times may even lead to contradictory criticism. In the process of legitimating new organisational forms, change agents may present the changes as an answer to at least some of the types of criticism presented. Another way of legitimating new organisational forms is to present the changes as answers to criticisms of already institutionalised organisational forms. Progressively the schemas of interpretation are reconstituted that permits one to make sense of the recent changes opening the way for a more specific criticism of the new forms of organisation, and for demands and propositions orientated to that specific new form of justice.

The criticism raised in relation to a new organisational form of capitalism may gradually lead to the formation of new normative points of reference for the renewed form of capitalism. This new compromise is affirmed in the expression of a new form of the capitalist spirit that includes the demands for justice made. To satisfy its need for legitimacy, the new spirit of capitalism has to be explicitly linked to general orders of justification, those that are identified under the concept of 'Worlds', or 'cités' in the original French expression.

A construction of a coherent world of justification becomes possible when a group of actors drawing on a coherent and stable set of instruments and objects sees their power grow. They then become able to claim that they make specific contributions to a common good. In this process, social science plays an important role in the construction of a coherent world of justification.

In this way, the development of a network perspective precedes the definition of a specific world of justice relevant to that perspective, the Project World. Following Boltanski and Chiapello, it is now urgent for social science to look closer into the present constitution of a network form of society to elaborate further on the development of mechanism, instruments and tests relevant for the emerging logic, the Project World.

Discussion

What are Boltanski and Chiapello's main contributions? What may be the ambiguities and problems that may be pointed to in their important attempt to understand the recent changes in recent capitalism?

First, in my opinion, a particularly important contribution made by Boltanski and Chiapello is to present a dynamic model of changes in capitalism that includes both structural (organisational models of capitalism) and cultural elements (the criticism of capitalism and the capitalist spirit). As demonstrated in their book, this model is quite helpful in understanding how capitalism has been able to include much of its criticism in new ways of organising capitalist production.

The general model of the change in capitalism presented by them points to the complex interplay of three different processes in the development of capitalism, processes related to competition (exit), to criticism of capitalism (voice), and to legitimacy. There may still be need for a better understanding of the interplay between these three factors. This interplay needs to be unpacked to a greater extent than Boltanski and Chiapello do. Nevertheless, the analysis undertaken by Boltanski and Chiapello may be a first important step toward such an unpacking of the dynamics in the model.

As an example, it might be important for understanding the more recent changes in the spirit of capitalism to produce a more refined understanding of the evolution of earlier spirits of capitalism and its relation to changes in capitalist organisation than presented in the book.

Another question in relation to the dynamic model of capitalist development is how to distinguish the spirit of capitalism (legitimating elements) from the ideas regarding successful strategies and models in the management of capitalist enterprises. As described by Fligstein (Fligstein 1990), in relation to the American case, there have been important changes made in the conceptions of control generally adhered to. How may these changing conceptions of management control be related to the capitalist spirit?

Second, Boltanski and Chiapello have made an important contribution to the understanding of the new spirit of capitalism and of recent forms of organisations by their description of the architecture of the Project World. This ideal typical description is probably the most elaborated model of the type of justification related to network forms of organisations. Less developed is the analysis of the actual compromises between the Project World and other forms of justifications in different types of organisations. As argued by Freyssenet (Freyssenet 2001) several forms of capitalism and several 'production models' exist simultaneously.[10] It is then a complex problem to establish the relative role of a specific spirit of capitalism vis-à-vis other forms of justification. Boltanski and Chiapello (Boltanski and Chiapello 2002) argue that between 10 to 20 per cent of French enterprises are dominated by the Project world. But as indicated by Boltanski and Chiapello, an analysis of how the Project World form of justification is related to other forms of justifications in actual organisations is an interesting and important object of study (Boltanski and Chiapello 2000).

---

[10] Freyssenet (Freyssenet 2001) argues that Boltanski and Chiapello by establishing the spirit of capitalism for one specific time period fall in the trap of mixing incompatible aspects of the different forms of capitalisms and 'productive models' existing simultaneously. While Freyssenet's argument is relating to the construction of the ideal typical model of the Project World, my argument concerns the problem of how this ideal typical model of the Project World is interacting with other forms of justification in real life organisations.

By pointing to some of the criticism that may be raised in relation to network forms of organisation Boltanski and Chiapello have contributed an important step toward developing a critical perspective on networks. There seems to be a growing awareness of the need of focusing on the potential problems arising from network forms of organisations not least due to the criticism formulated by Richard Sennett. Boltanski and Chiapello's book may serve as an important inspiration to develop such a perspective.

References

Boltanski, L. and Chiapello, E. (1999), *Le nouvel esprit du capitalisme*, Paris, Gallimard.
Boltanski, L. and Chiapello, E. (2000a), 'Befreiung vom Kapitalismus? Befreiung durch Kapitalismus?', *Blätter für deutsche und international Politik* (avril), pp. 476-88.
Boltanski, L. and Chiapello, E. (2000b). 'A Reply', *French Politics, Culture and Society* 18(3), pp. 129-36.
Boltanski, L. and Chiapello, E. (2001a), 'Comment interpréter les changements du capitalisme. Réponses à quelques critiques', *Sociologie du travail*, 43, pp. 409-21.
Boltanski, L. and Chiapello, E. (2001b), 'Die Rolle der Kritik in der Dynamik des Kapitalismus und der normative Wandel', *Berliner Journal der Soziologie*, 4, pp. 459-77.
Boltanski, L. and Chiapello, E. (2001c), 'The New Spirit of Capitalism', *Sociologie du travail* 43 (3), pp. 409-21.
Boltanski, L. and Chiapello, E. (2002), *The New Spirit of Capitalism*, Paper presented at the Conference of Europeanists, Chicago, March 14-16, 2002.
Boltanski, L. and Thévenot, L. (1991), *De la justification. Les économies de la grandeur*, Paris, Galimard.
Boltanski, L. and Thévenot, L. (1999), 'The Sociology of Critical Capacity', *European Journal of Social Theory*, 2 (3), pp. 359-77.
Boltanski, L. and Thévenot, L. (2000), 'The Reality of Moral Expectations: A sociology of situated judgment', Philosophical Explorations, 3(3).
Burt, R. S. (1992), *Structural Holes: The Social Structure of Competition*, Cambridge, Mass., Harvard University Press.
Castells, M. (1996), *The Rise of the Network Society*, Oxford, Blackwell Publishers.
Castells, M. (2000a). 'Materials for an Exploratory Theory of the Network Society', *British Journal of Sociology*, (Jan/Mar), pp. 5-24.
Castells, M. (2000b), *The Rise of the Network Society*, Oxford, Blackwell.
Chiapello, E. and Fairclough, N. (2002), 'Understanding the New Management Ideology: A transdisciplinary contribution from critical discourse analysis and new sociology of capitalism', *Discourse & Society*, 13(2), pp. 185-208.
DiMaggio, P. (ed.)(2001), *The Twenty-First-Century Firm: Changing economic organization in international perspective*, Princeton, Princeton University Press.
Emirbayer, M. and Goodwin, J. (1994), 'Network Analysis, Culture, and the Problem of Agency', *American Journal of Sociology*, 99(6), pp. 1411-54.
Fligstein, N. (1990), *The Transformation of Corporate Control*, Cambridge, MA, Harvard University Press.
Freyssenet, M. (2001), 'Le nouvel esprit du capitalisme de L. Boltanski et E. Chiapello. Esprit, es-tu-là?' *L'Annee de la Régulation*, 5, pp. 309-18.

Hatchuel, A. (2001), '"Le nouvel esprit du capitalisme": Grandeurs et limites d'un spiritualisme dialectique', *Sociologie du travail*, 43, pp. 402-09.

Hirschman, A. (1970), *Exit, Voice and Loyalty*, Cambridge, MA, Harvard University Press.

Lamont, M. and Thévenot, L. (eds) (2000), *Rethinking Comparative Cultural Sociology: Repertoires of evaluation in France and the United States*, Cambridge, Cambridge University Press.

Piore, M. (2000), 'Deconstructing the Reconstruction of Capitalism', *French Politics, Culture and Society*, 18(3), pp. 109-14.

Podolny, J. M. (2001), 'Networks as the Pipes and Prisms of the Market', *American Journal of Sociology*, 98, pp. 829-72.

Podolny, J. M. and Page, K. L. (1998), 'Network Forms of Organization', *Annual Review of Sociology*, 24, pp. 57-76.

Sennett, R. (1998), *The Corrosion of Character: The personal consequences of work in the new capitalism*, New York, W. W. Norton & Company.

Stark, D. (1999), 'Heterarchy: Distributing intelligence and organizing diversity', in J. Clippinger (ed.), *The Biology of Business: Decoding the natural laws of enterprise*, San Francisco, Jossey-Bass Publishers, pp. 153-79.

Stark, D. (2001), 'Ambiguous Assets for Uncertain Environments: Heterarchy' in P. DiMaggio (ed.), *Postsocialist Firms: The twenty-first-century firm. Changing Economic Organization in International Perspective*, Princeton, Princeton University Press, pp. 69-104.

Thévenot, L. (2001a), 'Organized Complexity: Conventions of coordination and the composition of economic arrangements', *European Journal of Social Theory*, 3, pp. 405-25.

Thévenot, L. (2001b), 'Pragmatic Regimes Governing the Engagement with the World', in K. Knorr-Cetina, T. Schatzki and E. v. Savigny (eds), *The Practice Turn in Contemporary Theory*, London, Routledge, pp. 56-73.

Thévenot, L. (2001c), 'Which Road to Follow? The Moral Complexity of an "Equipped" Humanity', in Law and A. Mol (eds), *Complexities in Science, Technology and Medicine*, J. Durham, NC, Duke University Press.

Thévenot, L. (2002), 'Conventions of Co-ordination and the Framing of Uncertainty', in E. Fullbrook (ed.), *Intersubjectivity in Economics*, London, Routledge, pp. 181-97.

Uzzi, B. (1996), 'Embeddedness and Economic Perfomance: The network effect', *American Sociological Review*, 61(4), pp. 674-98.

White, H. C. (2001), *Markets from Networks: Socioeconomic Models of Production*, Princeton, Princeton University Press.

Chapter 4

Social Capital, Trust and Dependency

Anne Kovalainen

Introduction

The concept of trust as part of the social capital has received relatively much attention in a variety of fields during the last few years. Social capital and trust have, within a short time, become hugely influential, truly global theoretical concepts in the analyses of current social and economic development, change and cohesion in various societies, communities and groups. Additionally, social capital is related to the description and explanation of social action. While the term 'social capital' features in much scholarly and interdisciplinary discourse, it also has parallels with political agendas, large-scale social and economic development and, in particular, social policy development. This issue is to a large extent visible in the influence of the World Bank and IMF, both in the defining of research areas and the framing of much of the discussion on social issues related to social capital analysis. The assumption of a positive relationship between democracy, participation and social capital and trust prevails in much of the research literature. The recent critique has taken up this positive 'furry animal' effect of social capital: only the positive effects of social capital are being focused on (e.g. Portes and Landolt 1996).

The emphasis of the social in the creation and shaping of social capital is important, thus making it a truly sociological concept. Also the intuitive appeal of the importance of the concepts of social capital and trust seems clear: the analytical concepts of social capital and trust do not seem burdened by the rigidity of classical sociological conceptual schemes, such as social class, power or stratification. The basic argument with the concept of social capital lies in its asset nature that inheres in all social relations and networks. Yet the concept finds its manifestation in contradicting ways in the literature (see, for example Coleman 1990; Putnam *et al.* 1993; Fukuyama 1995; Seligman 1997).

Social capital, as stated by all theorists in question, is not by any means a new phenomenon. What are the reasons for it to become a 'new' concept in explaining the social within the economy, for example? I believe that the elasticity of the term 'social capital' across disciplinary fields has led to a situation where it is used very differently, depending on the context and research purpose in question. What is common to much research in political science and sociology, is the use of the concept of 'social capital' to refer to a set of norms, networks, institutions and organisations. It is through these sets that the access to specific elements such as power, inequality or resources embedded within or available through these elements is gained. According to Coleman (1988, p. 598), 'Social capital is social structure which facilitates certain actions of actors within the structure', and, thus, it seems to create some sort of attribute of the network among groups, that may extend to the entire society.

In a rather similar fashion, trust, as defined as one of the three crucial components of social capital, has caught the interest of sociology, and especially social theory, in a new and appealing way. Coleman emphasises the importance of relationships; various relationships enable individuals to trust each other, while Putnam, for example, argues that it is the individual-level trust that enables institutions to work well. These ways of defining social capital and trust are not unique, as the fluidity of the notion of social capital has given rise to several definitions, captured through social relations, as well as through economic structures (Lin 2001). The metaphors of mobile activities such as glue and lubricant (borrowed from Arrow 1972) are most often used and repeated in articles on social capital.

The question then arises as to how and in what ways can social capital or trust be measured, when it is by the variety of definitions used also being placed on different levels, ranging from individual level to societal level. In a similar manner, the notion of trust has been defined in a variety of ways, ranging from 'public good' (e.g. Gambetta 1988) to 'moral good'. The questions of how to combine macro-level institutional arrangements, such as legislation, to micro-level activities such as interpersonal networks are of theoretical relevance only. This question is further developed later in this article in the description of the recent changes of the welfare services in Finland.

The argument developed in this chapter is that even if the present analyses and discourses on trust and social capital at large are based on other than strict notions of rational choice and contract theories, they fall short of theorising the agency in ways other than as free, independent individuals, thus also contradicting the importance of 'the social'. The argument developed further in this chapter is that there are gendered assumptions operating in the discussions on social capital, trust and networks building social capital. This becomes manifested in the empirical examples. One of these issues is the question of agency. The power imbalances and mutual dependencies that unavoidably exist in everyday life as well as in various institutional arrangements should be taken into account, when, for example, some main elements of civic society, such as the arrangements for care and the welfare state services are discussed. These inequalities become visible, when examples of power imbalances are being discussed.

While feminist analysis of social theory in general has worked to unsettle rigid and established categories and concepts, most mainstream sociological theorising still ignores the questions of gender. The main argument of this chapter is that this assumed gender neutrality of contemporary social theorising should be challenged and critically analysed. The intention is to examine the reasons why concepts of social capital and trust have lately become so influential in social theory. Secondly, the intention is to illuminate the possible reasons why the discussion on social capital and trust have not – even if considered as new theoretical agendas – been able to renew the kind of social theory where gender is disentangled and invisible, yet written into the theory in several ways. The Finnish welfare state restructuring and the new service purchaser-provider split model serves here as one empirical example of the dependencies within social capital and of the problematic nature of trust relationships in the service production seldom analysed in the literature.

Social Capital and Trust – the 'Glue' in Between Social Theory and Economics?

As mentioned in the introduction, social capital encapsulates a wide range of social mechanisms, individuals, networks and institutions, and their actions, from the variety of perspectives of social cohesion and struggle, economic activity and generalised exchange. The wide variation of interest in the concept is partly evident in early works by Pierre Bourdieu (1980), Bourdieu and Louis Wacquant (1992), James Coleman (1990) and Robert Putnam (1993, 2000), but even some references to Jane Jacobs' (1961) classic work on town planning can be found.

Even if the nature of these works is seen to be relatively similar, as argued by Burt (2001), calling attention to the similarity of approaches glosses over the different and contradictory theoretical commitments. They all address the notion of social capital from quite different perspectives, developing the idea further from two opposing sociological traditions, namely that of integration (Putnam) and struggle (Bourdieu). The recognition of the contextual nature of the discourses means acknowledging that the points of view of the above-mentioned authors seldom meet (e.g. see Siisiäinen 2000). To develop the key argument of this chapter, I will briefly present some of the main developments in the theorisation of social capital and trust.

In the social sciences, discussion of the overall theoretical attachment of social capital and trust is relatively dispersed. The body of theoretical discussion can be presented condensed within two extremes of social theory discourses: firstly, the search for a solution to the 'collective action dilemma', and secondly, 'inequalities of different kinds'. These two directions for discourse open up diverse perspectives and intangibles, ranging from rational action theory to social construction of social capital, as fields for discussion covered by research on social capital and trust. Even if the economic aspects have been importantly present in the analysis of social capital, it seems that the links to economic capital theory have historically been relatively weak. Among others, Solow (1997) has questioned whether social capital can be analysed within the similar conceptual scheme as capital.

Two most prominent authors, Bourdieu (1986) and Coleman (1988) differ in the ways they describe the development of social capital, and following from that, diversity in the use of social capital has increased. For Bourdieu, social capital mostly develops through the economic infrastructure. For Coleman social capital manifests itself through a process of negotiation of contracts, even if he emphasises also the importance of social structures that facilitate the social capital. The emphasis in the contracts varies from individual contract building to societal infrastructure. Whatever the origins of social capital are, there seems to be widespread agreement that the notion of social capital incorporates both the social and the economic in the explanation of it (Lin 2001; Fine 2001). To some extent, the theoretical question at stake here could also be expressed as the classical problem of rational choice theory, that is, being able to show how 'interdependent individual actions produce collective-level outcomes' (Abell 1992, p. 186).

The inherent appeal of social capital rests on the idea of its being at one and the same time an economic, political and sociological concept, thus, having interdisciplinary prominence and potential. Similarly, the concept of trust extends beyond economics and sociology to philosophical and political fields, describing the creation and maintenance of interaction between individuals and institutions, for example. Studies of social capital and trust do not form a coherent paradigm. On the contrary, they attempt to expand the disciplinary boundaries in a variety of directions. However, in the attempt to create an interdisciplinary field, the concepts of social capital and trust are given different positions in explanations of social, cultural and economic phenomena by different disciplines. Yet, the elusive nature of both concepts seems to have led to generalisations that are far from clear, and to the omission of both theoretical and historically specific insights (Fine 2001; Lin *et al.* 2001).

Bourdieu's main idea of social capital rests upon the idea of how cultural reproduction fosters the social reproduction of relations between groups and classes. Through a variety of connections, capital is used as a collective 'asset' within and outside the group (see also Schuller *et al.* 2000). For Bourdieu, social capital remains at the level of connectedness, even if it is part of symbolic power. He defines social capital as 'the aggregate of the actual or potential resources which are linked to possession of a durable network of more or less institutionalised relationships of mutual acquaintance and recognition' (Bourdieu 1986, p. 248). Bourdieu's use of social capital varies between realist and metaphorical, and remains, at least when thinking of the possibilities for empirical analysis, relatively 'sketchy' (as argued also by Schuller *et al.* 2000). How does an agent gain knowledge of the social capital he or she possesses? How is the usefulness measured? These questions are left unanswered in Bourdieu's texts.

Coleman and Putnam have published more explicit work pinpointing the definition and limits of the analytical power of social capital. Their theories seem to be the most influential in developing and directing the discussions of social capital within the field of economics. Putnam's work on the decline of social capital in the U.S. (2000) has recently been as influential as his earlier work on Italy (1993). Originally interested in the concept of social capital as a regional-level shoring-up of democratic institutions and economic development, Putnam defined it as 'trust, norms and networks' that facilitate co-operation for mutual benefit (1993, p. 167). The question of trust is inherently part of social capital. While Bourdieu's idea of the *recognition* of symbolic capital resembles the concept of trust in Coleman or

Putnam's theoretical framework, the concept of trust as such does not exist in Bourdieu's texts (see, e.g. Sztompka 1999; Hollis 1998).

Putnam's way of measuring social capital emphasises an individual's active participation in voluntary associations, which has never been the commonest form of social activity or public participation in many countries, compared with the United States. The problem here is that a causal link between participation in voluntary organisations and improved democratic institutions is simply assumed, but not contested (e.g. Harriss & de Renzio 1997), thus, giving a minor role to institutions or stability within institutions. For Putnam, the dense networks of horizontal interactions among relative equals (neighbourhood associations, football clubs, bowling leagues, PTAs) produce the norms of reciprocity, work as information channels and create a culturally favourable climate for future collaboration between those who participate. And those who participate are most often men, but also women, when home, PTAs and schools are being discussed. Putnam focuses on complex community, regional and national-level outcomes of social capital, related to political and economic development taking place at that level. Networks of civic engagement are the keys to the existence of social capital, as they foster norms of reciprocity. These norms, in turn, sanction those individuals who are not part of the reciprocal system. Putnam places men and women according to their 'natural' social order in homes, schools, football clubs and bowling leagues.

An additional problematic assumption in Putnam's theory is that both reciprocity and trust will follow from participation in such associations. Margret Levi (1998) has outlined several problems with the way social capital is produced and maintained in Putnam's work. Levi argues that football clubs, bowling leagues or churches may not be the types of organisations that are able to produce the trust needed to facilitate collective action, and that such trust would not enhance collaboration among a diverse set of stakeholders.

Putnam's thesis has been challenged as both theoretically gender-biased and empirically problematic (Skocpol 1996; Paxton 1999). Gender in Putnam's theory is to a large extent a middle-class-oriented dichotomous category of men and women. According to Putnam, women who moved out of the home into paid employment have, at least partially, been responsible for the decline in the accumulation of commodified social capital (Putnam 1995). Putnam largely ignores the idea that social capital can also accumulate in employment, and even more so, in comparison to having women as homemakers.[1] Typically, the visibility of women's active citizenship is absent in Putnam's analysis. Gender is defined as a rigid, stereotypically female notion; Putnam's writings focus more on the activity of men.

---

[1] Putnam's insensitivity to gender is visible in the fact that not all gender contracts globally have changed the way they have in the United States. In Nordic countries women have 'never' been at home, but always in the labour market. Adopting Putnam's theory as has been done in many countries would provide incorrect results in the Nordic national contexts.

Even if economics did not adopt social capital to any large extent, there are some prominent theorists arguing for the concept. Coleman brings economics closer to sociology in his theorisation on, and measurement of, social capital. In Coleman's theory economic prosperity follows from human capital, and not necessarily from social capital. Coleman (1988) differentiates between two broad intellectual streams in the discussions of social capital. One argues for a socialised actor, whose actions are governed by social norms, rules and obligations. The other stems from economics, where the actor is traditionally defined as seemingly neutral, as having achieved goals independently, and as fully self-interested (for a critique of this, see e.g. Folbre 1994).

Even if Coleman's characterisation is a somewhat time-bound analysis of social and economic theories, it carves out the essential question of existing tensions in the interdisciplinary project of social capital. Coleman's answer is to introduce rational action theory into the sociological analysis of social capital and trust. For Coleman, this means that social capital exists in 'the *relations* between actors and among actors' (1988, p. 100). Coleman argues that in contrast to other forms of capital, social capital is '*embodied in relations among persons*' (p. 120). These persons are individuals, who act rationally within specific, given constraints and on the basis of the information they have.

What elements do these relations consist of? Coleman argues for three key elements: the trustworthiness of the social environment (obligations to be met), and the extent of obligations held. In addition, norms accompanied with sanctions, are an integral part of the relations. The idea of trust as an integral part of social capital, together with norms and social networks, can receive different emphasis: trust can be seen as a rational way of dealing with exchange, as Diego Gambetta (1988) defines it, close to Coleman's definition.

Dependency and Trust – Gendering the Social Capital Theory?

So far there are many images of both social capital and trust, making it difficult to form a consensus regarding a definition, to say nothing of a coherent analysis. The environment of mutual trust creates 'a bank of resources' that can be used to support a whole variety of organisations and initiatives (Deakin 2001, p. 71), and which 'tend to be self-enforcing and cumulative', as Putnam argues (1993, p. 37). But is that pool of resources similarly open to everybody? The empirical evidence from the welfare service reorganisation in Finland strongly questions this assumption. When considering the elements of social capital, that is trust, norms and networks, all of them can be potentially problematic. Trust clearly serves as the 'lubricant' for economic transactions and, thus, creates the basis for economic development and prosperity, but just as easily trust can also serve as a basis for the black or grey economy, or a barrier to economic or societal development. This can in practice mean the importance of informal customs, behaviours and practices, as well as knowledge of the codes of conduct in specific situations.

In order to elaborate on the nature of trust, Annette Baier (1995) calls for further precision here: according to Baier, dependency and trust should be discussed as a question of reliance, that is, that in a trust relationship something will be entrusted to others. In caring and dependency relations, such as working in social and health care services, trust involves the opportunity for power and inequality relations. Within trust, bad things also take place, even in cases where the norms are shared by the members of the group or network. The feminist notion of relations within trust becomes visible in Baier (1995) and in Sevenhuijsen (1998). Both the dependency and competition can disable the trust relationships.

The introduction of rational action theory and rational choice into the debate within sociological theory predates the theorisation of social capital but is in many ways very relevant to it. Even if economics is actually based on the idea of rational agency, agency as such does not have a specific role in economic theory other than within decision-making situations. Agency in economics is about decision making. In economics, the critique of 'rational economic man' as one modification of the rational action theory's conception of agency has also taken a variety of forms. The critique extends from philosophical arguments of the idea of rational economic man (e.g. Hollis and Nell 1975), to feminist critique ranging from the pre-eminence of mathematical modelling, 'to its congruence with a particular image of masculinity, one created in the gender structure of dualism' (Longino 1993, p. 160; also e.g. England and Kilbourne 1990; Nelson 1993).

The feminist critique of this notion has been two-dimensional. The inadequacy of economic analyses of gendered issues such as invisible work and the wage gap is one line of critique. This has resulted information of the stability of the wage gap and gender differences in salaries across the nations. Another line of critique, theoretically perhaps more interesting and possibly even more important, focuses on the more theoretical set of problems within economics, which call for the redefinition of the subject of the discipline and bring up the questions of dependencies and power.

Economic theories are most often concerned with the ways in which the production, distribution and consumption of goods and services is organised through exchange and market mechanisms. Rational choice theorists have argued that the same general principles as in economics can be used to understand individual interactions in any disciplinary field where a form of exchange takes place, thus, extending the boundaries of the theoretical device as such. Rational choice theories hold that individuals must anticipate the outcomes of alternative courses of action and calculate what is best for them. Rational individuals choose alternatives likely to give them the greatest satisfaction, that being the principal guide in decision making (Coleman 1990). The actions of individuals form the starting point for the analysis; in principle, all other social phenomena are reducible to individual actions. What results does this have for individuals? First of all, it gives the impression that individuals are the omnipotent actors, without class boundaries or any personal, group related or societal restrictions.

Drawing one conclusion, when analysing social capital from a sociological point of view, neoclassical economics is basically 'asocial' by its approach, as are most of the rational action theory applications in other disciplinary fields. The core of methodological individualism is expressed in Coleman's definition, even if he acknowledges the role of social structure as facilitating social capital: 'Actors establish relations purposefully and continue them when they continue to provide benefits' (Coleman 1988, p. 105). The actor is general, abstract, detached from ties and dependencies, an omnipotent agent. The problematic nature of this perspective for sociology, at least for feminist sociology (e.g. Marshall 1994, p. 2000) is obvious: the agent is not only without social ties, but also presented as a socially atomic, abstract masculinity. Furthermore, the functionalist definition – social capital as a means of increasing an individual's resources – places more emphasis on the individual rather than on the societal level. The inherent problem in analysing social ties and networks comes forward. The individuals are embedded in social structures and the whole notion of social capital emphasises norms and networks, both of which assume and require the presence of the social. Social capital does not exist without the presence of the social, and of individuals that are embedded in the social networks, social relationships and social ties.

To summarise the above discussion, the contrast between the social capital theorists examined is between the emphases put on the level of analysis. For Bourdieu, it is individuals in a struggle, for Putnam it is community, region or even nation, while for Coleman it is individuals in a variety of structural settings (mainly family or community). The distinction and relationship between agency and structure is central for all the theorists. Flyvbjerg (2001, p. 138) argues that for Bourdieu, the use of the notion of *habitus* can be understood as a way of escaping the choice between 'a structuralism without a subject and the philosophy of the subject'. In their earlier work on Italy, Putnam *et al.* (1993) similarly combine individual and structural analysis in an attempt to explain democracy in Italy. This model of theorising follows the path of asking which structural factors influence individual actions, how these actions are constructed and what are their structural consequences (Flyvbjerg 2001). The notion of the individual is left untouched, however: the individual is mostly assumed, in the realist tradition, to be a rational decision-maker working within the given framework, that is, within the existing structures.

But is the structure/agency problem, in the way it has been understood in sociology, also the case for Coleman? While Coleman follows more clearly the tradition of economics in his strong programme for social capital, he also restricts his analytical perspective to rational action theory more so than his followers.[2] Attempts by economists, such as e.g. Dasgupta and Serageldin (2000), to treat social capital as a measurable entity, functioning as a relationship between the market and social interactions, and having positive implications for efficiency, are numerous. The application of social capital to mainstream economic theory might prove difficult, however, for the reasons as described, and for additional reasons as

---

[2] Francis Fukuyama (1995, 1999) argues, following Coleman, that social capital creates prosperity. Fukuyama's thesis on the relationship between social capital and economic wellbeing remains relatively problematic, and is keenly disputed.

well. Conventional economic theory is highly formalised and consists mainly of mathematical models containing few 'residual' variables, which is one of the explicit 'places' for social capital in regression models or other explanatory models used. This form of economics, the neoclassical, is not only non-gendered, but also fundamentally asocial. This naturally reflects upon the issue of dependency: dependency within trust is not seen as relevant.

But is trust a presupposition for economic relationships, such as argued above (e.g. Misztal 1996)? The reason for taking up the issue of economics so strongly here, is related to the multidisciplinary nature of social capital. The influence of economic theory in sociology in this specific question is visible, for example, in the works of Gary Becker (1996), who explicitly subsumes his concept of social capital as part of the theory of the utility-maximising individual, much without any social ties or dependencies. On the other hand, for example radical political economy rejects neo-classical economics' assumption that economic behaviour would be self-interested only. Within social theory, however, social capital is, or should be, a sociological concept, not an individually oriented, psychological one. Thus, social capital is not reducible to the individual, as it can only operate at the shared and collective level (Furstenberg 1998, p. 296). Several factors can be considered when we are analysing the emergent interest in economics within sociology. One influential discussion concerns the notion of 'risk society' (Beck 1992), another of globalisation. Perhaps more influential has been the fluctuating and changing economies and labour markets, and the 'corrosion of character' of the workforce (Sennett 1998), and where trust has become a commodity.

In related work, notions of globalisation have shifted interest away from cultural sociology and closer to economic sociology. This does not signify that there is only one way or level of analysing economics and economies sociologically, as the economy and its functioning can be seen as socially constructed phenomena, or fully embedded in society (Granovetter 1985).[3] According to Fine and Green (2000, p. 89), part of the attraction derives from the quantifiable nature of the economy: the result is, as they argue, an 'expanding list of studies that show, in some way or other, a non-economic factor having a substantive impact on economic performance'. One of these factors is social capital. At large, this is the issue of the embeddedness of the economic in the social. The discussions and studies of social capital and trust show, for their part, the increase in sociological analysis of the economy, despite possible limitations and related criticism. The underlying dilemma between sociology and economics is that the social cannot be identified as an independent factor separate from individual activities. In the social sciences, this dilemma is overshadowed or made to disappear specifically in those fields of sociological theorising where the rational choice is the meta-level theoretical choice for research, and no other perspectives are taken into account.

---

[3] The role of both Coleman and Becker in the new economic sociology is briefly described in Swedberg (1990).

In summary, the views on social capital include informal and local horizontal networks, hierarchical associations and institutions, ranging from informal to formal national and transnational organisations. While norms and values are seen as common belief systems, the views on trust relationships are not as settled. According to Barbara Misztal (2000, p. 107), many arguments about social capital have extended the idea of co-operation from an individual characteristic to one of societies. As Portes remarked (1998), 'Social capital has come to be applied to so many events and in so many different contexts that it has lost its distinct meaning'. It seems to include everything and yet precisely nothing. There is an existing definitional diversity among those doing research on social capital. Therefore, it is justified to ask whether we can talk about social capital as a single conceptual category or entity without dependencies that would be built into the concept or as inequalities that are built into the issues of networks and contacts, which are distributed differently, specifically by class and gender.

Gender, Trust and Changing Social Capital

Despite criticism targeted at functionalist, or even tautological, ways of defining social capital, the concept has found its field and audience. This is a key reason why the study of gender in the theoretical foundations and empirical grounds of social capital is crucially important. The questions of the influence of economics on social theory, the adoption of rational action theory (RAT) and, most of all, the realist epistemology of social theory can all make finding space for gendered analysis difficult. 'Coleman's interest in equity issues was combined with a curious blindness to gender, ethnicity and disability' (Field *et al.* 2000, p. 248). The confidence in abstract rationality as the general logic underlying the agency becomes visible in the role of the social in the analysis.

The social capital theorising as it currently exists is clearly strongly gendered. In the texts of Coleman, Putnam and Fukuyama, where exactly does the notion of gender become visible? It is mainly at home, within the family, where agency acquires its explicitly gendered expression of a mother or father. For both Putnam and Coleman, the social actor, in the process of creating, using and recreating social capital, is of crucial importance. This social actor is inherently male, and in this sense social capital theorists differ hardly at all from the theoretical assumptions of rational choice theorists, where the actor is omnipotent, without formal or informal ties to other actors other than are contract-related. In Coleman's analysis, less so than in Putnam's, social structure is a mere facilitator for social capital: the closure of social networks suggests the existence of norms, and it is through this idea that Coleman inserts the explicitly gendered agent into his theory. Coleman defines the importance of social capital taking place within the family, in the creation of human capital.

For Coleman, family is generalised, as is the aim in economics, and the contextual element is lacking. For both Putnam and Coleman, the birth and origin of social capital reside within the family, which comprises 'the most fundamental form of social capital' (Putnam 1995, p. 73). What the definition of family is and how it functions is not explicitly stated in any of these theories, yet it is present in the settings and starting point for the theory building. The idealisation of the family as the core of civic engagement and social capital rests on the assumption that families will provide good models for relationships and civic virtues (see e.g. Cox 1995, pp. 28-29).

For Putnam, gender is explicitly present only when he discusses women, their role and their contribution to the increase or decrease in social capital. While he acknowledges that in the United States, the movement of women into the labour force is not the main reason for the basic decline in American civic engagement, women are still culpable according to his analysis. According to Putnam (2000: 202), 'the long-term movement of women out of the category of affluent housewife into other social categories has tended to depress civic engagement'. What Putnam fails to acknowledge is that social capital might take other forms than the ones defined in his study. The social capital can accumulate at paid employment, and that the measurements used by Putnam, such as 'entertaining, club going, community projects, etc' are all empirical measures attached to time, culture, generation and place. It might well be that other measures such as use and frequencies of e-mails and mobile phones, SMS, etc. have replaced Putnam's ideal of the accumulation patterns and processes for social capital. There is clearly a generation shift going on, and more importantly, new technology might be blurring the boundaries between generations and creating new ones between nations.

However, we need to make a distinction here between theoretical debate stemming from economics and the debate that is closer to sociology. With respect to economics, two points are important. First, the idea of social capital is poorly dealt with in contemporary economic thinking, largely because of social capital's elusive nature. It is not easily defined as an economic good, or as a measurable variable, thus, escapes serious analysis. Therefore, it also tends to get a so-called 'residual' role in economic modelling. After all measurable variables that can be classified in modelling national development, etc., are accounted for, the residue remains. This residue consists of, for example, skills and knowledge or other forms of un-measurable dimensions such as caring, nurturing, dependencies, power imbalances and inequalities.

Secondly, being able to see social capital as a productive asset in economics means that the whole notion would have to be built upon problematic and deeply gendered assumptions about such things as the division of labour, invisible work and social networks. Thirdly, economic analysis skirts a fundamental problem when trying to use the concept of social capital: is social capital a public good, such as shared knowledge, or more of a private good, such as human skills? This question also calls up deeply rooted assumptions about gender, which beg a more sociological analysis.

The recent restructuring of the Finnish welfare state has created a situation, where the introduction of markets in the Finnish public sector in general during the 1990s became associated with political goals and new service provision systems. Several solutions have been put forward at the global level as solutions for the crisis of the welfare state. Perhaps best known is the idea of neo-liberalism with tax reductions and increased reliance on the market solutions. Entrepreneurship became the slogan at the social and health care services, where the purchaser-provider split became the prevalent form of service production. The markets, however, are regulated and function as quasi-markets: state and municipalities are purchasing the services, that is, they are providing the financing, and public and private contractors are providing the service. How does social capital relate to the restructuring of the welfare services?

The connection is to be found on at least two different levels: first, social capital becomes prevalent in the ways in which the negotiations between the purchaser of services and provider of services are being taken forward. Secondly, the purchasers of welfare services have most often previously held posts and positions in the public sector as employees, before becoming private service providers.[4] This puts them in a position where trust relationships between provider and purchaser are most often already established. This is evident in the empirical data from Finland. We have analysed national data from Finland gathered in 1999-2000, where the focus was on the questions of the state of generalised trust in Finland in the 1990s, and the maintenance and change of trust in privatised municipal services. As there was some evidence that an economic recession will weaken social capital, six municipalities were chosen as cases from different parts of Finland. In addition, a nation-wide survey was made on the issues of trust and social capital, including questions about the welfare services. Only the issues related to changing welfare service provisioning are reported here, where the theoretical focus has been on gender, changing societal networks, trust and cohesion in the social structures.

The background for the changes in trust and social capital in general lies in the severe economic recession Finland faced during the 1990s. This resulted in many changes, some of which were mainly focusing on the principles and practices of welfare service production. The increasing pressure to introduce neo-liberal politics into the welfare state policy governing in Finland resulted in relatively quickly changes in the amount and scope of the services provided by the state, thus changing the Nordic welfare model or regime. The economic recession intensified this development, which was already introduced before the recession, thus giving support to the neo-liberal hypothesis. The economic recession led to cuts in the expense structure of the welfare state system, thus increasing pressure at the municipal level to change the service provision system. This was legitimised by the change in state legislation in 1993, resulting in the formal quasi-market system in the Finnish welfare state.

The analysis of the changes within the welfare service provisioning, that is, the shift towards the quasi-market situation, and public/private mix in the service

---

[4] Following Putnam's idea it would be as important to relate the local civic democracy to decision making concerning the provision of social services. In case the decision making – as it does in our data – is made only by the professional civil servants, the local social capital will decline.

production, has resulted in a multifaceted picture of the changes in the welfare state. Even if the numbers are not yet large – less than 20 per cent of the publicly provided services are produced by private enterprises – the trend is upward. The changes have taken place 1) in the ways the services are being provided, 2) in the negotiation patterns between the service provider and purchaser, 3) in the local gender order, that is, in the ways women's work and its position have changed locally. The changes have taken place at different levels as well. First of all, the development has led to marketisation of the services in large cities. This means private services, which can be bought privately and at non-subsidised prices. Second, the development has lead to quasi-markets, where the municipal bureaucracy is the sole purchaser of privately produced services, and the price and contents of the services are controlled by the municipal sector. In small rural municipalities, the effects of marketisation are more difficult to locate. The 'enterprises', private firms within personal social services are mostly not for-profit, but for self-employment, thus not geared for maximisation of efficiency or returns on invested capital, but for good quality care and for possibility to employ oneself (Kovalainen 2001). We were specifically interested in analysing what happens in the new negotiation situations where private providers of care and public purchasing bodies (municipalities) are negotiating for the contract of the service production (Kovalainen 2002; Österberg 2002).

On the political level, we are able to talk about the confidence towards welfare mix arrangements in general and confidence in private social and health care provisioning, but in the municipalities at the 'grassroots' level it is more an issue of trust in both directions. In order for the care arrangements to function, there needs to be trust both between the municipal authorities and the care provider and also between care provider and client. What became evident in the interviews was that dependency is an integral part of the trust relationships: no contract exists without dependency, which is one-dimensional in the sense that usually there are several providers of care services, but only one purchaser, namely a municipal agency. The municipal authorities have the power of the contract negotiation situation, they have the opportunity to define the contents of the contract, and decide from whom the services are purchased. And it is in this situation, where the embedded dependencies and power relations become manifested.

The question of trust, thus, includes the dependency, which becomes visible only when private providers of care, who most often have been previously employed by the same municipal agency they are now negotiating with as private independent contracts, try to get their voices heard. It seems that in this negotiation, power is embedded in trust and also used in negotiations. However, the paradox of the trust becomes prevalent in the negotiations: it is much easier to become a contractor of services for those private providers, who have previous knowledge of the municipality as employees, and who are known from being previous employees. The mutual climate of trust, thus, lowers the threshold for such providers and may even raise it for those who are not known previously.

While the majority (over 75 per cent) of the private providers of care services are women, and while the vast majority of them have been working as employees in the public sector, before the restructuring, gender became an issue in many ways. The most visible way appeared in the interviews of municipal agencies. When the former employees became private providers, their status suddenly changed from employee to small business owner, which was not easily accepted: people representing strong professions such as nurses or kindergarten teachers suddenly turned out to be businesswomen, owning their own businesses and readily negotiating over the prices and costs of the services with the municipal bureaucracy. One of the results was that the trust, which was created in the earlier occupational position, extended to the new service provision activity as well. Having earlier worked in the public sector as employees, they were readily accepted as 'known' persons with a good occupational history and reputation. However, what was more difficult was to gain acceptance in the change of the roles, from employee to self-employed or even employer. Clearly, this transformation was more easily accepted and even praised for men than for women, who expressed in the interview data, the lack of credibility, due to the role change.

Conclusions

There has been a huge increase in research and attraction towards social capital in explaining the recent changes in the economies and societies. Social capital is embodied in relations among persons. Why would the trust and social capital be theoretically inadequate without the questions of dependencies and gender? In this chapter, the problematic relationship between economics and sociology when the question of social capital, trust and dependency are being analysed has been taken up. It is argued here, that knowledge of social capital is in fact very much socially created and constructed knowledge as well, which is shaped by gendered social relations and interactions and dependent upon the theoretical frame used in research. Clearly, in social capital theory, the gender difference *is* making a difference in terms of the transmission and acquisition of social capital, yet gendered agency remains completely untheorised. The crucial questions of power, dominance, or indeed of dependence and vulnerability are left aside.

The core of the concept of social capital rests with the household, and the key components of this concept are the least known, defined and debated by theorists. The definition of gender as a binary, biologically determined variable recalls the idea of gender prevalent in earlier theory. The manner in which social theory has treated gender is illuminated in a somewhat old quotation from Anthony Giddens, who defends structuration theory from criticism by several feminist authors, including Linda Murgatroyd (1989), as follows: 'Not all aspects of social life are gender-divided, and precisely one of the issues which has to be faced in social theory is how far, and in what ways, the difference that is gender "makes a difference"' (Giddens 1989, p. 282). To a large extent, this is reflected in the treatment of gender in mainstream social theory literature: gender is discussed as a pre-existing, binary distinction.

Therefore, the 'capital' of social capital research and theories of social capital cannot be conflated with the knowledge or possession of an atomic individual, and thus cannot be understood as deriving from solely individualistic processes. While the discussion of the 'nature of social capital' is still going on, whether it parallels the other forms of capital such as financial capital, physical capital or human capital, the notion of social being embedded in embodied person-related networks and dependencies within those networks is often forgotten. While the dominant voice in discussions of social capital currently comes from the Putnam-Coleman tradition, and increasingly wins the platform, the subject is, therefore, inherently and explicitly oriented towards economics and rational action theory. The epistemological assumptions in theories where formalism reigns allow very little margin for gender and/or feminist epistemological or social epistemological orientations. In conclusion, the proposal for analysing gender in social capital theory refers to, both, making the implicit gendered theoretical claims visible, by explicating the gender assumptions within the theoretical discussions encompassing social capital theories, and to empirical analyses of gender in the formation process of social capital and trust, as the examples from the Finnish case show.

With the acknowledgement of dependency in trust and social capital relationships comes that of vulnerability as well. Vulnerability indeed specifies the form of trust into relations in which we are dependent on others; what do we entrust to him or her. For example, Sevenhuijsen (1998) argues that care should be seen as a democratic practice, and that democratic citizenship supposes that everybody would be guaranteed equal access to the giving and receiving of care. Care implies responsibility, trust and reliance, and insists on the ethical salience of another person's condition. It is precisely in this that social capital, trust and dependency meet and need to be further analysed.

References

Abell, P. (1992), 'Is Rational Choice Theory a Rational Choice of Theory?', in J. Coleman and T. Fararo (eds), *Rational Choice Theory: Advocacy and Critique*, Newbury Park, Sage.

Arrow, K. (1972), 'Gifts and Exchanges', *Philosophy and Public Affairs*, 357.

Baier, A. C. (1995), *Moral Prejudices: Essays on Ethics*, Cambridge MA, Harvard University Press.

Beck, U. (1992), *Risk Society: Towards a New Modernity*, London, Sage.

Becker, G. (1996), *Accounting for Tastes*, Cambridge, MA, Harvard University Press.

Bourdieu, P. (1980), 'Le capital social: notes provisoires', *Actes de la Recherche en Sciences Sociales*, 3, pp. 2-3.

Bourdieu, P. (1986), 'The Forms of Capital', in J. Richardson (ed), *Handbook of Theory and Research for the Sociology of Education*, New York, Greenwood Press, pp. 241-258.

Bourdieu, P. and Wacquant, L. J. D. (1992), *An Invitation to Reflexive Sociology*, Chicago, University of Chicago Press.

Burt, R. S. (2001), 'Structural Holes versus Network Closure as Social Capital', in N. Lin,
    K. Cook and R.S. Burt (eds), *Social Capital. Theory and Research*, New York, Aldine
    de Gryuter, pp. 31-56.
Coleman, J. C. (2000), 'Social Capital in the Creation of Human Capital', in P. Dasgupta
    and I. Serageldin (eds), *Social Capita: A Multifaceted Perspective*, Washington, The
    World Bank.
Coleman, J. C. (1988), 'Social Capital in the Creation of Human Capital', *American Journal
    of Sociology*, 94, pp. S95-S120.
Coleman, J. C. (1990), *Foundations of Social Theory*, Cambridge MA, Harvard University
    Press.
Cox, E. (1995), *Truly Civil Society*, Sydney, ABC Books.
Dasgupta, P. (2000), 'Economic Progress and the Idea of Social Capital', in P. Dasgupta
    and I. Serageldin (eds), *Social Capital: A multifaceted perspective*, Washington, World
    Bank.
Dasgupta, P. and Serageldin, I. (2000), 'Preface', in P. Dasgupta and I. Serageldin (eds), *op
    cit.*
Deakin, N. (2001), *In Search of Civil Society*, London, Palgrave.
England, P. and Kilbourne, B. (1990), 'Feminist Critiques of the Separative Model of the
    Self: Implications for rational choice theory', *Rationality & Society*, Col. 2(2), pp. 156-
    72.
Field, J., Schuller, T. and Baron, S. (2000), 'Social Capital and Human Capital Revisited',
    in S. Baron, J. Field and T. Schuller (eds), *Social Capital: Critical Perspectives*,
    Oxford, Oxford University Press, pp. 243-63.
Fine, B. (2001), *Social Capital versus Social Theory: Political Economy and Social Science
    at the Turn of the Millennium*, New York, Routledge.
Fine, B. and Green, F. (2000), 'Economics, Social Capital and the Colonization of the
    Social Science', S. Baron, J. Field and T. Schuller (eds), *op cit.*, pp. 78-93.
Flyvbjerg, B. (2001), *Making Social Science Matter*, Cambridge, Cambridge University
    Press.
Folbre, N. (1994), *Who Pays for the Kids? Gender and the structures of constraint*, London,
    Routledge.
Fukuyama, F. (1995), *Trust: The Social Virtues and the Creation of Prosperity*, New York,
    Free Press.
Fukuyama, F. (1999), *The Great Disruption: Human nature and the reconstitution of social
    order*, London, Profile Books.
Furstenberg, F. (1998), 'Social Capital and the Role of Fathers in the Family', in A. Booth
    and A. Creuter (eds), *Men in Families: When do they get involved? What difference
    does it make?* New Jersey, Lawrence Erbaum.
Gambetta, D. (1988) (ed.), *Trust: Making and Breaking Cooperative Relations*, London,
    Blackwell.
Giddens, A. (1989), 'A Reply to my Critics', in D. Held and J. B. Thompson (eds), *Social
    Theory of Modern Societies*, Cambridge, Cambridge University Press, pp. 249-301.
Granovetter, M. (1985), 'Economic Action and Social Structure: The problem of
    embeddedness', *American Journal of Sociology*, 91(3), pp.481-519.
Harriss, J. and De Renzio, P. (1997), 'Missing Link or Analytically Missing? The concept of
    social capital', *Journal of International Development*, 5(7), pp. 919-37.
Hollis, M. (1998), *Trust Within Reason*, Cambridge, Cambridge University Press.
Hollis, M. and Nell, E. (1975), *Rational Economic Man: A philosophical critique of neo-
    classical economics*, Cambridge, Cambridge University Press.
Jacobs, J. (1961), *The Death and Life of Great American Cities*, New York, Vintage Books.

Kovalainen, A. (1994), *The Invisibility of Gender in Economics*, Turku, Publications of Turku School of Economics and Business Administration, Series A-2:1994.

Kovalainen, A. (2001), 'Restructuring and the New Economy', in 'Work, Employment and Society. Conference: "Winning" and "Losing in the New Economy"', Nottingham, Conference publications.

Levi, M. (1998), 'State of Trust', in V. Braithwaite, and M. Levi (eds), *Trust and Governance*, New York, Russell Sage Foundation.

Lin, N. (2001), *Social Capital: A Theory of Social Structure and Action*, Cambridge, Cambridge University Press.

Lin, N., Cook, K. and Burt, R. (eds.)(2001), *Social Capital: Theory and Research*, New York, Aldine de Gruyter.

Longino, H. (1993), 'Economics for Whom?', M. A. Ferber and J. A. Nelson (eds), in *Beyond Economic Man: Feminist Theory and Economics*, Chicago, University of Chicago Press, pp. 158-68.

Marshall, B. L. (1994), *Engendering Modernity: Feminism, Social Theory and Social Change*, Cambridge, Polity Press.

Marshall, B. L. (2000), 'Configuring Gender', in *Explorations in Theory and Politics*, Peterborough, Broadview Press.

Misztal, B. (1996), *Trust in Modern Societies: The Search for the Bases of Social Order*, Cambridge, Polity Press.

Murgatroyd, L. (1989), 'Only Half of the Story: Some blinkering effects of "mainstream" sociology', in D. Held and J. B. Thompson (eds), *Social Theory of Modern Societies*, Cambridge, Cambridge University Press, pp.147–161.

Nelson, J. (1993), 'The Study of Choice or the Study of Provisioning?', in M. A. Ferber and J. A. Nelson (eds.), *Beyond Economic Man: Feminist Theory and Economics*, Chicago, University of Chicago Press, pp. 23-36.

Österberg, J. (2001), 'Recession and New Care Entrepreneurs', in K. Ilmonen, A. Kovalainen and M. Siisiäinen (eds), *Recession and Trust*, Swedish School of Economics, Helsinki, Publications, Research Reports 55 (in Finnish).

Paxton, P. (1999), 'Is Social Capital Declining in the United States? A multiple indicator assessment', *American Journal of Sociology*, 105(1), pp. 88-127.

Portes, A. (1998), 'Social Capital: Its origins and applications in modern sociology', *Annual Review of Sociology*, 24(1), pp. 1-24.

Portes, A. and Landolt, P. (1996), 'The Downside of Social Capital', *The American Prospect*, 26 (May-June).

Putnam, R. D. (1995), 'Bowling Alone: America's declining social capital', *The Journal of Democracy*, 6(1), pp. 65-78.

Putnam, R. D. (2000), *Bowling Alone. The collapse and revival of American community*, New York, Simon and Schuster.

Putnam, R. D., Leonardi, R. and Nanetti, R. Y. (1993), *Making Democracy Work: Civic traditions in modern Italy*, Princeton, Princeton University Press.

Schuller, T., Baron, S. and Field, J. (2000), 'Social Capital: A Review and Critique', in S. Baron, J. Field, & T. Schuller (eds), *op cit.*, Oxford, Oxford University Press, pp. 1-38.

Seligman, A. B. (1997), *The Problem of Trust*, Princeton, Princeton University Press.

Sennett, Rd (1998), *The Corrosion of Character: The Personal Consequences of Work in the New Capitalism*, New York, Norton.

Sevenhuijsen, S. (1998), *Citizenship and the Ethics of Care: Feminist considerations on justice, morality and politics*, London, Routledge.

Siisiäinen, M. (2000), 'Two Concepts of Social Capital: Bourdieu vs. Putnam,' Paper presented at ISTR Fourth International Conference 'Third Sector: For What and For Whom', Trinity College, Dublin, Ireland, July 5-8, 2000.

Skocpol, T. (1996), *Social Revolutions in the Modern World*, Cambridge, Cambridge University Press.

Swedberg, R. (1990), *Economics and Sociology: Redefining their Boundaries: Conversations with Economists and Sociologists*, Princeton, Princeton University Press.

Sztompka, P. (2000), *Trust: A Sociological Theory*, Cambridge, Cambridge University Press.

PART B
INVESTIGATIONS OF
EMBEDDEDNESS

Chapter 5

The Social Foundations of Labour Markets: Foreign Immigration in Portugal[1]

João Peixoto

Introduction

One of the more interesting questions in the study of labour migrations is the role played by labour markets in the formation of flows. A simplistic view, not to be confused with some common sense or more stringent economic analysis, tends to explain the flows only on the basis of income imbalances in different labour markets. In this sense, migrations would function something like means conveying human agents from locations where employment is scarce or wages remuneration low, to other locations where employment is considerable or pay wages higher. Economic agents would, in one way or another, be aware of these imbalances and tend to move to locations where their labour capacity is better rewarded.

When criticising the simpler economic explanation, sociologists usually present an alternative view. They show that labour migrations in different parts of the world do not exactly correspond to income imbalances. There are richer zones with less immigration than others, and poorer zones with higher emigration figures. Furthermore, migratory routes seem to be based on more complex criteria than strictly economic ones: for example, individuals from ex-colonies mostly tend to move towards the hub of former empires, and areas far apart from each other are sometimes more in touch than proximate locations. An international observer has

[1] A first version of this paper was presented at the Fifth Conference of the European Sociological Association (ESA), Economic Sociology Research Network, University of Helsinki, Finland, 28th August – 1st September 2001. A Portuguese version was afterwards published as an academic report in ISEG (Peixoto, 2002a). Some of the material was also used in an article by the author published in the *Journal of Ethnic and Migration Studies (JEMS)* (Peixoto, 2002b). I thank the participants of the Helsinki conference, the academic evaluators in ISEG, the referees and editors of *JEMS* and several colleagues for their very useful comments. I also thank the Foundation for Science and Technology (*Programa de Financiamento Plurianual de Unidades de Investigação*), Calouste Gulbenkian Foundation, Technical University of Lisbon and SOCIUS for support in various occasions. Any errors and shortcomings are entirely my own responsibility.

difficulties in explaining, for instance, why a country like Portugal attracts mainly Portuguese-speaking Africans and Eastern Europeans, and why there are practically no immigrants from Morocco.

Discussions of economic and sociological explanations of reality have enjoyed broad scope in migration studies. Explanations using the intermediate perspective of economic sociology have often been considered preferable to antagonistic argumentation that may lead to nowhere. In the words of Alejandro Portes,

> seldom are the social underpinnings of economic action laid bare with such clarity as in the processes that give rise to immigration and determine its outcomes. (...) In the current climate of revived interest in what sociology has to say about economic life, the field of immigration represents, in Merton's term, a 'strategic research site' (SRS) – an area where processes of more general import are manifested with unusual clarity (Portes, 1995b, p. 2; for the importance of economic sociology to migration studies, see also Portes and Sensenbrenner, 1993; and Portes, 1995a).

Analysis of the social foundations of labour markets, and particularly of social factors accounting for human mobility in this context, is very relevant today for economic sociology and the explanation of specific migrations. The pioneering contribution of Granovetter (1973 and 1974) as well as many other recent studies have pointed to labour mobility within geographically well-defined labour markets. The processes of supply of and demand for work do not usually cross major geographical borders. When this does occur, migration analyses seldom consider it. The conclusions of Granovetter's and similar studies indicate that labour supply and demand does not result only from the rational attributes postulated by economists, but is frequently due to the intervention and interplay of social ties (for a synthesis of sociological research on labour markets, see Granovetter 1992; Tilly and Tilly 1994).

This study will concern itself with the mobility of agents between different labour markets, and focus mainly on the crossing of national borders – in other words, on international labour migration. The principal motive for the displacement revealed in these flows lies in the search for or acceptance of a job. Movements directly caused by non-economic factors (for example, refugee flows) will not be considered here.

If migrations generally are geographical displacements of individuals from one social space to another, labour migrations are displacements from one labour market to another, whether local, regional, or national. Movements of this kind tend to be a response to changes in the economic context (availability of jobs, level of wages and income, etc.) and/or in the social environment (aspirations, social mobility paths). If it is agreed that the most plausible explanation for flows is not purely economic but also related to a group of other factors, then we shall be justified to apply the perspective and concepts of economic sociology to the study of migrations.

Examination of one particular international migration flow may allow us to test the theoretical potential of a different set of factors. The empirical case under scrutiny will be that of foreign immigrants coming to Portugal. The history of this is very recent, but displays significant variety. Flows include not only, as might be expected, European migrants and people from Portuguese-speaking countries (Africans and Brazilians) but also more recently a wave of labour from Eastern Europe. The temporal concentration of these flows, and this rapid change and intertwining with a large number of variables ascribe to the Portuguese case certain qualities that may, to some extent, be regarded as proper to an experimental analysis.

In brief, this study will examine a major issue faced by economic sociology: the embeddedness of economic structures in social relations, and particularly the social factors accounting for mobility between labour markets. First, some of the main theories explaining migration will be reviewed, as well as, the relevant economic theories concerning labour markets, namely the economic push-pull model, dual labour-market theory, and internal labour market theory; the sociological approaches based on the functioning of social networks; also and the institutional theories that underpin the role played by the political factor. The purpose of this is to evaluate some of the more important variables that best explain contemporary migration flows. Then we shall look at the main trends of foreign immigration into Portugal. Finally, conclusions will be drawn from the Portuguese case to explain migratory flows more generally.

Migration Theories

There are many factors that explain labour migrations, or the absence of such flows. Interdisciplinary migration studies have shown the direct relevance economic, social and political circumstances (for a synthesis of available theories, see Massey *et al.* 1993; also Peixoto 1998, p. 39-68; Brettell and Hollifield 2000; for a panorama of recent research, King, 2002). In what follows, some of the more relevant theories on contemporary migration will be described, i.e. those that emphasise the role of labour markets, social networks, and the institutional activities of the State.

Labour Market Theories

Economic Push-pull Model

The push-pull analysis underlies the mainstream economic approaches on migration studies. The idea is that migration occurs whenever there is an imbalance of incomes or employment between two geographical areas. Typically, countries or regions with low incomes or high unemployment may potentially experience outflows to others with higher incomes or lower unemployment. The model acknowledges that at the core of migratory processes we may find decision-making by rational agents who, in possession of information on the relative characteristics of regions A and B and contextual data pertaining to their individual situation, opt for either staying or leaving. The theoretical premise of this reasoning is typical of neo-classical economics.

These explanations, widely supported by common sense, were the first to be developed in modern studies of migration, specifically by Ravenstein (1885 and 1889). The idea, more or less explicit in the author's work, that the prime motive for migration is an individual's desire for better personal economic circumstances, represents the essence of the push-pull model. The choice of a specific path is based on comparative information concerning about the region of origin and potential regions of destination, even when the decision is affected by other mechanisms, such as the distance involved and the possibility of a stage-by-stage movement. Ravenstein's reasoning was taken further by subsequent researchers, who considered that in the mind of individual economic agents, all migration is based on the combination of push- and pull- factors. Among these are intervening opportunities and certain obstacles to movement (such as distance). Later, human-capital theory developed this perspective further without denying its theoretical foundations (see Sjaastad 1962).

Dual Labour-market Theory

The push-pull theoretical framework is often opposed with a more structural approach, that of the dual or segmented labour market. This posits that we must overcome an explanatory framework based only on individual agents who make rational decisions about migration after having collected and evaluated the relevant information. Instead, we should recognise that there is often a structural imbalance that attracts migrants from specific countries or regions to secondary or marginal positions in host labour markets. These peripheralised jobs can be formal or, increasingly, mix with the unregulated and informal areas of labour markets (Piore, 1979; Portes 1981).

According to the dual labour-market theory, labour markets have two main characteristics – as the name suggests. The first and main attribute is that the 'primary' labour market enjoys stability of employment conditions and industrial relations, good wages, career prospects (through an internal labour market that is well developed within the employing organisation), and guaranteed social protection. Departments of the State administration and other major public and private organisations display a large number of these characteristics. The 'secondary' labour market is dominated by jobs with low skills, low skilled jobs, low wages, few possibilities of job promotion, job insecurity and, frequently, lack of social protection. Since the 1970s, structural economic changes and the development of new forms of regulation have led to a growing number of precarious sectors and the increasing need for a flexible labour force.

Dual labour-market theory quickly achieved significant acceptance among academics. It has been realised that a large number of specific international migration routes, particularly those from poorly to better developed countries, lead towards the secondary labour markets of the latter and, currently, to the informal zones of the economy. It is the existence of economic activities of this nature that, on the one hand, drives away most of the local native workers who possess the necessary social mobility or can get support from the welfare state. On the other hand it is responsible for attracting migrants from poorer regions who, even in precarious economic conditions, improve their former standard of living or, at least, can nurture expectations of future mobility. It is also this type of situation that gives rise to the statement that there is no immigration without a specific economic need for it in the host country.

However, migrant populations are not attracted to the secondary labour market only. As Portes (1981) has made clear, modes of incorporation are diverse. According to him, the main characteristics of migrants attracted to the *primary* labour market are their admission through legal channels; their access to employment by individual characteristics and not by ethnic origin; patterns of social mobility identical with those of the native population; and as a reinforcement of the national labour force. Typically, this type of flow is represented by the 'brain drain'. By contrast, the main attributes of those destined for the *secondary* labour market are a precarious juridical status (usually temporary or irregular); recruitment based on discriminating according to ethnic origin rather than skills (in view of the vulnerable status associated with the ethnic condition); filling very temporary jobs, with no prospects of upward mobility; and exercising a disciplinary function on the local labour force (by causing a reduction in the average wage). This type of recruitment applies the majority of migrant workers in the world context. Finally, a third form of incorporation must be considered: the one that links migrants to zones of ethnic homogeneity in the economy (ethnic enclaves).

Internal Labour-market Theory

Labour market structures can also be approached from the organisational angle. The main question is to know whether large companies recruit labour in their external labour markets (the usual view) or in internal ones (Doeringer and Piore 1971; Salt and Findlay 1989). The processes of labour circulation internal to large companies are based on their type of organisational structure and the circumstances on their human resources. Examination of these structures allows identification of the main labour flows. We have to must differentiate between vertical (going upward in the hierarchy), functional (related to changes in the function performed), lateral (moves to similar tasks), and geographical movements (between locations). Also the different hierarchical levels must be defined and the different channels in each one to which human resources have access. These channels constitute both 'internal ports' providing for the upward trend (promotion) in the internal labour markets; and 'ports of entry/exit' communicating with external labour market (see Salt and Findlay 1989, pp. 164-66).

The most frequent references by migration theory to the internal labour-market notion occur in analyses of promotion (vertical movement). Generally speaking, various forms of overlapping of labour flows can occur, and migrations (geographical moves) result from and express themselves as one or more of the above types (vertical, functional, lateral). Since each career path in a company's organisational structure depends not only on the agent's decision but also on the organisational framework, namely the company's need of allocating/re-allocating resources, this perspective combines a micro and a macro view on migrations. The internal labour-market approach has mainly been used to explain highly-skilled mobility. The possession of skills (or human capital) enables individuals to pursue job changes, and so to benefit from the given organisational framework.

In the case of international migrations studies, what is relevant is how business firms and other organisations engaged in international activities and possessing multiple establishments move their personnel. Here it is not the isolated relationship between individual workers and the national labour markets of host countries (the external markets), but their insertion in the internal market that most meaningfully explains their movement and modes of integration.

Social-network Theories

Theories based on the concept of social networks have in the last few years acquired growing importance in sociology and particularly in economic sociology. Networks are sets of repeated relations between individuals linked by occupational, family, cultural or affective ties. They may take diverse forms expressed in their different size (number of individuals involved) or the density of relations, for example. Whether they are presented as explanatory models of a qualitative type, or consist of rigorous quantitative methodologies as in social-network analysis, their potential is widely accepted to describe and explain human behaviour. The efficacy of these theories results from combining a sociological analysis of an individualistic type with a structuralist perspective. On the micro level, network theories stress the role of individual agents in releasing all forms of action; they do not deny the effectiveness of rational choice. At the macro level, they emphasise that all action is interaction between agents, as well as different modalities of positive and negative sanctions for individual behaviour as structural constraints to action (for a review of network theories in economic sociology, see Powell and Smith-Doerr 1994).

Particularly with regard to economic sociology, networks are seen as a crucial concept in current research. According to Portes,

> social networks are among the most important types of structures in which economic transactions are embedded. (...) Networks are important in economic life because they are sources for the acquisition of scarce means, such as capital and information, and because they simultaneously impose effective constraints on the unrestricted pursuit of personal gain (1995b, p. 8).

The network concept is also closely linked to that of social capital. The latter reflects the capability of individuals to obtain valued goods, information, or power as a result of their social membership, particularly the relationships and networks in which they are engaged. In Portes' words again, social capital 'refers to the capacity of individuals to command scarce resources by virtue of their membership in networks or broader social structures' (1995b, p. 12). The main dimensions of social capital are obligations, reciprocity, and solidarity (Faist 2000). Resources obtained by this means reflect the crucial characteristic that they are 'free', not paid for in money. As a result, transactions based on social capital are intrinsically different from market transactions.

Theories based on social networks are decisive for explaining migratory flows. Those most frequently referred to in migration literature are *informal* social networks (Portes 1995a, 1995b; Portes and Böröcz 1989; Faist 2000). It has been shown that personal ties create channels of information, frameworks for decision, and conditions for social support and integration that from the actual migration flows. Individual ties among family and kinship members, among friends and neighbours, help to spread information (whether correct or otherwise), act as economic and social support for migrants, and can even instil a culture of mobility (penetrating individual decisions). As postulated by Faist, migration networks activate the social capital of particular groups. Although social capital is initially a local asset mainly helping to explain immobility, networks break its territorial logic and invest it as a resource for geographical mobility. Under the command of networks social capital ceases to be a local asset and becomes a 'transnational transmission belt', diminishing the transaction costs of moving. When they are operating, migration networks become 'crystallized social capital' (Faist 2000, pp. 15-17).

Research on this type of network is presently widespread and has provided a convincing explanation of many of the questions concerning migration. It is also in this field that the linkage with the economic-sociology perspective has proved to be most effective (see Portes 1995b; Portes and Böröcz 1989). This line of reasoning, considers migrations not as individual actions between different geometric economic spaces, but rather as socially-oriented phenomena to be analysed by means of a relational perspective, functioning on the basis of chain migration.

This concept of networks has in the main been used to explain migration from the perspective of external labour markets. But it may also be argued that a specific type of informal social networks can be found in the study of internal labour markets. Until now, research on networks in organisational contexts has neglected the migratory dimension. A research area that remains to be explored would be to evaluate the extent to which networks inside large organisations are related to geographical movements of employees. Some observations already available suggest that a significant part of international corporate migrations – movements of highly-skilled personnel within transnational firms – is related to individual particularistic links. For example, a fraction of the highly-skilled personnel working as expatriates in foreign subsidiaries owes relocation to reasons of inter-personal trust and loyalty. It is the possibility of placing trusted employees in a foreign location that emerges as a motive for migration, as much as the need to allocate technical personnel (Peixoto 1999, 2001). It may be argued that the technical relocations too are related to the individual employee's position in networks of relations.

This means that the international circulation of staff in global organisations, including transnational corporations, seems to depend not only on rational considerations based on the allocation of staff according to specific shortages, but also on social factors. It is the roles played by trust and loyalty that may explain why certain functions are more subject than others to control by the organisation's centre and the personnel emanating from it. On the other hand, even the strictly technical personnel movements may be due to the fact that an individual is personally more closely in touch with, or better known to, the relevant decision-maker.

A second *formal* type of social networks has been increasingly emphasised in research. This relates particularly to migrant trafficking, which for the purposes of this study embraces both trafficking and smuggling. By using the term 'formal' we refer not to its legal but its organised nature (see Salt and Stein 1997; Salt 2000b). In fact, migrant trafficking positions itself at a theoretical crossroad, since it represents both the regular interaction of a relatively dispersed set of individuals (i.e., a network) and an increasingly organised economic activity. In other words, trafficking can be analysed either through the theoretical lens of social networks, or the perspective of institutional and organisational theories. What favours the network perspective is the fact that this activity requires different types of connection at different points along the path (agents, contacts, individuals liable to corruption...) and possesses highly flexible structures. What supports an institutional perspective is the fact that it is an organised intermediate agent facilitating and promoting migrations, thus rendering 'services' to migrants, the functioning of which is based on economic logic and not social capital (about the roots of the concept on the institutional perspective of migration, see Salt 1987, pp. 245-47).

It must be acknowledged that different forms of organised migration have existed for a considerable time – namely State-linked migration, labour brokers, and trafficking (Stalker 2000). Institutions such as migrants' associations may also play a role in this field, emerging as intermediary agents between the host country's administration and individual migrants. Whatever the notion held to be most appropriate for dealing with these entities, the truth is that trafficking nowadays is increasing. The organised support of migration through trafficking and smuggling is undeniable for any explanation of migratory flows from the 1990s onwards. It is responsible for a growing volume of human movement, especially as political restrictions to migration became more severe. It should also be acknowledged that this type of formal social network disrupts the traditional logic of migration systems, insofar as it does not depend on previous social (or other) connections. Moreover, it helps to speed up the whole process of migration (for more on this, see below).

The activities of informal as well as formal social networks implies both an individualistic and a structural view of migration, so avoiding rational explanations on the one hand, and social determination on the other, while still situating the migrants in their context of action. Networks also explain some of the apparent anomalies of migration. In this connection we should mention the durable character of migration, which lasts well beyond the short-term economic reasons that were the cause of it. This inertia of migration flows is best explained by evaluating the complex mechanisms of behaviour diffusion through networks (Faist 2000). Another apparent anomaly is the linkage between very specific geographical host and destination areas, the functioning of networks that maximises movements emerging from a particular location (village, town) to another particular location (neighbourhood, town). This occurs mainly in the case of informal networks, based on strong social ties between agents (as opposed to the weak ties mentioned by Granovetter 1973). With respect to formal networks, their capacity to disperse migrants in response to concrete labour requests is higher.

Institutional and Political Theories

Institutional theories of migration have been applied to many analyses, including that of business firms, the State, migrants' associations, employment agencies, migrants' support agencies, and trafficking networks (see Salt 1987, pp. 245-47; Massey *et al.* 1993, pp. 450-51). The role of business firms in their capacity as employer organisations, and that of trafficking networks regarded as organisers and facilitators of flows, have already been mentioned. At this point we shall consider the role of the State and, simultaneously, the political nature of migrations.

As Zolberg (1981) has stated, it is nation-states and their territorial sovereignty that define the range of international migrations. National immigration policies erect concrete barriers in the economic labour market – which, from a purely economic perspective, would be proximate to a geometric and abstract space. National policies act in a number of ways. They intervene directly through control of borders (the entry of foreigners), granting the right to stay (concession of residence and work permits), and the granting of citizenship (naturalisation and nationality policies). Indirectly they make themselves felt in the concession of particular rights as a result of sectoral policies in areas such as housing, employment, or in whether or not they recognise the immigrant's academic qualification, diplomas, etc. With respect to the last point, even if a foreigner is permitted by the host country to stay, the process of his or her skills being accepted and the recognition of the true potential of his/her human capital is a complex one; the institutional nature of skills has deep roots in nation-states and restrains labour changes (Marsden 1992). Recently, the link between national migration policies and international regulations has also been stressed. Multilateral agreements, the constitution of supra-national entities such as the European Union (EU), and international principles on human rights – all must be taken into account in a country's policy-making and all play a growing role in international migration nowadays (Cornelius *et al.* 1994; Sassen 1998; Faist 2000).

Just how efficient national political regulations control over international migration has been the object of intense scrutiny. It is widely acknowledged that nation-states have always devoted attention to the subject, either for practical labour-market reasons or because the large movements of people can erode a country's administrative and social basis. Immigrants may not only become a problem in terms of host-country's welfare arrangements, they may also disrupt the cultural and ethnic basis on which national identity is built. It is not by chance that migration issues have resisted attempts to subject them to international regulation, contrary to what has happened in trade or finance. It is also not accidental that migration is one of the areas where supra-national entities like the EU have the greatest difficulties in defining a common policy.

Another point that is generally accepted is that, after a period when different national immigration policies diverged in several respects, a more common trend towards restriction then emerged. Considering only the period since World War II until the 1970s, we find that labour-importing countries at first presented a long list of regulations. Gradually, inflows – whether temporary (guest workers) or permanent – were more widely tolerated. Then, from the mid-1970s onwards, the policies of different countries became more alike and a generally more restrictive climate emerged, both in the former settlement countries such as the United States and Canada, and in the new European host countries (Cornelius *et al.* 1994).

Cornelius *et al.* developed the idea of a crisis of political control over immigration in the 1990s. It concerns the time lag between policies and actual migration movements, and states their 'the gap between the *goals* of national immigration policy (laws, regulations, executive actions, etc.) and the actual results of policies in this area (policy *outcomes*) is wide and growing wider in all major industrialized democracies' (1994, p. 3). According to the authors, the declining efficiency of control measures was due to the continuous demand for migrant labour in host countries, the supply mechanisms in the workers' country of origin, the activities of social networks, and the rise of rights-based politics. This last-named variable was emphasised by authors such as Faist (2000). He posits that after a first phase, where nation-states can exert significant control over inflows, the acquisition of a legal status and subsequently of rights by the first migrants makes it possible for new and self-feeding movements to develop. Family, marriage, and illegal migration (not to mention refugees) all follow the first migrants and benefit from the protection of human, civil, and social rights in democratic host countries.

The setbacks of immigration policy can also be viewed under the dual action of economic globalisation and the new international human-rights regime. According to Sassen (1998), the novel 'transnational regimes' – capital and human rights – challenge traditional national policy-making and oblige the State to adapt to a new framework for action. In brief, the increasingly restrictive national policies on migration are not always effective. Rather, 'it is the confluence of *markets* [the push–pull factors] and *rights* that explains much of the contemporary difficulty of immigration control in Europe and the United States' (Cornelius *et al.* 1994, p. 10).

Migration Flows to Portugal

Immigration in Recent Decades

Foreign immigrants coming to Portugal did not reach significant numbers until the late 1970s, although even before that some foreign inflows and communities existed. The most important of these groups was that of western Europeans. Minor inflows of Spaniards were traditional, and followed either certain frontier lines of attraction (e.g., entry from Galicia) or political disturbances in their country (e.g., the Spanish civil war of the 1930s). Other Europeans came traditionally in connection with specific economic activities (e.g., the production of Oporto wine) or again due to political disturbances (World War II). In the 1960s, the number and variety of foreigners increased, following the economic opening-up of Portugal, which had become a member of the European Free Trade Association (EFTA) and begun to attract more tourism. The number of foreign professionals working for multinational firms, and retired individuals living in sunny resorts of the country became larger. There was a relatively large inflow in the late 1960s, bringing individuals from Cape Verde, then a Portuguese colony in Africa. Although they were all Portuguese citizens, this was the beginning of a major 'foreign' inflow in the next decade.

Foreign immigration reached sizeable numbers in the mid-1970s, when the country became politically modernised with the establishment of democracy, when the economy was opened up to a more intense exchange with foreign countries, and when the ex-colonies became independent. Immediately afterwards and following civil disturbances (or even civil war) in these new countries, a mass departure of Portuguese individuals occurred to the home country. This mostly consisted of people born in Portugal (as now defined) or of Portuguese descent, although some 'native' individuals – mainly from the middle or high social strata – also emigrated. Very quickly the number of so-called *retornados* had reached half a million people (1974 and 1975). The inflow from the ex-colonies continued during the later 1970s, but was now composed of foreigners who owed their new political status to that of their countries' and the change in nationality rules in Portugal (which had deprived them of their former Portuguese citizenship). Although many gave economic motives for departure, they did leave their countries at a time of political turbulence and therefore did not represent a typical labour migration. They were really a continuation of earlier flows, either these of the 1960s from Cape Verde or those immediately following independence. In any case, they were responsible for the first strong upsurge in the total number of foreigners in Portugal.

The numbers of foreign individuals legally living in Portugal from 1980 to 2001 is given in Table 5.1. It seems quite clear how the migratory influx of different foreign nationalities evolved during this time.

In 1980, foreigners amounted to almost 51,000, or 0.5 per cent of the total Portuguese population. Africans constituted the major foreign group, accounting for just under half of all legal foreigners (48.8 per cent). Europeans were the second major group, with 30.3 per cent of the total; and Americans (North and

South) the third, with 18.5 per cent of the total. Taking single nationalities, the predominance of Cape Verde was very clear, with 41.4 per cent of the total, followed at some distance by Spain and Brazil (13 per cent and 7.1 per cent, respectively). By 2001, the total number of foreigners had increased more than fourfold to almost 224,000, or 2.2 per cent of the whole population. Regarding relative positions, little had changed: Africa was still the major group, with 47.8 per cent, followed by Europe (30 per cent) and America (17.5 per cent). Taking single nationalities, Cape Verdeans were still the leading group – but now with only 22.3 per cent of the total (down from 41 per cent) – followed by Brazil (10.5 per cent). These figures express the three major components of foreign immigration in this period: African labour migrants, mostly coming from the ex-colonies; European professionals (often working in the framework of transnational corporations) and retired citizens; and a direct counter-current of former Portuguese emigration coming from America (many of these individuals were of Portuguese descent).

Despite broad stability in the quantitative evolution of the major groups of nationalities over the last two decades, some qualitative changes were verified. First, a true economic migration directed to the Portuguese labour market was established in the early 1980s, mostly grouping low-skilled workers coming from the ex-colonies in Africa. This flow was initially dominated by Cape Verdeans who availed themselves of strong social networks already in place, but then progressively gave way to migrants from Angola and Guinea-Bissau. These latter initiated new migratory cycles, compensating for the relative exhaustion of the inflow coming from Cape Verde, stimulated by political and economic motives.

Portugal's entrance into the European Economic Community in 1986 created a strong stimulus for both new and existing flows. The surge in foreign direct investment and the availability of European structural funds after 1986 created new economic initiatives and sparked off an overall economic expansion. This reinforced inflows of European professionals, often within the framework of multinational corporations. The economic boom also increased the numbers of low-skilled Africans, and gave new reasons for the entrance of Brazilians. The latter, attracted by the country's new European status, possessed skills necessary for the new economic environment (for example, marketing skills). Along with the economic rationale for moving, migrant groups quickly became self-renewing, a mechanism which guaranteed their continuous increase.

Table 5.1 Foreigners with full legal residence in Portugal, 1980-2001

Nationality	1980 Total	%	1990 Total	%	2001 (a) Total	%
Total	**50,750**	**100**	**107,767**	**100**	**223,602**	**100**
Europe	**15,380**	**30.3**	**31,412**	**29.1**	**66,973**	**30.0**
EU/15	*14,830*	*29.2*	*29,901*	*27.7*	*61,575*	*27.5*
Germany	1,959	3.9	4,845	4.5	11,143	5.0
Spain	6,597	13.0	7,462	6.9	13,584	6.1
United Kingdom	2,648	5.2	8,457	7.8	14,952	6.7
Other EU	3,626	7.1	9,137	8.5	21,896	9.8
Other Europe	*550*	*1.1*	*1,511*	*1.4*	*5,398*	*2.4*
Africa	**24,788**	**48.8**	**45,255**	**42.0**	**106,978**	**47.8**
PALOP (b)	*24,491*	*48.3*	*43,297*	*40.2*	*101,119*	*45.2*
Angola	1,482	2.9	5,306	4.9	22,630	10.1
Cape Verde	21,022	41.4	28,796	26.7	49,930	22.3
Guinea Bissau	678	1.3	3,986	3.7	17,580	7.9
Mozambique	594	1.2	3,175	2.9	4,749	2.1
São Tomé Principe	715	1.4	2,034	1.9	6,230	2.8
Other Africa	*297*	*0.6*	*1,958*	*1.8*	*5,859*	*2.6*
America	**9,405**	**18.5**	**26,369**	**24.5**	**39,214**	**17.5**
North America	*3,826*	*7.5*	*8,993*	*8.3*	*10,229*	*4.6*
Canada	754	1.5	2,058	1.9	1,956	0.9
USA	3,072	6.1	6,935	6.4	8,058	3.6
Other	-	-	-	-	215	0.1
Latin America	*5,579*	*11.0*	*17,376*	*16.1*	*28,985*	*13.0*
Brazil	3,608	7.1	11,413	10.6	23,541	10.5
Venezuela	1,705	3.4	5,145	4.8	3,547	1.6
Other	266	0.5	818	0.8	1,897	0.8
Asia and Oceania	**1,053**	**2.1**	**4,509**	**4.2**	**10,160**	**4.5**
Other	**124**	**0.2**	**222**	**0.2**	**277**	**0.1**

Notes (a) Provisional data.
(b) Portuguese-speaking African countries.

Source: National Statistical Institute (INE).

Meanwhile, there was strong pressure for irregular immigration. Growing labour demand, the new era of economic flexibility, the lack of regulation in the civil-construction sector, more stringent immigration policies, and continuous difficulties in the migrants' home countries – all led to the growing presence of illegal immigration. A contradiction was evident between, on the one hand, an economic logic that favoured the informalisation of the labour market and, with it, the recruitment of illegal immigrants; and on the other, a political discourse promoting immigration control. The intensification of civil construction and public works, including an extensive network of highways and the building of the Expo-98 site (for the Universal Exhibition of Lisbon), was ultimately responsible for increased informalisation. At that time it seemed to be informal social networks that were the main vehicle for immigration. It was, in a sense, the interests of individual actors (the employers' or even the migrants' ones) that prevailed over the generic call for citizenship. As a result, there was a growing component of illegal immigration throughout this period, most of which was included in the legal segment after two legalisation processes in 1992-1993 and 1996. (For a more detailed picture of foreign immigration until the late 1990s, see Pires 1993, 1999; Malheiros 1996; Machado 1997; Baganha 1998, 2000, 2001; Baganha and Góis 1998/1999; Baganha, Ferrão and Malheiros 1999; Peixoto 1999; Fonseca 2000).

Recent Flows

In the mid-1990s, a significant new inflow began from the Eastern European countries, which are practically absent from the numbers of legal foreigners given above. Officially, there were very few Eastern Europeans living in Portugal legally in 2001. However, Portuguese media estimates during 2000 pointed to the existence of around 50,000 Eastern Europeans at the turn of the millennium (see Portella 2000 and several references in the mass media). A process of legalisation launched in January 2001, based on the grant of temporary 'permits to stay', quickly produced that figure. The process of regularisation, which consisted of temporary (one year) legalisation of individuals able to present valid labour contracts or who could show employed status, represented an important change in the country's immigration policy (although this process was interrupted in 2002). The new law created juridical status for the 'permits to stay' (which, in practice, constituted labour permits), established penalties for supporting illegal immigration, and laid down basis for an immigration policy which allowed previously defined labour shortages to be filled by immigrants (the definition of shortages was to be established by the government in collaboration with other institutions related to the labour market).

Statistics for March 2002 on 'permits to stay' that had been renewed after the first year of legalisation, are presented in Table 5.2. Since the new temporary status does not entitle the immigrant to the full right of residence, it does not add to the total number of foreigners presented in Table 5.1 (of individuals holding the full residence permit). In March 2002, immigrants from Eastern Europe numbered more than 80,000, and represented the bulk of recent immigration into Portugal (*circa* 55 per cent of all foreigners with 'permits to stay'). The clear majority of them came from the Ukraine (more than 52,000, i.e., 35.6 per cent of the total), followed at some distance by Moldovans, Romanians and Russians (7.3 per cent, 6 per cent and 3.9 per cent, respectively). The figures also show a general change in recent immigration. The traditional sources – Brazil and Portuguese-speaking Africa – are represented, by lesser weight than before (especially Africa). Brazilians (who in 2001 accounted for 10.5 per cent of fully resident foreigners) now make up 18.5 per cent of the legal contingent – a number that suggests the beginning of a new and less skilled migration wave towards the informal sector of the economy, but Africans amount to barely 14 per cent, far less than their traditional presence in the country. On the other hand, new sources of labour are evident, namely from Asia. Considering the rapid increase of these numbers, it is generally accepted that the process of regularisation has covered a high proportion of formerly informal labour (for a review of recent changes in immigration, see Pires 2002).

Given that Eastern European migration to Portugal is of very recent date, little systematic research is yet available on it, and only some generalisations can help elucidate certain of its features. Concerning the *timing* of these flows from Eastern Europe the first came into Portugal in the mid-1990s, partially in response to opportunities at the Expo-98 building sites, or trying to benefit from more relaxed immigration policies. Initially, the only country of origin was Romania. After the 1996 regularisation (itself a motive for new entries), the number increased. Concerning *economic* activity, Eastern European migrants are overwhelmingly engaged in the informal labour market. The large majority of them are employed in construction (Pires 2002), where opportunities remain abundant, and the prospects for the future are promising. (For instance, Portugal has been awarded the organisation of the European Football Championships in 2004, which involves substantial modifications of existing stadiums and the construction of new ones, aside from adjacent urban renewals.) Concerning *demographic* structure, the first wave of immigrants consisted mainly of adult men, but some women are now coming to the service sector (restaurants, domestic cleaning). Concerning permanent *settlement* in Portugal, it is still too early to ascertain whether this migration is a truly temporary one, characterised by frequent inward and outward movements, or may alternatively achieve a permanent character, based on the functioning of networks and family reunions.

It must be emphasised that the Eastern European inflow was a complete novelty in Portuguese immigration history. All previous inflows were, in one way or another, linked to former Portuguese connections. African immigrants came mostly from the Portuguese ex-colonies (at its peak, some other African migrants came from border countries, like Senegal or the Congo). Brazilian immigrants came from a country with many historical links with Portugal and sharing the same language, or were themselves of Portuguese descent. Inflows from America mainly resulted from Portuguese diasporas, and that from Asia was also linked in various ways to the Portuguese colonial past (Malheiros 1996). All these flows constituted what we may call an international migratory system united by the Portuguese language.

Finally, immigration from Western Europe has a long economic, social and cultural history. However, no significant relationship ever linked Portugal to the Ukraine, Moldova, Romania or Russia, the origin of the new flows. It is interestingly that this novelty is a dual one. Not only did Portugal never have contacts with these countries, but these countries have had no significant international emigration in recent times.

Table 5.2 Foreigners with 'permits to stay' (issued from 22 January 2001 until 5 March 2002)

Nationality (a)	Total	%
Total	147,515	100
Europe		
Belarus	899	0.6
Bulgaria	2,002	1.4
Moldova	10,783	7.3
Romania	8,882	6.0
Russia	5,737	3.9
Ukraine	52,578	35.6
Africa		
PALOP		
Angola	5,725	3.9
Cape Verde	6,296	4.3
Guinea Bissau	3,788	2.6
São Tomé Principe	1,779	1.2
Other Africa		
Guinea	1,456	1.0
Morocco	1,306	0.9
America		
Brazil	27,296	18.5
Asia and Oceania		
Bangladesh	943	0.6
China	3,838	2.6
India	3,355	2.3
Pakistan	3,242	2.2

Note (a) Only the largest nationalities are presented.

Source: Serviço de Estrangeiros e Fronteiras (SEF).

The obvious question is: why did such a flow occur? The probable answer: this is the first immigration flow predominantly linked to Portugal's new European status resulting from her EU membership, as well as from the new global economic and political framework. On the one hand are the push factors in the sending-countries: economic weakness, together with the collapse of the pre-existing social and economic fabric, has resulted in widespread poverty and explains people leaving (for instance, wages in some skilled occupations in those countries are inferior to low-skilled wages in the Portuguese economy). On the other hand there is Portugal's intrinsic attraction as an EU member, the (real or perceived) idea that the immigration rules are less stringently enforced there than in other EU countries, or that the acquisition of legal status is easier there than elsewhere, and Portugal's buoyant labour demand (partially as a result of EU funds) that collectively help to explain the flows. Additionally, it was perhaps also the full implementation of the Schengen Convention in 1995 that made the granting of visas to Eastern European nationals more straightforward and allowed free circulation in the Schengen space, that explained the inflows (Malheiros and Baganha 2000). In fact, the typical way for East Europeans to enter the country seems to be by through tourist visas to Austria, Germany, the Netherlands or France (all of which belong to the Schengen area), and then coming to Portugal overland (Portella 2000).

These inflows are also changing the nature of illegal immigration – and the role of migrant social networks – in Portugal. As Malheiros and Baganha (2000, p. 190) have stated,

> (...) illegal immigration in Portugal seems to be undergoing remarkable structural changes. It seems to be changing from a flow mostly constituted by individual and volunteer movements, based on migratory networks active at both ends of the migration pathway, to another flow mainly composed of immigrants whose entrance and stay are linked to trafficking networks of labour migrants, orchestrated from the sending (or distributing) areas.

The authors add that this situation ha to do not only with the changed origins of the illegal immigrants (from Africa to Eastern Europe), but also with the inefficiency of the control mechanisms of the national labour market. Nevertheless, migrant trafficking has increasingly come to public attention in Portugal as a result of police actions and court of justice trials. It is also trafficking that apparently explains the reduced associative behaviour of this migratory group, as well as its high circulation and dissemination in the country (see also Pires 2002).

I would add two further observations. *First*, it is the action of formal trafficking networks that channels the migrants from specific countries of origin to this (formerly) unknown destiny, following a strict logic of effective labour placement. Salt and Stein (1997), referring to other geographical contexts, have already stated that, as a consequence of trafficking, the decisions about the geography of flows have moved from migrants to the organisations that transport them. The latter decide the routes to follow, based on the existence of labour supply, but also on the relative ease of operations. In this sense, trafficking disrupts the traditional logic of migration systems whereby most migration proceeds within the framework of an established system of relationships. *Secondly*, trafficking speeds up the process of migration. The sharp increase in Eastern European immigrants in Portugal would probably have been impossible in the context of informal social networks whose circulation of information, contacts, and migrants' support develop more slowly.

The Paradoxes

The current situation of foreign immigration into Portugal may be viewed as displaying a double paradox. Firstly, the flows can hardly be explained by the push-pull theory alone. If economic criteria based on income and employment levels were really the main motives for migration, how should one account for the specific origins of these flows, let alone the fact that Portugal is the preferred destination? During the traditional phase of migration, the country attracted mainly Portuguese-speaking migrants from the African ex-colonies and from Brazil. But from a rational standpoint there is nothing to suggest that Portugal was really the best possible destination for these migrants, given that nearby European states (mainly Spain), offered the same cultural and linguistic similarities and better economic conditions. The same applies to the more recent wave from Eastern Europe. What comparative advantages has Portugal as a labour employer, considering its relatively low economic standard, compared to other potential destinations in the EU?

Whatever the specific factors that make Portugal attractive to migrants are even more bizarre from a strictly economic point of view when if we consider the large pool of labour and potential emigrants to be found in North Africa, particularly in Morocco. An international observer with no knowledge of migration mechanisms would have difficulty explaining why Portugal registers practically no inflows from Morocco, although the two countries are geographically close and there are strong migratory flows from the latter to Spain. It can hardly be that social agents in Morocco are behaving irrationally in terms of migratory options, when they disregard Portugal. It is certain that many of the jobs that Portuguese-speaking and Eastern-European immigrants perform in Portugal would have equal appeal for many Moroccans.

Immigration flows into Portugal are just as difficult to explain if we take into account some of the best-established sociological theories on the phenomenon. For example, Portes points out that,

> in general, migratory waves are directed from peripheral countries to those central countries with which they possess more historical links and are responsible for the diffusion of new desires and aspirations. As a result, current migration flows directed to the United States mainly comes from Mexico, Philippines, Puerto Rico, South Korea and Vietnam. All these nations are profoundly affected by North America's economic presence and political interference. Similarly, migration towards Portugal mainly occurs from its former colonies, Angola, Cape Verde, etc. (Portes 1999, p. 3).

In other words and generally speaking, migrations channel individuals between countries that historically knew and met each other before – between former imperial hubs and their colonies, dominant world powers and peripheries.

Portes' argument is based on the migration-systems theory. This explains that frequent contacts between countries produce exchanges at diverse levels that eventually acquire the contours of a system (see Kritz *et al.* 1992). Military, political, administrative, social, and cultural contacts afford better knowledge between countries; these contacts imply the transfer of human resources and allow the diffusion of 'desires and aspirations'. The fact that the peripheral society absorbs resources and institutions from the central country leads to some de-structuring of its local economic and social fabric and so to activation of the migratory potential. Migrants choose the central country because information about it is more easily accessible or the entrance into its labour market is more straightforward. They know the administrative streams, they have already encountered institutions and employer organisations from the country of attraction, and they feel a certain social, cultural and linguistic affinity with it. In a word, the 'system' contains favourable conditions for self-renewal of diverse type of exchanges, be they migratory or otherwise.

Portes' assertion above (from the introduction to a recent Portuguese edition of some of his writings) does not, however, adequately reflect the current reality of immigration in Portugal. In fact, in the last few years the unprecedented immigration flux from Eastern Europe acquired a volume equivalent to that of some of the largest foreign communities in the country. It would be another complex exercise to explain to an international observer why countries that mutually ignored each other in the mid-1990s – Portugal and Ukraine, or Portugal and Moldova, for example – are today important partners in the European migratory system. Their respective populations witness increasing exchanges, including at the symbolic level. This is really astonishing, given that the leading western destinations for Eastern European migrants are mainly located right next to their geographical borders – Germany, Austria, and Finland (Salt 2000a) – Portugal being the only (and most extreme) anomaly.

Ignoring the juridical differences between nationalised foreigners enjoying legal residence (Table 5.1) and those (Table 5.2) in possession of only temporary permits to stay (strictly speaking, these numbers cannot be added together, as a permit to stay does not entitle the migrant to the full rights of residence) a comparison between the two shows some striking quantitative factors. The bulk of the legally residing, formerly foreign nationals in Portugal in 2001 are from Cape Verde, with some 50,000 individuals, and Brazil, with about 24,000. These numbers represent the sediment of immigration waves accumulated over at least two to three decades – although their total volume is somewhat higher, since many of the immigrants have in the meanwhile merged with the Portuguese population through acquisition of nationality. Concerning immigrants with temporary permits to stay, in the very short time of little more than five years the population from the Ukraine has reached almost 53,000 individuals (data of March 2002).

If we add legal residents to those in possession of permits to stay – a situation that could occur if all the holders of permits to stay were to apply for the right of residence – we shall obtain a clearer idea of the relative volumes. The addition would give us Cape-Verdeans numbering amount to more than 56,000 (50,000 enjoying legal residence and 6,000 holding permits); Brazilians totalling over 50,000 (24,000 and 27,000 respectively), and Ukrainians almost 53,000 (permits only). These figures clearly show the weight of the new Eastern European migration, besides confirming that among the traditional flows it is mainly that from Brazil which continues to be active, as the recent flow from Africa is very low. According to these figures, the Ukrainians are today the second-largest foreign nationality in Portugal, not far behind Cape Verdeans (although the numbers do not include the progressive absorption of the latter into the Portuguese population). As already stated, the historical connections between Portugal and the Ukraine are scarce compared to the country's traditional sources of migrant flows. It remains to be seen why Portugal was responsible for the diffusion of desires and aspirations in that country.

The Explanation: Labour Markets and Social Factors

The labour market in Portugal has been unquestionably dynamic in recent decades. In terms of international labour mobility alone, the country has witnessed diverse types of flows. Immigration inflows never ceased since the late 1970s, although some of the movements are not related to the labour market (political refugees, family flows, students). The linkage between migrant labour and certain economic sectors is quite obvious – for instance in civil construction and domestic cleaning. Aside from that, immigration has also been closely connected with the growth of informal mechanisms of labour organisation, mainly in those two sectors (Baganha 1998, 2000, 2001).

The difference between Africans and Eastern Europeans is not very marked at this level, since both are part and parcel of similar labour market segments. At the most, it could be posited that although the latter, can often produce academic and professional credentials they are not always recognised in Portugal. This devaluation of credentials also occurs in the case of African migrants, although perhaps to a lesser extent, even if it is not widely known. Brazilians constitute a partial exception to this pattern, given their positions in other service industries and the acceptance of their greater academic and professional skills. However, there have been some problems with recognising Brazilians diplomas too, for instance in the case of dentists.

From the emigration standpoint the labour market in Portugal has also been active. The emigration of Portuguese citizens is not yet over, although the reasons for it and the strategies for departure have changed (see Baganha and Peixoto 1997). The last outflow of considerable size occurred during the 1990s, when migrants left to seek employment in the civil-construction sector of the reunified Germany. A considerable volume of this flow was organised by Portuguese firms, which transported their own workers to the jobs for which the company was responsible (a situation favoured by EU directives on posted workers). This led to cost reductions, since social-security dues and taxation were paid in the country of origin (see Baganha 2000; Hunger 2000). In the majority of instances, outflows were strictly temporary, but that they could take place at all shows that the rationale for emigration still exists. It is significant that the sector that attracted most of these Portuguese emigrants is the same that absorbs foreign workers in Portugal – civil construction. The fact that in Portugal it is poorly regulated has made it less attractive for nationals and more appealing for foreigners. This simultaneity of emigration and immigration sectors has give rise to discussions about the possibility of substitution or complementariness of foreign and national workers.

If we put the theories presented above together with the descriptions of labour immigration into Portugal, certain assertions can be made about the main explanations for these flows. The synthesis shows that the theoretical potential of each factor by itself is not high. It is rather from a whole complex of factors, economic as well as non-economic, that mobility derives its characteristics.

Firstly, migration can be accounted for by strictly economic factors. It is economic reasoning by individuals in the sending-countries that makes them search for more rewarding job opportunities abroad. This has always been so, but the context in which the decisions are made is new compared to a few decades ago. The greater inter-linking of the world's economies in the process of globalisation has brought more countries into the international economic circuits including an enlarged international labour market. Although the migratory connections between Portugal and its former colonies is a sign of both past and present, the influx from Eastern Europe is clearly a present-day symptom. Information on job opportunities in Portugal, available to social agents in Portuguese-speaking countries as well as in Eastern Europe, coupled with the fact that Portuguese employers require workers willing to accept precarious working conditions, has favourably contributed to the process of immigratory flows.

Political and institutional factors are also crucial for explaining flows. Here various factors played a role. First and foremost, Portugal's entry in 1986 into what is now the European Union, and its incorporation into the group of countries that first established European monetary union, has conferred upon it a new status in the international arena. On the one hand this was linked to the growth of foreign direct investment and the influx of structural funds from the EU, which between them have generated a process of economic growth and increased labour demand. The latter has been directly (in the case of civil construction and public works) or indirectly connected to labour inflows. On the other hand, EU membership has tied the country to political regulations regarding foreign labour. These are globally restrictive, with limited possibilities for positive discrimination towards traditional flows, and have created specific constraints. Here the Schengen Convention should be mentioned, which has made national frontiers more difficult to control. As noted already, many of the Eastern European immigrants to Portugal are assisted by Schengen space – they obtain a visa to a country neighbouring Portugal and then merely cross the border. Finally, as a result of EU membership the international image of Portugal has improved: its new status provides the country with a new symbolic value and international appeal.

They are yet other elements of institutional and political regulation that are relevant to our explanation of migrations. In the domain of internal regulations, the weak mechanisms designed to control Portugal's labour markets, including the difficulty of controlling the informal use of labour, creates a *de facto* situation that has proved to be in the migrants' interests. The specific type of regulations in particular sectors or professions may also make Portugal attractive: the fact that many jobs in civil construction do not demand credentials (contrary to the situation in some in other countries) facilitates migrant absorption (they are not subjected to the filter of having their credentials recognised). Finally, the fact that many immigrant groups admit that the Portuguese State's ability to enforce immigration policies is less effective than that of other 'central' countries bestows on Portugal yet more appeal (since it counterbalances the country's lower economic standard).

Informal social networks have long been actively channelled migrant labour. In the main, they emerged with the first inflow from Africa, namely from Cape Verde, in the late 1960s. Since then, all Portuguese-speaking African countries have benefited from the mobilisation of social capital – or, in other terms, the 'relatives, friends and neighbours' effect set in motion by these networks. Migratory chains built in this way have availed themselves of growing political tolerance towards family reunion and brought about a significant momentum of inflows. Communities other than African have consolidated migration with the help of networks – for instance Brazilians, both of lower or high qualifications, and Indians (Malheiros 1996). Informal networks typically develop their potential only after the beginning of the migratory cycle, which is why this type of network is only now emerging for Eastern migrants.

Informal networks of this kind were also active among international firms and organisations transporting their own personnel to Portugal, and internal labour markets of this type benefited from the highly skilled inflows. Empirical research data show that it was actual job relationships between particular individuals in transnational corporations that often caused the moves. More than any economic logic of staff distribution in certain technical functions, it was the need to fill certain positions, including top management and financial functions, with trusted personnel from headquarters that played a pivotal role in explaining flows (Peixoto 1999).

The role of formal social networks, and particularly trafficking networks must also be mentioned. Organised support of illegal migration has a long history, and has even targeted traditional flows and sending-countries. In the case of Eastern Europe it is very plainly evident. There seems to be no doubt that the large majority of Eastern European immigrants have, in one way or another, been helped by such networks to enter Portuguese territory. As mentioned before, it is this type of support that accounts for the following migratory features: the choice of an unknown, remote host country (as seen from the migrant's standpoint); the geographical area of departures (the Ukraine, Moldova and Romania are neighbouring countries, and out-migration from these seems to affect certain regions within them); and the enormous pace and volume acquired so quickly by these flows. Concerning the latter, hardly any non-organised migration could, in so short a time, have attained the quantitative dimension of the Eastern European one in Portugal.

It has been argued with regard to formal social networks that the consolidation and circulation of information processed through informal ones is usually slower, being based on individual experiences alone, which are not always well interlinked. Individual contacts and support of migratory streams too acquire greater speed if they are formally organised. Informal migrant networks are based on a slow mechanism of pioneer migration, the emergence of brokers, diffusion of migration and self-feeding movements (for the various stages of the migration process, see Faist 2000, pp. 145-71). It can be hypothesised that formal networks as a form of organised industry – though frequently an illegal one – speed up the process and render it more effective. These formal networks are also the best way to explain why there was suddenly a large inflow into a host country where no former social or symbolic contacts existed.

Certain technological factors have reinforced some of the constraints mentioned above. As for transportation technologies, the possibility of frequent air connections and the straightforward use of land transportation (via highways) tend to make locations more accessible that were once regarded as remote, and so give fluidity to migration. In the case of communication technologies, information tends to spread far more quickly between potential sending and host countries. A television report presented in the Ukraine about Portugal and its job opportunities, in which some relative advantages were highlighted may, compared to alternative destinations (friendly population, attractive climate, etc.), be the proximate origin of many flows linking these countries.[2] The increasing ease of information circulating through modern communication technologies may also partly explain the swift pace of the Eastern European inflow into Portugal.

Conclusion

The main conclusion from the points discussed above is that human mobility between national labour markets or, in another words, international labour migration, is only explainable through a complex set of economic, social and political variables. Firstly, it results from the effective dynamics of national labour markets. The worldwide imbalance of income and employment constitutes a powerful stimulus for flows. Although it must be admitted that the classical push-pull model is never in itself sufficient to explain migration flows, it seems to be a good general frame for them. From the individual's perspective, the notion that his/her human capital can be elsewhere for a better reward is in itself a potential a reason to move, although other factors must be added to explain it happening in

---

[2] I thank this information to Olga Ivashchenko, from the National Academy of Sciences of the Ukraine.

practice. From a structural perspective, the presence of a 'dual' labour market, which exerts a specific attraction for migrants, completes that line of explanation.

On the other hand, we must emphasise the key role of the internal labour markets of large companies and organisations. Although this argument is mainly targeted to highly-skilled migrants like those employed by transnational corporations, the formation of organisational paths (and a homogeneous organisational space) across international frontiers creates a new logic for migration. The notion that the same organisation exists in different countries brings familiarity to what was once regarded an abrupt change. The possibility of international careers reinforces the possibility of moving when promotion within the organisation becomes linked to a geographical move.

Secondly, migration is significantly constrained by State action and the institutional regulation of labour markets. It is certainly true that a large part of migratory flows tends to ignore political barriers and gives in to the appeals of precarious segments of the labour market, thus swelling the ranks of illegal migration and informal labour. It is also true that, in a somewhat pragmatic manner, national States ultimately reward these initiatives through processes of regularisation. In this sense, we may contrast the strength of labour markets with the weakness of States in the current panorama of international migrations (Peixoto 2002b). But the fact that migrants are excluded, at least temporarily, from entitlement to citizenship and confined to non-regulated segments of the labour market (which operate by disregarding legal status or skill qualifications) demonstrates the importance of the political factor in the migrants' mode of entry and subsequent integration.

Third, it should be stressed that labour-market forces are closely articulated with social relationships. In the migration field, this articulation may be found in two contrasting forms. On the one hand, the role of informal social networks has long been emphasised as an explanation of migration flows. Such networks are useful for analysing how personal contacts transmit information and give support to migrants and social groups in both the sending and receiving areas. As they rely on social capital and become a form of such capital, networks are highly relevant in accounting for some of the contours of migration. Networks allow us to understand the strategic use of political mechanisms favourable to migrants (such as the right to family reunion); they establish the basis for a continuous migration flow developing beyond State control; they help us to comprehend the momentum of such movements even when the economic rationale for migration ceases to exist; and they provide an explanation for the linkage of specific geographic origin and destination areas. Although most of the references to informal social networks mention external labour markets, a specialised form can be said to occur in organisations (internal labour markets). Here, networks are used to lubricate some organisational channels, mainly those involving the movement of highly-skilled personnel, by means of personal relationships of trust or personal acquaintance.

On the other hand, formal social networks, particularly trafficking networks, are becoming closely involved today with the migratory phenomenon. The case of migrant trafficking is increasingly referred to in the literature, and explains some of the effectiveness of labour circulation, official barriers notwithstanding. These formal networks also seem to subvert and escape the traditional paths of migration, by linking formerly unknown receiving and sending-countries and speeding up the whole migration process.

In summary, the explanation of international labour migrations is subject to a set of factors that, to a large extent, transcend individual scientific disciplines. Empirical observation of foreign immigration into Portugal demonstrates that the variables that must be considered to explain flows in their multiple dimensions are simultaneously economic, political and social. It is their conjunction and interrelationship that accounts for the origin of flows, the phases and rhythms of evolution, and how immigrants are inserted into the labour market (sectors, occupations, level of informality).

The contribution of economic sociology to an understanding of the mobility of social agents between labour markets must be acknowledged as decisive. The explanatory role of the economic functioning of markets over human behaviour is very strong, but at the same time political, institutional and social mechanisms trigger off and constrain movements. In other words, and to use the terms of Granovetter (1973), labour markets not only function on the basis of the individual rationality of agents, but are also driven by powerful (not always weak) social ties.

References

Baganha, M. I. (1998), 'Immigrant Involvement in the Informal Economy: The Portuguese case', *Journal of Ethnic and Migration Studies*, 24 (2), pp. 367-85.

Baganha, M. I. (2000), 'Immigrants' Social Citizenship and Labour Market Dynamics in Portugal', in M. Bommes and A. Geddes (eds), *Immigration and Welfare: Challenging the Borders of the Welfare State*, London, Routledge.

Baganha, M. I. (2001), 'A Cada Sul o seu Norte: Dinâmicas migratórias em Portugal', in B. S. Santos (ed.), *Globalização: Fatalidade ou Utopia?*, Porto, Afrontamento, pp. 135-59.

Baganha, M. I. and Góis, P. (1998/1999), 'Migrações Internacionais de e para Portugal: O que sabemos e para onde vamos?', *Revista Crítica de Ciências Sociais*, 52/53, pp. 229-80.

Baganha, M. I. and Peixoto, J. (1997), 'Trends in the 90s: The Portuguese migratory experience', in M. I. Baganha (ed.), *Immigration in Southern Europe*, Oeiras, Celta Editora, pp. 15-40.

Baganha, M. I., Ferrão, J. and Malheiros, J. M. (1999), 'Os Imigrantes e o Mercado de Trabalho: O caso português', *Análise Social*, 34 (150), pp. 147-73.

Brettell, C. B. and Hollifield, J. F. (eds) (2000), *Migration Theory: Talking across disciplines*, New York, Routledge.

Cornelius, W. A., Martin, P. L. and Hollifield, J. F. (1994), *Controlling Immigration: A global perspective*, Stanford, Stanford University Press.

Doeringer, P. B. and Piore, M. (1971), *Internal Labour Markets and Manpower Analysis*, Lexington, Heath Lexington Books.

Faist, T. (2000), *The Volume and Dynamics of International Migration and Transnational Social Spaces*, Oxford, Oxford University Press.

Fonseca, M. L. (2000), 'The Geography of Recent Immigration to Portugal', in R. King, P. De Mas and J. M. Beck (eds), *Geography, Environment and Development in the Mediterranean*, Brighton, Sussex Academic Press, pp. 137-55.

Granovetter, M. (1973), 'The Strength of Weak Ties', *American Journal of Sociology*, 78 (6), pp. 1360-80.

Granovetter, M. (1974), *Getting a Job: A study of contacts and careers*, Cambridge, Harvard University Press.

Granovetter, M. (1992), 'The Sociological and Economic Approaches to Labor Market Analysis: A social structural view', in M. Granovetter and R. Swedberg (eds), *The Sociology of Economic Life*, Boulder, Westview Press, pp. 233-63.

Hunger, U. (2000), 'Temporary Transnational Labour Migration in an Integrating Europe and the Challenge to the German Welfare State', in M. Bommes and A. Geddes (ed.), *Immigration and Welfare: Challenging the borders of the welfare state*, London, Routledge.

King, R. (2002), 'Towards a New Map of European Migration', *International Journal of Population Geography*, 8 (2).

Kritz, M. M., Lim, L. L. and Zlotnik, H. (eds) (1992), *International Migration Systems. A Global Approach*, Oxford, Clarendon Press.

Machado, F. L. (1997), 'Contornos e Especificidades da Imigração em Portugal', *Sociologia – Problemas e Práticas*, 24, pp. 9-44.

Malheiros, J. M. (1996), *Imigrantes na Região de Lisboa: os Anos da Mudança: Imigração e Processo de Integração das Comunidades de Origem Indiana*, Lisbon, Edições Colibri.

Malheiros, J. M. and Baganha M. I. (2000), 'Imigração Ilegal em Portugal: Padrões emergentes em inícios do século XXI', in *Janus 2001 - Anuário de Relações Exteriores*, Lisbon, Público and Universidade Autónoma de Lisboa, pp. 190-91.

Marsden, D. (1992), 'European integration and the integration of European labour markets', *Labour – Review of Labour Economics and Industrial Relations*, 6 (1), pp. 3-35.

Massey, D. S. *et al.* (1993), 'Theories of international migration: a review and appraisal', *Population and Development Review*, 19 (3), pp. 431-66.

Peixoto, J. (1998), *As Migrações dos Quadros Altamente Qualificados em Portugal – Fluxos Migratórios Inter-Regionais e Internacionais e Mobilidade Intra-Organizacional*, Lisbon, Instituto Superior de Economia e Gestão (ISEG), Universidade Técnica de Lisboa.

Peixoto, J. (1999), *A Mobilidade Internacional dos Quadros – Migrações Internacionais, Quadros e Empresas Transnacionais em Portugal*, Oeiras, Celta Editora.

Peixoto, J. (2001), 'The International Mobility of Highly Skilled Workers in Transnational Corporations: The macro and micro factors of the organizational migration of cadres', *International Migration Review*, 35 (4), pp. 1030-53.

Peixoto, J. (2002a), *Os Fundamentos Sociais dos Mercados de Trabalho: O Caso da Imigração Estrangeira em Portugal*, Lição Síntese para Provas de Agregação, Lisbon, Instituto Superior de Economia e Gestão (ISEG), Universidade Técnica de Lisboa.

Peixoto, J. (2002b), 'Strong Market and Weak State: The case of foreign immigration in Portugal', *Journal of Ethnic and Migration Studies*, 28 (3), pp. 483-97.

Piore, M. J. (1979), *Birds of Passage. Migrant Labour and Industrial Societies*, Cambridge, Cambridge University Press.

Pires, R. P. (1993), 'Immigration in Portugal: A typology', in M. B. Rocha-Trindade (ed.), *Recent Migration Trends in Europe*, Lisbon, Universidade Aberta / Instituto de Estudos para o Desenvolvimento, pp. 179-94.

Pires, R. P. (1999), 'A Imigração', in F. Bethencourt and K. Chaudhuri (eds), *História da Expansão Portuguesa*, Vol. 5, Lisbon, Círculo de Leitores, pp. 197-211.

Pires, R. P. (2002), 'Mudanças na Imigração – Uma análise das estatísticas sobre a população estrangeira em Portugal, 1998-2001', *Sociologia, Problemas e Práticas*, 39, pp. 151-66.

Portella, C. (2000), 'Imigrantes da Europa de Leste', in *Janus 2001 - Anuário de Relações Exteriores*, Lisbon, Público and Universidade Autónoma de Lisboa, pp. 184-85.

Portes, A (1999), *Migrações Internacionais – Origens, Tipos e Modos de Incorporação*, Oeiras, Celta Editora.

Portes, A. (1981), 'Modes of Structural Incorporation and Present Theories of Labor Immigration', in M. M. Kritz *et al.* (eds), *Global Trends in Migration: Theory and research on international population movements*, New York, Center for Migration Studies, pp. 279-97.

Portes, A. (1995b), 'Economic Sociology and the Sociology of Immigration: A conceptual overview', in A. Portes (ed.), *The Economic Sociology of Immigration. Essays on networks, ethnicity and entrepreneurship*, New York, Russell Sage Foundation, pp. 1-41.

Portes, A. (ed.) (1995a), *The Economic Sociology of Immigration. Essays on networks, ethnicity and entrepreneurship*, New York, Russell Sage Foundation.

Portes, A. and Böröcz, J. (1989), 'Contemporary Immigration: Theoretical perspectives on its determinants and modes of incorporation', *International Migration Review*, 28 (3), pp. 606-30.

Portes, A. and Sensenbrenner, J. (1993), 'Embeddedness and Immigration: Notes on the social determinants of economic action', *American Journal of Sociology*, 98 (6), pp. 1320-50.

Powell, W. W. and Smith-Doerr, L. (1994), 'Networks and Economic Life', in N. J. Smelser and R. Swedberg (eds), *The Handbook of Economic Sociology*, Princeton, Princeton University Press, pp. 368-402.

Ravenstein, E. G. (1885), 'The Laws of Migration', *Journal of the Royal Statistical Society*, 48, Part II, pp. 167-227.

Ravenstein, E. G. (1889), 'The Laws of Migration', *Journal of the Royal Statistical Society*, 52, Part II, pp. 241-301.

Salt, J. (1987), 'Contemporary Trends in International Migration Study', *International Migration*, 25(3), pp. 241-51.

Salt, J. (2000a), *Current Trends in International Migration in Europe*, Strasbourg, Council of Europe, CDMG (2000) 31.

Salt, J. (2000b), 'Trafficking and Human Smuggling: A European perspective', *International Migration*, 38 (3), pp. 31-56.

Salt, J. and Findlay, A. M. (1989), 'International Migration of Highly-skilled Manpower: Theoretical and developmental issues', in R. T. Appleyard (ed.), *The Impact of International Migration on Developing Countries*, Paris, OECD, pp. 159-80.

Salt, J. and Stein, J. (1997), 'Migration as a Business: The case of trafficking', *International Migration*, 35 (4), pp. 467-94.

Sassen, S. (1998), 'The *de facto* Transnationalizing of Immigration Policy', in S. Sassen, *Globalization and Its Discontents*, New York, The New Press, pp. 5-30.

Sjaastad, L. A. (1962), 'The Costs and Returns of Human Migration', *The Journal of Political Economy*, 70 (5), Part 2 (Supplement), pp. 80-93.

Stalker, P. (2000), *Workers Without Frontiers: The impact of globalization on international migration*, Boulder, Lynne Rienner Publishers and Geneva, ILO.

Tilly, C. and Tilly, C. (1994), 'Capitalist Work and Labor Markets', in N. J. Smelser and R. Swedberg (eds), *The Handbook of Economic Sociology*, Princeton, Princeton University Press, pp. 283-312.

Zolberg, A. R. (1981), 'International Migrations in Political Perspective', in M. M. Kritz *et al.* (eds), *Global Trends in Migration: Theory and Research on International Population Movements*, New York, Center for Migration Studies, pp. 3-27.

Chapter 6

Social Networks, Collective Action and Public Policy: The Embeddedness Idea Reconsidered

Filippo Barbera

Introduction

The theory of social capital is frequently criticised for its negative aspects given that social networks do not always support economic development and democracy (Portes 1998). The literature of collective action shows how game theory can help to explain such unwanted effects, because 'in a social dilemma, actors may sometimes find it attractive to utilise social relations for personal ends that are unrelated to or even in conflict with collective goals' (Flache 1996, p. 3). Another, less explored weak point in the theory of social capital concerns the relationship between social capital and public policies (cf. Montgomery et al. 2001). For instance, research in industrial districts has shown how social capital can be a crucial resource for local development,[1] as well as that the collective-action approach does not necessarily benefit everybody. There is no systematic exploration, however, of the role of public policies in social-capital creation,[2] although the subject is of major importance today. The crisis of the industrial districts (Cossentino et al. 1996) and the new role of the state in economic growth, require finding out the mechanisms with which public policies can increase local social capital. The most interesting point here is one that has hardly been considered, namely the deliberate promotion of social capital through social

---

[1] Bagnasco's work relates how the Middle and North-East Italian regions have followed development paths different from both the North-West 'fordist' and the South state-assisted development (Bagnasco 1977). Small and medium-size enterprises, widespread entrepreneurship and good economic performance are closely linked to characteristics such as trust, reciprocity relations, and shared local identity. In the words of Bagnasco and Trigilia, the institutional preconditions in these regions have allowed for communitarian rather than individualistic market behaviour (Bagnasco and Trigilia 1984, 1985; Trigilia 1986 and 1997).

[2] Usually, research into collective action and social dilemmas focuses on the fact that social capital 'is rarely taken into account in policy analyses' (Ostrom 1994, p. 548). Nonetheless, it is useful for examining the problem discussed here.

engineering by the state. So, 'if social capital is a self-organising system with many actors connected in an amorphous web or network, it cannot be controlled with the tool kit of rational utilitarian instrumental planning' (Wilson 1997, p. 748). I disagree, and would argue that the new local-development policies are a possible link between self-organising systems and state regulation.

From a theoretical viewpoint, these are (i) an important example of the growing 'contractualisation' of public projects (Bobbio 2000), and (ii) they represent an example of policy-based production of trust and social capital (Trigilia 1997). In a nutshell, this points to the genesis of social capital through a particular kind of formal contracts and financial incentives. As a theoretical consequence of it, the embeddedness perspective is turned upside down (Granovetter 1985). It is not always social networks that explain economic transactions, but rather that formal contracts and economic exchange can be a possible source of social relations. The customary perspective on the embeddedness of economic action has shown much explanatory power, being at the heart of the lively 'new economic sociology' (Swedberg 1997). For all that, exclusive attention to only one direction of the causal chain (embeddedness as a independent variable, and economic action as a dependent variable) may obscure the picture if the previous level of social networks has been low. The same is true for the policy relevance of the 'new economic sociology'. The social embeddedness level, as Williamson calls it, is described as a rather sluggish institutional level, where medium and short-term policy intervention are difficult to perform.

> Institutions at this level change very slowly – on the order of century or millennia (…).
> An identification and explication of the *mechanisms* through which informal institutions arise and are maintained would especially help to understand the slow change in Level 1 institutions (Williamson 2000, p. 597).

I do not think that this is due to the embeddedness thesis as such. Instead, the denial of the political construction of social networks or of quick change in the institutional environment is mainly due to *conflating* the embeddedness perspective with that of social capital, as happened during the 1990s. In this essay, I shall extensively use the former, and specify the latter as contrasting a 'causal' perspective with an 'intentional' one (Bagnasco 1999).

Territorial Pacts and Local Development

The new local development policies seem to possess the crucial features for testing the thesis outlined. Among these policies, the so-called Italian Territorial Pacts (TPs) are perhaps the most innovative and promising. Their core features are the promotion of local-level concertation, along with supporting local development. The local-level concertation is built on a shared idea of economic development, and the financial aspect of the TP involves a number of entrepreneurial projects and public infrastructures financed by the central government. The TPs are carried out by:

- public actors at local level,
- local corporations,
- local entrepreneurs associations and unions,
- private actors.

Financial resources are allocated to depressed areas eligible for the EU structural funds, i.e.:

- the underdeveloped areas of South Italy (objective 1 of the structural EU funds),
- the areas affected by industrial decline in the Middle-North (objective 2 of the EU funds).
- A TP can use specific government resources to the amount of about € 500 million maximum, and investments in public infrastructures may not exceed 30 per cent of the total. The law specifies that public infrastructure must be strictly functional to the entrepreneurial initiatives. Formally, the activation of TPs and of government resources must be based on two qualifications:
- the making of an effective partnership network, in the form of local-level concertation certified through a specific agreement protocol;
- consistency of the private entrepreneurial and public infrastructure projects with the general aim of the TP, as decided through the local-level concertation process.

In synthesis, from a formal viewpoint, we can define TPs as *contractual exchanges* between local areas and the central government. Local actors agree to use and develop the concertation method and principles to select those entrepreneurial projects and public infrastructures that are coherent with the local-development design. The central government supplies financial resources for such projects.

To understand the effects of the TPs on the local social capital, it is necessary to focus on their incentives structure, which acts on the context conditions supposedly useful for local development. Two points are important here: social context matters (i.e. economic results depend on contextual factors), and social context can be positively affected by public polices. This means that it is not only the long history that counts, the cultural inheritance, the civic traditions inherited by the far past. What is also important is the short history, 'the role of the political factors, and the most recent causalities' (Cersosimo 2000b, p. 173, my translation). Therefore, as mentioned already, formal contracts and economic transactions are possible sources of social relations (Franzini 1999, p. 18).

After briefly outlining the distinctive incentives structure set up by the TPs, I shall illustrate certain results of TPs, along with their possible perverse effects and note the factors that can explain their success or failure. The conclusions will summarise four empirical cases to support the hypotheses. I shall adhere to the analytical schema proposed by Goldthorpe (2000, p. 151), which consists of:

- establishing the phenomena that form the *explananda* – i.e. identifying a macro-regularity that requires and allows explanation;
- hypothesising the generative process at the level of social action that would be able to produce this macro-regularity;
- testing the hypotheses.

The Italian Territorial Pacts: Establishing the Phenomenon

Territorial Pact funding applies to almost the *entire territory of Italy, with two* macro-regularities (Cersosimo 2000a; Cersosimo and Wolleb 2000; Iter 2000): Integrative pacts and Distributive pacts.

---

1) The TP speeds up formation of an already developing local system
2) Information about the initiative has been diffused
3) The concertation process strengthened the social partners' relationships
4) The agreement is solid and stable
5) All important local actors are represented in the group of supporters

weak consensus

–
_____+

                                                   strong consensus

1) The information was partial
2) The concertation did not improve local actors' relationships
3) The agreement is weak and unsettled
4) The group of supporters lacks important local actors

Source: Iter 2000

Figure 6.1 First factor

A quantitative examination on the first 46 TPs on Italian territory shows three macro-variables, which have been determined by means of a multiple correspondences analysis of 20 indicators of perception. The first macro-variable refers to local-level concertation. It covers all situations – from those where the concertation process has strengthened the trust existing among social partners and activated solid and stable relationships of agreement between them, to cases where 'the concertation process had no effects on the actors' relationships, and the agreement appears weak and unsettled' (Iter 2000, p. 46, my translation).

The first factor (see Figure 6.1) brings together the characteristics and the results of the territorial concertation process. Other extensive national research on the Pacts presents the same picture (Cersosimo and Wolleb 2001).

A further question concerns the *territorial distribution* of these two macro-regularities: are the Integrative pacts diffused only in those areas that already showed important territorial micro-concertation capacities (Regini 2000) – in those areas where the local actors were already able to produce goods by means of local collective competition?[3] And are the Distributive pacts a prevailing characteristic of South Italy? Empirical evidence is not clear on this point: some qualitative studies (Mirabelli 2000) on the Pacts in Calabria (South Italy) provide a picture very close to the Distributive case, while some systematic researches show that the South has also examples of Integrative pacts (Cersosimo and Wolleb 2001; Sviluppo Italia-Iter 2000). Finally, this territorial distribution applies to a sub-regional area, and in the last few years several cases of a solid micro-institutional context were found in South Italy (Cersosimo 2000b; Viesti 2000).

But the central question of this work does not lie with the territorial distribution of the two macro-regularities, but concerns the explanation of the mechanisms underlying the two macro-regularities. After briefly having established a macro-distinction between two modalities, what follows will examine the mechanisms that may explain these different regularities at the macro-level.

Hypothesising the Mechanism: Institutional Incentives, Social Resources, and Local-level Concertation in the New Development Policies

The Territorial Pacts set up an innovative incentives structure quite different from the incentives that characterised the extraordinary public intervention in South Italy. These were essentially individual incentives for capital and work, whose chief limitation was to have increased only income and consumption levels without positively affecting the institutional context (Trigilia 1999; Cersosimo 2000). By

---

[3] Le Galès and Voelzkow differentiate between two kinds of these goods: intangible and tangible. The first refers to the normative and cognitive resources (tacit knowledge, specialized languages, conventions and trust) in the local context, while the second includes infrastructures and services. Production of tangible goods by small-to-medium size enterprises can be difficult, especially if the units are isolated. Therefore, institutional devices which make possible local collective competition are crucial (Crouch *et al.* 2001).

contrast, Territorial Pacts are explicitly planned to influence the institutional context and to exogenously promote endogenous development (Crouch *et al.* 2001). One of their main ambitions is to promote cooperation, to increase social capital and trust, in order to facilitate the resolution of collective action dilemmas in the local economies. In this respect I suggest that the incentives structure of TPs can be represented through an assurance game (AG) or 'stag-hunt' game. It can be useful to compare the pay-off matrix of the AG with the well-known game of prisoner's dilemma (PD) (see Figure 6.2):

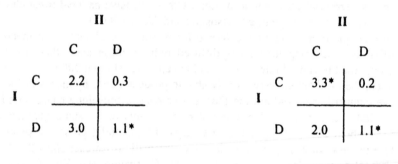

a. Prisoner's Dilemma (PD)   b. Assurance Game (AG)

* = Nash equilibrium

Figure 6.2   Two dilemmas of strategic interaction: Pay-off matrix for two players

DP. The best possible outcome is defecting while Alter co-operates (DC). The next best possible outcome is mutual co-operation (CC) followed by mutual defection (DD); the worst outcome is when Ego cooperates while Alter defects (CD). Thus, in prisoner's dilemma, DC>CC>DD>CD. The equilibrium is the DD combination (Nash equilibrium).
AG. The mutual co-operation leads to a better situation of unilateral defection (CC>DC>DD>CD). A strictly dominating strategy does not exist, the game has two equilibrium points: CC (mutual co-operation), and DD (mutual defection).

At least two points characterise the AG: (i) Ego's expectations about Alter's strategy matters (Macy 1997), and (ii) there are exclusion mechanisms for free riders (Taylor 1987). The first element refers to the fact that the goods-production function is a 'step-level production function'. In other words: a critical mass is necessary to produce the goods. TP law is not very clear on this point, but it does consider *at least* local councils, entrepreneurial associations and unions, as prerequisites for funding the local actors' mobilisation. There is no financing without a local council, nor without the agreement of the most representative unions or entrepreneurial associations. Other authors (Taylor *op. cit.*) argued that the two games produce two different kinds of goods: club goods and public goods. In the former case, some institutional barriers exist against free riding; in the latter, consuming the goods is possible even without having taken part in their production supply (Olson 1965). This is a somewhat ambiguous aspect of the TPs. On the one hand, it is true that there are exclusion mechanisms for those who do not participate (e.g. enterprises located in a town that did not sign the TP agreement protocol are not admitted to the funding). On the other hand, it is also true that participation can have very low costs (perhaps only the signature of the agreement protocol and may never require active participation in the concertation). Moreover, TPs lack real *ex-ante* selection mechanisms among the territories admitted to the funding, as well as serious *ex-post* sanctioning mechanisms. From a public-policy viewpoint, this means that incentives to co-operation can also stimulate collusive or distributive behaviour.

In analytical terms we could say that the concrete results of the Pact depend on the interaction of two strategic problems: a game-theoretical strategic interaction between the local actors (horizontal opportunism), and a principal-agent strategic relationship between the central government and the local areas (vertical opportunism). Vertical opportunism is assumed to have the same effect in all the national territory. But (Figure 6.1) the local areas performed the TP very differently: from Distributive pacts to Integrative pacts. The reason for this difference must, I would argue, be found in the different solutions given by the local areas to horizontal opportunism. In other words, the concrete application of TPs can enable co-operation coherently with the aims of the policy. But (also without 'reciprocal assurance mechanisms') the local actors may find it convenient to participate solely to distribute financial resources. In that case the TP does not modify any institutional elements.

Integrative TPs, where local actors have found an effective solution to horizontal opportunism, pose a further question – namely whether and when the experience of rational co-operation can support the learning of reciprocity rules and the creation of stable relational structures, whether and when the exogenously promoted co-operation is able to implement a co-operation not strictly depending on the incentives structure. Here the problem of the Pact as a social institution is important (Vino 1998). In theoretical terms, it means that if local actors are to learn to trust one another depends on whether a public-policy schema has increased the benefits of reciprocal co-operation. Then, the experience of co-operation has somehow implemented co-operation rules not strictly dependent on the incentives structure. If this really happens, we can agree with the suggestion that co-operation does not necessarily need previous trust. On the other hand, trust can be the result of a monitored co-operation among rational actors (Sabel 1994; Pichierri 1999, p. 32).

Public Incentives and Inherited Social Capital

I have argued that the distributive or integrative features of TPs depend on the interaction between the outlined incentives structure with the actors' expectations about reciprocal co-operation (which prevents horizontal opportunism). But on which elements do the actors' expectations depend? There are two most plausible and interesting rival hypotheses. The first regards inherited social-capital endowments; the second refers to social-capital creation in the policy process itself. To support the importance of inherited social-capital endowments requires some specification. R. Putnam (1993) has strongly emphasised this aspect, provoking critical remarks too well known to repeat here (*cf.* Goldberg 1996; Tarrow 1996). At the same time one should not over-react and pretend that public policies intervene in an 'empty situation' – nearly pre-institutional – where the past is of no account at all. The proper role of inherited social capital is to pass from a causal perspective to an intentional one (Bagnasco 1999),[4] that is, to shift analytical attention from the effects behind the social structure to the consequence of this structure for the reciprocally oriented social action.

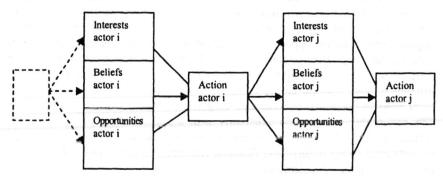

From: Hedström and Swedberg 1998, p. 73 in H. P. Blossfeld and G. Prein (eds).

Figure 6.3 Social capital as macro-to-micro mechanism

It goes beyond the confines of this work to examine in detail the endless and well-known debate about social capital and trust. For the present purposes, social capital will be specified as a pattern of relations tendentially horizontal, which facilitate the attainment of co-operative interactions. Trust, for its part, is to be understood as a behavioural disposition, which reduces the risk of opportunistic behaviour (for an excellent discussion of this, see Torsvik 2000). In these terms, the relationship between social capital and trust is very close (both are capable of promoting co-operation), and this explains the often-indistinct use of the two concepts. Therefore, social capital is a property of social structure and can make action easier within that structure (Coleman 1990; Lin 2001, p. 23), while trust regards the *action schema* of a specific actor. More precisely, from an intentional perspective, social capital affects the action schema impinging on three distinct elements (for a very informative discussion, see Abell 2001; Mansky 2000). These are expectations, constraints, and preferences. In the first case, social capital carries information; in the second social sanctions; and in the third influence. Information

---

[4] For a clear distinction between these two perspectives, see Elster (1983).

changes the probability distribution and the expectations; social sanctions increase the costs, and the existent opportunities lead to a certain course of action; influence directly changes the preferences. Social structure affects the action schema through *other* actions, or, as some economists put it: 'Agents interact through their chosen actions. An action chosen by one agent may affect the actions of other agents through three channels: constraints, expectations, and preferences' (Manski 2000). An intentional interactionist view of social capital would be as given in Figure 6.3 below:

Two of these cases have been very effectively illustrated by Torvsik (2000). In the first case, social capital influences the actor's behaviour through activating sanctioning mechanisms, and excluding Alter from future transactions. In this way, co-operative behaviour becomes a rational strategy. In the second case, social capital acts through group-identity creation and establishes solidarity and pro-social motivations. Here co-operation does not depend on costs-benefit calculations, but relies on non-consequentialist mechanisms of group identification (Pizzorno 2000). Here striving and attaining are intimately fused (Hirschman 1982). It has been argued convincingly (Torsvik 2000) that both modalities are important for an explanation of the development processes and for related policy suggestions. But in the AG set up by the Pacts it is not sanctions that are requested nor altruists actors, since co-operation can be convenient. Knowing or expecting that the other is willing to co-operate in such a game is enough to induce an egoistic and rational actor to co-operate. In this case, information carried by social networks about the probability of Alter's co-operative behaviour is sufficient to induce Ego's reciprocal co-operation (Gulati 1999, 623). We may imagine two cases: in the first, we have a local system rich in inherited social capital, with horizontal relations and reciprocal co-operation ventures. Here local actors have positive expectations about others' intention to co-operate. In this case we are likely to find an integrative TP. In the second case we have a territory with scarce social-capital endowments, expectations toward co-operative behaviour are at a low level, and the TP assumes a distributive form. A corollary of the outlined hypotheses is that TPs produce governance *only* where the local society is *already* rich in inherited social capital. If this were true, the new policies for the local development would have perverse effects tending to increase the inequalities between the territories – a point I shall investigate in the section below.

But, as I have argued before, in an 'intentional' perspective the effect of the social capital has to be linked to the reciprocally oriented social action. In this respect, it is crucial to explore the interactional and structural dynamics established in the new experimental context set up by the TP (Wolleb and Cersosimo 2000). Among the dynamics activated by the local-level concertation, in other words, it is possible to identify some factors that affect the trust level positively, even where the inherited social capital is at a low level. But before coming to this, let me outline the possible perverse effects of TP policy.

Public Policies and Local Development

Let me now introduce two variations of the game. In the first, the local coalition faces other problems, different from the Pact but with the same incentives structure (Assurance Game). This is the case of the various European projects for retraining or funding of activities to alleviate social problems or to counter industrial decline. Now let us again cases of AG where the already described conditional co-operation is crucial. Let's now consider the second variation of the game and assume that the local actors are facing a prisoner's dilemma. The financial resources obtained through several local-developments policies can create public goods and reproduce a pure free-riding strategy. For instance: (i) the production of a 'positive industrial atmosphere' has consequences for *all* of the area; (ii) the territorial area can become eligible for regional or European projects, whose consequences concern *all* the local actors; (iii) the decrease industrial-relations conflicts, has positive effects also for economic and social actors who did not participate in the territorial coalition, or did so only formally. But non-excludable goods are produced also for economic actors: the increased occupation in the territory makes easier the creation of generic human capital (a non-excludable good) easier;[5] and the positive reputation of the territory in the foreign markets involves *all* of the economic actors and not only those participate in the TP.

For this kind of mechanisms we may assume that the AG set by the TP will turn into a prisoner's dilemma, but the information carried by the social networks is no longer sufficient to solve it. Other mechanisms are necessary. Two that were illustrated earlier are of importance here: social sanctions which increase the cost of opportunism, or a change in the actors' preferences. In other words, those territorial areas that have strengthened the prior social-capital resources would be better able to face the new collective-action dilemmas. As pointed out already, the Integrative pacts made possible a reinforcement of the prior social resources. But if they exclusively involve those territories already supplied with social resources, and the Distributive pacts characterise only the territories with a low level of prior resources, then the new local-development policies could increase inequality between territorial areas.

This point can be illustrated by linking social-network characteristics to the possible emergence of *social* norms-social/sanctions. The territories that played an Integrative pact – which in the hypothesis as now developed correspond to the territories already supplied with inherited social capital – have also improved the context conditions.[6] The territories that played a Distributive pact – for this argument identified with the cases in which the prior social resources were at a low level – did not augment the degree of closure of their social networks. What effects has social-network closure on the formation of social norms?

---

[5] On this point, see Streeck (1988).

[6] For this example, we identify this improvement with the degree of closure of social networks among local actors.

In the (a) figure (Figure 6.4,), the A1-action has negative externalities on A2 and A3 which. however, are not in contact with each other but only with A4 and A5. In the (b) figure, the action of A1 has the same effect as in (a), but A2 and A3 are linked. In the first case any sanction toward A1 must be applied *independently* from A2 and A3: it must be a 'heroic' sanction. In the second case the presence of social relation between A2 and A3 makes it possible 'to impose a sanction on A1 through some form of joint action that neither A2 nor A3 could impose alone' If, in the case depicted in figure (b), 'A2 has obligations toward A3, then A2 may pay off a portion of those obligations by sanctioning A1' (Coleman, 1990, 270). If social structures are segmented, they cannot be co-ordinated to mutually participate in the sanctioning process. This example shows how territories that improve their endowment of social resources are also better capable of solving new collective-action dilemmas. Conversely, territories that are poorly provided with such resources, and have not improved them in the policy process, are not ready yet to face these problems.

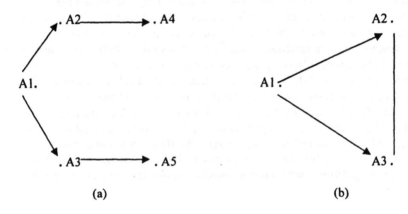

(a)   (b)

Source: Coleman (1990, 269).

Figure 6.4 Social relations, collective action and norms

Face-to-Face Interaction, Trust and Co-operation

Let us now turn our attention to those circumstances where it is possible to reduce uncertainty in reciprocal co-operation even if there is a shortage of inherited social capital. Here the analytical focus moves from the inherited social capital to the mobilisation process and to the interaction dynamics created by local-level concertation.

The first step towards this end comes about through institutional leadership, which helps the actors 'to reformulate their interest, moving from the short term to the middle-long term' (Parri 1997, pp. 122-24). The AG has a powerful solution mechanism in the institutional leader, who is able to figure out the mutual co-operation advantages (Taylor 1987). That being so, it is crucial to understand the processes and conditions for building consensual leadership. In the opposite case, of management by a leadership that is not consensual, the TP would be expected to fail, being unable to stimulate the necessary co-operation.

The subject of institutional leadership points to two further questions, one of them empirical and the other analytical. Concerning the first it is not completely clear why consensus in respect of the leader requires developing trust among the actors of the coalition. One hypothesis that will be examined is that both depend on the peculiar features of the decision-making process and on the power balances characterising the local coalition. The second, analytical point refers to the term 'social entrepreneur' as someone in a structural hole and, by joining up disconnected parts of the social structure, creates new aggregations (Granovetter, 2000).

The AG pay-off structure also points to the role of interactionist factors, easy to develop in face-to-face situations like local-level concertation, which constitute the quintessence of the 'interaction order' as studied by Goffman (1983). As the laboratory experiments on collective action have repeatedly shown, it can be argued that the co-operation level grows considerably if the players can communicate in 'interaction contexts' (Ledyard 1995). By means of communication, people build up a shared vision of the problem, search for the most effective solutions, and show their disappointment when collective action fails. The effects are not the same if communication is computer mediated and so it does not take place face-to-face (Ostrom 2000). Finally, face-to-face interaction gives a dynamic character to the theory of structural holes, widely applied to explain the strategic advantage of social entrepreneurs. The theory has a major weak point as regards the reproduction of structural holes. This is that the maintenance of a network configuration allows a *tertius gaudens* to manage and reproduce a strategic advantage:

> Burt's argument lends itself better to understanding power and compliance, based on control of uncertainty (...). Sustaining this control over time depends, however, on preventing structural holes from being closed up, an aspect that requires more sustained analysis (Granovetter 2000).

The local-level settings, therefore, can express novel coalitions between social actors who used to have conflictual relationships.

These considerations – at least from a theoretical viewpoint – make clear the hypothesis that local actors can develop fiduciary expectations even *without* inherited social capital. There are however several mechanisms for this, however, which must be empirically investigated.

Research Design: Testing the Hypothesis

The third phase of the explanatory model previously illustrated consists of empirically testing the micro-mechanism expected to produce the macro-regularity of Distributive pacts vs. Integrative pacts. Moreover, the inquiry is explicitly directed toward two rival hypotheses – namely, inherited social capital vs. created social capital. The relevant variables for the empirical research are:

(1) the level of social capital in the TP area before the TP,
(2) characteristics of the mobilisation process and of territorial concertation dynamics,
(3) composition and activity of local-level concertation institutes, created during and after the TP.

The following indicators are used to specify the first dimension at time T0, *before* the local-level concertation process (T1):

- formal partnership institutions in the area and their composition,
- formal and informal co-operation events among the local actors.

Concerning point (2), the mobilisation can be more or less diffused in the local area, it can require only a short time and involve few actors, or take longer and involve a large number of local actors. Others aspects to be considered will be how to plan the agenda, actors' evaluation of the concertation process, conflicts and their different resolutions. Point (3) looks at the effects, if any, of the TP on the local coalition and the local actors. Have they created new governing structures? Has the concertation coalition survived its contingent function? Why?

In my research I interviewed 30 key informants among the local actors, namely mayors, local politicians, trade unionist and representatives of local firms. I also collected various kinds of documents (e.g. agreement protocols, research reports), useful for reconstructing the local socio-economic context. This research was concentrated on TPs in the Turin area,[7] and analyses four cases, which seem to cover the two macro-regularities previously discussed.[8] These are more precisely the Canavese Pact and the Pact of Turin's West Zone, described as Integrative pacts; Turin's South-West Pact (the Sangone) labelled a Distributive pact; and the Pinerolese pact which shows features of both.

---

[7] Turin is Piedmont's main city; it is situated in North-West Italy.
[8] This has been called 'retrospective research design' (see: King, Kehoane and Verba 1994, p. 141).

Empirical Findings

The crux of this work is contained in answers to the two questions: 'Can public incentives increase social capital?', and 'How important are inherited context conditions vis-à-vis face-to-face interaction dynamics in local-level concertation'? Put succinctly: in the cases examined the interactionist factors exercise the most influential role; less crucial, but not unimportant, seems to be the role of inherited social capital. Where this was very limited, the TP became integrative (e.g. in the West Zone). Where the TP was built upon pre-existing co-operative elements, mobilisation and local-level concertation dynamics were important explanatory factors for the final result (Canavese). An analytical emphasis on social capital does not lead to deterministic explanations, leaving the possibility that *trust is produced in the cooperative process itself.*

What follows is a discussion of the empirical results summarised in table 6.1 for the most crucial phases of the four TPs cited. I shall deal with an empirical result not foreseen by the analytical model, i.e. the consumption of social capital, in the conclusion.

Inherited Social Capital

In the Canavese TP, the prior presence of social capital was significant only in the Ivrea neighbourhood (the Canavese main town), due to the localisation there of the Olivetti factory and activities by of the Province of Turin; it did not involve the rest of the Canavese. Thanks to a joined initiative by the Olivetti factory, the Ivrea Council and the provincial administration of Turin, some important collective actors appeared well before the TP. Among them we find the consortium for the training of human resources, 'Carlo Ghiglieno' (now FO.R.UM), a technological consortium for the district, the Bio-Industry Park, and the Institute for Mechanical Technology and Automation Research (R.T.M). There was a local elite in the Ivrea and its environs which acted through partnership agreements, as is clear from prior cases of co-operative ventures that involved several protagonists of the forthcoming TP coalition. One of these events was the signing of a regional document for economic planning (DOCUP 1997-1999), in which industrial associations, unions and public administrations made joint proposals for the Canavese area. However, partnership agreements and cooperative ventures were concentrated around the town of Ivrea and more or less monopolised by just a few actors. It can therefore be said that the 'inheritance' of Olivetti contributed to the creation of a kind of local elite. At the same time the Canavese TP involves a much wider territory and the concertation coalition is made up of local actors that were never before or only marginally involved in the governance of the Canavese area.

In the West Zone of the metropolitan area of Turin, the inherited social capital also evinced opposite trends alongside initial co-operation attempts by local actors. The main difference from the Canavese is that instead of one naturally leading town here are four small towns, all equally strong. To begin with, public actors did co-operate on various occasions, but always in the face of strong competition for the leadership among the four main towns. In the interviews the early co-operative ventures are described as 'blocked' or 'never fully effective' and, furthermore, there were no active public-private partnerships. In fact, joint action was mainly limited to react to already existing crises, with very few strategic discussions or forward-looking projects of local development.

Table 6.1 Main features of TPs examined

	Canavese	West Zone	Pinerolese	Sangone
Inherited Social Capital	High level, but chiefly around the Canavese main town (Ivrea). Relevant presence of prior formal partnerships.	Mix of cooperation and conflict. No formal partnerships.	Very low, apart from a recent experience (Forum). No formal partnerships.	Very low. No formal partnerships.
Mobili-zation	Open and polycentric process.	Substantially open.	Substantially open.	Closed.
Concer-tation	Effective discussion, no conflicts and legitimated leadership.	Effective discussion, constructive conflict and legitimated leadership	Effective for the public actors of the coalition, but to a minor extent also for the private ones.	Quite ineffective, both for public and private actors. No legitimated leadership.
Effect on the Coalition	Coalition very active. Many meetings to discuss forward-looking projects.	Coalition very active. Many meetings to discuss forward-looking projects.	Coalition most active in the private than in public part.	Coalition not very active. Few meetings, and discussion mainly about today's issues.

Not only is there no natural leader in the Sangone TP but the towns in this area are much smaller than in the Canavese. As in the rest of the Turin metropolitan area (excepting the Canavese) the presence of prior social resources is very poor. No co-operative relationships existed among the local actors, or only such as were oriented towards managing industrial and employment crises. Again the prevailing common activities were reactive and not proactive, tailored for specific urgent situations.

The TP in the Pinerolese area, finally, was not characterised by formal local partnerships, and public-public as well as public-private relationships were very ordinary. The Pinerolese did not effectively discuss local development until the beginning of the 1990s. Also, the relationships and activities of the local collective actors were extemporaneous and again mainly directed toward the management of various economic emergencies. Moreover, the main town (Pinerolo) was largely unconcerned with the local development of the territory. Pinerolo used to be notable for its absence from a territory comprising the mountain communities of small villages, the town of Pinerolo itself, and the consortium of the towns close to the Turin area. The existence of so few autonomous actors was one of the elements that conduced to the territory's fragmentation until the middle of the 1990s. Thereafter the situation began to change: a new political class along with a new mayor was elected, and the mountain communities started to activate co-operative relations that involve the whole territory. The main result of this new process is the Forum for the Development of the Pinerolese. It includes the area's two parliamentarians, the Pinerolo mayor, the representatives of three mountain communities, a representative of the other councils, and a representative of the administration of Turin. Unions and business associations were very soon invited to join the Forum, whose activities are mostly political and programmatic, and the coalition is responsible for certain documents on the problems of local development.

All in all, only the Canavese areas showed a high level of social capital, while in the other three cases co-operative practices and horizontal social relationships were either negligible or absent altogether.

Mobilisation

Two modalities can be distinguished in the mobilisation process: closed and open mobilisation. In the first case one or a few local actors elaborate the Pact proposal, in the second case the ideation process is more polycentric. The four types can be placed along a continuum from the more open to the more closed. For instance, in the case of the Sangone, the idea was elaborated by the managers of the ASSOT public agency for local development, who saw the TP as the first chance to widely legitimate the new public agency, which had just been set up. Their decision to activate a TP was then communicated to the other local actors.

In the West Zone case, an integrative TP, the early phase of the mobilisation process again took place among the restricted group of local public administrators. This was necessary to solve certain internal conflicts that had characterised the area for some time. Once this was achieved, the next step was the choice of a consensual leadership, and thereafter the process was opened up to other actors who entered the local coalition and participated in the actually drawing up of the TP proposal.

An interesting characteristic of these two cases (The Sangore and the West Zone) is that they are both areas without a natural leader. An important difference is that in the Sangone we find small tows with an undersized administrative apparatus and where local politicians have no skilled staff to rely on. In the West Zone, by contrast, there are medium-size cities whose councils have a larger administrative apparatus and local politicians dispose of highly-skilled staff. It is in the second case, therefore, that it is more likely that local politicians or the mayor himself will care about a new policy, since they have both the resources and the time to do so. This means that the process inevitably assumes political characteristics, not only technical ones.

This is rather less of a problem if the area has a town, bigger than the others, that is a natural leader. Such is the case of the Canavese as well as the Pinerolese TPs. In both, in fact, the mayors and assessors directly managed the process. In the Canavese the mayor of the biggest town in the area, Ivrea, led the mobilisation. Besides, one of the main characteristics of the inherited social capital in this area was the very centrality of Ivrea, whose importance derives from being the seat of the once biggest Italian computer factory (Olivetti). However, the mobilisation process involved a wider area (western Canavese and Chivassese), previously excluded from strategic decision-making. In the Pinerolese TP, too, the mayor played a central role from the very start of the process. In both these cases the local councils took *direct political responsibility for the* process. Also, in the Pinerolese the mobilisation was opened up from the beginning to involve trade unions, entrepreneurial representatives and the other councils of the area. This created horizontal connections among previously separate areas of the territory. During this phase the role of social entrepreneur – one who connects disparate parts of the social structure – was crucial.

Local-Level Concertation

The concertation process forms the second phase of TP development. Here it is the institutional leader who is most important. It is he who draws up the cognitive maps of local actors, he who prefigures the size of the reward for reciprocal cooperation (Parri, p. 1997). The second most important factor is the development of 'a concertation process with costs' (Cersosimo and Wolleb 2001). The local actors, in other words, must be able to take a risk, because *taking a risk is an act of trust, which can stimulate further trust.* To accept such risks, the local actors must be able to *decide.* Some of the conditions that support polycentric decision-making, are (i) the presence of power-balanced relationships and interlocking ties, that limit the opportunism of a *tertius gaudens*; (ii) obliging the leader to legitimate himself to the local coalition and to use the concertation as a means of such legitimisation; (iii) a reasonably long period for developing the concertation process, allowing time to resolve possible conflicts. Related to this is the creation of *horizontal* trust among members of the coalition, and the role of *vertical* ties between them and the leader: 'Where such chains exist, reassurance about the leader's intentions flow along them, (...) in part because one has the possibility of exerting influence through the chain in ways that restrain self-seeking (...)' (Granovetter 2000, p.371).

Where such a chains exists, therefore, the actors feel able to take some risks in their decision-making. In the Canavese and in the West Zone all the actors sublimated their own particular interests to those of other local actors. In the Canavese, the operation was quite simple, given the inheritance of co-operative ventures. In the West Zone things were rather more complex. For example, the entrepreneurs' representatives and the trade unionists had literally never met before. During the concertation process, however, they were endowed with real decision autonomy, and this allowed them to risk their resources, thus showing trust and producing further trust. In the Pinerolese, the costs were partial. On the one hand, the Pinerolo mayor did not abuse his position of natural leader. On the other, the dialogue between unions and business associations was not so worthwhile and effective. In the Sangone, finally, decision-making was set up with bilateral meetings between the public agency and the other local actors, along with assembly meetings of a semi-public kind. In this kind of context nobody risked anything in the course of local-level concertation.

In the comparative evaluation of the territorial concertation process, one important element remains: namely, the various conflict-resolution procedures that emerged in the course of local-level concertation. In the cases examined, two distinct conflict-resolutions devices were noticed. First, through *vertical ties* that connected the local actors to a 'third' actor *outside* the territory; second, by means of *horizontal* ties connecting the conflict to a third actor *inside* the territory (Locke 1995). Let us consider this second case. In the Canavese TP there were no remarkable conflicts, while the Pinerolese and the West Zone did have some conflicts, as reported in the interviews; in both cases they were settled through the intervention of a third actor. In the Pinerolese a local committee mediated the conflict between the mayor and the unions. In the case of the West Zone, the conflict emerged at the beginning of the process and one important town left the coalition for more than six months; mediation by another town in the coalition was required to solve the matter. By contrast, the case of Sangone is an example of intervention by vertical ties. A strong conflict between the public agency and the unions was solved by means of a discussion at the provincial level of the unions. Symbolically, this took place outside the Pact territory. In all cases the process was unblocked, but the modalities employed were quite different. As has been asserted very effectively (Granovetter 2000), horizontal ties carry trust and co-operation, while vertical ones transmit power and compliance.

TP Effects on Local Coalitions

Let us now look at local coalition activities once the TP was funded. In the Canavese, the coalition assumed functions of *governing* the territory, and met twice a week to discuss common strategies to this end. All interviewees are agreed: the local-level concertation coalition meets frequently, and discusses subjects of local importance and plans co-ordinated action.

In the West Zone too the local-level concertation process has contributed to create a local governing coalition that discusses and plans strategies for the area's local development. The actors' judgements on the activity of the coalition are very positive, in terms of both the quantity and quality of the projects undertaken (which range from urban regeneration projects to training programmes and local welfare measures). Local actors, however, are always keeping open the possibility of exiting from the coalition. The leadership is continuously negotiated among the partners and its legitimacy must be confirmed for every single decision.

In the Sangone the concertation process was feebler and more conflictual. What consequences did this have for the sustained activity of the coalition? At zero level it could be argued that the conflictual dynamics had a positive effect by creating unexpected alliances. As stated by the former manager of the public agency, the Pact 'created some relationships which did not exist at all before'. This is actually an innovative element in the context, an element that recalls the well-known social function of conflict. The conflict involving a 'third' creates new interactions. But, as already noted, this happened without specific risk-taking and with conflict-resolution networks extended outside the local area in a vertical configuration. The actors' judgement about the effectiveness of the coalition is still quite negative, and confirms that the local-level concertation process did not create co-operative relationships. The issues discussed at the meetings concern mainly short-term topics, seldom strategic measures oriented towards the future. This indicates that the local coalition has not been able to go beyond the contingency of TP funding.

Finally, in the Pinerolese the activity of the coalition is not as positive as in the Canavese and the West Zone, nor as weak as in the Sangone. Unexpectedly, the private actors (unions, business associations) are more active than the public ones. This is surprising because the concertation process was quite positive in terms of the public components and pretty poor for the private ones. To understand this we must look at *social-capital consumption*.

Consumption of Social Capital, and Conclusion

The unexpected element – according to the theoretical model previously outlined – is that, even if the local-level concertation creates trust, it is the incentives structure that remains crucial for explaining the local coalition's subsequent activities. We have two instances of empirical evidences for this. In the Pinerolese TP, the local coalition shows a lack of cohesion in its most active component, that of the public actors. A possible explanation for this lies in the institutional circumstances: the territory shows a considerable number of alternative coalitions, and this decreases the exit cost from the TP coalition. Furthermore the TP coalition can weaken even if the exit cost is high, due to strategic bargaining to remain inside the coalition. As I have illustrated in the case of the West Zone, decision-making implies continuous bargaining between actors equally powerful. This has two important consequences. On the one hand it prevents a more powerful actor from assuming a privileged role in the decision-making process and gives everyone a chance to decide and risk the resources in the process. On the other hand it legitimates contractual negotiations to remain inside the coalition. In a nutshell: *social capital and trust created during the local-level concertation phase can be consumed.*

The problem of the consumption of social capital and trust would require more thorough investigation. However, at this stage two analytical consequences are already quite evident. With respect to the consumption of trust, it has been argued that trust actually becomes exhausted when not used (Hirschman 1984). Greater analytical detail is required to specify the particular ways of *using trust* that are, at the same time, also great destroyers of it. So an exclusively contractual use of trust relationships − like 'I trust you according to the incentives structure' − aside from being debatable theoretically (Granovetter 2000, p. 356), can also have deleterious practical consequences. The same argument has been put forward with regard to social-capital consumption. Economic results obtained through social networks are described as a secondary effect of relationships activated for expressive or affective purposes (Bagnasco 1999, p. 117; Steiner 1999). An instrumental use of social networks, therefore, would tend to destroy the real source of the economic advantage (Blau 1963).

From an empirical viewpoint, these considerations suggest the conclusion that the Pacts have to face a double challenge: the first is to make convenient reciprocal co-operation, preventing collusion and effortless distribution. For this aim a greater attention for *ex-ante* selection mechanisms and *ex-post* control devices remains crucial, as is argued by all the economics of incentives (Milgrom and Roberts 1992). The second challenge is to activate co-operative and stable relationships apart from any contingent advantage. Promoting co-operation that goes beyond the narrow incentives alignment and activating the 'Pact as institution' is the second challenge for these policies. To survive the contingency of incentives, the TP process must be able *to create a new collective actor* whose parts do *not come together only through the incentives structure.* Pichierri (2001) called this process the 'creation of organisational implementation structures', and the new economic sociology refers to it with the expression 'embedded ties' (Uzzi 1997). Podolny and Page described it as the network form of governance:

> We define a network form of organisation as any collection of actors (N≥2) that pursue repeated, enduring exchange relations with one another and, at the same time, lack a legitimate organisational authority to arbitrate and resolve disputes that may arise during the exchange (Podolny and Page 1998, p. 59).

In Pichierri's terms, a change in the strategy of local development entails a shift in the organisational structure of local development. From the viewpoint of the micro-foundations, the crucial element is to stimulate non-consequentialist motivations (Granovetter 2000), motivations that allow continued co-operation even if it is against the short-term interest.

Actually, it's not only that local actors must have a long-term perspective for co-operative activities. It is rather that they must be willing to suspend rational calculation and to act as if incentives existed and co-operation were always convenient. Where Industrial Districts have been successful, it has been as the result of such attitudes. Co-operative behaviour in these districts has been due to not only a correct incentives alignment. Co-operation has been an end in itself. It constitutes an actor's identity, and to defect means to deny this identity. In terms of the local actors in TPs, long-term co-operation becomes possible by actors *being politically aware of* the process. In other words Integrative pacts that last beyond the funding are those where local actors have assumed political functions of governance of their territory. Finally, from a theoretical viewpoint, the interplay between social networks and public incentives can be heuristically fruitful. I have argued that the embeddedness perspective is too limited only if interpreted in the narrow light of the theory of social capital, as has been done extensively in recent years. The embeddedness argument is much broader than that of social capital and, above all, can easily include a specific role for public action.

References

Abell, P. (2001), 'On the Prospect for a Unified Social Science: Economics and sociology', Paper presented at the 13th Annual Meeting of SASE, Amsterdam University of Amsterdam, June 28-July 1.

Bagnasco, A. (1977), *Tre Italie: la problematica territoriale dello sviluppo italiano*, Bologna, Il Mulino.

Bagnasco, A. (1999), *Tracce di comunità*, Bologna, Il Mulino.

Bagnasco, A. and Negri, N. (1994), *Classi, ceti, persone*, Napoli, Liguori.

Bagnasco, A. and Trigilia, C. (1984), *Società e politica nelle aree di piccola impresa. Il caso di Bassano*, Venezia, Arsenale Editrice.

Bagnasco, A. and Trigilia, C. (a cura di) (1985), *Società e politica nelle aree di piccola impresa. Il caso della Valdelsa*, Milano, Angeli.

Blau, P. (1963), *Exchange and Power in Social Life*, New York, Wiley.

Blossfeld, H. P. and Prein, G. (eds) (1998), *Rational Choice Theory and Large-Scale Data Analysis*, Boulder, Westview Press.

Bobbio, L. (2000), 'Produzione di politiche a mezzo di contratti nella pubblica amministrazione italiana', *Stato e mercato*, 1.

Burt, R. (1992), *Structural Holes*, Cambridge MA, Harvard University Press.

Cersosimo, D. (2000), 'I Patti territoriali', in Cersosimo D. e Donzelli, C. *Mezzo Giorno*, Roma, Donzelli.

Cersosimo, D. and Wolleb, G. (2000), 'Politiche pubbliche e contesti sociali. L'esperienza dei Patti territoriali', *Stato e mercato*.

Coleman, J.S. (1990), *Foundations of Social Theory*, Cambridge Mass., Harvard University Press.

Cossentino, F., Pike, F. and Sengerberger, W. (eds) (1996), *Local and Regional Response to Global Pressare: the case of Italy and its industrial districts*, Geneva, ILO Publications.

Crouch, C., Le Galès, P., Trigilia, C., Voeltskow, H. (eds) (2001), *Local Production Systems in Europe: Rise or Demise?*, Oxford University Press.

Degenne, A. and Forsé, M. (1994), *Les Rèseaux Sociaux*, Paris, Armand Colin.

Flache, A. (1996), *The Double Edge of Networks*, Amsterdam, Thesis Publishers.

Franzini, M. (1999), 'Cooperazione, scelte pubbliche e sviluppo locale', *Meridiana*, n. 34-35.

Goffman, E. (1983), 'The Interaction Order', *American Sociological Review*, 48.

Goldberg, E. (1996), 'Thinking about how democracy work', *Politics & Society*, 24.

Goldthorpe, J. (2000), *On Sociology*, Oxford University Press.

Granovetter, M. (2000), 'Un'agenda teorica per la sociologia economica', *Stato e mercato*, n. 60, dicembre.

Hedström, P. and Swedberg, R. (1998), 'Rational Choice, Empirical Research and the Sociological Tradition', in H. P. Blossfeld and G. Prein (eds), *Rational Choice Theory and Large-Scale Data Analysis*, Boulder, Westview Press.

Hirschman, A. (1982), *Shifting Involvements: Private Interest and Public Action*, Princeton, Princeton University Press.

ITER for Sviluppo Italia (2000), 'Caratteristiche e potenzialità dei Patti territoriali', Roma, mimeo.

King, G. Kehoane, L. and Verba, S. (1994), *Designing Social Inquiry*, Princeton, Princeton University Press.

Kollock, P. (1998), 'Social Dilemmas: the Anatomy of Co-operation', *Annual Review of Sociology*, 24.

Le Galès, P. (with Aniello V.) (2001), 'Between Large Firms and Marginal Local Economies. The Making of Systems of Local Governance to develop SME's in France?', in C. Crouch, P. Le Galès, C. Trigiliaand H. Voeltskow (eds), *Local Production Systems in Europe: Rise or demise?*, Oxford, Oxford University Press.

Ledyard, J. O. (1995), "Public Goods: A Survey of Experimental Research", in Nagel, J. H., Roth, A., *The Handbook of Experimental Economics*, Princeton, Princeton University Press.

Lin, N. (2001), *Social Capital*, Cambridge, Cambridge University Press.

Macy, M. (1997), 'Identity, Interest and Emergent Rationality', *Rationality and Society*, 9(4).

Manski, C. (2000), 'The Economic Analysis of Social Interactions', in *Journal of Economic Perspectives*, 3.

Milgrom, P. and Roberts, J. (1992), *Economics, Organization and Management*, Prentice Hall.

Mirabelli, C. (2000), 'Concertazione e sviluppo locale: l'esperienza dei Patti territoriali in Calabria', *Rassegna Italiana di Sociologia*, n.3.

Montgomery, J. D. and Inkeles, A. (2001), *Social Capital as a Policy Resource*, Kluwer Academic Publishers.

Olson, M. (1965), *The Logic of Collective Action: Public Goods and the Theory of Groups*, Cambridge, Cambridge University Press.

Ostrom, E. (1994), 'Constituting Social Capital and Collective Action', *Journal of Theoretical Politics*, 6(4).

Ostrom, E. (2000), 'Collective Action and the Evolution of Social Norms', *Journal of Economic Perspectives*, 3.

Parri, L. (1997), 'I giochi della cooperazione tra piccoli imprenditori: i consorzi di vendita come istituzioni', *Quaderni di sociologia*, XLI.

Pichierri, A. (1999), 'Organizzazioni rete, reti di organizzazioni: dal caso anseatico alle organizzazioni contemporanee', *Studi organizzativi*, n. 3.

Pichierri, A. (2001), *Strategie e strutture dello sviluppo locale*, Bologna, Il Mulino.

Pizzorno, A. (1999), 'Nota per una teoria del capitale sociale', *Stato e mercato*, n. 57.

Podolny, J. M. and Page, K. L. (1998), 'Network Forms of Organization', *Annual Review of Sociology*, 24.

Portes, A. (1998), 'Social Capital: its Origin and Application in Modern Sociology', *Annual Review of Sociology*, 24.

Putnam, R. D. (1993), *Making Democracy Work: Civic traditions in modern Italy*, New York, Princeton University Press.

Regini, M. (2000), *Modelli di capitalismo*, Bologna, Il Mulino.

Sabel, C. (1994), 'Learning by Monitoring', in N. Smelser and R. Swedberg (eds), *The Handbook of Economic Sociology*, Princeton/New York, Princeton University Press and Russell Sage Foundation.

Steiner, P (1999), *La Sociologie Économique*, Paris, La Découverte.

Streeck, W. (1988), 'L'impresa come luogo di formazione e apprendimento', in P. Ceri (a cura di), *Impresa e lavoro in trasformazione. Italia-Europa*. Bologna, Il Mulino.

Sviluppo Italia (in collaborazione con ITER) (2000), *Caratteristiche e potenzialità dei Patti territoriali*, Roma, mimeo.

Swedberg, R. (1997), 'New Economic Sociology: What Has Been Accomplished, What Is Ahead', *Acta Sociologica*, vol. 40.

Tarrow, S. (1996), 'Making Social Science Work Across Space and Time: A critical reflection on Robert Putnam's "Making Democracy Work"', *American Political Science Review*, 90.

Taylor, M. (1987), *The possibility of Co-operation*, Cambridge, Cambridge University Press

Torsvik, G. (2000), 'Social Capital and Economic Development', *Rationality and Society*, n. 4.

Trigilia, C. (1986), 'Small Firms Development and Political Subcultures in Italy', *European Sociological Review*, l(2), n. 3.

Trigilia, C. (1992), *Sviluppo senza autonomia*, Bologna, Il Mulino.

Trigilia, C. (1997), 'Italy: The Political Economy of a Regionalized Capitalism', *South European Society and Politics*, n. 3.

Trigilia, C. (1999), 'Capitale sociale e sviluppo locale', *Stato e mercato*, n. 57.

Uzzi, B. (1997), 'Social Structure and Competition in Interfirm Networks: The paradox of embeddedness', *Administrative Science Quarterly*, 42.

Viesti, G. (2000), *Come nasce un distretto industriale*, Bari, Laterza.

Vino, A. (1998), 'Patti territoriali e progettazione istituzionale', *Nord e Sud*, anno XLV, Settembre.

Williamson, O. (2000), 'The New Institutional Economics: Taking stock, looking ahead', *Journal of Economic Literature*, 38, September.

Wilson, P. A. (1997), 'Building Social Capital: A learning agenda for the twenty-first century', *Urban Studies*, 34, 5-6.

Chapter 7

The Insignificance of Weak Social Ties and the Uselessness of Strong Ones (With Two Case Histories of Low-income Families in Naples)

Enrica Morlicchio

Premise

The attention of the social scientific community in the last two decades has been increasingly drawn towards the concept of social capital. Nevertheless, in spite of the large amount of theoretical work on the subject, there is still no real agreement about the scope and the implications of the concept, which need to be known when measuring its frequency. Indeed, sometimes it seems almost that its very existence requires an act of faith rather than a strict empirical verification.

These difficulties are a consequence of the peculiar characteristics of social capital as a form of intangible 'capital' made up of such intangible factors as the availability of trust-based relationships, the limiting of personal interests for the benefit of the collective, or for what might be termed civic engagement, the possibility of transferring the right of control, and the use of a network of relationships for reducing the cost of information or increasing its effectiveness. The concept also includes the type of resources that individuals, or a specific social structure, partly inherit on the basis of pre-existing relationships and partly build up in time through new relationships. As Fortunata Piselli has observed, social capital 'becomes concrete in the creative actions of the actors, in the realisation of practical projects. It is a potential of resources that exist, becoming social capital only when it is activated' (Piselli 1999, p. 399).

Social capital is, then, a general concept that refers to a large range of phenomena, and because of this it can assume contradictory shapes. This variability does not depend only on the availability of relational resources, but is also influenced by the significance such resources have for the individual and by what use s/he is able to make of them. In other words, the concept can be characterised as ambivalent. For this reason I shall use it selectively, concentrating in particular on the subject in micro-level and informal contexts. The focus is on the importance of personal and informal relationships, such as those between friends, relatives, or neighbours that may be of help to people who are poor or/and unemployed and need to find work.

The study is designed to clarify and exemplify the role played by social capital in the context of unemployment and poverty. The two sections that follow examine a number of academic studies on social networks and various labour-market outcomes. The subsequent two sections present findings from two case histories of low-income families living in Naples that exemplify the usefulness of social capital (or lack of such) for reducing poverty. The final section presents concluding remarks to the research.

The Importance of Personal Networks in the Labour Market

The labour market has been one of the fields of research where the concept of social capital has been applied more systematically, and which therefore has produced the main results by which it can be evaluated (for a review see Barbieri 1997). Research results seems to demonstrate that personal networks – of relatives, friends, neighbours, and workplace colleagues – continue to play an important role in obtaining a job, even in situations where the labour market is, at least formally, governed by institutions. In the first half of the 1970s Granovetter (1974) examined the use of personal ties to investigate changes in the labour market in the city of Boston, which is characterised by medium or high levels of professional and occupational mobility. In the course of this research he interviewed a sample of 282 men performing professional, technical or managerial work, who had acquired their first job or changed jobs or within the last five years. He began with defining and isolating two specific kinds of ties. The first he termed 'strong' ties – those with a high intensity of control and emotional content, such as family ties, or links within the neighbourhood. The second kind of he termed 'weak' ties – which are characterised by less frequent contact and a lower emotional content, such as relationships established among acquaintances.[1] Granovetter showed that the majority of the people interviewed had acquired information about their new job thanks to individuals with whom they had a relatively loose relationship. The explanation for this peculiar 'strength of weak ties' (Granovetter 1973) relates to the fact that where the personal network is less dense, the subjects tend to move in different circles and so are more likely to provide information not previously encountered by their interlocutors, or better able to become useful contacts in their search for work. Granovetter concludes his analysis by stressing the importance of establishing ties outside the restricted circle of relatives and friends. Where individuals meet each other frequently, the type and degree of information is likely to be too restrictive to be of useful for finding work or better work.

---

[1] We do not enter into the merit of the debate on the operationalisation of the concept of strength within such ties such as intended by Granovetter. For a detailed discussion of these issues see Barbieri 1997, p. 77 ff.

Granovetter was one of the first to employ the concept of personal networks as an operative instrument in academic research and, in particular, to use the notion in a way that demonstrates the limitations of analysing the elements of awareness, rationality, and selection of action, which at that time represented the conventional wisdom. Fortunata Piselli argues that Granovetter's research is important because he clearly demonstrates that:

> individuals do not change jobs because they act according to criteria such as economic rationality – comparing the full range of benefits and related costs in order to choose the utility-maximising option, in the context of which there is little or no active research to support – but because they take advantage of information that they acquire accidentally every time their contacts offer it (Piselli 1994, p. 81).

Granovetter's work shows the relevance of context for in understanding the relationship between information and choice. Now 'context' can be translated as specifically the kind of social relationships typical of the modern industrial society: relationships with a high bureaucratic and formal content, functioning in a highly developed way. In its choice of specific classes of worker, the research was typical of a social Fordist environment. The subjects interviewed – all men with high levels of professional social mobility – were, in the majority of cases, not looking for their first job but wished to change the one they already had. This meant that almost all of them were already deeply involved in the informal networks available in their work environment.

In *Getting a Job* (Granovetter 1974) Granovetter further demonstrates that those of his research subjects who that knew each other during their first job and who stay in contact, keep on representing an important resource of information through the entire course of their working life. The research suggests that ties created at the beginning of one's career (thanks to the fact of working in the same enterprise for a given time) allow further ties to be developed which become useful at the moment of changing jobs, having something of a snow-ball effect. The results of Granovetter's research, though unquestioningly important, cannot be easily generalised or developed into a social policy. The social situation of the poor and in particular those that subsist through casual work, marked for instance by a succession of small informal activities and irregular periods of work for low wages, does not permit weak ties of any utility to be built up. In such cases, individuals can only rely on strong ties, in particular those with their family and other close relatives or close friends, which provide far less information on finding regular and well-paid work.

In addition to Granovetter's study of weak ties, two studies focussing on strong ties – namely the research of Larissa Adler Lomnitz (1977) and that of Margaret Grieco (1987) – are important in that they supply evidence with which to assess the effectiveness of impact of different types of network in providing practical information about employment possibilities. In the first of these studies, Lomnitz shows how poor families from a shantytown on the outskirts of Mexico City can to find work exclusively through either family ties or other close ties that presuppose a system of reciprocal obligation (such as neighbourly help) or of symbolic roles (of godfather or godmother). Jobs acquired by these strong ties, Lomnitz argues, enable the family to survive, but are not sufficient to lead it out of poverty. Furthermore, such networks generate strong occupational segregation. For example, in one family that was interviewed all the male adults work as upholsterers, while in another they all clean tombstones for a living. This type of segregation can be problematic, especially when there are periods of instability in these market sectors.

While strong (family) ties are valuable in certain social contexts, Margaret Grieco, who evaluated the results of three research projects developed in different British industrial areas, shows the importance of the family network as a form of social capital too. Grieco's research clarifies what exactly strong or weak ties imply. She documents, for example, that infrequent face-to-face contact is not a specific of weak ties as Granovetter argued, because through the migratory chain of groups of relatives or friends information on job vacancies can be transmitted even over a long distance. Secondly, Grieco shows that at the same time as such family ties make labour migration possible (initial hospitality for the new immigrants, information on work opportunities and other essential information), it is these same ties that contribute to the segregation of different professions. As she notes *à propos* her research in Scotland, specialisation that represented a useful resource when the occupational sector was expanding became a big disadvantage when the steel-industry crisis came and the tied workers found themselves isolated *via-à-vis* in respect the local social system.

This ambivalent character of strong ties as compared to other occupational strategies also appears in a survey examining the relationship between work and family ties in three areas in Southern Italy (Fondazione Brodolini 1997). The project revealed that more than two-thirds of the workers interviewed had found their jobs through mediation by family members or through close strict friends. Indeed, all the interviewed individuals employed in one specific sector had found their jobs in this way, and in one factory all the workers interviewed were linked by either family or neighbourhood relationships.[2] The majority of studies in other, more traditional fields of employment (for example, canal reclamation work) arrive at conclusion different from Granovetter's. Research in these traditional sectors shows that individuals searching for work more frequently turn to family relationships than to acquaintances. This is not surprising when many people compete for the same scarce opportunities, the role of the family becomes stronger

---

[2] In a factory that produces DIY kitchens for the local and export markets, all nine workers are linked by kinship or neighbourhood ties, either directly between the workers or with the head of the factory. The existence of this paternalistic and trust network among the workers and the head of the factory might be an advantage on the level of trust and reliability, but it also represents a restriction for the development or delocalisation of the enterprise. As the manager said: 'It is clear that to expand we have a problem. We work a lot like a family, the workers are all locals, and the majority are my relatives. It would be difficult to do a full transfer because I feel responsible for their families.'

and so does the family-structure model of the management of the job market. In this way, a family-structure model is not necessarily regressive. When it bonds with other elements that support individual micro-enterprises, it can become an element of activation and development, as happened in the 'Third Italy' (Centre/North-East regions). However, this does not seem to be the prevalent situation in the area to which the research results refer. That study supports the opinion that strong ties tend to be consolidated as a form of occupational segregation, and that they suffice to guarantee access to specific sectors of the job market. For this to be the case it is necessary, of course, that occupations of this type are available in the local economic system, and that such work is actually accessible to unemployed looking for jobs.

Unemployment and Social Isolation

All four of the studies quoted above show that for career development, individuals can effectively exploit the strength of weak ties (in particular, indirect relations with people in powerful positions) as well as also strong ties (particularly family ties), although the latter give access mainly to the locally prevailing occupations typical of the secondary segment of the labour market. The long-term unemployed are not, however, able to build relationships of the first kind, nor are they able to mobilise their strong ties to any great advantage. They enter a long irreversible phase of professional deskilling. Indeed, a prolonged period of unemployment results in not only economic and human-capital impoverishment, or as Sen argues: 'such as people "learn doing" so "they forget not doing"' (Sen 1997, p. 5). It also has repercussions at the level of social capital, principally by weakening the quality and quality of the relationships. Before discussing this further, let me look in greater detail at the course of events as shown by related research.

Paugam, for example, documents that in France, the long-term unemployed do have special family, friendship and community ties, but these are less numerous than in other categories, and as represented in the scores such individuals attain on a scale used to evaluate the degree of 'relational poverty' (see Paugam 1995). A study conducted by Gallie, Marsh and Vogler on long- and short-term unemployment in England and Scotland shows that fewer than one-third of the unemployed sampled were able to think of someone they knew who would be able to help them in their searching for a job, compared to two-thirds of the employed and self-employed sampled (see Gallie, Marsh and Vogler 1994). The unemployed are caught in something of a vicious circle, where unemployment itself creates growing social segregation and where the networks consist mainly of people who are unemployed themselves or at risk of unemployment, and so can provide little help in finding new job opportunities. Such networks do not correspond to any preference for a particular lifestyle but reflects the consequences of lack of resources and the demoralisation induced by unemployment, which do not allow the long-term unemployed to keep reciprocal relationships for very long. In Britain, moreover, as Ray Pahl has shown, social segregation expresses itself even in growing social polarisation between families where husband and wife are both unemployed, and families where both are employed in stable occupations. This 'spouse effect' (Benoit, Guilbot and Gallie 1992) has impoverished the network of social relationships for unemployed families, to such an extent as to preclude access to occasional and informal work like painting and decorating or maintenance jobs. Instead, access to information about work opportunities of this kind is chiefly through relationships established in the workplace or the forms of association related to it. Lydia Morris arrives at a very similar kind of conclusion in her research on unemployment in Hartlepool. In this city in the North of England, Morris discovers that,

> the long-term unemployed tend to live on public-sector housing estates with high levels of unemployment; to have partners who are also unemployed; to show concentrations of unemployment in their extended kin networks; and to name close friends who are also unemployed (Morris 1995, p. 27).

She points out that the majority of unemployed people rely on strong ties in their search for work. Indeed, Morris notes that 'when competition for jobs is high, i.e. in areas where the unemployment level is high, then a system of preferential channelling may assert itself' (Morris 1995, p. 33), a system based exactly on the type of ties described earlier by Lomnitz and Grieco.

In Italy, where the hard core of the unemployed (Pugliese 1993) is not represented by adult male breadwinners but by youths, generally with low education and without relevant work experience, such family ties are of little help in the search for work for their unemployed family members. Frequently the relational resources of the family network, when they are of assistance in finding work, function mainly for the male members of the family, making help for the women a secondary matter. Alessandro Cavalli has demonstrated that families 'invest less in the education of the females and they worry less about their proper working allocation than they do with the males' (1990, p. 375). This is corroborated by a research sample of young unemployed in Naples; it revealed that a much larger proportion of families are active in the search for a job for men (82 per cent) than for women (56 per cent) (see Cerase, Morlicchio and Spano 1991). More recent research (conducted by means of the narrative biographical method), has also found that a family tries harder to mobilise relational resources to help its boys than its girls (Zaccaria 2002, p. 289).

In addition, it seems that political channels in Italy do not seem to have taken the unemployed into consideration.[3] Evidently, the deep crisis of the traditionally

---

[3] Let me note here that if the terms weak and strong ties, or what is here referred to as political channels were used instead for 'bridging', 'bonding' and 'linking' social capital, the contents of this chapter would not be substantially different. Indeed 'bridging' social capital refers to cross-cutting or weak ties between workplace colleagues, members of civic organisations, business associates; 'bonding' social capital represents the strong ties within homogenous groups, families, small communities; and 'linking' social capital implies vertical ties linking people of unequal status (political elites and the poor, for instance).

clientelistic political parties has created a vacuum that has not yet been filled by other organisations save – in part, by the family. Recent evidence suggests that the labour-market situation is an arena of competition for a particularly scarce resource. For those in the most hazardous and precarious positions, relationships outside the family and close friendship group are of little use in providing access to information about the availability of work or any other type of job opportunities.

The Esposito Family, Living in Mercato Pendino (Naples)

The next two sections, which investigate a number of issues of general significance, are based on an empirical enquiry designed to explore further the various question raised above. The histories of two families in which the male breadwinner is currently unemployed should reveal how social capital is barely made available and utilised in the daily routine.[4] The study does not seek to draw universalistic conclusion but attempts to comprehend how each single family, without being able to avoid the vicious circle of intergenerational transfer of poverty, manages to survive without falling apart. In particular, it tried to find out how an event such as poverty – clearly of a levelling nature – was absorbed and metabolised by different families, and what role is played by social capital in this process.

The two selected families live in different neighbourhoods: in Scampia on the northeast fringe of the city of Naples, and in Mercato-Pendino in the historical city centre. Both are characterised as poor areas (their population includes a high percentage of low-income households). However, the latter is a pre-World War II area with a relatively large number of privately rented dwellings, while Scampia is a neighbourhood that originated in the post-World War II period characterised by high-rise public housing and a severe lack of public services.

I shall begin with give a description of the two families, starting with the Esposito family (my case A).

The Esposito family is going through its economically most difficult phase, that of expansion. At present the family consists of five people: mother, father and three sons: ten, five and one years old. Ciro, the male head of the family, is 30 years old, and obtained his secondary-school certificate at the age of twenty-six through a

---

[4] Semi-structured open interviews with the adult members of the families revealed their incomes and expenditures, their strategies for obtaining the necessary daily and durable consumer goods, and the spatial dimension of these strategies, including the use of family and kinship networks, local private and public welfare provisions, and neighbourhood-related assets. The reconstruction of the social genealogy of each of the two families – i.e. a genealogy in which not only a person's name but also her/his main (past or present) occupation appears on the graph (Bertaux 1995; Bertaux and Thompson 1997) – was made possible by prolonging the interviews. Each genealogy goes back to the two grandparents of the person interviewed and of her/his spouse. Its principal aim is to examine the household economy from the point of view of family history, and to explore to what extent poverty and the leading male's occupational instability are fixed characteristics of different generations.

scholastic rehabilitation (night school) course; his wife Maria holds only a primary-school certificate.

Maria used to live in the same neighbourhood of Ciro and they used to see each other frequently. They were married in 1990 when both were 20 years old. Ciro considers this early marriage a mistake because it has made the decision of migrating in search of work difficult.

> She was pregnant. I felt an obligation, a moral obligation ... . If I hadn't married at the age of twenty I'd have moved elsewhere to look for work. I'd have a lot of experience by now ... . These years of marriage have been a never-ending effort to try and live decently (C. Esposito).

The family lives in a very small apartment owned by a housing company, sublet to them by the elderly lady who is the legitimate titleholder.

> This is quite common around here. When [you've looking for something here to live and] it's known that someone has gone away and abandoned the home, you make contact with that person and take the place over. Then you don't have to move away from the neighbourhood where the family lives and one doesn't pay a lot of money (C. Esposito).

Ciro Esposito's family is a family of irregular workers (people working outside the framework of public regulation). His father Vincenzo, 52 years old, has always worked as a street vendor, selling socks or T-shirts; his mother is a housewife. Ciro has a sister (Luisa) and a brother (Giovanni). The first is a housewife married to an unauthorised night-time parking attendant, who is about to lose this job as the parking area is to be transformed into a park. Ciro's brother is unemployed, but three times a week transports mattresses for a small firm. Few of Ciro's cousins have held stable jobs, except for two (Gennaro and Maria) who have moved to Ravenna (in the North of Italy) where they work in metallurgical and textile factories respectively. These two have been the family's only success stories, in employment terms. Although the job experiences of Ciro's other cousins have been varied, many of them have failed to move out of the secondary labour market.

Ciro himself has never had regular employment. As a boy he worked as a bricklayer and street vendor. Aged 17 he started to work as an unauthorised parking attendant, a job he still holds. He earns about €150 a week.

> I started working as an unauthorised parking attendant twelve-thirteen years ago. One morning, I and some friends of mine from the neighbourhood who also had no work, we left the bar where we went every day, and began to look after the cars in the small square near the hospital where patients and visitors are always parked (C. Esposito).

In the family of Ciro's wife Maria, the dominant occupation is wholesale or street vendor of table and bed linen or detergents. Maria's father died at the age of 38 in a car accident. Uncles and aunts who are also trades-people have helped Maria, but she herself has never worked in this line. Although there is enough evidence for arguing that in her family the men's economic contribution is not enough to cover the needs of the household she is not looking for work. She defines herself as a housewife.

> I have never worked, I'm housewife! With three children and not much education I've no chance to get a job. I look after my children's and I do all I can to stretch what we have so nobody has to suffer (M. Esposito).

The Esposito family has a very low level of consumption:

> Now the children put on the jumpers other people give us. But when they grow up and begin to understand that those jumpers are second-hand, they won't want them any more (M. Esposito).

> When we don't have enough money to buy meet or fish, my wife knows how to prepare *gnocchi* (fresh pasta made with flour and water) or a pizza, so my children aren't hungry and we can save money (C. Esposito).

The Esposito family is in daily, weekly or monthly contact with close relatives (parents, brothers and sisters) and with maternal and paternal uncles, aunts, and cousins living in the same neighbourhood. For all that they are not given much material help, because the people who make up the network of family and friends find themselves in similar economic difficulties. Relatives do provide the children with food, shoes, and money occasionally, but only in emergencies.

Ciro and Maria are strongly attached to their neighbourhood, though they are fully aware of the neglect and lack of public services that characterise it.

> Given my work I'm always in the street. I know quite a few who live round here, I am part of this neighbourhood. I've friends who I've known since I was little, and they've stayed on ever after they got married. We meet everyday, we're having a coffee at the bar and talk of this and that ... The neighbourhood around here is ruined, everything is missing. I can't see how the social services we don't have could come here, there are buildings everywhere and no space. In the last ten years criminal activity round here has grown, there are more serious crimes now than there used to be, like more shootings. At first there was only cigarette smuggling, now they smuggle drugs too (C. Esposito).

> If I could, I'd look for somewhere else to live where it's better for my family, especially the children ... . But for the moment that's out of the question, so it's better that we don't even think of it (M. Esposito).

The possibilities for the Esposito family receiving welfare services and transfers are limited, both because of the lack of public services offered, and the characteristic of the Italian welfare system which does not provide substantial support for families with young children (see Saraceno, 1994). Although the Esposito family gets free medical service and medicines through the National Health Service they sometimes have additional expenses of this kind. The family also receives vouchers for the purchase of schoolbooks, after the municipality conducted a means test. Between July 1999 and December 2000 the family benefited from the minimum supplementary grant of €500 monthly. They heard about the possibility from their network of kin.

> It was my mother who found out about it from my sister, because the district councilman had told her that I should try ... and so I found myself in receipt of this sum, thanks to my mother who came alongside with me to apply (C. Esposito).

At present, however, the payment of this grant has been blocked, leaving the family in difficulty again.

> When we had the grant we comfortable, not having to count every single lira as we'd done ... The first time I received the grant it was summer, and I got a lot of shopping (food and detergents), and I took the children to the seaside. I'd been in arrears with the rent too, and I took care of this. Then I bought shoes for the children, the washing machine broke down ... all things you need. But the chief thing was food. On my way home I'd think of the shopping. Then I got a book or two for my son, for example, that the school didn't provide. I had to buy it for him myself because they give you a certain sum [vouchers for the purchase of school books], the rest you must get on your own. Schoolbag, exercise books, all those things. I did everything possible, unthinkable that I wouldn't (Mrs Esposito).

> We hope we'll go on getting it. We know its an experiment they're doing, but in the rest of Europe they already give unemployment benefit, and so why not in Italy too? (Mr Esposito).

The monetary grant has in no way affected Signor Esposito's commitment to look for work, which he perceives as a central issue, the key element for changing his life's prospects. Despite the difficult occupational history and the lack of regular jobs, there is no sign of refusal or self-exclusion from the sphere of work on his part.

> Together with other people round here who have the money grant we're trying to organise ourselves to see if, instead of giving us cash they'd give us a job so we can feel easier about the future. We keep in contact between us, we visit other neighbourhoods and talk to other young people, we're even gone on unauthorised strike (C. Esposito).

> Let's say that unfortunately there just isn't any work, there's no job that lets you to work properly. I don't know whose fault that is. Not my husband's because what he is able to bring home to let us go on, even that little bit, is already a lot. And it's not only my husband, there are lots of others like him who're without work (M. Esposito).

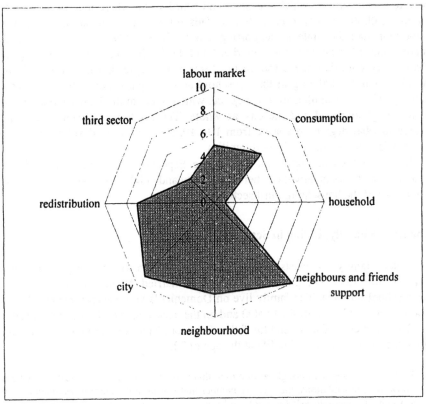

Labour market	5
Consumption	6
Household	1
Neighbours and friends support	10
Neighbourhood	8
City	9
Redistribution	7
Third sector	3

Figure 7.1 Esposito family

In order to make the coping strategies of the two families more explicit and to show the importance of different options for action we have made use of diagrams (see Figures 7.1 and 7.2). The spider-web diagrams are divided into four areas: market, redistribution, reciprocity, and space. Each option is further broken down into more specific aspects. Using the interviews as the main source, we have attributed scores from 0 to 10 (see Appendix I for the key to the criteria used). The higher the score, the more widely it is used. *Redistribution* includes a public and private social service, which are State and 'third sector' (here mainly represented by the Catholic charity organisations). This third sector can, at times be more important than the State in supporting a poor family. *Market* includes both the regular and informal, the labour market,[5] and the family's pattern of consumption. *Reciprocity* considers the presence or absence of people (kinship or friendship), whether or not cohabiting in the household and – in particular – their supporting activity. The same applies to urban *space*, which refers to the family's relationship to the neighbourhood and the city as whole. The resulting diagram, shows at a glance to what degree on a scale from 1 to 10, each option to develop one's own strategy is used by each of the two families.

It can be seen in Figure 7.1 that in the Esposito-family graph (case A) the shaded area covers mainly the sphere of the city and neighbourhood, and to a lesser extent that of the household, third sector, and market.

The Buono Family, Living in Scampia (Naples)

The Buono family is consists of Domenico, aged 60, his wife Maria (53), and their son Salvatore (27). The daughter Tina (30) is married. Neither husband nor wife has a school diploma. The family live on Domenico's very meagre income (he has a permanent job but is off the books) and on the occasional earnings of Salvatore.

Both Domenico Buono and his father Salvatore have worked in a glass factory. Domenico started his working life at the age of 22.

> I found the job easily enough; at that time there weren't so many complications, who to know, recommendations, money. I remember that I went to the glass-works factory with a group of friends to ask for a job and they gave it to us, and until the crises in this sector I've never had any problem (D. Buono).

The crises he mentions were in 1974 when the factory laid off many of its employees, in 1975 it closed down altogether. In 1978, at the age of 38, Mr Buono found his present job as store-man in a goods-haulage company but as he is not hired legally he has no pension contributions paid, holidays, or sickness benefit. His working life has, therefore, been a process of 'skidding' from a regular occupation to an irregular one with a lower level of qualification and pay. This skidding process meant deterioration in his family's living conditions.

> Today many people have to live on €400-500 a month. They are making us go back fifty years to when I was a boy ... but what sort of life is this? (D. Buono).

---

[5] Other distinctions are, of course possible, within the labour market – for instance between the formal and informal market, where working condition differ greatly. There the divisions are if anything more complicated in terms of job stability or wage levels, which have important effects on strategic action. But including these would make the diagram too complicated, so only the first divide will be considered. For more details about this methodology of analysis, see Andreotti and Kaazepov 2001, pp. 13-16.

The family is able in one way or another to make ends meet, but the level of consumption is very low. Shopping is done where prices are lowest and is almost exclusively limited to food. The choice of what food to buy depends on how much money is available that week. Almost no money is spent on culture, leisure or social activities. The home itself is poorly equipped with electrical domestic appliances apart from colour television, radio, fridge and washing machine. There is no sign of evident consumer goods, although these can be found among the marginal population of Naples (mostly obtained illegally or by hire purchases).

Domenico's demotion from relatively favourable working conditions to a secondary segment of the labour market has not only brought a net reduction in the family's consumption but also major uncertainty about the future. This is made worse by the absence of 'component wages' capable of compensating for the drop in the only breadwinner's income. Signora Maria Buono is a housewife without an outside job. She comes from a family of precarious workers. Her paternal grandfather worked as an unloader in the fruit and vegetable market and his son, Maria's father, inherited this job when he died at the age of 48. One of Maria's brothers also works in the fruit and vegetable market as an unloader. One of her father's sisters emigrated to England with her husband, while another brother collected scrap metal from the streets. Both are now dead. Maria's maternal grandfather works as a street fishmonger. Her sister is handicapped with crippled arm due to polio but works twice a week as a domestic help, and the sister's husband acts as unqualified night nurse at the Camaldoli Hospital, being paid by the families of the patients in his care.

Salvatore, the son of Domenico and Maria, started work at the age of 12 as a helper in a mechanical workshop, then at 14 he switched to parquettery. At 19 he was called up for his military service and sent to Somalia. There he was wounded in the knee, and the injury impedes his work. His employer dismissed him. At present he does occasional jobs as a house painter. He has applied to the Italian navy for compensation.

The Buono family has changed neighbourhood several times. When Domenico and Maria were newly married in 1969 they stayed with Domenico's parents, where they were not charged any rent. They then went to live with Maria's mother in another of Naples' neighbourhoods, and she too did not ask for rent. Domenico's occupation in the glass-works, while it continued the same, had become less secure. In 1974 the Buonos moved to Miano (in the Neapolitan hinterland) to live on their own for the first time. They. By this time they already had two children, and Domenico was experiencing problems at work. After the earthquake of 1980 they moved as squatters into a flat in Scampia.[6] It is obvious from the way they talk about it that Maria was very active at all stages of the struggles by the inhabitants of Scampia for obtaining the supply of public services (water, etc.) and the urban infrastructure. In 1985 they were formally allocated the flat they were occupying.

---

[6] In the early 1980s there was a wave of squatters taking over unfinished council houses in Scampia.

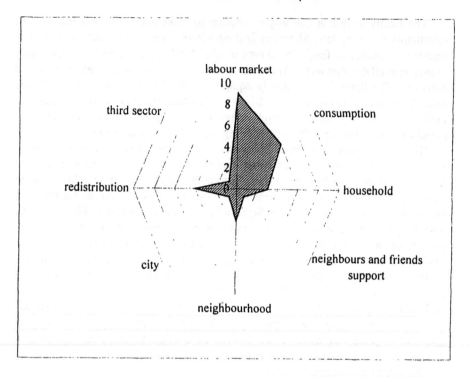

Labour market	9
Consumption	6
Household	3
Neighbours and friends support	1
Neighbourhood	3
City	1
Redistribution	4
Third sector	1

Figure 7.2 Buono family

They then paid €34 in rent a month, at present they pay €50. Maria is still busy and directly concerned with improving their flat and the neighbourhood.

> Our flat doesn't have windows in the bathroom, and not on the stairs either. That's why three years ago we decided not to pay the rent. We wanted the people from the Institute of Public Housing to fix the building first, but then we found that ten families – there are forty-two here – paid the rent anyway. So we couldn't do battle and everyone started paying again (M. Buono).

Other members of the family have similarly precarious housing situation. For instance, one of Maria Buono's sisters lives in a house occupied inside the area of the Frullone Psychiatric Hospital. The occupied house has been ceded to her from her mother seven years ago after the latter obtained public housing in Melito.

The Buono family receives less help from relatives than the Esposito family and receives no financial support from the state. The family maintains good relations with the neighbourhood, as can be seen by a remark of Signiora Buono's:

> Living opposite there is a very nice young lady who lets me put my washing out from her balcony in the morning when the sun is shining. With the neighbours on the other stairway we get on well too, and with all the other people living in the building (M. Buono).

However, these neighbourhood relationships cannot help in the search for work and are limited to friendly exchanges of mutual assistance. The socio-economic background is similar for everyone in this neighbourhood, so people who have a job and might act as intermediaries with prospective employers are scarce. This makes it impossible to seize any opportunities for work, which – even though they are few and far between – do exist in the outlying areas and municipalities.

Compared to the previous diagram (Figure 7.1), the diagram for the Buono family (Figure 7.2) tends to the north-end side (labour market) whereas neighbourhood and redistribution play a relative unimportant role. It is quite evident that the spheres most usual are labour market and family and neighbours' support. As we have seen, resources are provided for mainly from the irregular income of Domenico Buono.

Final Remarks

An analysis based solely on two case studies does not, of course, permit any generalisations. However, if these two studies are seen as supporting evidence for the results of the research referred to earlier, then it may be argued that the perspective of social capital can be very useful when analysing differences of opportunity in breaking the vicious circle of unemployment and poverty. These differences are not analysed merely in terms of 'residual' factors – which cannot be explained by merely referring to individual attributes so require a network analysis – but also in terms of a contextual reduction of the possibility of finding work and the resulting social relationships.   Indeed (independently of any individual inclinations), other factors, such as the level of the family's cohesion, or racial discrimination will, of course, have an effect on a person's life and job opportunities. However, someone born in an area in which the majority of the people are unemployed starts off at a great disadvantage: there are not likely to be many positive role models with which to identify, or useful contacts for finding work. While someone in this kind of situation is capable as anyone else to develop relationships, they will probably be with people who are equally disadvantaged and equally unable to mobilise useful resources to break the vicious cycle of unemployment, and to overcome the segregating context that the area perpetuates.

Appendix 7.I: Key to case A and case B

1. Reciprocity

1.1. Household

1-2 = co-habitants over 18 do not give any support, and no support is given by relatives;
3-4 = co-habitants over 18 give some support but no other support from their family is given;
5-6 = co-habitants over 18 give support and some support from the parents is given too;
7-8 = co-habitants over 18 give support and also support from parents and other relatives is given;
9-10 = strong support from the whole kinship network.

1.2. Neighbours and Friends

1-2 = Almost no contact with friends and neighbours;
3-4 = few support contacts with neighbours and almost no support from friends;
5-6 = support relations with selected neighbours and few friends;
7-8 = good support relations with neighbours and some friends;
9-10 = large support networks composed by neighbours and friends.

2. Market

2.1 Labour

1-2 = Almost out of the labour market;
3-4 = unstable jobs, working once in a while;
5-6 = stable job working part time; unstable job working enough to have a decent income;
7-8 = stable job working full time but not regularly hired;
9-10 = stable job working full time and regularly hired.

2.2. Consumption

1-2 = Market is used for buying food only;
3-4 = market is used for food and other primary needs only;
5-6 = market is used for buying food, clothes, furniture (all every day goods);
7-8 = market is used not only for buying every day goods but also for some durable goods (car, p.c., mobile phone, etc.);
9-10 = everything is bought on the market from the little things to the house.

3. Redistribution

3.1. Public Services and Provisions

1-2 = Almost no use of public services (neither schools or hospitals);
3-4 = Use of basic public social services (schools, hospitals, transports, etc.);
5-6 = Use of social services for getting information and bureaucratic support (e.g. filling in forms for in the rent);
7-8 = Use of social services for getting monetary and non monetary support besides other supports;
9-10 = Full use of public institutions and social assistance services for every kind of need.

3.2. Private No-profit Services and Provisions

1-2 = Almost no use of any third sector service or provision;
3-4 = Rare use of third sector agencies in the neighbourhood for information;
5-6 = Use of private non-profit social agencies for information and bureaucratic support (e.g. filling in application forms);
7-8 = Use of private non-profit social agencies for getting monetary and in-kind support besides other supports;
9-10 = Full use of private non-profit social agencies for monetary and in-kind support to meet every kind of need.

4. Space

4.1. Neighbourhood

1-2 = The neighbourhood is not used in any of the spheres of regulation. There are no knots there;
3-4 = The local space is used only rarely and in an instrumental way (e.g. shopping, but not for jobs). Few knots are there;
5-6 = In the neighbourhood there are some interviewee network knots (a mix, but with more informal networks);
7-8 = In the neighbourhood there are many interviewee network knots (a mix, with more institutionalised networks);
9-10 = The person makes full use of the local space in all spheres (e.g. also having a job in the area).

4.2. City

1-2 = There is almost no relation with the city (the person does not leave the neighbourhood);
3-4 = The city is used only for services and provisions (in one sphere of regulation, e.g. "she goes to her mother in another neighbourhood for child care") that are not available in the neighbourhood;
5-6 = The city is used only for services and provisions (in at least two spheres of regulation) that are only party available in the neighbourhood (it's a choice not to use them all);
7-8 = The city is used for services and provisions in all spheres, that are also available in the neighbourhood (it's a choice not to use them, e.g. the child is brought to a school in a better off neighbourhood to foster upwards mobility);
9-10 = Full use of the city, taking advantage of services and provisions in all spheres of regulation available.

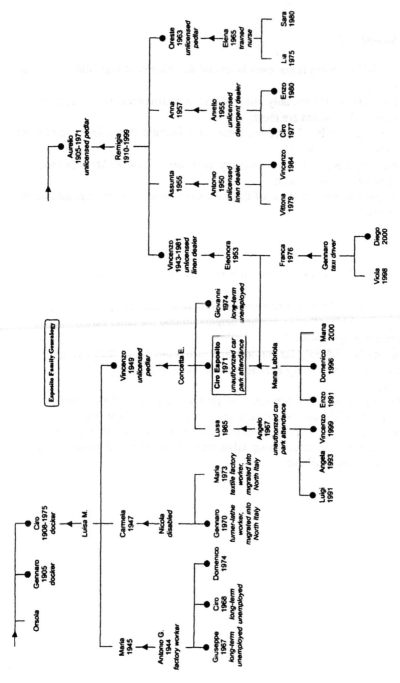

Appendix 7. II The Esposito and Buono family social genealogies

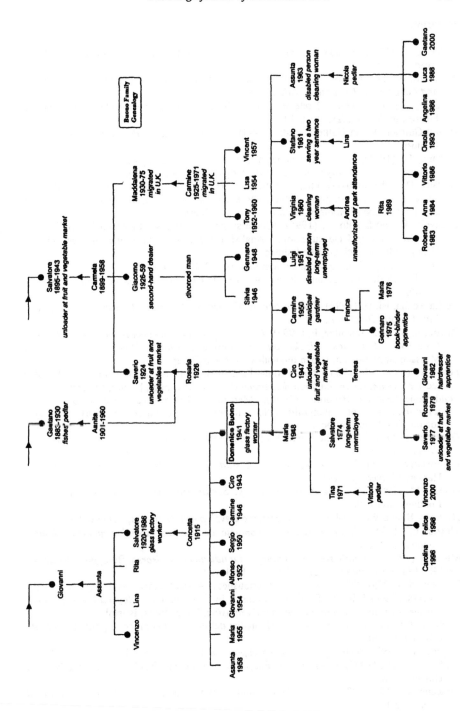

References

Adler, L. (1977), *Networks and Marginality: Life in a Mexican shantytown*, New York, Academic Press.

Andreotti, A. and Kazepov, Y. (eds) (2001), *Spatial Dimensions of Urban Social Exclusion and Integration: The case of Milan*, Amsterdam, Ame.

Barbieri, P. (1997), 'Non c'è rete senza nodi. Il ruolo del capitale sociale nel mercato del lavoro', in *Stato e Mercato*, n.49 .

Benoit-Guilbot O. and Gallie D. (eds) (1995), *La disoccupazione di lunga durata*, Napoli, Liguori,.

Bertaux, D. (1995), 'Social Genealogies Commented and Compared: An instrument for studying social mobility processes in the long durée', *Current Sociology*, No.43.

Bertaux, D. and Bertaux-Wiame, I. (1997), 'Social Mobility over Five Generations', in D. Bertaux and P. Thompson (eds) (1997), *Pathways to Social Class: A Qualitative approach to social mobility*, Oxford, Clarendon Press.

Casavola, P. and Sestito, P. (1995), 'Come si cerca e come si ottiene un lavoro?', in A. Amendola (ed.), Disoccupazione. Analisi Macroeconomica e mercato del lavoro, Napoli, Edizioni Scientifiche Italiane.

Cavalli, A. (ed.) (1990), *I giovani del Mezzogiorno*, Bologna, Il Mulino.

Cerase, F., Morlicchio, E. and Spanò, A. (1991), *Disoccupati e disoccupate a Napoli*, Napoli, Cuen.

De La Rocha, M. G. (1994), *The Resources of Poverty: Women and survival in a Mexican City*, Oxford. Blackwell.

Falcon, L. M. and Melendez, E. (1996), *The Role of Social Networks in the Labour Market: Outcomes of latinos, blacks and non-hispanic whites*, Boston, University of Massachusetts-Boston, Urban Inequality Research Group.

Follis, M. (1998), 'Perché contano i contatti personali nel mercato del lavoro?', in M. Follis (ed.), *M. Granovetter: La forza dei legami deboli e altri saggi*, Napoli, Liguori.

Fondazione Giacomo Brodolini (1997), 'Mercati del lavoro locali, occupazione e beni relazionali. I fattori intangibili dello sviluppo e dell'occupazione', Parte II-Analisi sociologica, Roma, mimeo.

Granovetter, M. (1973), 'The Strength of Weak Ties', *American Journal of Sociology*, 78 (6), pp. 1360-80.

Granovetter, M. (1974), *Getting a Job. A study of contacts and careers*, Cambridge, Harvard University Press.

Grieco, M. (1987), *Keeping it in the Family: Social networks and employment chance*, London, Tavistock.

Harrison, B. and Weiss, M. (1998), *Workforce Development Networks*, London, Sage.

Morris, L. (1995), *Social Divisions: Economic decline and social structural change*, London, UCL Press.

Mutti, A. (1998), *Capitale sociale e sviluppo. La fiducia come risorsa*, Bologna, Il Mulino.

Pahl R. (1984), *Division of Labour*, Oxford, Blackwell.

Paugam, S. (1995), 'The Spiral of Precariousness: A multidimensional approach to the process of social disqualification in France', in G. Room (ed.), *Beyond the Threshold: The measurement and analysis of social exclusion*, Policy Press, Bristol.

Piselli, F. (1997), 'Il network sociale nell'analisi del potere e dei processi politici', in *Stato e Mercato*, n.50.

Pugliese, E. (1992), *Sociologia della Disoccupazione*, Bologna, Il Mulino.

Pugliese, E. (ed.) (1999), *Oltre le Vele. Rapporto su Scampia*, Napoli, Fridericiana Editrice Universitaria.

Saraceno, C. (1994), 'The Ambivalent Familism of the Italian Welfare State', in *Social Policies*, n.1.

Sen, A. (1997), 'L'occupazione: le ragioni di una priorità per la politica economica', in P. Ciocca, (ed.), *Disoccupazione di fine secolo*, Torino, Bollati Boringhieri

Zaccaria A. M. (2001), 'Una lettura di rete', in A.Spanò (ed.), *Tra esclusione e inserimento. Giovani inoccupati a bassa scolarità e politiche del lavoro a Napoli*, Milano, F. Angeli.

Chapter 8

Informal Support Networks in the Making of Small Independent Businesses: Beyond 'Strong' and 'Weak' Ties?[*]

Sokratis M. Koniordos

Introduction

In Greece (the country from which I draw my empirical material) as in so many other countries, most economists and State authorities consider so-called informal business practices an abomination that restricts the country's growth and development.[1] Whether this is true or not, I am more interested in showing that the continuing reproduction of very small ('micro') and small manufacturing businesses, which the European Union (EU) perceives as a key locus of new employment (European Commission 1994, pp. 93-94; European Commission 1995, p. 3), depends to a very substantial extent on the widespread prevalence of informal practices. In particular, I would claim that the setting up of independent very small enterprises is premised on the support provided by informal support networks of close relatives, workmates, friends, ex-bosses, suppliers and even clients, in addition to the support offered by acquaintances sharing the same neighbourhood or village background. This is support given to working-class agents when they attempt to set themselves up as independent business proprietors in manufacturing. The support being informal means that at this level such networks do not enjoy an

[*] Parts of an earlier version of this paper have been presented at the following conferences: EKKE-SEK Conference on 'Social Developments in Contemporary Greece and Europe', Panteion University, Athens 24-26 May 2001; Fifth Conference of the European Sociological Association (Economic Sociology Research Network) – 'Visions and Divisions', University of Helsinki, 28 Aug. – 1 Sept. 2001; *Work, Employment & Society* Conference on 'Winning and Losing in the New Economy', at the University of Nottingham, 11 – 13 Sept. 2001. I would like to thank the conference participants for comments received. Also, I am most grateful to Roe Panagiotopoulou for her critique.
[1] In the particular context, 'informal' refers to various undeclared economic practices that evade registration. Of course, non-registration means that they remain untaxed and are beyond State control and supervision.

officially acknowledged status, without this implying that they are negatively appraised or morally unacceptable at the local (micro-) level at which they unfold.

Two other terms should be clarified: 'support' and 'network'. By support I mean assistance that may take a material, economic form, but also more intangibly the form of psychological and moral encouragement; both kinds are indispensable for 'becoming independent'. In addition, support may take the form of a mobilisation in which the organisational and technical skills of close kin, friends and acquaintances and their (informal) social capital – which may be seen as trust-infused networks of relations (see Trigilia 2001; Burt 1997; Coleman 1988) – are drawn in to benefit the person(s) attempting to become independent. In this sense, support appears to stem from relations of a mostly 'strong' kind, i.e. direct and personal, between those who extend and those who receive it. Running parallel to this, the very idea of support, both given and received, is continually generated and fed by a *habitus* where instances of mutual assistance are praised, independence is glorified, and being your own boss (by having your own business) is highly approved and very positively sanctioned. [2]

The type of networks referred to here is the so-called egocentric or personal one (see McCarty, 2002), in which the point of reference is the individual small business person. It is around her/him that the network of individuals is anchored. At the same time, the pattern of connections of the personal network has a systemic element that calls for a more socio-centric approach (see Scott 2000, pp. 74-79). [3] This approach may not cover all members of such networks, but it does affect a substantial number of them, i.e. all those sharing a similar 'us-them' imagery of class and class identity. It is this latter group of participating network members who operate with the notion of mutuality: either paying back support that was given to them in the past, or extending support in the expectation that it will be reciprocated at some later time (see Portes 1998). [4]

If the general statement made by economic sociology (old or new), which claims that the economy is embedded in social institutions (Granovetter 1985; Smelser in Swedberg 1990) is to remain valid, then it will have to be continually and concretely demonstrated that this is indeed the case. Therefore, when considering an economy such as that of Greece, which is marked by the fact that

---

[2] This is a point noted by other authors, i.e. R. Panayiotopoulou (1996), and K. Tsoukalas (2000). For a fuller development and discussion, see Koniordos 2005-forthcoming.

[3] I shall not embark here on a matrix data-generating exercise, as is often the case with mathematised structural analyses. I shall abstain from doing so for several reasons. One, when the material was collected and processed no provision was made for generating matrix data for individual respondents. Two, while such a task could be attempted on the basis of the data available, this seems to me to be both too tedious and expensive. Third, the responses received from the interviewees concerning their relations with network members entail their own perception of the relations dimension and these, in agreement with McCarty (2002), I consider as sufficiently accurate for present purposes.

[4] A third option would be to extend support as a form of give-away present. See the relevant discussion in Papataxiarchis 1992; also, Rafael Marques' article on reciprocity in this volume, and in Portes 1998.

small and very small businesses never lost their importance and even today retain much of their significance (European Commission 2000, pp. 32, 64-65, Koniordos 2000b), the empirical question must be asked: Where are the institutions to be found in which this specifically structured economy is supposed to be embedded? To be more precise, the question I shall try attempt to answer is: How is it possible for wage-workers to move upwards to become small independent entrepreneurs in the contemporary time-frame, in an EU member-country, albeit one that apparently retains its semi-peripheral position (see Mouzelis 1987, pp. 17-78)?

I should add that the existence of an official framework that facilitates such economic activity, and of a set of accommodating official economic institutions is not in question nor is it discussed here. What matters here is to map the operation of what may be considered social institutions that alongside their formal mode have an informal one – apprenticeship, work and class, friendship and kinship – and provide would-be independent business people with that informal support network which I consider absolutely necessary for establishing independent business. In other words, I shall try to show how this particular set of largely informal social institutions lies at the root of the said kind of economic activity, at least in the early stages of setting up and consolidating a new micro or very small business – a period that typically lasts for about two years.

The making of small independent proprietors may also be seen as a process of 'getting a job' for those concerned. The difference from other ways of finding a job is that here it takes the form of self-employment. The point is that informal support networks act as bridges that render such a development possible for skilled wage-workers in the manufacturing sector (specifically in Greece). However, in contrast to Mark Granovetter's thesis about 'the strength of weak ties', this does not come about primarily or exclusively through either weak or strong ties.[5] Let me stress that both kinds of ties are necessary and indeed indispensable, but that the key factor in getting the kind of job I am here concerned with (becoming the independent proprietor of a small business) is personal agency – which is rooted in a benign social context and continually bred by it. This then is the basic issue explored in the present paper.

---

[5] The reader is reminded that, building on earlier empirical work (1995 – initially published in 1974), Granovetter has argued that *weak* ties – meaning relationships limited in intensity and frequency, such as with acquaintances or friends of friends – are nevertheless very useful to lower-class people in search of a job. The reason is that the people with whom someone is linked by such weak ties live, work and operate in different social circles from those of the person concerned. They can therefore operate as viaducts or local bridges by means of which information about jobs is acquired. This exactly is the value such weak ties have for those whose limiting circumstances leave them with both very little information about what is happening beyond their immediate milieu and with poor opportunities. By contrast, *strong* ties refer to the close relations one has with kin, friends, close workmates, or perhaps neighbours, in other words with one's in-group members. Strong ties are particularly helpful in finding a job for members of the socially better established middle classes (see Granovetter 1973, 1983).

I shall now proceed to say a few things about the empirical samples and present some aspects of the morphological characteristics of those surveyed. This will be followed by a discussion of the levels of skill and other prerequisites for becoming independent. Thereafter, the composition of the support networks will be presented, and the support function of certain of their member clusters; I shall also look at their character (weak/strong ties) and impact. Finally, the points made earlier will be drawn together to show how they conduce to the continuing creation of formally independent positions.

The Empirical Samples: The Sampled and their Skills

The material on which I have drawn was collected in the course of empirical investigations made fifteen years ago (late 1988 to early 1989) and more recently (late 1998 to early 1999).[6] In all, three samples are involved. The first is the oldest, the other two are from the late1998 and early 1999 period.

The first sample consisted of 100 working proprietors of small manufacturing concerns in the Athens basin. Of these, 50 had machining shops and the remainders were involved with garments; this first sample forms the base of comparison. The second, part of a follow-up survey of the initial sample, involved 41 working proprietors (35 machinists and 6 in garments) from the Athens area. The third sample is from the Heraklion area on the island of Crete; It consists of 32 very small units in various branches of manufacturing. The bulk of the interviewees i.e. all of the machinists and most of the remainder were men, and the information was obtained by means of identical questionnaires.

The three panels are not identical, which somewhat affects the overall validity of comparisons. However, the members of the panels are homologous, which for present purposes I consider a sufficient condition for making possible the particular comparisons I wish to draw.[7]

The independent units whose proprietors were surveyed were all primarily engaged in small manufacturing. The businesses as well as their proprietors are grouped into three categories on the basis of the ratio of working proprietors to hired employees: as *very small* or *artisanal*, those of *smaller employers*, and of *larger employers*. The very small (artisanal) enterprises refer here to manufacturing units employing 6-8 persons (so belonging into the EU category of micro-enterprises), in which the labour contribution of hired hands does not exceed that of the working owners and their working family-members. At the other end of the spectrum the larger employers operate small but already capitalist enterprises, while the smaller employers that stand in between engage in simple-commodity

---

[6] The 1988-89 survey was reported initially in Koniordos (1996). Certain data from that survey presented here have undergone further processing. Data presented here from the 1998-99 survey have not been published before.

[7] The first two samples were researched by myself; students of the Social Work Department of the TEI of Crete did the third in the course of a research-methods class.

production and/or capitalist production. These three categories are merely strata of the officially designated 'small' units or 'small' enterprises category; this includes all units, artisanal and other, employing up to 50 persons. (All but two of the units researched employ from 1 to 18 persons.)

In terms of the social origin of the interviewees (as gauged by their fathers' occupation), most of the sampled came from humble backgrounds: from artisan families (15 per cent), peasants (38 per cent), wage-workers (18 per cent), and petty merchants (8 per cent). The proprietors of the smaller units (artisans and smaller employers) both were over-represented in terms of their family backgrounds and attended school for a substantially fewer years than officially suggested. Such interviewees had to undergo apprenticeships lasting on average about 4.5 years. Due to poverty their families could neither support them for the usual period of schooling, nor pass on to them substantial material support (e.g. savings or other property), nor yet the prospect of a family business to inherit. They therefore had to find work for wages. Especially the older among them reported starting wage-work while they were still children, only nine or ten years of age. As a rule they had no expectations of financial assistance from their families nor did they receive any.

These interviewees were, therefore, forced to rely on whatever assets they could muster themselves and had to work for wages for a long number of years before they were in a position to attempt becoming independent – on the average 11.6 years in the case of the first sample (Koniordos 1996: 285), and 10.1 years in the second and third one.[8] Excluding those who were occupied in family businesses, the remainder often changed employers – on average at least four times, but they basically continued working in the same trade. With the partial exception of those who inherited their businesses (27 per cent of the total of interviewees), virtually all of the rest worked for wages for a considerable period of time.

At the same time, working for wages also meant acquiring skills. Skills were the interviewees' FIRST and prime asset, the means for obtaining the increase in wages that would allow for some savings, which in the course of time could be used as the capital to set up a business of their own. Once this was established, skills were again the key factor: they safeguarded technical independence and kept down labour costs. While the sums needed to start the businesses were relatively small, it was skills that were the main asset of the small independents, and were picked up largely in the course of long apprenticeships, mostly on the job.

Of course, to be of maximum use to the would-be independent, the skills acquired in the course of apprenticeships and working prior to establishing an independent workshop had to range across a broad spectrum to allow tackling newly encountered work problems successfully (see Piore and Sabel 1984, p. 115). In this way an artisan or small employer acquired a good name in the trade and attracted potential clients. Without such a comprehensive grasp of skills the

---

[8] It may interest the reader to note that in the first sample, 26 of the 100 businesses researched were pre-existing family businesses, before the interviewees came to work in them. In the newer samples, 21 of the 73 businesses researched (almost 29 per cent) pre-existed the interviewees entering them; the remainder numbered 52 (71 per cent).

prospective independent could not expect to survive as such for long. Of course, the range of skills these individuals possessed also largely determined the particular type of goods they could produce as independents. So a machinist who set up to make general repairs had to be exceptionally multi-skilled, in contrast to, say, a seamstress who sewed only sleeves or some other part of shirts. A broad range of skills obtained over many years of wage-work in different places – in other words, extensive work experience – is a feature that, in comparison with the two other types of proprietor, marks especially the artisans.

The apprenticeships and overall work experience of the sampled larger employers, which usually took place in a family business context, was very different from the analogous experience of those of a more humble background. While for the former it was primarily a matter of learning how to run an enterprise and the ways of commerce, whatever administrative competence the latter managed to obtain were limited to what they could pick up by observing their bosses, or the more entrepreneurial members of their family, and their own limited formal education. The sum of administrative competence so acquired was entirely insufficient for a successful business career – as proved by the continual and severe difficulties artisans are facing in the business world today.[9] However, since at their beginning of their working life the artisans and smaller employers had to focus chiefly on their technical training, it is not surprising that they do not feel at home in the business world. It is surely this lack of early socialisation into specific abilities and competences of a general managerial/administrative nature that now blocks them from expanding of their enterprises. This suggests that there is a qualitative difference between the apprenticeships of today's artisans and small employers on the one hand, and larger employers on the other.

The broad outlines given above indicate that the individuals who became artisans and small employers were initially working-class and ended up being highly skilled in their particular trade and in very good command of their craft. Those who inherited their businesses and mostly belong to the larger-employer category also had, in many instances but not all, first-hand experience of their trade because they had for long years worked manually in their family business or elsewhere as wage-workers (Cavounidis 1985; Koniordos 1996).

What kind of enterprise the interviewees were trained in also carries importance. It is no accident that artisans in all the trades, and roughly to the same extent, more often reported to have worked for wages in small than in medium-sized or large firms. The reverse was true for larger employers in both trades, with small employers standing between the two.

The numerical prevalence of small firms in the interviewees' work experience is in part explained by how the various industrial branches are structured in Greece, by the fact that in all of them small units greatly outnumber medium or large ones. This does not, however, explain the fact that artisans tend to have a background of working in small units, and larger employers in larger ones. The prevalence of

---

[9] The situation of those categorised as small employers was somewhat better than that of the artisans. This may be due to their relatively longer years of schooling.

small businesses is such as to elevate this feature into a principal structural particularity of the country's manufacturing sector (Greece hold the record on this in the EU-25). The pattern becomes meaningful when we consider that bosses/small-firm proprietors are quite similar to our artisan interviewees. The bosses, it is assumed, provided a model that a good number of their workers evaluated as positive and so attempted to emulate. It is understandable, therefore, that would-be artisans wanted to work in an environment similar to the one they hoped to establish themselves one day. If close working proximity made it possible for their employers to have them under constant surveillance, the reverse was also true. As employees observed their artisan-bosses they learned how workshops operated and how the business was organised – they picked up elements of a managerial/administrative know-how they could later put to use in their own businesses. I should add that the power of example and imitation might also be invoked, including the sample's petty capitalists. In their case, however, the end result was to continue a family business or replicate a more organised bigger one, but certainly one with which they were familiar.

From the perspective of skill too, small workshops have advantages for workers who aspire to become independent one day. Since they are routinely short of mechanised equipment, they invite unorthodox and innovative solutions to technical problems. This then encourages the workers to develop a more comprehensive breadth of specific traits (as well as general technical skills), to become multi-skilled and equipped with the ability to find solutions to problems encountered for the first time. In other words, it provides them with the technical prerequisites of artisanship, which involve possession of a range of skills.

Skilled workers then, by building their skill base, acquire the ability to do good work. This they will utilise later in their career when they make themselves independent and attract friends of friends and other acquaintances to them (weak ties). These latter may then operate as bridges to customers, who in turn will allow the skilled artisans to keep their new independence. Skill acquisition is indeed all-important. Without a wide range of skills, becoming self-employed is impossible.

We may, therefore, refer to a degree of 'path dependence' in the making of the small independents as both macro- and micro-level features converge to produce an effect. At the macro level there is wide diffusion of the smallish business firms and the capacity of the country's economy to sustain them. At the micro level are patterns of personal trajectories that are typical for artisans and smaller employers: impoverished background, little education, working from an early age, on-the-job skill development in technical and managerial matters. In such a context, independence becomes a viable and real option.

Other Prerequisites for Starting Up as an Independent

No artisan or other small business person set up independently on the spur of the moment. Leaving aside those who joined or were co-opted into a family-owned enterprise, or who bought shares in and joined an already functioning business (a rarity), the thought of becoming independent has been in the minds of smaller business proprietors since their first days as wage workers, as they themselves pointed out time and again during the interviews. However, once the decision to actually set up their own business was taken, the average time that elapsed until the new enterprise could be launched was reported to be from five to twelve months.[10]

Collecting Information

To establish a new artisanal workshop requires more than technical skill. The SECOND most vital element is information about matters such as the overall current market situation in one's particular trade, the location where demand is likely to be satisfactory, the availability and cost of the raw materials needed, and the means for financing the venture.

Passing on such information is informal and casual, taking place during working and leisure hours, right from the first day and throughout the interviewees' apprenticeships. The master craftsmen presented the long years of apprenticeship and then working as paid craftsmen as indispensable for their employees one day reaching, as themselves had done, the socially hallowed goal of becoming independent artisans. For the apprentices the person (usually a man) who had achieved this goal figured as a role model, and their proximity to him attested to the possibility that the ambition to become independent was indeed realisable. Detailed information circulated all the time, covering virtually all aspects of setting up on one's own. The subject of becoming and remaining independent was discussed every day with other workers on the job and elsewhere, with members of the family, or with colleagues who had more or less successfully taken the big leap already. It was an essential aspect of being socialised into the craft.

In addition, exposure to a particular trade was widespread even when there was no craft lore involvement. In the course of our research, data was collected rather systematically on the linkages between a would-be independent business person and someone closely related to him/her with inner knowledge of the job.[11] It was established that in the great majority of cases (roughly in 3 out of 4) there was at least one person, a close relation, who had introduced the artisan interviewee into that particular line of business – here excluding those with the same-trade family-business background. With the latter, in all instances of course, strong ties with such a person or persons, invariably a relative, operated as the bridge to independent proprietorship.

It was startling therefore when 45-50 per cent in both trades in both surveys answered my question 'Whom did you consult when you were planning to set up

---

[10] However, the starting-up period may be said to extend over another 12 to 18 months after launching the new enterprise, and throughout this time the survival of the young business remained an open issue.

[11] The strong/weak link dimension surfaced in the course of interviewing, but a number of respondents from the first sample were not surveyed directly on this. However, it is possible on the basis of fieldwork notes to trace for most cases the existence of such links.

independently?' with: 'Nobody.' However, most of them explained this by adding: 'I knew all about it already.' Since the relevant information had been steadily supplied over a number of years, this makes sense. It also verifies that collecting information, as part of the preparation for becoming independent, is a long-drawn process. The remaining half of the interviewees said they had discussed the issue with family members; a disproportionately high number of whom were among those involved with a family business. About 20 per cent of all machinist artisans specifically acknowledged asking the advice of fellow workers, and another 15 per cent had spoken to other artisans they knew personally. In other words, would-be independents surveyed their immediate milieu to obtain a precise picture of their likely prospects.

With the time of the decisive step approaching the need and usefulness of trusted relations in most cases became increasingly important. Once the picture had clarified through observation and casual discussions with acquaintances they had to proceed with the utmost circumspection because many of their prospective clients were already clients of their current bosses. They could trust only family members, close friends and workmates, with whom they often jointly set up in business. The support of close relations during this period took the form of supplying them with requisite information about various aspects of trading, organisation, legal stipulations and suchlike, as well as being psychological. The strong-tie relations also spread the word to potential customers about the high skill and workmanship of the budding entrepreneur. All these activities were intensified in the days just before start-up as well as immediately after, and included introductions to potentially useful people – perhaps someone with machinery to sell, or a potential wage-worker.

The Logistics of Setting Up Shop – Financing the Venture

Having acquired the necessary skills and information, the artisan or smaller employer now had to establish the actual workshop and to ensure its legalisation. The meant setting up a firm and registering it with the tax authorities, being issued with books for invoicing, accounting, etc., and a licence from the Ministry of Industry. A licence from the Fire Brigade is also needed. Registration with the appropriate insurance fund (TEBE) and payment of its dues is compulsory, and itself a prerequisite for registering for tax purposes: only then will the licence to operate be issued by the Ministry. This specifies the horse-power capacity of the machinery that may be installed, and in the area covered by my research has in the last fifteen years required complying with anti-pollution ordinances. Sooner or later a new firm must also register with the local Chamber of Artisans (for the samples in the Athens-Piraeus region) or regional Chamber (elsewhere). Registration with a Chamber may be postponed until a bank loan or an export/import license is needed, or the new entrepreneur wishes to bid for a State tender, all of which require such membership.

In some instances, especially when the workshop was part of an existing residential building, not all the legal stipulations for starting up were observed, even though the sums of money involved to conform with them were quite small. It was not unusual that, once a license had been obtained, initial compliance with the absolutely indispensable requirements was followed by the systematic evasion of official rules and regulations.

What could not be dodged in the physical establishment of the workshop was paying the rent for the premises (usually several months in advance), installing a telephone (which used to be a long-drawn out affair, but is not so any more), arranging for the supply of the lower-price industrial electricity, and the purchase of at least a minimum of machinery and hand-tools which, with only two exceptions, all interviewees said they had in their possession when they launched their new business. The bulk of this mechanical equipment was second-hand. Raw materials could be bought on credit until the first cash payments from customers came in. While the necessary start-up capital was not very large, some cash had to be available at the outset. In addition, a certain financial reserve was needed to carry newly independent artisan through the first period when regular work was not yet assured. How these funds were procured represents the THIRD key-factor in setting up on one's own.

A partial solution lay in the some artisans working two jobs for a time both before and after the foundation of their new business. A significant segment of machinist artisans (about 30 per cent), a smaller one in the garment trade (11 per cent), and a sizeable one (17 per cent) among those in other trades acknowledged that while they were still wage-working they also did some work of their own.

Many of them reported that their boss knew about this and even supported them by allowing them the use of his machinery. It appears that here we have the operation of craft-lore norms of conduct between masters and employees. Also, these side activities played a significant role in acquiring for the prospective entrepreneur both customers and a reputation, and later helped to make the new independent enterprise a success. Overall, however, it was personal labour that was the chief element for securing the necessary start-up funds.

The interviewees were asked how they had managed to obtain the money to purchase their mechanical equipment, which was one of their main expenditures, of course. The reported sources of finance were as follows. Among artisans and small employers, savings were by far the most frequently mentioned source of paying for equipment. This was followed by bills of exchange, a widely available credit facility. The difference between the artisans and small employers was that the former did not report receiving any financial assistance from their families. For the larger employers, taking out bank loans and obtaining financing from 'other' sources prevailed over financing derived from ability to work manually. Only a few of the interviewees said they took out loans to establish their business, and they were mostly among those that had inherited a business. All generalisations can only be tentative, but two things do stand out: (i) larger employers secured bank loans much more often than did the other categories; and (ii), the artisans obtained their (very limited) loans mostly from relatives or friends and rarely from banks. This indicates the different opportunities open to the different types of proprietor.

It is worth noting that a good part of the machine tools purchased by the machinists while setting up shop, especially brand-new ones, were of cheap technologically mature East European make. Equipment of this kind was resold a number of times. Both the new and second-hand machine tools were either automatic or semi-automatic; no instances were reported of purchases during the starting-up period of the technologically advanced CNC (computer numerically controlled) machine tools. The representatives of the companies concerned, or those who resold the equipment, accepted payment by bills of exchange. On the other hand, most mechanical equipment for setting up independently in garment production and other trades was purchased new or second hand, and was of various West-European or Japanese makes. These too were not very advanced technologically, and did not usually incorporate electronics in their control mechanisms. For the most part they consisted of heavy-duty sewing machines, specialist sewing machines, and cutting equipment. Again, the sellers of brand-new or used machine equipment accepted payment by bills of exchange.

One may well wonder how the seller could feel certain that payment would eventually be made. It is here that the network of ex-bosses, customers, friends or workmates who were already independent came into full operation. The links had to be of the strong-tie type; this was an absolute must. Why? Because what was at stake for such persons bridging for the perspective independents involved the advancement of credit. In such instances strong-tie relations act as a guarantee that the money will be paid, even though in many cases such intermediaries take no personal legal responsibility. It is extremely rare for an acquaintance to be asked to act as guarantor, and only possible if the link with such a person is a strong one.

It may be concluded from the above that purchasing machinery, and by extension setting up an independent business, was arduous for the artisans but not impossible. The availability of credit facilities did, of course, play a very important role. Particularly bills of exchange were indispensable for the establishment of new and independent workshops. I should add that in the second survey the situation with respect to the financing of purchases of machinery and even of working capital had changed dramatically. As a result of changes in the banking system associated with Greece's membership in the European Union, it was quite easy to obtain small sums of bank financing, and the formal or informal need for a guarantor being much reduced.

Another factor that kept the overall capital requirements for starting up relatively low was the existence in Greek manufacturing of a plethora of small and very small units, as mentioned already.[12] Being uniformly ill-equipped and with little constant capital, they effected a low level of entry costs that made starting-up

---

[12] According to the available statistical evidence, the largest concentration of artisans in European Union and the rest of Europe is to be found in Greece, Italy coming a close second: Statistical evidence on micro-enterprises (businesses employing from 1 to 10 persons) in manufacturing indicates that in 1988 their share in Greece was 93.7 per cent (ESYE 1994), while in 1996 in Italy it stood at 83.6 per cent (Eurostat 1998).

for prospective independent artisans and smaller employers quite feasible financially.[13]

Finally, the interviewees' initial labour costs were also very low since, as already noted, newly independent artisans relied heavily on their own and the all-important if poorly remunerated but widely available family labour. In summary, therefore, financing the new venture was made possible, in the initial survey, by extra work, access to semi-formal credit (bills of exchange), and low start-up costs. In the subsequent survey, the hiring of workers had become very probable for new start-ups as a plethora of newly available and inexpensive, mostly unskilled, illegal/semi-legal foreign workers had become available and were desperately searching for a job (see Koniordos 2000a). Therefore, while start-up costs remained limited, the work capacity of the newly independent could be expanded.

As already noted, the role of close kin is negligible with respect to financial assistance for artisans and smaller employers (for instance when purchasing machinery), although it is more important with larger employers. With the latter, strong relations were able to give them some help by assuring that credit was extended to them. This indicates an alignment with Granovetter's thesis about a class-connectedness in the impact that the distribution of strong/weak ties has. To put it differently, it indicates a class-connectedness in the impact that the distribution of benefits from participating in social structures, i.e. social capital (see Portes 1998), has.

The Customers

Attracting customers is the FOURTH key element for establishing an independent workshop. Although many interviewees decided to set up on their own at a time the country was experiencing a period of economic expansion, this in itself could not guarantee customers for the new business. Besides, attracting customers is no easy matter for yesterday's wage-workers with almost non-existent linkages to the market. For most of them, a major approach to customers, and often the only one, is through their former employers. These can help actively, either by placing orders with the new workshop themselves or, when specialities do not overlap, by

---

[13] The small start-up sums are illustrated in the following two instances. Although as a rule interviewees showed a marked aversion to giving actual figures, two of them did mention the amounts with which they had launched their enterprises, and these were extremely modest. In the first case (machinist artisan No. 225), the interviewee set up with 45,000 drachmas in 1966 (then *ca* 130 euros) he had inherited from his father and with some bills of exchange. In the second case (machinist No. 235) the four partners who jointly started on their own in 1969 each contributed 40,000 drachmas (*ca* 115 euros), and took out one million drachmas (*ca* 2,882 euros) in bills of exchange to buy their mechanical equipment (at the time the U.S. dollar-drachma parity was 1:30). From allusions and remarks made in passing, and from the general picture of mechanised equipment in the workshops, I received the strong impression that start-up costs in the garment and other industries were much lower still than in machining.

referring some of their own customers and bringing the new business together with various subcontracting networks and the market generally.

Another way for the new independents to acquire a clientele of their own is to try to 'steal' or lure away their ex-employers' customers and/or pursue a similar specialisation – which of course means competing with them. The new entrepreneurs' strongpoint is their lower price, which goes hand in hand with faster work and especially with longer working hours. For their ex-employers and competitors, who invariably are artisans and small employers themselves, such a practice represents a very serious challenge and – at least in some cases when a craftsman had set up a new concern or more rarely left a partnership to become independent – had led to an all-out war.

On the other hand, the fact that newly established proprietors try to do business with clients they originally met while working for their former masters is something generally acknowledged and recognised. As seen from the interviews, the small employers quite take it for granted that this will happen at the end of a lengthy apprenticeship and training. Some of them even mentioned that they pass on some of their customers to the newly independent ex-workers of theirs because, after all, 's/he is one of us'. As it has been already indicated, this suggests the existence of craft lore and of antecedent strong ties between ex-workers and their ex-bosses; ties that are significant in supporting the former in the course of planning, preparing, and setting up workshops of their own.

Whatever the circumstances, the departure of core workers who make themselves independent entails an element of threat for their former masters, and in some instances puts an abrupt end to the personal relationship between artisan and master craftsman. The worker's eventual departure is a possibility that hangs over every small business, of course, and once it has happened, that newly independent artisans exert constant competitive pressure on the established ones because their main competition comes precisely from their former employers. The ambivalence of the situation is well expressed in the response of a machinist artisan when asked whether he ever referred any of his customers to his newly independent ex-workers. 'Yes', he said. 'After we've come to a brotherly understanding' (No. 224).

It becomes clear from the interviews that in both machining and the garments trades, as well as in the remaining ones, help in securing customers also came via the widespread networks of subcontracting, that link small producers to one another as well as to larger producers – even though, as we shall see in the next section, my interviewees did not realise the extent of the subcontracting nexus. Subcontracting relations often contain an element of patronage. They are not business exchanges simply on the basis of mutuality, but rather business exchanges on the basis of favour and obligation. For example, in return for help from the erstwhile employer, the newly independent artisan may undertake to do work for him, even for very low remuneration. Depending on circumstances, this unequal relationship sometimes extends well beyond the initial period of starting up the independent business. This can happen when the new business has not managed to attract sufficient customers of its own, and/or is actively prevented from doing so by the putter-out patron (particularly so, I found, in the case of women homeworkers in garment-making).

Weak ties were also extensively utilised for attracting a clientele. In several instances, especially when strong ties had proved insufficient, acquaintances were actively mobilised to introduce the new shop to their own network.

Organisational Patterns

The transition to independent proprietorship usually took place in one of two organisational contexts, which in many cases overlapped: that of the family, and that of partnerships. Because this involved a pooling of resources and skills, it made it much easier to set up the new venture than if a prospective independent went about it alone. Such arrangements also provided a more efficient matrix for eventually expanding the firm, given that they allowed elementary divisions of labour among the partners and/or family members.

In roughly half of all cases, the organisational form for setting up shop independently was that of partnership. It is interesting that partnership is the dominant organisational form among machinists of all types – i.e. for 67 per cent of them. This may mean that when, as in their case, a more substantial starting-up capital is required, only partnerships are able to pull together the necessary resources. While preparing to be independent, 40 per cent of all my interviewed artisans formed partnerships, 64 per cent of the small employers, and 71 per cent of the larger employers.

Moreover, roughly 45 per cent of the interviewees of both surveys had been partners in at least one business prior to their current one, which as a rule, manufactured the same or similar items. Regardless of the causes of the break-up of the earlier partnership, this will have provided them with some practical experience in administration while it lasted, and in this sense made them somewhat better equipped for their new venture. Each partnership involved two or (less often) three partners; in 70-80 per cent of the cases at least one partner was kin. Apart from family members, partners may be former workmates or former bosses (which indicates co-option into a partnership); or they may have met in the army and become friends.

This means that for half of the interviewees finding a job by creating one themselves by means of becoming independent is clearly dependent for forming partnerships on the prior existence of strong ties. The remainder were attempts at single proprietorship and independence.[14] It appears that even among those who embarked on a solo business career, strong ties were the most important factor for

---

[14] Analytically the patterns of organisation are as follows. In the *first sample*, 49 out of 100 businesses were formed as partnerships (much more often in machining). In 39 of these (or 80 per cent) at least one partner was kin. Sole proprietors numbered 51 (more often in garments). In the *second sample*, 38 out of 73 businesses (52 per cent) were formed as partnerships (again, much more often in machining), in 28 of which (71 per cent) at least one partner was kin. Sole proprietors numbered 35 (48 per cent).

establishing themselves independently. If for instance, their ex-bosses relinquished clients or put out work with them, this may not have supplied them with enough orders to become independent in all cases, but it certainly will have greatly assisted them with surviving in the early and most crucial months.

Why Independence?

When considering the difficulties skilled craftsmen encounter in setting up and operating their workshops, it becomes understandable why they regard it as an achievement and personal triumph. This brings us to the reasons why artisans and other independents become independent, and what alternatives were at their disposal at the time when they were considering their future career.

The available alternatives were both limited and not at all promising. The majority of the artisans and half of the small employers, but very few of the larger employers, thought that they would have had to go on working for wages had they not become independent. The remainder did not know what else they could have done, and said that due to their lack of education they had no viable alternative. A mere handful of the interviewees thought that they might have found some kind of commercial position. Evidently, none of these prospects were considered as acceptable alternatives at the time of changing from wage-labour to becoming independent.

The most pervasive reason why both artisans and small employers opted for becoming independent was an extrinsic one: namely, to improve their income. Also, it was important for them to know they were able to stand on their own feet. In addition, artisans were impelled towards independence because it would allow them to do creative and innovative work without constant supervision.

Women artisans also emphasised that independence gave them the possibility to care for their dependants. The existence of the pertinent skills and a family tradition were also of some significance. To a limited extent small employers were motivated by the prospect of independence because it permitted doing 'creative', i.e. their *own* work.

There is a difference in emphasis between the main two trades researched, which centres on the attitude to the work as such. Machinist craftsmen gave far greater importance to the work experience than did artisans/small employers in garment production. No such considerations applied to the larger employers, whose motives were different altogether. They were mostly concerned with maintaining their social position by following the course ready laid out for them in the existing family-owned firm. Indeed, the much higher frequency with which the self-employed and the smaller among my interviewees expressed a strong work ethic agrees with the psychologist C. N. Weaver's (1997) thesis that the prevalence of a strong work ethic amongst these social categories is not a myth. It also makes sense: since it is their own personal labour and skills that constitute their prime assets it is reasonable for them to stress these factors on which their individual agency largely rests when setting out to carve a life career.

Overall it was a variety of factors that made my interviewees reject other options in favour of setting up as independent artisans. The emergent pattern clearly shows that the most persuasive motive concerned the good economic prospects they hoped this would open up. While this was justified up to a point, the artisans' expectations were probably somewhat exaggerated, because they had already decided against skilled wage-labour as an alternative.

The second motivation mentioned was the intrinsic satisfaction felt by employees at the prospect of being freed of the authority of the boss or/and foreman. Moreover, being one's own master is perceived in Greece as a positive social value, and at least ideologically helps a prospective entrepreneur to achieve independence. To put their abilities and skills to work creatively and for their own benefit was found to be psychologically fulfilling for the small business person and to foster a sense of self-respect. This is also true of the overall improvement in social position that results from business independence, which is evident in comments such as 'I became the master of my household' that interviewees very often voiced. Increased self-respect and social respectability were an intrinsic part of what they expected from setting up on their own as independents. For the rest, the composite nature of their motives reflects the opportunities that were open to them.

Discussion and Concluding Remarks

Because its fragmented structure and the small size makes the market in Greece of only limited interest for powerful and well organised investors, these features act to effectively protect the small business proprietors from a potentially very threatening competition. It also means that it is possible to set up and go on operating small manufacturing businesses, but only for those who are themselves skilled craftsmen in their field. Skill by itself is not enough to go up the social ladder. For skilled workers getting a job, or getting a better job, means one of two things: to move to a bigger company, preferably a State-owned one, or to create one. The latter means crating a job for themselves by establishing a very small business. To do so they need all the support they can muster.

What has been said above shows that would-be independent small entrepreneurs have extensively employed pre-existing social ties. Kin, friends and workmates have been utilised, sometimes even ex-bosses, but also more distant relations to collect information. In addition, the interviewees systematically used these direct strong-tie relations to develop indirect weak ones (transivity). It was, therefore, not only psychological support, personal guarantees, and information that strong ties themselves offered to my interviewees directly, but they also acted as bridges across social boundaries and brought for instance suppliers or customers to the prospective independent enterprises, which were indispensable if the business was to survive.[15]

While therefore, strong ties are an absolute must for certain type of bridging (for instance when credit is an issue or for forming partnerships), weak ties have also been utilised (e.g. to attract customers). Therefore, these networks of support are heterogeneous.

Could my interviewees have achieved their independent position without the benefit and support extended to them by their social networks? I think that the answer is no. It seems that in this instance especially the strong-type ties were instrumental in generating jobs via setting up independent businesses. This marks a divergence from Granovetter's thesis that lower-class people rely more on weak ties for obtaining information on how to find a job. This will depend, of course, on the specific type of job being sought, which in our case is that of a self-employed person. It should not, therefore, be seen as an outright rejection of the usefulness about the strength of weak ties argument.

In the cases here studied, obtaining a job means primarily to rely on oneself, on one's individual agency, skills, workmanship, and dexterity. Ties are important, but getting a job as a self-employed person is not that much an issue of strong or weak ties, or of the degree of social capital benefits that membership to the corresponding networks may secure. Yes, skilled workers do draw from their milieu whatever assistance they can get their hands on, but their particular network of relations both weak and strong, despite having its uses, is not decisive for obtaining the status of the independent self-employed (and the job that goes with it) – as is it in the original strong/weak-ties discussion. What is of key importance here is the different socio-economic context of the job-opening that is being sought. The original Granovetter analysis implied that this context was that of a bureaucratic Fordist work-organisation in an advanced capitalist country. In the cases I have been discussing, the macro-level context is that of a country of the semi-periphery, and the micro-level context that of personalistic independent small businesses.[16]

It is noteworthy that not only were the interviewees anxious to utilise their ties for becoming independent, but that those with whom they were linked accepted being 'exploited' and indeed appear to have been quite energetically active to that end. It may be that because the Greek social context is less formal-bureaucratic, the methods used for recruitment are personalistic, certainly more personalistic than those of the developed western countries.

---

[15] Granovetter's point that weak ties 'are significant in that they are far more likely to be bridges than are strong ties' (Granovetter 1983, p. 208) does not seem to apply in the case of the support networks under discussion.

[16] I will therefore argue that although Granovetter's approach is very useful in the search for deep structures (Wellman 1983, p. 157), its limits must be acknowledged. These limits are evident in his first analysis of 1973, but are rather lost, because of overextending their explanatory radius of his thesis, in his second analysis on strong/weak ties of 1983 (a rather similar point is implied by E. Morlicchio, see this volume).

I do not think this explanation goes far enough. The patterns of activating network members are such as to suggest the existence of a common cultural parameter, according to which being independent is a highly appraised positive value. Furthermore, I think that there is a common awareness of this cultural dimension. It is this common cultural element rooted in the tradition of petty ownership that has remained intact over time in Greece,[17] which explains why, although the two surveys discussed are ten years apart, the support both extended and received has not diminished or changed in identifiable manner.

References

Baines, S. and Wheelock, J. (1998), 'Reinventing Traditional Solutions: Job creation, gender and the micro-business household', *Work, Employment & Society* 12(4), pp. 579-601.

Burt, R. S. (1997), 'The Contingent Value of Social Capital', *Administrative Science Quarterly*, 42, pp. 339-65.

Cavounidis, J. (1985), 'Family and Productive Relations: Artisan and Worker Households in Athens', unpublished Ph.D. Thesis, University of London (LSE).

Coleman, J. S. (1988), 'Social Capital in the Creation of Human Capital', *American Journal of Sociology*, 94 (Supplement), pp. S95-S120.

ESYE (1994), *Statistical Yearbook of Greece 1990-91*, Athens, National Statistical Service of Greece.

European Commission (1994), *Development, Competitiveness Employment – White Book*, Luxembourg, Official Publications Service of the European Communities (in Greek).

European Commission (1995), *Commission Report on Recent Policy Initiatives at Member State Level for Small and Medium-sized Enterprises* [Report presented by the Commission to the Madrid European Council], CSE (95) 2087.

European Commission (2000), *The European Observatory for SMEs – Sixth Report*, Luxembourg, Official Publications Service of the European Communities.

EUROSTAT (1998), *Database 'SBS size class'*, Luxembourg: Statistical Service of European Communities.

Granovetter, M. (1973), 'The Strength of Weak Ties', *American Journal of Sociology*, 78 (6), pp. 1360-1380.

Granovetter, M. (1983), 'The Strength of Weak Ties: A network theory revisited', *Sociological Theory*, 1, pp. 201-233.

Granovetter, M. (1985), 'Economic Action and Social Structure: The problem of embeddedness', *American Journal of Sociology*, 91, pp. 481-510.

Granovetter, M. (1995[1974]), *Getting A Job: A study of contacts and careers*, 2nd edition, Chicago, University of Chicago Press.

---

[17] This unbroken link may be contrasted with other instances (such as those referred to by Baines and Wheelock (1998)) in which the 'traditional' solution of self-employment was discovered anew, often enough under the guidance and active assistance of an ultra-modern, supra-national entity, i.e. the EU apparatus of small and medium-sized enterprises (European Commission 1995).

Koniordos, S. M. (1996), 'Artisans in Late Development: An investigation of Athenian small producers in the machining and garments industries', Unpublished PhD thesis, University of London.

Koniordos, S. M. (2000a), 'Power Structures in Labour Relations: Continuities and Discontinuities in employer control strategies in small manufacturing enterprises', in *Power Structures and Relations in Contemporary Greece*, Athens, Sakis Karagiorgas Foundation, pp. 818-37 (in Greek).

Koniordos, S. M. (2000b), 'Development, Artisans and the 1967-1974 Dictatorship', *Review of Social Research* 103, pp. 27-56 (in Greek).

Koniordos, S. M. (2001), *Towards a Sociology of Artisans*, Aldershot, Ashgate.

Koniordos, S. M. (2005-forthcoming), *Comparative Investigation of Greek Artisans*, Athens, Gutenberg (in Greek).

McCarty, C. (2002), 'Structure in Personal Networks', *Journal of Social Structure*, 3(1), March 20.

Mouzelis, N. (1987), *Parliamentarism and Industrialisation in the Semi-Periphery: Greece, the Balkans, Latin America*, Athens, Themelio (in Greek).

Panayiotopoulou, R. (1996), 'Rational Self-centered Practices in the Context of an "Irrational" Political System', in Ch. Lyritzis, E. Nikolakopoulos and D. Sotiropoulos (eds), *Society and Politics: Facets of the third Greek democracy 1974-1994*, Athens, Themelio, pp. 119-38 (in Greek).

Papataxiarchis, E. (1992), 'The World of the Coffee-house: Identity and exchange in male commensalism', in E. Papataxiarchis and T. Paradellis (eds), *Identities and Gender in Contemporary Greece*, Athens, Kastaniotis Editions and University of the Aegean, pp. 209-50 (in Greek).

Piore, M. and Sabel, C. (1984), *The Second Industrial Divide: Possibilities for prosperity*. New York, Basic Books.

Portes, A. (1998), 'Social Capital: Its origins and applications in modern sociology', *Annual Review of Sociology*, 24, pp. 1-24.

Scott, J. (2000), *Social Networks Analysis: A handbook*, second edition, London, Sage.

Swedberg, R. (1990), *Economics and Sociology. Redefining their Boundaries: Conversations with economics and sociologist*, Princeton, Princeton University Press.

Trigilia, C. (2001), 'Social Capital and Local Development', *European Journal of Social Theory*, 4 (4).

Tsoukalas, K. (2000), '"Free-riders" in Wonderland', in P. Kafetzis (ed.), K. Tsoukalas, *Journey in Discourse and History: Texts 1969-1996*, volume two, Athens, Plethron Editions, pp. 143-82 (in Greek).

Weaver, C. N. (1997), 'Examining a Work Ethic Myth about Self-employed People', *Psychological Reports*, 81, pp. 1075-81.

Wellman, B. (1983), 'Network Analysis: Some basic principles', in R. Collins (ed.), *Sociological Theory - 1983*, San Francisco, Jossey-Bass, pp. 155-200.

PART C
INVESTIGATIONS OF EASTERN EUROPEAN CAPITALISM

Chapter 9

Informal Institutional Arrangements and Tax Evasion in the Russian Economy[*]

Vadim Radaev

Informalisation of Rules: Analytical Model

It has been widely acknowledged in the last decade that the state of the post-communist Russia is weak and disorganised while the economy suffers from the lack of formal rules. Establishing of the rule of law and increasing formalisation of rules are seen as the core element of market building. According to this view, the main progress is to be achieved by filling the gaps in the legislative and regulatory basis. Recently, this view was challenged by new expert claims that transitional period has been completed in Russia: nearly all-necessary formal institutional arrangements have already emerged, and the main task is to set the new legislation at work (Nesterenko 2001).

In my opinion, both views overestimate the significance of the generalised legal norms. We would argue that the main problem today lies neither with an 'institutional vacuum', nor the abundance of formal rules, but rather with the structure of these rules and the way they are introduced into the economy. Thus, principal links between formal and informal rules are to be at the core of our analysis (on this issue, see North 1992, p. 6).

Since the well-known study by Ernando De Soto 'The Other Path', many scholars tend to treat emergence of the efficient formal rules as a consequence of the formalisation of customary rules and informal practices developed by economic agents on a spontaneous basis. According to this view, new formal rules are not viable if they are not embedded in the norms and practices of everyday life. We think that this insight is very productive. However, it does not grasp all the complexity of the institutional dynamics. And we would consider a different approach of establishing links between formal and informal rules which looks at the

---

[*] This paper was presented at the 5th Annual Meeting of International Society for New Institutional Economics, Session II-B 'Taxation as an Institution' (Berkeley, USA, 13-15 September 2001).
I would like to thank Masha Dobryakova for her kind support in the English language editing of this paper.

things right the other way round. To characterise this approach, we introduce the notion of the informalisation of rules.

Let us start with a principal definition we base our arguments on. *The informalisation of rules is a continuous transformation of institutions when formal rules are largely substituted by informal ones and built into informal relationships.*

It is assumed that the actors know the existing formal rules but avoid them on a day-to-day basis.[1] It does not mean that these rules are entirely rejected. Rather they are built into a sophisticated system of informal arrangements and widely used as an umbrella for flexible informal strategies.

Our analytical model of *the logic of informalisation* includes the following main elements:

1. Formal rules are imposed by public officials in a way that leaves room to act at ones' discretion and create a situation of uncertainty for economic agents.
2. Compliance with formal rules is associated with high cost, the result being that economic agents create innovative governance structures to avoid formal rules systematically.
3. Public officials establish selective control, in which formal rules are used to create conditions for extortion and to set selective pressures on economic agents.
4. Economic agents bargain with the public officials on the conditions, on which formal rules are implemented.
5. Multiple arguments and interpretations are produced to justify practices of informalisation.

In this paper, we go through all these consequent elements of informalisation. An evidence from entrepreneurial behaviour with regard to tax avoidance and tax evasion illustrates all major statements.[2]

Data sources. Empirical part of our analysis is based on the data collected in the course of two 1997-1998 surveys. These include a standardised survey of 227 entrepreneurs and top managers in 21 regions of Russia and a set of 96 in-depth interviews with entrepreneurs and top managers. The author and a research team of the Centre Political Technologies (Moscow) conducted the surveys.[3] The research was supported by the U.S. Centre for International Private Enterprise (CIPE) (for detailed description of research outcomes, see Radaev 1998b).

In this paper, we use mainly qualitative data of the in-depth interviews (96 in total). They were conducted from May 1997 to April 1998. The main focus was

---

[1] Facts of concealment of taxable legal transactions should not be confused with criminal activity involving transactions forbidden by the law (in more detail, see Radaev 2001, pp. 334-7).

[2] For a detailed review of the literature on tax evasion in transitional economies, see Pirttila 1999.

[3] We would like to thank colleagues from the Centre for Political Technologies headed by Igor Bunin for the organization of surveys and discussion of the first research outcomes.

made upon the emerging areas of non-state businesses. The sample also included 27 interviews conducted by the Centre for Political Technologies previously in 1993. It gave an opportunity to trace changes in the five-year period that preceded the survey.

Introduction of Formal Rules

The first element of our analytical model is the introduction of new formal rules by the authorities. In our opinion, it corresponds to the principal logic of institutional changes, at least for the case of Russia. Most of these changes have been normally initiated by the state, while economic agents used to adapt to the new conditions in a flexible way.

According to a conventional statement of the new institutional economics, new law is introduced to specify property rights in some area of activity, and therefore, decreases transaction costs (Eggertsson 1990, p. 16). Russian experience often demonstrates quite the opposite. An obtrusion of formal rules by the authorities leads to additional transaction costs. These rules are formulated and enforced in a way that leaves a large room for uncertainty and even creates uncertainty itself. The main reason for this is that legislative and regulatory documents include very general or/and ambivalent statements, which become subject to different interpretations. We would not insist that Russian lawmakers consciously bring controversial wording into the law provisions. However, we would argue that after lengthy negotiations (*soglasovaniya*) between legislative and governmental bodies these documents do contain statements with uncertain meanings, which are used later by civil servants to produce diverse evaluations and accounts. Given that property rights are not properly specified and the whole regulatory system is complicated, economic agents are not able to follow all formal rules. And all their failures are interpreted as violations of the law.

> Laws contradict each other... One accounting officer would insist on one mode of accounting. Another would come and say it must be different. A third one would suggest a third way. And everyone would be right. It is pretty convenient for tax inspectors. They can impose fines on any enterprise (co-owner of a retail chain).

The Russian system of taxation is a most apt illustration to this. Speaking about their most burning problems, businessmen normally rank taxation issues first: (1) The total tax burden for the Russian firms is considered prohibitive (although many tax rates in Russia are comparable with the level adopted in many other European countries); (2) Tax reporting and payment procedures are complicated and non-transparent, the number of taxes and exemptions is large; (3) Excessive taxation is accompanied by excessive regulation. Numerous regulations are issued to instruct on how to report on revenues and calculate payments. Not surprisingly, these rules are often interpreted in a way unfavourable for economic agents; (4) The Russian tax system is subject to frequent changes, and it is difficult, especially for small enterprises unable to cover the costs of expensive accounting services, to follow all the requirements.

> One has to hire a dozen of accountants and auditors just to fill in all the forms properly (director of a consulting firm).

Periodically, attempts to restructure the tax system are made. For instance, an abridged system of taxation and reporting was introduced for a certain category of small enterprises in 1995. Later, in 1999, a single tax for imputed income was adopted for small firms in many regions of Russia. However, all these partial reforms led to rather ambiguous outcomes.

This situation has a negative impact on long-term business strategies. Large enterprises suffer primarily from the high taxation rates because it is difficult for them to hide their significant cash flows, while small companies suffer rather from the complexity of the tax system and the lack of skilled accounting support. All in all, there is a well-established view that it is absolutely impossible to pay all the taxes without ruining the enterprise.

> Any enterprise, if it just started to pay all the taxes, *would be ruined in a couple of months* (manager of a financial audit firm).

Adaptive Strategies of Economic Agents

What is a normal response of economic agents to the uncertainty created by the new formal rules? In terms of A. Hirschman, they may pursue three types of strategy: exit, voice, and loyalty (Hirshman 1970). In our case loyalty means compliance to formal rules. Voice strategy is defined as public (political or legal) questioning of formal rules and ways of their enforcement. Exit strategy presumes silent avoidance of these rules.

Russian entrepreneurs do not express much loyalty with regard to formal rules and regulatory agencies, which issue and enforce them. On the contrary, according to many surveys of Russian entrepreneurs in the 1990s, pressures implied by the tax system present the main issue of complaints (Chepurenko 1998). At the same time, it is not often that entrepreneurs so discriminated challenge the inconsistencies through formal political and legal channels. Institutions representing their political interests are not well developed. Arbitration Courts are not very efficient and hardly can be considered independent. Thus, it is the opportunistic exit strategy that becomes the main mode of action for the entrepreneur. As it is impossible either to follow all the rules, or prove the discriminatory character of their enforcement, economic agents start to avoid them systematically. Even if numerous complaints and public voice strategy are ever used, they are but a camouflage for the exit strategy.

Russian entrepreneurs have proved to be very innovative in inventing informal schemes, which allow to overcome the discrepancies of formal rules and not to confront the authorities at that. Normally, after a new formal rule constraining entrepreneurial activity has been adopted, it takes less than one week to find a way to evade it. The best corporate and free-lance lawyers and accountants are invited to build such a 'coping scheme'.

By and large, economic actors respond to the discrepancies of taxation system rationally. They build up flexible governance structures that facilitate tax avoidance and evasion. Such structures include sophisticated *chains of affiliated firms*, which are formally independent but actually present different parts of the same business group (on business groups, see Granovetter 1994; Pappe 2000). So called 'grey schemes' (semi-legal modes of activity) are worked out to achieve organised diversity (Stark 2001), which produces ambiguity of assets and numerous modes of evaluation of resources. In the Russian economy, business groups are normally illegible and non-transparent for the outsiders (controlling bodies, competitors, and potential investors). They become an instrument stimulating capital flight, assets stripping, tax evasion, and money laundering.

Long chains of firms within one business group make it difficult to trace the origin of money and the destination of the cash flow. Each transaction is legal while the entire business scheme obviously violates the law.

Tax avoidance and tax evasion practices within business groups are based on three distinct strategies, namely:

- illegal activity;
- concealment of legal activity outcomes;
- political bargaining.

Let us consider these strategies briefly. We omit *illegal activity*, as firms not officially registered and therefore not reporting to the tax authorities carry it out.

Concealment of the legal activity outcomes is the most important strategy in this respect. It is implemented with the help of the following instruments:

- corruption deals;
- institutional fictions;
- games of exchange.

Corruption deals consist in direct bribing of the tax inspectors, their bosses, and powerful officials who are able to influence tax inspections. Bribery is a widely spread and extensively debated though not necessary strategy. There are strategies that do not attract so much public attention as corruption but are very important as well. They use institutional fictions and games of exchange.

Most prominent example of the *institutional fiction* is the pseudo-firm or 'one-day' firm (*firma-odnodnevka*), which is established especially for shadow dealings. It operates for less than three months, and then it is simply abandoned without reporting to the tax authorities.

They establish a new firm, which is to disappear in three months without tax reporting... Major law firms that know all the details of our inconsistent legislation are involved in that... The regular chain is the following: a Russian firm – a western firm. Money is transferred to the West. And everything is absolutely in accordance with the law. They charge from 2 to 5 per cent for their services (head of a multiprofile firm).

Such one-day firms are used to obtain bank loans and advance payments, which are never paid back. They accumulate debts for tax payments and then disappear. No bribes are required here. And the costs of registration and operation are minimal.

Games of exchange, in their turn, provide effective methods of concealing revenues by balancing on the edge between legal and illegal transactions. Most frequent methods are listed below:

- fictitious transactions;
- non-equivalent exchanges;
- intended sanctions.

We call *transactions fictitious* when accounting books fix non-existing deals between the firm and a market intermediary or an institutional fiction. Such transactions may involve advance payments for the goods no one is going to deliver, or payments for marketing research, which has never been done. False export transfers are arranged to recover VAT payments. Insurance premiums are paid for contingencies that are very unlikely to ever happen (i.e. the money inevitably goes away) or, on the contrary, happen with one hundred per cent probability (i.e. the money inevitably comes back).

- *Non-equivalent exchange* may happen when the following actions are undertaken.
- Contracts are signed to the benefit of an 'outside' affiliated firm and the value of transferred goods and services is under- or overestimated.
- Barter exchanges and mutual set-offs are convenient for buying and selling goods above and below their market value.
- Business dealers speculate on the differences in internal transfer prices, and gaps between nominal and real value of the bills of exchange.
- Stocks of different liquidity are exchanged.
- Loans are provided at interest rates, which are higher than those in the market.

The schemes described above help to conceal the real value and contribute to asset stripping.

Finally, *intended sanctions* are applied. Unrealistic contract obligations are taken on, which entail serious fines in favour of affiliated firms. Transfer of mortgage to these firms is practiced as a means for the false debt repayment.

Most tax evasion strategies are based on the following principles:

- separation of companies adding value from sales and financial flows which are passed over to affiliated firms;
- stripping of assets from producing companies to affiliated firms;
- double accounting or destruction of accounting documents by affiliated firms.

Entrepreneurs publicly called such strategies an 'optimisation of tax payments'. Some entrepreneurs admit in their interviews rather openly that successful tax optimisation allows them to conceal a significant share of their profit and wages from taxation claims.

> Only lazy people do not get away with tax payments. Everyone turns to legal or illegal ways of tax evasion (director of a marketing firm).

> Today, the Russians live in conditions of mass civil disobedience (said with respect to tax payments – VR) (head of a group of companies).

There are considerable discrepancies in the words of entrepreneurs. In public, they used to complain about the high level of taxation. At the same time, in the interviews, they easily admit that they are very far from paying all the taxes. There is a feeling that public complaints are largely of a ritual character while many agents are satisfied with the current situation.

> Not all commercial dealers would like to see the tax system changed. Its imperfections allow them to justify their minor financial tricks (owner of a trading firm).

Thus, discrepancies in the tax system are reflected in and maintained by the incentives of economic agents.

Selective Control of Opportunistic Behaviour

It should be noted that public officials are well aware of governance structures and financial schemes designed for tax evasion and money laundering. From the formal viewpoint, the authorities are supposed to check all the enterprises and stop their illegal and semi-legal activity. There is a *regular (planned) control*, which is carried out in accordance with predetermined administrative rules and covers all economic entities. However, this sort of control is rather superficial. Well aware of the opportunism of economic agents, public officials are still unable to monitor all their operations adequately. Inspectors often lack technical equipment, comprehensive databases, and the necessary professional skills. Above all, they are not very much interested in such a total surveillance because it is costly. As a result, there are more evadable and less evadable sectors in the economy in terms of taxes (Jung, Snow and Trandel 1994). For example, firms with small sales are not very attractive to control. Besides, small firms and their managers are often difficult to find. It takes much time to inspect them, while revenues including tax payments recovered for the state budget and bribes for the inspectors are not significant. As a result, small firms have more chances to avoid careful investigations of their activity (Yakovlev 2000).

For the same reasons, in case of personal income tax, state inspectors are much more interested in surveying revenues of individual entrepreneurs (registered as self-employed) rather than rank-and-file corporate employees.

Instead of total control, the authorities establish *selective control*, which is focused on some businesses and overlooks the others. Selective control is divided into random and non-random (aimed) audits. *Random control* means that the inspector attacks the first target at hand. Many firms easily get away with it, because inspectors cannot (and are not supposed to) to come down on everyone. *Non-random control*, on the contrary, is not spontaneous. It fulfils certain political or/and economic tasks, which go beyond controlling functions as such. It is carried out not only for fiscal reasons (such as additional payments to the state budget), but also is used informally as an effective weapon against competitors.

Aimed control is sometimes implemented as *ordered checks (zakaznye proverki)*, when commercial or political organisations send teams from Tax Inspection or armed Tax Police to their competitors and rivals. This method of non-economic pressure has become very popular since the mid-90s. At that time entrepreneurs realised that rather than to deal with bandits and criminal groupings, it could be much more cost-effective and less risky to use official bodies as informal means to get information and set disputes. It is less expensive because the costs of exploiting the state repressive bodies are covered from the state budget while the revenues are privatised. It is less risky than dealing with the *Mafia* because public inspectors present legal bodies protected by the law.

Ordered checks by the Tax Police have become really famous in Russia in the recent years. State authorities help to disclose confidential information (*compromat*) about the firm and its owners. This information, in turn, is used to establish control over the firm or just to decrease its competitiveness making it spend its time on the checks and thus hindering its regular activity.

In most cases, selective control procedures hit their target. In conditions when nearly all-economic agents violate at least some of the formal rules, each of them is seen as a potential subject to formal sanctions. And they easily become subject to penalties if selected for the in-depth investigation.

> All Russian business is working under the threat of penalties. Some measures taken by the controlling bodies can ruin virtually any firm. I mean the intervention of the Tax authorities first of all (Chairman of the Board of Directors of a bank).

We should admit that selective control is not aimed at eliminating illegal and semi-legal activities. Rather it serves the goals of the powerful groups dividing their areas of interests.

Informal Arrangements of Formal Rules

The simplest way to escape selective control is to pay the officials off. However, this involves important aspects, which cannot be reduced to corruption and bribery. In our opinion, they neither can be encompassed by the three Hirschman's strategies (exit, voice, and loyalty). We would add a fourth element into this typology: a *strategy of bargain*. It describes a situation when economic agents do not just escape from control but try to influence the decisions and outcomes of the control to their advantage. This is achieved most effectively through informal lobbying of their individual and collective interests rather than through courts or mass media. The main instrument is bilateral and collective informal negotiations with the authorities on particular conditions under which formal rules would be implemented use to take place.

Formally, adopted legal norms are not subject to bilateral negotiations. But real life is no doubt different. Representatives of the state and business negotiate and reach institutional compromises defining the extent to which formal rules should be followed. At the same time both parties play rituals of compliance to formal rules, which are used as a camouflage for their latent strategies. It is obviously a paradox when implementation of formal rules largely depends on informal conventions between economic agents supposed to obey these rules and state bodies authorised to control their obedience.

Strategy of political bargaining is aimed at the following objectives:

- getting official tax exemptions;
- negotiating on semi-official tax trade-offs;
- delaying and restructuring tax payments.

Normally, some firms in the business group get official *tax exemptions*. They are registered in offshore areas or employ disabled persons. Tax privileges could be also acquired as investment credits. According to the Russian Ministry of Finance data, tax privileges acquired as investment credits should have made 227 billion roubles (about $7.8 billion) in 2001. However, this sort of privileges is not very popular at the moment. It requires much effort in bargaining with the state authorities. Besides, those who benefit from it may attract an extra attention from the controlling bodies. Thus, it is more efficient to apply informal strategies of tax optimisation.

As it was mentioned above, large companies / big business is able to negotiate with the authorities on some *tax trade-offs* not fixed by the law. In this political bargaining, they refer to the crucially important ('systemic') role of their enterprise for the region, including its large sales volume, 'strategic' products, facilitation of employment and social welfare/protection programs.

Finally, a firm can *delay payments* referring to payment arrears and the absence of money on its bank accounts. In this case, it can maintain its cash flow through the accounts of other firms or simply evade bank accounts altogether with black cash.

Depending on the scale of business, bargaining over formal rules may lead to public or tacit agreements. Bargaining of the large companies for tax privileges is arranged as top-level *political agreements*. At least some of their outcomes become known to the mass media. What is remarkable, instead of exercising legitimate violence to non-payers, the state representatives negotiate with them to compromise and recover a part of taxation debts. Willingness to fill the budget is often traded by the public officials for privileges and non-competitive advantages for the large company. It is principally important that this sort of politicisation of the economy (Johnson, Kaufmann and Shleifer 1997) does not merely replace the formal rule by the informal agreement. It brings fundamental changes to the formal rule itself. Formal rules are processed by the mechanisms of political and commercial trade-offs. In this institutional frame, exclusive rights and specific privileges are exchanged for political and financial support. This does not necessarily imply corruption but rather a capture of the state (though of course there is something in common with corruption here).

With smaller firms, *tacit agreements* between the state and business agents are widely spread. The tax inspector can check up a firm in an in-depth or in a superficial manner. The firm accountants often suggest an informal trade-off. The tax inspector is allowed to disclose some minor discrepancies in the accounting books and impose small fines, which would prove that the tax inspector did not waste his/her working time. The communication is also fed by a reasonable amount of bribes and gifts, which make the inspector dissemble more serious 'mistakes'.

Public and tacit trade-offs with regard to tax benefits go far beyond one-time agreements among perfect strangers. They become a basis for *strategic alliances* among business and state agencies. These alliances are maintained both on the institutional level with 'friendly organisations' and on the personal level with 'friendly people'. They help to reach relative stability in the highly fluid institutional environment of the Russian economy.

The existence of public and tacit agreements points to an important fact that economic agents are actually allowed not to pay all the taxes to the full. It becomes a part of broader institutional compromises with the authorities when business dealers pay only part of taxes, which they themselves decide to pay.

Who pays taxes today? Only people who want to pay and who decide to contribute a little bit to the state (manager of a financial auditing firm).

Folks do not pay real taxes. They pay some part, which they are able to pay... It makes sense to pay some reasonable rate of taxes (manager of a trading firm).

We have all the grounds to conclude that the source of tax evasion is not just the opportunism of economic agents. It is encouraged and often initiated by the authorities. Many tax evasion schemes have been developed under the patronage of state bodies and influential civil servants. As a result, a part of tax payments are substituted by informal fees and bribes (Shleifer and Vishny 1993, pp. 602, 611-612).

Legitimisation of Informal Practices

The increasing informalisation of rules resulted in a situation when tax evasion has become a very wide spread phenomenon in the Russian business, and this fact is stressed by a vast majority of entrepreneurs (Radaev 1998b). Such a situation impedes tax collection. The share of tax payments non-collected to the state budget in the recent years makes from 25 to 40 per cent, including direct concealment of revenues, which amounts to 20 per cent (Russian Ministry of Finance estimates).

Nearly all firms under-report at least part of their true revenues and conceal profits (Glinkina 1997, p. 50). There is a famous saying that the owner must fire his/her chief accountant if the firm becomes profitable. Social security taxes paid to the off-budget funds are also largely avoided through quasi-insurance and quasi-credit schemes, which are welcomed both by the employers and employees. Custom duties present another important subject for 'optimisation'. Even according to the official data, 30 per cent of imported goods were smuggled into Russia at the end of the 1990s. Meanwhile, market dealers estimate the average share of goods imported with some violations of custom rules as 80 per cent.

Widely spread informalisation practices require substantial legitimisation. The latter does not resolve the problem in terms of the legal code but nevertheless provides a necessary means for public justification of the continuous violation of formal rules by the officials and entrepreneurs. Without such a legitimisation, the informalisation of rules would not last long. There are multiple modes of the justification argument, which support and reinforce each other. They include:

- legalistic argument;
- we-are-like-the-others argument;
- distrust argument;
- survival argument;
- public benefit argument;
- external pressure argument.

The legalistic argument refers to discrepancies in the system of formal rules, including gaps and controversies in the legislation. For example, it is asserted that it is impossible to follow all formal changes in the tax system.

The we-are-like-the-others argument appeals to the standard modes of behaviour adopted by a majority of economic agents: 'No one is going to pay all the taxes, why should we?'[4]

---

[4] In his public lecture, A. Pashin, a judge from Moscow, gave a good example of the informalisation of the court legal decisions. The Russian jury often demonstrate surprising tolerance towards bribe-takers, even when they are proved guilty in the court. They usually

A special kind of the *distrust argument* is also resorted to. It is claimed that to pay high taxes one should trust the state institutions and believe that the money would be used for public benefit. Many argue that the Russian state always tries to squeeze revenues from the business without a parallel provision of public goods to Russian citizens. In other words, why should we pay taxes to a non-reliable government?

The survival argument is even more straightforward. It is argued it is impossible to follow formal rules on rational economic grounds. For example, paying all the taxes would lead to drastic results for the firm – in conditions when its rivals do not pay taxes, it would lose its competitiveness and simply be driven out from the market.

> I would be happy to pay one hundred percent of taxes... But I cannot survive if a small company next to me successfully avoids paying either taxes or customs. It doesn't pay anything at all (president of a computer firm).

Still another type of argument is the public benefit argument. The agents affirm that tax evasion allows to decreases the costs of the operation of the firm, which can thus keep lower prices for its customers. According to expert estimates, an optimisation of custom duties allows to keep prices on consumer goods lower by 20 per cent at least.

Finally, the *external pressure argument* is used. It appeals to the frequent facts of extortion by the civil servants and protection agencies. Its proponents argue that it is corrupt civil servants that make entrepreneurs violate the formal rules. One cannot run a business without giving bribes, and bribes require 'black cash'. Therefore, some part of cash flow needs to be hidden in the shadow.

All these modes of legitimisation are mutually complimentary. They reinforce each other and help to maintain a high level of criticism among entrepreneurs and in public opinion towards formal rules. All these sorts of argument are developed to justify informalisation practices and depict them as absolutely unavoidable.

As a result, both tax avoidance and tax evasion have become quite a common phenomenon. And failures of tax collectors do not surprise anyone. But the most exciting point here is that tax evasion is seen as a legitimate practice not only by the business people but also by the public opinion. To cheat the 'grabbing state' is a widely shared norm if not a business virtue.

Is There a Way Out?

It is widely acknowledged that informal arrangements contribute to the stability of the situation and resolve many tensions engendered by the formal order. At the same time, they lead to an erosion of legal norms and commercialisation of the

---

justify their actions saying, 'Civil servants do take bribes. Why should we punish this particular person?' (InterCentre International Symposium, Moscow, January 20, 2001).

corrupt state. Economy is stuck in a bad equilibrium (Johnson, Kaufmann and Shleifer 1997). Is it at all possible to get out of this vicious circle, in which rational actions of economic agents escaping from the formal rules are backed by norms and customs that stimulate further exit strategies? We would suggest several approaches of the development of company compliance, namely:

- legal approach;
- utilitarian approach;
- administrative approach;
- negotiation approach;
- normative approach.

The legal approach is associated with a serious improvement of legislative and regulatory basis. No one would deny a necessity of such legislative efforts. However, views differ with respect to ways as to how to formalise the rules. There is an enduring debate on whether it would be more efficient to import institutions from the West (or even from the East) or to legalise the existing informal norms and customs. We would not consider this issue here. What is more important, we need to achieve a greater simplicity and transparency of formal rules to avoid their dubious interpretations. Doing this, we have to take into account that inclinations to informal exit and bargain strategies are highly inertial. Therefore, the adoption of a 'good law' is never enough for the real institutional change to take place.

An improvement of formal rules should also be based on the *utilitarian approach*, which exploits economic interests of the rational agents. In the field of taxation, it is assumed that a reduction of taxation rates would lead to increasing legalisation of businesses. The latter would find it more beneficial to avoid risks of double accounting. In 2001, the Russian Government in this respect undertook some positive measures, when it slightly reduced the rates of customs duties and social security payments to the off-budget funds. Official reports claim that this tax reduction allowed to improve the collection of these taxes and duties in 2001. However, we would not impute the improvement in tax collection solely to the fair tax rate policy. Either would we not expect that the firms fully legalise their activity after some taxation rates have been lowered. The costs of legalisation are still very high while the risks of tax evasion are still low.

The *administrative approach*, in its turn, is based on severe penalties against detected evaders. This sort of pressures on business on behalf of the state authorities has increased within the recent years. And it may produce some positive results (in some studies, penalty rate is pointed as the most effective measure (Hepburn 1992). However, we should not rely on heavy penalties and high fines alone. It is better to raise the detection rate, and therefore, reduce the selective character of the control (Pirttila 1999). Besides, there is a significant danger that administrative methods would be abused. The firms that are relatively more legal, and therefore more open for external selective control may become victims of this control if inspectors choose the easiest ways for themselves. Thus, this policy could lead to the opposite outcomes and prevent the best-open firms from their further legalisation. A more difficult for public officials but a more efficient way to use 'administrative methods', is to eliminate tax privileges and dismantle the market infrastructure that supports illegal and semi-legal activities. The last point is most delicate because at least a part of these agencies serve the financial interests of influential state and political forces. In this respect, tax evasion is by no means an unforeseen event. It means a direct involvement of political and state institutions and their leaders in the process of the facilitation of shadow dealings, one of the major reasons for the low risks of tax evasion in Russia today (Yakovlev 2000, pp. 142-6). For a real change to occur, we need to exercise control over controllers. And today, it would be far-fetched to argue that political will is strong enough to impose such a control.

The negotiation approach offers different solutions. In the situation of instability and multiple interpretations of formal rules, it focuses on the development of agreements and codes of conduct on the micro-level. Economic agents should negotiate over particular conditions and steps, which would allow them to proceed gradually towards legalisation. In other words, it means establishing informal conventions about formal rules. Negotiation starts on the business-to-business level to overcome a traditional free-rider problem and unwillingness to take extra costs of legalisation. Then it proceeds to the level of business-to-government relationships. Conventions with public officials are vitally important for securing stability and transparency of rules and ensuring legalisation attempts.

The normative approach is also important. It is aimed at developing loyalty towards the state and voluntary self-compliance. Serious efforts are to be made to break stereotypes about the inevitability of tax evasion. We also need much more public support for the state fiscal policy. At the same time, semi-legal arrangements are deeply embedded in norms and habits of the Russian society. And trying to reduce the 'tax immorality', one should not expect quick positive results.

Our final remark is that there is no panacea in this area, therefore a combination of these approaches is needed for the policy efforts to be a success.

References

Chepurenko, A. *et al.* (1998), 'Malyi Biznes Posle Avgusta 1998 g.: Problemy, Tendentsii, Adaptatsionnye Vozmozhnosti' (Small Business after August 1998, Problems, Trends, Adaptive Capacities), in M. K. Gorshkov, A. Yu. Chepurenko, and F. E. Sheregi (eds), *Osennyi Krizis 1998 goda: Rossiiskoye obschestvo do i posle* (1998 Fall Crisis: The Russian society before and after), Moscow, ROSSPEN, pp. 101-183.

Eggertsson, T. (1990), *Economic Behavior and Institutions*, Cambridge, Cambridge University Press.

Glinkina, S. K. (1997), 'Voprosu o kriminalizatsii rossiiskoi ekonomiki' (On the Issue of Criminalization of the Russian Economy), *Politekonom*, No. 1, pp. 56-63.

Granovetter, M. (1994), 'Business Groups', in N. Smelser, and R. Swedberg (eds), *The Handbook of Economic Sociology*, Princeton: Princeton University Press, pp. 453-475.

Hepburn, G. (1992), 'Estimates of Cash-Based Income Tax Evasion in Australia', *The Australian Economic Review*, 2nd Quarter, pp. 54-62.

Hirschman, A. O. (1970), *Exit, Voice, and Loyalty: Response to Decline in Firms, Organizations, and States*, Cambridge, MA, Harvard University Press.

Johnson, S., Kaufmann, D., and Shleifer, A. (1997), 'The Unofficial Economy in Transition', *Brookings Papers on Economic Activity*, No. 2, pp. 159-239.

Jung, Y. H., Snow, A., and Trandel G. A. (1994), 'Tax Evasion and the Size of the Underground Economy', *Journal of Public Economics*, 54, pp. 391-402.

Nesterenko, A. (2000), 'Perekhodny period zakonchilsya. Chto dal'she?' (Transitional Period Is Over. What Is Ahead?), *Voprosy Ekonomiki*, No. 6, pp. 4-17.

North, D. C. (1992), *Institutions, Institutional Change and Economic Performance*, Cambridge, Cambridge University Press.

Pappe, Ya. (2000), *Oligarkhy: Ekonomicheaskaya khronika. 1992-2000* (Oligarchs: An Economic Chronicle of 1992-2000), Moscow, State University-Higher School of Economics.

Pirttila, J. (1999), 'Tax Evasion and Economics in Transition: Lessons from tax theory' (manuscript).

Radaev, V. (1997), 'Practicing and Potential Entrepreneurs in Russia', *International Journal of Sociology*, Fall, 27 (3), pp. 15-50.

Radaev, V. (1998a), 'Regional Entrepreneurship: The State of Small Business', in *A Regional Approach to Industrial Restructuring in the Tomsk Region, Russian Federation*, Paris, Organisation of Economic Co-Operation and Development Proceedings, pp. 275-319.

Radaev, V. (1998b), *Formirovaniye novykh rossiiskikh rynkov: transaktsionnye izderzhki, formy kontrolya i delovaya etika* (Formation of New Russian Markets: Transaction Costs, Forms of Control and Business Ethics), Moscow, Centre for Political Technologies.

Radaev, V. (2001), 'Urban Households in the Informal Economy', in K. Segbers (ed.), *Explaining Post-Soviet Patchworks*, volume 2, Aldershot, Ashgate, pp. 333-61.

Shleifer, A. and Vishny, R. W. (1993), 'Corruption', *Quarterly Journal of Economics*, CVIII, August (3), 5, pp. 99-617.

Stark, D. (2000), 'Ambiguous Assets for Uncertain Environment: Heterarchy in Postsocialist Firms', *Ekonomicheskaya Sotsiologiya* (Economic Sociology), 1 (2), pp. 7-36, http://www.ecsoc.msses.ru .

Yakovlev, A. (2000), 'Pochemu v Rossii vozmozhen bezriskovy ukhod ot nalogov?' (Why Is the No-Risk Tax Evasion Possible in Russia?), *Voprosy Ekonomiki*, No. 11, pp. 142-146.

Chapter 10

Security, Trust, and Cultural Resources: Hungarian Manufacturing Enterprises in the Post-Socialist Transformation

György Lengyel and Béla Janky

Introduction: The Problem

This study aims at investigating the impact of material, cultural and social resources on perceived security of business environment. The analysis puts special emphasis on the role of cultural resources and trust in fostering the sense of security in a transition economy. Moreover, we point to the complex interrelations between perceived security, social resources and managerial decisions. Namely, we hypothesise that strong social ties tend to reduce uncertainty in business transactions if managers are worse off in terms of material and cultural resources. The empirical analysis is based on a representative survey among top managers of Hungarian manufacturing firms.

The role of security and trust in economic transactions has been studied with special emphasis in economic sociology. Max Weber ascribed salient importance to the elimination of dual morals in the emergence of capitalism because the spread of the rational calculative behaviour delimits a great source of insecurity: rude acquisitiveness, while it also weakens the norms of solidarity (Weber 1981 (1927)) In this theory, generalised trust is the precondition for the spread of business transactions and the moderation of a sense of insecurity. Researches on the social bases of trust and on the issues of how does trust influence human resources, ontological security, and the quality of life seem to deliberately shape current sociological discourse (Coleman 1988; Giddens 1990; Fukuyama 1995; Seligman 1997; Putnam 2000; Yamagishi et al. 1998; Hardin, 2001). What substitutive mechanisms are facilitated by the lack of trust under the conditions of limited social mobility and rudimentary political institutions is explored by researchers into the Mafia (Gambetta 1998). Studies into the role of social resources and trust formation in economic life based on the Weberian tradition led equally important results (Zucker 1986; Whitley 1991; Sako 1993; Lane-Bachmann 1998).

The low level of trust in market interactions may be one of the important decelerating factors of economic growth in emerging market economies. Both theoretical sociology and empirical researches suggest that post-socialist countries in the transition period are characterised by a lack of trust (Sztompka 1999; Rose and Haerpfer 1998; Utasi 2002). Earlier researches support the assumption that in East-Central European countries the spread of entrepreneurial inclination was also hindered by the lack of trust, in addition to the lack of funds (Róna, Tas and Lengyel 1997/98; Radaev 1999; Kuczi and Lengyel 2001). That is primarily related to the weakness of civil society, the lack of adequate market institutions and social capital that could be accumulated with the help of the former. Optimistic scenarios of the transition to a market economy may hope for the gradually strengthening of civil society, the selective influence of the market and the spread of business culture introduced by the penetrating multinational companies. This would suggest that a continuous increase of trust can be witnessed in these countries. Mistrust in partners, in the market and institutional environment affects the actors of transitional economies to varying degrees. In this paper, a closer look is taken at the range of factors that influence the firm managers' sense of security besides market position and sector specificity. Special emphasis is laid on the specific features of transitional economies. We hypothesise that in post-socialist economies a salient role is assigned in the lessening of business insecurity to cultural and social capital in addition to material resources.

Earlier, the role of cultural and social capital in the transition economy was principally studied in connection with enterprise strategy and performance. A fundamental finding of Hungarian empirical observations was that enterprise behaviour failed to adopt the patterns typical of market economies within a year or two's time. A kind of 'wait-'n'-see' attitude, the postponement of settling problems (Laki 1992, 1993, 1994; Török 1994; Szanyi 1998), or a relapse to the customary patterns of the 1980s (Voszka 1996) was typical of the economic actors. These phenomena call attention to the role of cultural resources. On the one hand: in vain is the institutional environment new, it can only function on the basis of the knowledge and values accumulated during its predecessor's time. On the other hand, at times of rapid changes, enterprises can only adapt to short-term changes, which also delays the adoption of new behavioural patterns (Laki 1994). It is an important factor that the transformational recession (Kornai 1993) hitting the transitional economies endows the enterprise crises with a peculiar character (Hoványi 1995a). It is far harder to find points for breaking out under such circumstances as offensive crisis management has far less scope. Some claim that precisely in accord with the situation, enterprises consciously kept their activity on pin-point flame in the first half of the '90s, as that helped them best adapt to the unfavourable circumstances and prepare for possible privatisation (Török 1994). In Grosfeld and Roland's view (1995) the deferment of typical market economy strategies was part of a conscious strategy. Two phases of adaptation are differentiated by them: in the first firms respond passively, and when they realise that no help is to be expected, and the new structures will be lasting, they begin to manoeuvre in accord with the new circumstances.

Researches related to enterprise efficiency and contractual relations emphasise the role of social resources (Whitley *et al.* 1996; Batjargal 2000b; Sako 1998; Csabina *et al.* 2002). In an earlier longitudinal survey among Hungarian small and middle-range entrepreneurs it was inquired how the initial state of material, cultural and social capital influenced the survival chances of the enterprises. It was concluded that these factors more strongly explained survival than growth, with social resources being the most powerful explanatory factor. Those who relied on friends for important decisions at the beginning – that is, who were characterised by solidarity-based personal relations – were overrepresented at two outer poles: among the defunct firms and among the expanding enterprises (Lengyel 2000). The possible explanation was that while in the first case the network of relations shrank, in the second a concord of personal solidarity and generalised trust was typical for the firm.

In his longitudinal survey of a small sample of Russian entrepreneurs, Bat Batjargal highlighted the interrelation of firm performance and social resources. Inspired by the embeddedness thesis of economic sociology, he wished to see how the entrepreneurs' networks of personal relations and the social capital that could be mobilised with their help contributed to firm performance. He concluded that the extent of the network of relations and the friendship relations did not influence performance, whereas heterogeneous economic knowledge did. Since the examination took place during the Russian economic crisis in 1995/98, the author was also prompted to state that social capital was especially valuable under the conditions of extreme insecurity (Batjargal 2000a, c).

Using the experiences of empirical researches, we wish to examine how the profile of entrepreneurial activity, various types of resources, the trust level of market relations and the entrepreneurial goals influence the perception of the security of the business environment. Instead of firm performance, we wish to explore the extent to which economic leaders deem the economic environment insecure, how the sense of insecurity relates to contractual trust and to the leaders' concept of success, and to other structural, institutional and cultural factors that influence the functioning of an enterprise. The target of research is not the relation between generalised trust and insecurity, but the correlation between material and cultural resources, forms of trust based on solidarity and interest, as well as the perception of insecurity.

Hypotheses

We assume that the material, cultural and social resources at the disposal of a firm have a key role in decreasing insecurity. Material resources may provide security for cases of sudden changes in the market conditions or the institutional environment, or when the partners do not behave co-operatively. It is up to the management and the professional groups to use their cultural capital to prepare for the above challenges and respond to them adequately. These two kinds of capital assume special importance in post-socialist economies because, on the one hand, the institutions of a market economy do not function adequately, and on the other, the qualifications and experiences gained in a socialist economy only give limited props for the development of successful market economy strategies. If the available material and cultural resources cannot reduce insecurity in business transactions, the management can moderate insecurity by restricting business activity and screening the transactions.

Material resources are gauged by capital and other indicators of thè size of the enterprise. We assume that larger firms can more easily weather the crises generated by unexpected market developments. We also take ownership as an institutional indicator of the material resources at the back of the enterprise. It is more likely to find parent companies well equipped with funds behind foreign-owned firms. Also, state or local government-owned companies have more means than the average to ward off risks.

The nature of a firm's cultural resources is measured by the school qualifications of the managers in the first place. We hypothesise that those who began their careers in the 1990s were faced less sharply with problems caused by the survival of firm management methods of non-market economies. In our hypothesis the kind of qualifications the management has contributes to the pace at which managers adapted to the market economy conditions. Graduates of business, economics and law can more easily observe the aspects of profit-orientation in directing the enterprise than graduates of other branches. The hypothesised influence of the type of qualifications can also be retraced to the lack of market traditions. With age and schooling we inserted factors determining management skills in the model. We also examine directly how the outlook of company managers satisfies the principles of a market economy. Here we analyse if managers judge the performance of their respective companies in terms of the market economy environment or rather, in terms dictated by the socialist economy. In a centrally directed economy based on plan directives, the goals to be achieved were laid down for the state enterprises in diverse financial and natural indices. They were sometimes contradictory and in conflict with the principle of maximising profit in many cases. To assess this attitude, we asked the company managers how they measured the success of their companies. The respondents had to narrate in their own words what they deemed as important criteria of success. The replies concerning success criteria can be subsumed in three categories. Profit is one of the clear categories, liquidity is the other and the broad umbrella concept of growth, expansion, technical improvement is the third.

Apart from the above-said, an important indicator of cultural capital is the use of the computer and the Internet. It is incorporated in the model as a sort of proxy variable referring partly to the skills of management and personnel that cannot be accurately measured by school qualifications and partly to innovative ability and flexibility not explained by other variables.

Social capital informs research mainly of long-term co-operative relations. They assume significance mostly with firms that do not have sufficient material resources to protect them from grave jeopardy caused by opportunist partners. In our empirical investigation, the related term was contractual trust. The category introduced by Mari Sako (Sako 1993) can be characterised by the duality of obligatory vs. arms-length contractual relations. Under obligatory contractual relations, the partners may act upon oral agreements, starting production prior to written contracts, controlling the quality of delivered goods less frequently. They are characterised by greater trust based on obligations. Under arms-length contractual conditions, the partners insist on written contracts and the observation of the terms laid down in them.

An indicator of another type of social capital is the use of solidarity-based relations in the running of the firm. A typical example is the employment of relatives as labour. Since it implies several drawbacks, its application is more strongly tied up with the lack of other resources.

To sum up: we presume that the perception of insecurity is fundamentally influenced by a few cultural resources inherited from the socialist economy, in addition to the lack of material resources. For want of these, the contraction of the circle of business transactions may decrease the perceived insecurity of the business environment. Those managers who pursue extensive business activity involving many partners despite having insufficient resources perceive the insecurity of the environment more acutely than the average. We expect to find a sort of dualization of enterprises, and to see that medium and large companies display far lower levels of perceived insecurity than micro- and small ventures. Added to the company size and material and institutional resources, this dualization is also supported by the unequal distribution of cultural and social resources.

In keeping with the above assumption, the following hypotheses were tested in the empirical survey:

H1. Material resources behind the firm reduce the chance that its managers might perceive the business setting as insecure.

Hypothesis 1 is to be operationalized with the following statements:

H1.1. Foreign- and state-owned firms perceive the environment as more secure while private Hungarian owners (including employee ownership) entail greater insecurity.

H.1.2. Enterprises of larger capital, staff and turnover perceive less insecurity in the business environment.

H.2. Cultural resources play at least as strong a role in the perception of insecurity as material resources do. Professional qualifications and market-conform knowledge and attitude help reduce the sense of insecurity.

The second hypothesis is operationalized with the following statements:

H.2.1. Perception of insecurity will be underrepresented among who managers formulate success in financial terms.

H.2.2. If computer culture is prevalent in the firm (there is intranet) management will perceive less insecurity, and this correlation applies independently of material resources.

H.2.3.a. The university diploma of the manager reduces perceived insecurity because the transferable intellectual skills can be put to good use under the conditions of insecurity.

H.2.3.b. The manager's qualifications in economics or law will reduce the sense of insecurity, because these types of knowledge make easy adaptation to market behavioural patterns more likely.

H.2.4. Those who started their professional careers in a market economy will perceive the business environment less insecure as they take competition for a natural context.

H.3. Obligatory relations and primordial ties are more binding in smaller firms, and among them they contribute to the moderation of insecurity.

Firms disposing over less material and cultural resources try to reduce the insecurity characterising their business activity to more intensely mobilising their social resources.

H.3.1. Obligatory relations with business partners mainly characterise small firms among whom they may lower the level of perceived insecurity.

H.3.2. Entrepreneurship relying on kinship relations in the first place mainly characterises firms with little material and cultural capital, reducing the perceived insecurity below average level. It is not merely hypothesised that solidarity-based trust will reduce the perception of insecurity, but also that it primarily serves to compensate for the lack of material and cultural resources.

Data and Methods

The investigation was made using the Hungarian Enterprise Panel survey for 2000. The Enterprise Panel programme has been alive since 1992 under the aegis of BUESPA (Budapest University of Economic Sciences and Public Administration), Department of Sociology and Social Policy (see Lengyel 1999; Janky 1999; Janky and Lengyel 2000). The observed population is composed of the Hungarian manufacturing enterprises. The interviewee was the manager of the enterprise. Sampling was based on the enterprise list of the Central Statistical Office (CSO). 383 firms were included in the sample. Owing to the systematic bias in denial to reply, we used two-dimensional weighting based on the CSO data. The figures were weighted along the capital-countryside dimension and by enterprise size.

The dependent variable is measured with the question 'How secure do you think the firm's economic environment is today?' on a five-point scale, where 1 is very insecure and 5 is very secure. Then later, in the models we focus in a variable constructed from the answers on those who have found the environment secure and very secure. As for other factors included in the examination, structural and institutional conditions include the character of ownership, size of firm and market radius, sector, technology, relative wages costs. No separate hypothesis is proposed for each factor, but they are included as control variables in the analysis. As for proprietorship, we wish to see if the firm is foreign- or Hungarian-, state- or private-owned, and within that, what is the rate of individual, employee and institutional ownership.

The cultural and social endowments of a firm include the qualifications of the employees and managers, the spread of computer culture, the strong ties cohering the firm, the trust in partners and the management's concept of success. As regards the perception of success, we wish to explore how successful the managers judge their firm, to what extent they express their enterprise success in material and financial terms, and within that, what weight they ascribe to expansion, profit and liquidity as criteria of success.

Several variables were used to measure how secure the manager saw his business environment, how safely he could move on the market. On the one hand, as mentioned above, we put a direct question to elicit an answer about how secure they deemed their business environment. We also put other questions in an attempt to grasp other aspects of security. We inquired into their attitudes to the employees and the regulatory context. We also tried to assess their risk aversion, which measures more unequivocally than the other variables a company leader's willingness to take risks.

We also inquired into trust towards market partners. We were not only curious to know the respondent's opinion but also his practice. We asked how typical it was to start production or render a service before they had signed a written contract with the partner.

In testing our hypotheses, we adopted various strategies. First we checked the strength of the correlation with two- or three-dimensional tables (see Appendix). Then with the help of the described variables we tried to define a general dimension of perceived security which was attached to each variable concerned but none expressed it without fail.

This task was carried out by the principal component analysis. We took for the general dimension of security the first factor that explained most of the variance of the variables. It was used as the dependent variable of the linear regression model applied in testing our hypotheses.

A further strategy was used to select the variable that was tied most directly to security perceived in the business environment. We divided the respondents into two groups along this dimension: marking off those who perceived their environment as secure from those who expressed ambivalent feelings or deemed the context insecure. With this dichotomous variable we built up a logit model which was also suitable to test our hypotheses. For the latter strategies we used the same explanatory variables. In addition to the variables directly needed for the examination of the hypotheses, we also built control variables in the model. They are in part basic characteristics of the enterprise that may influence (at times inexplicably for us) the sense of insecurity of a leader. Some of these variables, on the other hand, give information of the market position of the enterprise, which may also influence of the perception of insecurity. Control variables were the sector, nature of product, radius of market, share of turnover of the single greatest buyer, exploitation of capacity, profit fluctuation, rate of new clients and the recent changes of demand in the firm's main market.

Empirical Findings

The first test of the hypotheses is based on table statistics (see Appendix) to reveal the interrelations of variables. This is followed by an analysis of some logit-models in which perceived security serves as a dichotomous dependent variable. Separate models are used to test the hypotheses referring to the impacts of material, cultural and social resources, respectively. Then the variables attached those hypotheses are incorporated in an integrated model (control variables are included in all of the models).

The cross tables suggest that leaders of foreign- and state-owned firms perceive less than average insecurity in the business environment (foreign ownership even boosts the sense of security), but this is not a significant correlation, given the low rate of such firms and the asymmetry of distribution.

Firms disposing of considerable wealth and having above average returns from sales tend to feel their environment secure, while the categories of employment do not correlate with insecurity perception. Besides, firms in the lower two-fifths by wealth perceive security in their environment above the average.

Those who measure success in financial terms do not perceive above-average security. This derives from the fact that those who gauge success by profit perceive both security and insecurity in an above average rate. (The mention of the interim category is infrequent among them.) Those who claim that liquidity is already success deem their environment insecure around the average, while those who find it secure are massively underrepresented among them.

The hypothesis that firms having computer networks perceive far less insecurity in their environment holds true. Controlling it against material resources, one finds that materially less equipped firms are underrepresented among those who perceive insecurity, while the rate of those of them who perceive security is also slightly below the average. This correlation is not significant for richer firms.

As regards the assumptions about the utilisation of management knowledge, table statistics reveal that the one about university qualifications is proved true but the one about specific economic and legal knowledge is not. So it seems that transferable intellectual knowledge facilitating universal orientation is more important for the perceived security of the business environment than specific market-oriented knowledge.

Those who most probably began work in the market-economy phase perceive the business environment far more secure than the average. This is partly owing to the lack of pre-market economy routines, and partly to young age. This is supported by the fact that if the entry into the labour market is in the eighties instead of the years around the great turn, the correlation still applies. Young managers are underrepresented among those who think employing foreign labour entails trouble, and that growth is hindered or too risky.

Obligatory relations indeed characterise smaller firms: two-fifths of the companies depend on them, but in the upper fifth by wealth one one-sixth of the companies prove to be of this kind. Similar is the correlation found along the variable of returns from sales. There is a positive correlation between obligatory contacts and perceived security: one-third of the firms on the whole perceive their environment as secure, while the corresponding rate among enterprises with obligatory relations is over two-fifths. The correlation is especially strong among firms with little wealth, and is insignificant among rich companies. Table analyses thus confirm hypothesis H3.1. In the logistic regression analysis in which property and obligatory relations are the explanatory factors only the latter remained significant.

Firms based on kinship relations are over presented among companies with limited material and cultural resources. But the managers of companies that also employ relatives perceive their environment less secure than the average. That is true for the control variables of material and cultural resources as well. The table statistics thus disproved our hypothesis about the compensative security enhancing function of kinship relations. The logistic regression model including kinship relations and material-cultural resources as explanatory factors of perceived security revealed that the kinship ties preserved their negative influence but the material and cultural variables did not.

As far as the results of the logit-models concerned, the empirical evidence does not support the hypothesis on material resources. Compared to the model including only the control variables, the goodness of fit of the model hardly improved, and the null hypothesis cannot be rejected for any of the indicators.

The goodness of fit of the model incorporating the cultural resources is better than that of the regression on material resources or the model containing the control variables alone. Moreover, the effects of some variables are significant. According to the results, younger managers are more likely to feel their business environment secure. Moreover, education also matters. Those, who possess an MA degree from one of the universities, are more likely to see more security in their business environment. Studies (at any level) in the fields of business, economics or law, however, do not result in higher level of perceived security. That is – as table statistics also show – general skills seem to play a more important role than specific professional knowledge does. Because of the multicollinearity of material and cultural resources in this model more advanced computer infrastructure makes insecurity more likely, but the connection is not significant.

The logistic regression on social resources partly reinforces our hypotheses. The goodness of fit of the model is at least as good as in the case of the regression on cultural resources. The coefficient of obligatory relationship is positive but not significant. The same is true for the interaction variable that indicates that kind of relationships at small firms. According to the results, in medium size and large firms, the presence of relatives at the company cannot compensate for the insecurity that urged the managers to employ their close ties. In other words, those managers of medium size or large companies who employ their relatives, perceive their business environment less secure. In small companies, however, this compensation effect seems to be significant. That is, the negative value of the coefficient is suppressed among the managers of those firms.

The separate models of each of the types of the resources can show the relative importance of material, cultural and social resources (or to put it more precisely: the relative importance of the selected indicators of them). The estimations of the coefficients of the variables are less likely to be biased, however, if one incorporates all of the possible indicators into the model. The coefficients of age and the employment of relatives are significantly differ from zero in the integrated model. The null-hypothesis on the effect of education, however, cannot be rejected. The effect of most of the disturbingly behaving cultural variables is not significant.

The regression analysis shows that the material resources has a weak impact on perceived security, while cultural and social resources play a more important role in decreasing uncertainty. Age – as a proxy of learned social skills – has a strong effect. Among social resources, employment of relatives indicates lower level of perceived security. This negative effect is suppressed among small companies.

At this point the empirical results of table statistics and logit models contradict each other. According to Table 12.6. based on the size capital there is no significant connection between the sense of security and relatives in business if one controls for the size of the firm. According to the 3rd and 4th models of Table 12.7 the general negative effect of kinship is compensated for in the case of small enterprises measured by the number of employees. Similarly: according to Table 12.5. the obligatory contractual relations enhance the sense of security, especially among enterprises with limited capital sources. In models 3rd and 4th of Table 12.7 – where obligatory and kinship relations were put together – the effect of both obligatory relations and their interaction with the number of employees proved to be insignificant.

Discussion

The study aimed to examine the material, cultural and social resources influencing the perception of security. The findings primarily confirm the role of cultural capital played in a transitional economy. In other words, the lack of high-level convertible knowledge may largely contribute to the lack of a feeling of security typical of the economies of the region. This is a finding which may contribute to the literature devoted to the theme mainly concentrating on the role of the institutional environment (Szelényi and Kostello, 1998). At the same time, the studied effect mechanisms of cultural resources predict a slow growth in the sense of security indispensable for prosperity in the post-socialist economies (as against the prognoses of a more uncertain future by research highlighting social capital). A little appreciated structural component of the post-socialist transition was namely the explosive expansion of tertiary education.

Our data confirm our thesis that the security of the economic environment can be studied in terms of the individuals' knowledge and skills. The thesis also reveals that an important source of insecurity is the individual's lack of knowledge to solve problem situations, and this automatically increases the risks of certain decisions. Consequently, it is the increase in the (adequate) qualifications and experience of the economic actors, besides the objective market and institutional conditions, that might contribute to the increase of trust and security.

However, a deeper analysis of the hypothesised connections and the empirical results of the research warn that caution must be administered lest trust should be viewed oversimplified. Some international researches into trust (Lianos and Douglas 2000) also call attention to that. Though the data on East-European post-socialist countries do refer to a low level of trust in keeping with theoretical considerations, there are some societies where on the basis of theories, lack of trust might be expected, but international researches measured high level of trust (Bonell and Gold 2002). Economic sociological researches e.g. in Japan have revealed how many-sided the concept of trust may be. While some investigations have shown that a high-level obligatory trust characterises the interrelations between Japanese economic organisations (Sako 1993), other researchers who have differentiated between generalised trust and personal commitment tend to characterise the Japanese society with lack of trust (Yamagichi *et al*. 1998).

When we presume that the level of trust in business transactions between strangers is low and the economic environment is insecure in general, then a part of the potential transactions can be expected to remain unrealised, since actors intend to test few interactions (Yamagishi 2001). In this case the trust as 'encapsulated interest' (Hardin 2001) works only in their close surroundings. This process, in turn, may result in a high level of trust characterising business transactions and security perceived in the immediate vicinity of the economic activity despite the overall lack of trust, as interactions take place mainly within the network of relations implying high level of trust. However, the actors of the economy differ according to the extent to which they are hit by the insecurity of the institutional system, to which they can restrict their economic connections and to which they strive for expansion (which necessarily implies the widening of the circle of transactions). In the emerging market economies, these differences have salient importance. With the institutions and actors changing rapidly, the role of resources that may reduce the insecurity of extensive transactions, and those that may ensure co-operative relations of high trust level in place of these transactions may increase. When these resources are missing, several actors may find that low trust-level transactions and a perception of general insecurity are enduring components of their activity. On the basis of the above-said, we presume that enterprises can reduce the insecurity by their activity. On the one hand, they can consolidate their positions in the emerging markets by relying on the cultural resources, material capital and broad social resources of the management and the enterprise. Or, they can also reorient their activity relying primarily on their narrow social resources so that they may avoid insecure market transactions.

Thus, the economic actors can themselves influence what risks they face. The increase of the security of the environment can be achieved not only by the growth of necessary knowledge but also by the avoidance of risky transactions. It is, however, to be realised that the two strategies are not on a par for the future perspectives of an enterprise. The first option is an offensive strategy which, when successful, may expand the firm's scope of action, while the latter is more on the defensive side, a strategy chosen out of necessity to survive. Profit-oriented enterprises aim primarily to widen their activity, and only for want of sufficient material and cultural resources do they try to mobilise their social resources to establish a narrower circle of transactions and partners.

Thus besides the cultural resources, we also took a look at the role of social resources. The aim was not to examine the security-enhancing role of social capital in general. We analysed whether or not firms devoid of other resources did rely more heavily on the social resources implied by their environment. We also studied whether these social resources did indeed boost the entrepreneurs' perception of security. The findings are less unambiguous than those concerning cultural resources. It is, however, to be remembered that the effect mechanism concerned is far more difficult to measure. Obligatory relations are efficient in the case of smaller enterprises, but the role of relatives in business is contradictory.

Conclusion

The aim of the paper was to examine how the material and cultural resources as well as trust relations of an enterprise influenced the perception of security in the post-socialist period.

Contrarily to our hypotheses, the material resources of an enterprise – property, staff size, foreign or state ownership – does not play a significant role in the perception of security. The main factor that counts in this respect is whether or not the firm has a wide enough market. The indicators of the cultural resources proved more important than the material resources. This is not surprising since though the questions were about the enterprises, the answers were part of the subjective opinion of the management which is obviously more deeply influenced by personal conditions than by the endowments of the firm. What is indeed striking is the fact that the computer intranet of a firm proved just as important as the university diploma of the leader and the period in which his career started. Confuting our expectations, specific market knowledge and the interpretation of success in financial terms did not influence the perception of security as university graduation, which made convertible general intellectual knowledge probable, did. It seems likely that in the period of post-socialism it is not specialised but generalised knowledge exploitable in a variety of contexts that contributes to a higher level of perceived security. Age and the beginning of a career have demonstrable influence on security perception. The younger one is and hence the less experience one might have from the period of state socialism, the more safely one moves in the new context and less risky one will find growth and enterprising beyond kinship relations. It must be noted that the two effects are inextricably intertwined. One roots in age, reflecting the 'optimism of youth'. The other is the coincidence of young age with a historical period, making the presence or absence of certain experience (routine, fears, skills) probable.

Obligatory relations with partners implying peculiar trust characterise smaller enterprises, among whom they strongly enhance the sense of security. However running a business on the basis of kinship relations does not contribute to the perception of a more secure environment – quite to the contrary. Solidarity-based kinship relations weaken the perception of security and this strong negative connection weakens among small enterprises only. Trust based on kinship, friendship, old personal acquaintances replace higher-level generalised trust, and may also shackle the spread of profit-oriented calculative behaviour.

It is also important what sets of persons and transactions the extent of trust and insecurity refers to. Obviously, the level of trust in transactions will considerably change depending on the partners being close relatives and utter strangers. Our findings thus indirectly tally with the connections exposed by a research in different context (Yamagishi *et al.* 1998). The wide extent of solidarity-based trust may indicate that the level of preliminary trust in unknown actors and institutions is low.

Our paper shows the special importance of cultural resources in business transactions of a transition economy. Moreover, the empirical evidence supports a more complex view of the impact of trust and solidarity-based social resources on security. Future empirical research (quantitative as well as qualitative) may shed more light on the mechanism that connect cultural capital and perceived security. The elaboration of the hypotheses on social resources, however, requires further theoretical efforts in the research on trust and business security. The relation between trust and the perception of insecurity does not necessarily postulate unidirectional causality. Trust may reduce the feeling of insecurity, but enhanced security may just as well increase trust. It seems to be plausible that both trust and the perception of security are to be retraced to common causes, to the general state of affairs in business, politics and media, or to a combination of contextual and personal factors we could not take into account yet.

References

Batjargal, B. (2000a), 'The Dynamics of Entrepreneurial Networks in a Transitional Economy: The case of Russia', University of Michigan Business School, William Davidson Institute Working Paper No. 350.

Batjargal, B. (2000b), 'Entrepreneurial Versatility Resources and Firm Performance in Russia: A panel study', University of Michigan Business School, William Davidson Institute, Working Papers No. 351.

Batjargal, B. (2000c), 'Social Capital and Entrepreneurial Performance in Russia: A panel study', University of Michigan Business School, William Davidson Institute, Working Papers No. 352

Bonell, V. and Gold T. B. (eds) (2002), *New Entrepreneurs of Europe and Asia. Patterns of Business Development in Russia, Eastern Europe and China*, Armonk/London, M.E. Sharpe.

Brinton, M. C. and Nee, V. (eds) (1998), *The New Institutionalism in Sociology*, New York, Russell Sage Foundation.

Coleman, J. S. (1988), 'Social Capital in the Creation of Human Capital', *American Journal of Sociology*, 94, pp. 95-120.

Csabina, Z., Kopasz, M. and Leveleki, M. (2002), 'Contractual Trust in the Trading Relationship of Hungarian Manufacturing Firms', *Review of Sociology of the Hungarian Sociological Association*, 8(1), pp. 79-97.

Fukuyama, F. (1995), *Trust*, New York, Basic Books.

Gambetta, D. (1998 (1993)), *The Sicilian Mafia. The Business of Private Protection*, Cambridge, MA, Harvard University Press.

Giddens, A. (1990), *The Consequences of Modernity*, Stanford, Stanford University Press.

218   *Networks, Trust and Social Capital*

Grosfeld, I. and Roland, G. (1995), 'Defensive and Strategic Restructuring in Central European Enterprises'. CEPR Discussion Paper No. 1135, London, CEPR.
Hardin, R. (2001), 'Conceptions and Explanations of Trust', in K. S. Cook (ed.), *Trust in Society*, New York, Russell Sage Foundation, pp. 3-39.
Hoványi G. (1995a), 'A vállalati válságmenedzselés néhány objektív és szubjektív tényezője', (Some Objective and Subjective Aspects of Corporate Crisis Management), *Ipargazdasági Szemle*, 1-2.
Janky, B. (1999), 'Adjustment Strategies of Hungarian Industrial Firms in the 1990s', *Acta Oeconomica*, 50 (3-4), pp. 283-96.
Janky, B. and Lengyel G. (szerk.) (2000), Bizalom, tulajdon, nyereség, (A Vállalati Panelvizsgálat elemzése – gazdasági szereplők és magatartások), (Trust, Property, Profit, (Analysis of the Enterprise Panel Data – Economic Actors and Attitudes)), Budapest, BKÁE.
Kornai, J. (1993), 'Transzformációs visszaesés' (Transformational Recession) *Közgazdasági Szemle*, 40(7-8), pp. 569-99.
Kuczi, T. and Lengyel, G. (2001), 'The Spread of Entrepreneurship in Eastern Europe', in P.- H. Jöns Meusberger (eds), *Transformations in Hungary. Essays in Economy and Society*, Heidelberg, Physica Verlag, pp. 157-72.
Laki, M. (1992), 'A vállalati magatartás változása és a gazdasági válság' (Changes in Enterprise Behaviour, and the Economic Crisis), *Közgazdasági Szemle*, 39(6), pp. 565-578.
Laki, M. (1993), 'Vállalati viselkedés elhúzódó gazdasági visszaesés idején', (Firm Behaviour During a Long Transitional Recession), *Külgazdaság*, 37(11), pp. 23-34.
Laki, M. (1994a), '*Vállalatok a szocializmus után*' (Firms after the Socialism), Dissertation, Budapest.
Laki, M. (1994b), 'Firm Behaviour During a Long Transitional Recession', *Acta Oeconomica*, 46 (3-4), pp. 347-70.
Lane, C. and Bachmann, R. (eds) (1998), *Trust Within and Between Orgarnizations. Conceptual and Empirical Applications*, Oxford, Oxford University Press.
Lengyel, G. (1999b), 'How Do Managers Interpret Economic Success? Some Experiences from an Empirical Investigation', *Acta Oeconomica*, 50 (3-4), pp. 297-310.
Lengyel, G. (2002), 'Social Capital and Entrepreneurial Success. Hungarian Small Enterprises between 1993 and 1996', in V. E Bonell and T. B. Gold (eds), *The New Entrepreneurs of Europe and Asia. Patterns of Business Development in Russia, Eastern Europe and China*, Armonk/ London, M.E. Sharpe, pp. 256-77.
Lengyel, G. (ed.) (1999), *New Economic Actors, Institutions and Attitudes in Central and Eastern Europe* (A volume workshop proceedings), Budapest, BUESP.
Lianos, M. and Douglas, M. (2000), 'Dangerization and the End of Deviance. The Institutional Environment', *British Journal of Criminology*, 40, pp. 261-78.
Putnam, R. D. (2000), *Bowling Alone. The Collapse and Revival of American Community*, New York/London, Simon and Schuster.
Radaev, V. (1999), 'The Building up of New Markets and the State in the Post-Communist Russia', in G. Lengyel (ed.), *New Economic Actors, Institutions and Attitudes in Central and Eastern Europe (A volume of workshop proceedings)*, Budapest, BUESPA.
Rona-Tas, Ákos and Lengyel, G. (eds) (1997/98), 'Entrepreneurship in Eastern Europe I-II', *International Journal of Sociology*, 27(3-4).
Rose, R. and Haerpfer, C. (1998), 'New Democracies Barometer V. A 12-Nation Survey', *Studies in Public Policy* 306, Glasgow.
Sako, M. (1993), *Prices, Quality and Trust. Interfirm Relations in Britain and Japan*, New York, Cambridge University Press.

Sako, M. (1998), 'Does Trust Improve Business Performance?', in C. Lane and R. Bachmann (eds), *Trust Within and Between Orgarnizations. Conceptual and Empirical Applications*, Oxford, Oxford University Press, pp. 88-117.

Seligman, A. S. (1997), *The Problem of Trust*, Princeton, Princeton University Press.

Szanyi, M. (1998), 'Ipari beruházások az átalakuló országokban' (Industrial Investments in the Transition Countries), *Közgazdasági Szemle*, 45(9), pp. 851-68.

Szelényi, I. and Kostello, E. (1998), 'Outline of an Institutionalist Theory of Inequality: The case of socialist and postcommunist Eastern Europe', in M. C. Brinton and V. Nee (eds), *The New Institutionalism in Sociology*, New York, Russell Sage Foundation, pp. 305-26.

Sztompka, P. (1999), *Trust: A sociological theory*, Cambridge, Cambridge University Press.

Török, Á. (1994), 'Stratégia-e a vállalati sodródás?' (Is Enterprise Drifting a Strategy?), *Közgazdasági Szemle*, 41(10), pp. 878-89.

Utasi, Á. (2002), *A bizalom hálója. Mikrotársadalmi kapcsolatok, szolidaritás* (The Net of Trust. Micro-societal connections, solidarity), Uj Mandátum K., Budapest.

Voszka, É. (1996), 'Az utánzó állam és az innovatív vállalatok találkozási pontja – az újraelosztás tradíciója' (The Meeting Point of the Imitating State and the Innovative Firms: The tradition of redistribution), *Közgazdasági Szemle*, 43(6), pp. 553-60.

Weber, M. (1981 (1927)), *General Economic History*, New Brunswick, NJ, Transaction Books.

Whitley, R. (1991), 'The Social Construction of Business Systems in East Asia', *Organization Studies*, 12 (1), pp. 1-28.

Whitley, R., Henderson, J., Czabán, L. and Lengyel, G. (1996), 'Trust and Contractual Relations in an Emerging Capitalist Economy: Changing relationship of then large Hungarian enterprises', *Organization Studies*, No 3.

Yamagishi, T. (2001), 'Trust as a Form of Social Intelligence', in K. S. Cook (ed.), *Trust in Society*, New York, Russell Sage Foundation, pp. 121-47.

Yamagishi, T., Cook, K. S. and Watabe, M. (1998), 'Uncertainty, Trust and Commitment Formation in the United States and Japan', *American Journal of Sociology*, 104 (1), pp. 165-94.

Zucker, L. G. (1986), 'Production of Trust: Institutional sources of economic structure, 1840-1920', *Organizational Behavior*, 8, pp. 53-111.

Appendix

Table 10.1 Perception of security and variables of property, market and economic setting

Variable	Who deem the business environs secure (%)	Phi/ Cramers 'V	N
Mean	34.7		373
Foreign owners	45.0	n.s.	60
State ownership	33.8	n.s.	40
Employee ownership	33.7	n.s.	162
Size of employment 21 +	36.7	n.s.	83
Firm produces profit	35.9	n.s.	267
National or international market	41.0	.17**	209
Sector: light industry	33.2	n.s.	111

Table 10.2 Perceived security and the cultural resources of the firm

Variable	Who deem the business environment secure (%)	Phi/ Cramers 'V	N
Mean	34.7		375
Are diploma holders in the firm: yes	35.2	n.s.	250
Are there computers in the firm: yes	33.0	n.s.	311
Is there intranet in the firm: yes	34.0	.14*	114
Are there employees of the firm (or do they plan to employ some) who speak foreign languages: yes,	36.3	n.s.	240
Age of manager: 45 + years	31.0	.17***	257
Manager has university diploma	42.9	.17*	90
Manager has business diploma in college or university	31.5	n.s.	67
Measures success in financial terms	39.4	n.s	176

Table 10.3 Perceived security and the social resources of the firm

Variable	Who deem their economic environment secure (%)	Phi/ Cramers'V	N
Mean	34.7		375
Relatives of manager work for the firm	26.4	.13*	129
Obligatory relations (delivery prior to contract)	43.7	.19***	144

Table 10.4 Opinions about security and insecurity factors among older and younger managers (%)

	Year of birth: 1964	Year of birth: 1965	Phi/ Cramers's V	N
Finds business environs safe	32.6	52.4	.14*	368
Thinks the employment of foreign labour would cause problems	38.0	18.9	.12*	375
Thinks expansion would bump into too many restricting rule	54.2	34.5	.12*	375
Thinks growth is risky because everything could be lost	48.5	30.2	.11*	375

Table 10.5 Rate of firms finding the business environment secure by obligatory relations and firm property (%)

	Is it typical to deliver to partners prior to signing written contract			Phi/ Cramers'V	N
	No	Someti-mes	Yes		
Property below 60 million HUF	26.5	19.1	44.3	.26***	297
Property at or above 60 million HUF	41.6	46.2	37.6	n.s.	74

Table 10.6 Rate of firms finding the business environment secure by kinship relations and firm resources (%)

	Do relatives work in firm?		Phi/ Cramers'V	N
	No	Yes		
Property below 60 million HUF, no computer network	40.0	26.6	n.s.	235
Property at or above 60 million HUF, or there is computer intranet	37.8	25.8	n.s.	140

Table 10.7 Coefficients of material, cultural and social resources from the logistic regressions (LOGIT-models) of perceived security

Independent Variables	\multicolumn{4}{c}{*Coefficients (and standard errors)*}			
	Model 1	*Model 2*	*Model 3*	*Model 4*
Constant	-1,386*	-3,752***	-1,623**	-4,379***
	(,552)	(,946)	(,572)	(1,032)
Material resources				
State- or foreign owned company	,185			,084
	(,326)			(,384)
Assets (M HUF)	,001			,000
	(,001)			(,000)
Turnover (M HUF)	,001			,000
	(,001)			(,000)
Number of employees	,001			,002
	(,001)			(,001)
Cultural resources				
Success-perception in financial terms		,356		,300
		(,248)		(,262)
Intranet at the company		-,501		-,475
		(,293)		(,331)
University (MA) degree		,643*		-,467
		(,309)		(,346)
Degree: business, econ. or law		-,364		,335
		(,319)		(,336)
Year of birth		,041**		,048**
		(,014)		(,015)
Social resources				
Obligatory contractual relationships			,475	,503
			(,286)	(,305)
Interaction var.: obl. rel*small company (0-5 employees)			,791	,729
			(,458)	(,483)
Managers relatives among the employees			-1,131***	-1,118**
			(,336)	(,363)
Interaction var.: relatives*small company (0-5 employees)			1,404**	1,635**
			(,503)	(,526)
-2 log-likelihood	442,866	416,565	417,272	382,038
Nagelkerke – pseudo R²	13,0%	17,9%	22,4%	27,6%
Proportion of correct predictions	68%	67%	70%	72%
N	374	365	376	363

Notes Standard errors are in parentheses under the coefficients. Beside the presented variables, some control variables are included in all of the models. The estimated coefficients and standard errors of those control variables are presented in Table 10.8.
* $p < 0,05$ ** $p < 0,01$ *** $p < 0,001$

Table 10.8 Coefficients of control variables from the logistic regressions (LOGIT-models) of perceived security

Independent Variables	Coefficients (and standard errors)			
	Model 1	Model 2	Model 3	Model 4
Control variables				
Sector and technology				
Light-industry	-,036	,189	-,251	-,169
	(,458)	(,489)	(,481)	(,533)
Heavy industry	,204	,375	,283	,434
	(,475)	(,501)	(,489)	(,539)
Machine industry	,011	,082	,095	,163
	(,492)	(,525)	(,508)	(,560)
Other	,117	,141	,163	,197
	(,508)	(,541)	(,513)	(,570)
Production technology: continuous	,426	,519*	,454	,494
	(,266)	(,272)	(,278)	(,301)
Market characteristics				
Nation-wide or international market-area	,620*	,572*	,669**	,636*
	(,248)	(,261)	(,253)	(,279)
The main customer's share (per cent)	,006	,007	,006	,007
	(,004)	(,004)	(,004)	(,004)
Decline of demand	-,722*	-,658*	-,860**	-,683*
	(,286)	(,293)	(,296)	(,315)
Success				
Use of capacities (per cent)	,005	,004	,008	,008
	(,004)	(,004)	(,004)	(,005)
High volatility of profit	-,485*	-,517*	-,449	-,511*
	(,234)	(,243)	(,243)	(,258)

Notes Standard errors are in parentheses under the coefficients. For the explanatory variables of the four models see Table 10.7.
* $p < 0,05$ ** $p < 0,01$

Young Entrepreneurs in the New Market Economies: Cultural and Social Capital as a Basis for Economic Capital

Jochen Tholen

Introduction

This paper arises from interviews in 1996 and 1997 with 550 under 30-year-old entrepreneurs in seven former communist countries. Four of them are in East-Central Europe (Bulgaria, Hungary, Slovakia and Poland), and three in the Commonwealth of Independent States (Armenia, Georgia and Ukraine); the latter act as a kind of control group to make clear the different developments although all seven societies started their new beginning in 1989 from the same line. Some distinctive features of small businesses in all the ex-communist countries are noted: the youth of the businesses and the inexperience of their proprietors, the absence of formal business support services, the radical outlooks of the entrepreneurs, their work-centred lifestyles, and the possibility of extremely rapid progress.

However, most important are the *differences* between the three GUS countries on the one hand (to be called CIS) and the four Middle and Eastern European countries with the focus on South-East European countries (to be called CEE) on the other, regarding young entrepreneurs and their businesses. In East-Central Europe the new business classes were being recruited from the wider range of social backgrounds, most businesses were based on the proprietors' specialised education and training, self-employment had been the majority's aim prior to completing their education, and when achieved it was nearly always a full-time occupation. In the former Soviet Union trading was the pivotal business activity, more business was in the second economies, bribery was more widespread, businesses were usually partnerships, genuinely independent female entrepreneurs were rare, and businessmen tended to act on the assumption that they needed to succeed quickly, by striking the big deal, because the gradual step-by-step development of their enterprises was likely to be thwarted by changes in the political and economic environments.

In the form of a matrix the research hypotheses and the resulting interpretation of the empirical findings in the final conclusions will be expounded in the following. Essentially our starting points are two independent and four dependent variables, with which help the results to put, not ideally typical in Weber's classical sense, but systematically, in order.

As independent variables we have defined:

1. the status quo of the market reforms and the implementation of the rule of law (sustainable or ambivalent) as macro variable, which cannot be influenced by the young entrepreneurs as individuals,
2. the type of school and vocational education of the focus group (craftsmen / artisans or academics), positioned on the micro level and decided *before* jumping in the self-employment.

11.1 Matrix: The development of the economic independence in the CIS and CEE countries

	Interfaces of Vocational Education with Type of Business		Legal Position of Business		Rank of self-employment		Stability of aims/ Trust in Future	
	1. *Yes*	*2.* *No*	*1.* *Regis tra- tion*	*2.* *Shadow Econo- my*	*1.* *Main Work*	*2.* *Side job*	*1.* *Yes*	*2.* *No*
Market Reforms/Rule of Law								
1. Sustainable	CEE		CEE		CEE		CEE	
2. Ambivalent		CIS		CIS		CIS		CIS
Type of Vocational Education								
1. Artisans	CEE		CEE		CEE		CEE	
2. Academic		CIS		CIS		CIS		CIS

Dependent variables are all positioned on the micro level and encompass the objective data as well as subjective (personal) attitudes of the young self-employed; but *both* are essentially shaped and influenced *during* their time as self-employed.

Of importance are here:

a) The types of business or the type of work of the young entrepreneurs (related to or no interfaces with the type of their previous vocational education);
b) legal position of the business / enterprise (official registration or hidden in the shadow economy);
c) rank of self-employment in the frame of the total activity of the focus group (main work or side job);

d) stability of the aims/trust in the future of the young self-employed (positive or negative).

Even if this matrix cannot include certain exceptions (so a few of the CEE independent entrepreneurs have a classical academic education), nevertheless the decisive criteria becomes clear, with which on the basis of our empirical results two different types of young entrepreneurs can be defined in the transformation societies of the East:

The 'Westernised' Young Entrepreneur

Growth and progress in the area of the founding of new companies have been substantially promoted in the CEE states because of their orientation to the core states of the European Union and therefore 'westernised'.

Generational experiences with at least rudimentary civil societies, even if they were not linked with democracy everywhere in the time between the wars, combined with certain knowledge of industrial production, are obviously resounding in the CEE countries even today. Characteristics of this type of young entrepreneur, which obviously can be empirically differentiated in the four CEE states, are the big intersections of vocational training with the type of business, the official registration of the company, the self-employment as main source of income and a positive outlook on the future.

The Post-Soviet Young Self-employed

In the CIS a substantially different development in society has emerged since 1989 (even though those countries are specifically different as well), which can be called as 'post Soviet capitalism'.

This capitalism is characterised on the political level by a patrimonial democracy, on the economic level by a system of oligarchic clans. Both levels are multifariously connected with each other. Compared with the CEE states, the small trade structures, in which the young self-employed 'move', are, more or less, no organic part of the macro-economic and social structures, but sealed off from the large companies, banks and their ruling elites. Thus it is understandable, why in the CIS states, the young self-employed have to 'move' in small niches, which are characterised, among others, that there are only a few intersections between vocational training (mostly academics) and the objectives of their business (mostly (street) trade). The business remains in the shadow economy and is only a side job of the young people, which as a result (as a consequence one could say), hardly have confidence in the future stability of their societies.

In this contribution the argumentation is thus, that in the future those politics and programs, which initiate and promote the emergence of new self-employment in the new market economies and which are often supported by the west politically and financially, should take into account the differences of the various societies more often.

Cultural and Social capital as a Basis for Economic Capital of the Post-Soviet Young Self-employed

I would like to focus on the young self-employed in the three ex-Soviet Union countries (Armenia, Georgia, Ukraine).

Hypothesis: Cultural and Social Capital as a Basis for Economic Capital in the Three Countries

The following analysis draws on Pierre Bourdieu's thesis on the differences between economic, cultural and social capital (Bourdieu 1986); furthermore we follow Coleman (1988) and other scholars like Putnam (1993, 1995) who have conceptualised social capital a bit more precisely.

With the help of their terms we will explain our data. In an a kind of inductive approach, we generate and defend a hypothesis, which turns Bourdieu's general framework – that economic capital will create and foster cultural and social capital – a little bit from the feet to the head: According to our empirical results, cultural and social capital are a basis for economic capital.

Finally at the end of this paper we construct a kind of typology of Soviet-style self-employment, which indicates major differences to entrepreneurship in CEE countries.

Theory

Economic capital is capital in the traditional and purely economic sense (possessing money and property). Naturally, this is the central form of capital in capitalistic societies. However, even in these highly developed societies (according to what are common criteria), economic capital alone does not necessarily guarantee power, or rather no longer guarantees power. A general science of the economy of practices must endeavour to grasp capital and profit in all their forms and to establish the laws whereby the different types of capital (or power) (which amounts to the same thing) change into one another (Bourdieu 1986: pp. 242-243). Only in connection with the other forms of capital (cultural and social) can someone exercise real power.

This is especially the case for transformation societies where, up until 1992 and sometimes even beyond this date, the state or rather the old and new *nomenclatura* held or still hold most capital in their hands. This capital can only be retained or increased when it is prepared to take on competition in the world economy. This means that the original economic capital plays a much smaller role in the development of countries undergoing transformation than in the 'old' market societies.

Cultural capital is the capital, which someone has at his/her disposal thanks to his/her vocational training and education. Cultural capital can exist in three forms: in the *embodied* state, i.e., in the form of long-lasting dispositions of the mind and the body; in the *objectified* state, in the form of cultural goods (pictures, dictionaries, instruments, machines, etc.), which are the embodiment of theories or critiques of these theories, problematics, etc.; and in the *institutionalised* state, specifically educational qualifications, whereby it confers entirely original properties on the cultural capital which it is presumed to guarantee (Bourdieu 1986, p. 243). However, cultural capital is not just an individual quality; it can be inherited and increased through family tradition. If higher education and university have been taken for granted in a family for generations, then this could lead to a 'natural' contact with educational and cultural institutions as if this was the most normal thing in the world.

Cultural capital is always reproduced through the system of teaching of a given society (schools and universities) and family inheritance. The incorporation, internalisation of cultural capital plays an important role in this situation as it costs time. The incorporation of cultural capital always has to be repeated by each individual; it cannot be delegated.

Social capital includes *relationships* that someone can fall back upon. Unlike economic capital, social capital functions purely symbolically and immaterially.

Social capital is the aggregate of the actual or potential resources which are linked to possessions of a durable network of more or less institutionalised relationships of mutual acquaintance and recognition – or in other words, to membership in a group – which provides each of its members with the backing of collectivity-owned capital, a 'credential' which entitles them to credit, in the various senses of the word (Bourdieu 1986, pp. 248-249).

We follow the extensions of this term by Coleman (1988) and Putnam (1995), which include not only social relationships, but also the norms and values associated with them.

Proceeding with Bourdieu, social capital acts as a 'capital of honour and prestige', being credit-worthy in the broadest sense of the term. Social capital is the form of capital, which all societies – pre-capitalistic societies such as the Berber in North-West Africa, state socialist societies such as the former USSR, transformation societies (our three countries for example) and western capitalist societies – have in common.

There is a tight connection between the different forms of capital and how a society is governed. Furthermore, the different forms of capital are mutually convertible. Social and cultural capital can be converted into economic capital.

The economic capital, which was controlled by state socialism, is eroding in the present transformation societies. Thus, cultural and social capital occupies central positions in the development of these societies.

The Young Self-employed in Armenia, Georgia and Ukraine – the Empirical Results

Aims and methods During 1996 to 1997 we interviewed 150 young entrepreneurs in three countries of the former Soviet Union – Armenia, Georgia and Ukraine. The young people were aged up to 30 and were all 'doing business' as their main economic activity. All but one of the businesses were officially registered in the countries concerned and they all had turnovers of at least the equivalent of 1000 USA dollars per year. A few of the businesses were privatised former state enterprises but these were not large factories. They were smaller units such as an architect' practice and a meat processing factory, and most of the businesses had no earlier history but had been created *de novo* by our respondents since 1991.

Most of the entrepreneurs who were interviewed in Armenia were in the capital city, Yerevan. In Georgia 40 were living and had businesses based in Tbilisi, and 10 in Telavi, a provincial city. In Ukraine there were 25 from Donetsk and 25 from Lviv, cities in east and west Ukraine respectively.

Despite the research aiming to study young male and female entrepreneurs the vast majority of the respondents were male. In Georgia and Ukraine respectively there were just eight and nine females among the 50 individuals who were interviewed in each country. In Armenia all but four out of the 50 respondents were male. The business women who were identified and interviewed were usually in enterprises that had been established with the assistance of, and/or were being run with male partners or 'protectors' – almost always a father, brother, husband or boyfriend. Some of the female interviewees in Georgia and Ukraine explained that they themselves could not answer all our questions – about dealing with tax and registration offices for example – because their male associates handled all such matters. In all three countries business was a masculine sphere. The following passages, therefore, refer to businessmen not as a sexist slip, but because this was the term used locally when speaking of the self-employed in general, and this reflected the reality of the situations. In the parallel studies of support services for the self-employed we encountered no high profile projects that specifically targeted independent business-women, let alone self-help women's groups operating effectively in this sphere.

The respondents were identified haphazardly rather than sampled systematically. 'Snowball' methods were used in all three countries but within guidelines which insisted that, in addition to the parameters outlined above, those selected should be from a range of construction, manufacturing, and buy-sell businesses, plus consumer, financial and other business services, that both males and females should be included, and that the respondents should be scattered across the age range up to 30.

Prior to embarking on this study we knew that small private businesses which had been created *de novo* or had emerged from the second economies were growing rapidly in number and strength in all the former communist countries, and had become responsible for most of the job generation in these places while state sector jobs were being lost (see Bilsen and Konings 1996; European Bank for Reconstruction and Development 1996; Konings et al 1995). We also knew that young people were well represented among the post-communist societies' new business classes. High levels of unemployment, combined with the generally positive, developmental, pro-reform and entrepreneurial attitudes of the age group, appeared to be responsible for this (see Buncak 1996; Genov 1996; Machacek 1996; Roberts and Jung 1995).

From a previous study of management in Russia (carried out between 1989-1993), we expected entrepreneurs to be supporters of the market economy as well as of extensive privatisation. The entrepreneur can mainly be found in the trade and service sectors, mostly in small or middle-sized companies. As a rule he is interested in short-term gains, in quick profits and less interested in a longer-term continual change in structure to a social market economy. Looking at him in a social-political way, the entrepreneur is usually a keen advocate of liberal Mancunian ideas, and in the end, of dispensing with an active social policy because of the costs to him personally. In a sociological sense the entrepreneur is from many more groups than the market manager is. Here there are members of the former political and economic *nomenklatura*, and scientists and artists, and from all possible further groups of the population (Eberwein and Tholen 1997, p. 227).

The fieldworkers had little difficulty in gaining the co-operation of the young entrepreneurs who were approached in Georgia and Ukraine. Our initial approaches were usually made by telephone followed by interviews at the respondents' places of work. In each country locally based postgraduates conducted the fieldwork, and in Ukraine and Georgia there were hardly any refusals. The situation in Armenia was rather different. In fact the Armenian fieldworkers found it very difficult to operate outside Yerevan, the city where they were based. Even in Yerevan they were suspected of being agents of the government and some respondents refused to answer any 'dangerous' questions – all those about money and political attitudes. Armenia had acquired new rulers on gaining independence but the old political structures and *de facto* one party rule were retained (see Fischer and Grigorian 1993). This was in the context of a war situation: Armenia was engaged in a military struggle with Azerbaijan over the status of Nagorno Karabakh. Armenia's then new rulers gained power on a platform of settling (winning) this dispute, and in the process established quasi-totalitarian control in Armenia. This was the country where no one complained about a crime problem. A reverse situation existed in Georgia where there were widespread complaints about crime and political instability.

The interviews were semi-structured. Certain topics were always covered, but with open-ended questions. Information was sought about each individual's family and educational backgrounds, and his or her history in business and any other work experience. The development of each respondent's business career was explored in some detail – how and why the individual had become self-employed, his or her successes and failures, obstacles encountered and how these had been negotiated. There were further questions on each respondent's out-of-work lifestyle and political opinions.

Cultural capital as a springboard for creating economic capital The accumulation of cultural capital in the '*embodied state*, i.e., in the form called culture, cultivation, *Bildung*, presupposes a process of embodiment, incorporation, which, insofar as it implies a laboratory of inculcation and assimilation, costs time, time which must be invested personally by the investor. Cultural capital, in the *objectified state*, has a number of properties that are defined only in the relationship with cultural capital in the embodied form. The owner of the means of production must find a way of appropriating either the embodied capital, which is a precondition of specific appropriation, or the services of the holders of this capital. By conferring *institutional* recognition on the cultural capital possessed by any given agent, the academic qualification also makes it possible to compare qualification holders and even to exchange them (by establishing one for another in succession). Furthermore, it makes it possible to establish conversion rates between cultural capital and economic capital by guaranteeing the monetary value of a given academic capital (Bourdieu 1986, pp. 244-248).

Most of the young entrepreneurs, around 80 percent in all three countries, had either graduated from or were still in higher education. Studies in other ex-communist countries have noted that their young self-employed are generally well educated (see Genov 1996), but mainly in the fields of pure sciences and engineering. In our investigation there was usually no direct connection between the courses that the respondents had studied and their business activities. Higher education was more likely to have acted as a springboard for business careers by creating space in which the young people could widen their social networks, and review their career aspirations and strategies.

In some ways the young entrepreneurs in Ukraine, Georgia and Armenia resembled, while in other respects there were stark contrasts with the profiles of the self-employed in more mature Western market economics. In the West there is now a tendency for business to be a family tradition. Males are over-represented among the self-employed in Western countries, though not to the same extent as in the former Soviet Union. The self-employed in the West are drawn from all educational and occupational levels. Marginal groups, ethnic minorities for example, are sometimes over-represented (see Blanchflower et al 1987; Labour Market Quarterly Report 1993; Taylor 1994). In contrast, in so far as our respondents offer reliable indications, the relatively successful young self-employed in the countries concerned tended to be from mainstream, high status groups. Whether the profiles of the self-employed in these countries will change as their market economies mature is a question that only time will settle.

There was rarely a close connection between the respondents' 'specialities' the subjects they had studied at secondary school and subsequently, and their lines of business. In Ukraine just eight out of the 50 entrepreneurs said that there was a total coincidence, though another 23 claimed that there was some overlap. The proportions were very similar in Georgia and Armenia. However, the tendency over time, as the respondents' business careers had developed, had been for the overlap to widen.

Not a single respondent had aimed for a business career when at secondary school. Self-employment had been no-one's original intention. Some had completed their secondary education under communism, but even those who had left school since 1991 had expected and wanted to become employees, usually in state departments or enterprises, almost always according to their specialities. A few who had completed their courses in the 1990s had hoped to obtain jobs in private (usually Western based or linked) companies.

Virtually everyone had made an initial transition from education into jobs where they had expected to remain. Everyone had some experience of being an employee. A few had experienced spells of unemployment, but generally these young people had always remained active. Most had 'prospective' rather than 'adaptive' or 'survival' orientations amidst the changes that were underway in their countries (see Koridze 1995; Tarkowska 1994). None of those who reported spells of unemployment had registered at a Labour Office. They had known that registration would not lead to offers of jobs that they wanted, and that they would either have been ineligible for benefits or, if they were eligible, that the payments would have been derisory.

Virtually everyone explained how they had been 'pushed' into depending mainly on self-employment for their incomes when the state economies collapsed and their salaries became non-existent or nominal. Very few Western businesses opened plants or even offices in any of the cities where our research was conducted so seeking such employment was not a real option. The young people explained that, if they had wanted to earn money, there had been no alternative but to try to work on their own accounts. In Tbilisi in 1992 40 percent of the workforce was judged to be unemployed and most factories were estimated to be operating at around 15 percent of their full capacity (Europa Publications 1994). The situation was similar in Armenia. In Ukraine conditions were less extreme, but not fundamentally different. Of course, when they had started to work for themselves our respondents were aware that business could be a route to riches. Self-employment was basically their survival tactic in the first instance, but some had hoped that eventually it might become their enrichment strategy.

Researchers have noted similar combinations of push and pull forces operating in initial decisions to become self-employed in Western countries (see Bögenhold and Stabler 1991; Meager 1992; MacDonald 1996). In Ukraine, Georgia and Armenia both forces were unusually intense. For most young people there was simply no other way in which they could earn any money. Simultaneously, in the early stages of marketisation spectacular progress was possible.

Initial steps into self-employment had usually been made tentatively. When they had started out in business most respondents were still in education or jobs, usually in the state sector. Many had begun in business when they were students and had continued after entering employment. At the time of our study some were still formally employees in state companies and departments even though they had been making most of their money through business for several years. The commitment that could be expected of public sector employees had become extremely modest when salaries were often unpaid, or, if paid, extremely low. There were several reasons why some of the self-employed had been keen to hold on to their original jobs. First, at the outset they had known that their own businesses were insecure. Second, even in the mid-1990s business was not always regarded as a proper profession and individuals could be reluctant to abandon the 'prestige' of a state sector job. Third, such jobs could be a useful source of additional income. Fourth, the jobs could preserve contacts which could be useful in the self-employed's dealings with state officials and departments. Fifth, and over-arching everything else, there had been a feeling that eventually 'normality' would be restored and that the young people would be able to resume their real careers. This feeling was weakening but it was still alive in 1996.

Typically the young people's first steps into business had been by 'trading', straightforward buying and selling. In its most basic form this involved the street sale of personal or household items, or farm or garden produce. When traders had sufficient capital they could buy in bulk. Those who had the means could go on 'shopping tours' to countries where the products were cheaper than at home. In the cities where our research was based the cheaper places were usually Arab states or other middle-east countries. One individual could do everything or, more commonly, by partners who pooled their resources and labour. As turnover rose imported goods could be sold to other street traders, shops or kiosks, or the partners could establish fixed sites of their own.

The skills of trading were usually learnt, in the first instance, by doing odd jobs for someone else, but before long the young people in this study had begun to trade on their own accounts. The attractions of this kind of business were that the overheads and start-up costs could be very low, turnover could be high, and profits made quickly. Moreover, the businesses did not require sophisticated machinery, marketing or anything else. Virtually anyone could trade if they had the need and drive, and could ensure their own safety on the streets and when travelling. In the aftermath of communism trading soon became ubiquitous. Merchants became visible on all international rail and bus routes, and on air flights to and from former communist countries. Virtually all young people seemed to become involved in a major or minor way, at some time or another (see Roberts and Jung 1995).

Traders were in fact the largest group among the respondents in all the countries in this research. This was despite the fieldworkers endeavouring to cover a 'good spread' of businesses. In Ukraine 26 out of the 50 enterprises had trading as a main activity, and the proportions in Georgia and Armenia, were similar. However, trading was not necessarily these young people's sole line of business. Many were operating in several 'business sectors' simultaneously, and it had been common for individuals to switch between different kinds of enterprise as their business careers developed. And during these switches there had been a general movement away from relying exclusively on buying and selling, and into other lines of business.

That means that there is a dynamic process of different steps toward self-employment. Confronted with the lack of economic capital (including the lack of job vacancies), young people use their cultural (and their social, see below) capital, especially their academic qualifications, to set up businesses of their own. But two remarks will modify this general picture.

The academic qualifications, which are used for starting a business of their own, are focussed only on the abstract, personal related aspect of qualifications (i.e. abstract training in thinking and acting etc.). It leaves out the vocational part of the academic qualifications. In other words, there is a very weak relationship between the qualifications (mostly as engineers) and the kind of business (mostly trading).

There is a danger, that the young self-employed will remain in the sector of trading, due not only to the lack of economic capital, but also to the lack of a good and reliable infrastructure in the societies (including the rule of the law), which will not allow the traders to move into other sectors of business (industry, other services). As a result, the tendency toward a 'normal' role for entrepreneurs in a Western sense as a backbone of the economy cannot be seen in the CIS countries so far.

Sources of Assistance – Social Capital as a Springboard for Developing Economic Capital

> The volume of the social capital possessed by a given agent ... depends on the size of the network of connections he can effectively mobilise and on the volume of the capital (economic, cultural or symbolic) possessed in his own right by each of those to whom he is connected. ... The profits, which accrue from membership in a group, are the basis of the solidarity that makes them possible. ... The reproduction of social capital presupposes an unceasing effort of sociability, a continuous series of exchanges in which recognition is endlessly affirmed and reaffirmed (Bourdieu 1986, pp. 249-250).

This kind of reproduction can lead to Mafia-like networks, which are widespread in the transformation societies; so unassailable and – in a certain sense – so successful.

Coming back to the centre of our argument, we will follow the distinction of Granovetter (1992) between the *structural* and the *relational* dimensions of social capital.

The *structural* dimension includes social action. The location of an actor's contacts in a social structure of interactions provides certain advantages for the actor (to get jobs, to obtain information, to access specific resources). The *relational* dimension of social capital refers to assets that are rooted in these relationships, such as trust and trustworthiness. Both dimensions are important to understand social capital as a main resource for young people in the CIS countries to set up their own businesses.

Few of the businessmen reported having received or sought assistance from any of the state or non-governmental organisations that operated relevant programs in their cities. Many respondents clearly felt that the idea of state officials offering assistance to businesses must surely be a joke. Some had used private consultants or mediators. Very few had sufficient trust in banks to deposit funds or use their foreign transaction services let alone seek their advice. Business was always in cash or on a barter basis.

None of the respondents were from long established business families. Open careers in business had been impossible for their parents. However, most of the parents had worked in management, professional or intellectual occupations under communism. Many of these parents had assisted their children's business start-ups though only a minority was directly involved as partners. It was usually more a matter of parents having been able and willing to finance their children's initial steps into self-employment, and otherwise offer advice and encouragement. Some of the parents had contacts with government departments and state enterprises that could be used to their children's advantage. Research in other countries has found that the members of older generations who have opted for self-employment since the collapse of communism have often been able to use experience, information and contacts built-up under the old systems (see Kusa and Tirpakova 1993), and in our study some had been able to pursue surrogate careers in business through their children.

Families and friends were far and away the main, and normally the only sources of assistance that the young people had received. Some attributed their success, such as they had achieved, entirely to their own efforts. They explained how they had saved start-up capital from earnings in their jobs and how they had learnt the arts of business in the 'school of life'. Many were proud of this. However, most had received some assistance, usually from close friends or family members. Families had been the most common source of start-up capital. Some respondents explained how flats or cars had been sold in order to raise the funds. If it was from within a family the money was almost always a gift, albeit one, which reinforced reciprocal obligations. When money had been raised from friends this was invariably as a (short-term) loan.

Friends had been the most common source of business information, advice and contacts. Often, but not always, these were the same friends who became business partners. Families had played a secondary role in offering advice and information on how to operate in a market economy. Market institutions – banks, trade directories, business associations and suchlike – were still emergent in the 1990s. The first generation businessmen in the former Soviet countries had found that the most reliable advice and information, often the only advice and information that they could trust, was from people who were already known and trusted, and who had first-hand experience in business.

On the basis of our interviews and referring to Coleman's distinction of social capital, the families represent both the structural *and* the relational dimensions, whereas the friends are more linked to the relational dimension of social capital.

The development of economic capital as a result of deploying cultural and social capital   Considering that nearly all of our respondents had created their business *de novo* (which means with a very small amount of starting capital) and none of them had access and/or could use the old state companies (in the process of a mysterious 'privatisation') to set up their own businesses, their economic success is rather remarkable.

At this point it may be useful to emphasise that all our respondents ran at least moderately successful businesses. We know from other research (Roberts 1996) that in Armenia, Georgia and Ukraine young males from all social backgrounds were more or less equally likely to try to make money by doing business. The generally advantaged backgrounds of the young people in this study, therefore, should be viewed as characteristics of those who had been relatively successful. Their educational and family backgrounds will help to explain their success rather than their starting-out in business.

All the respondents had reasonably substantial businesses with turnovers of at least $1,000 per year, and their career histories will exaggerate the success chances of all the young people in Ukraine, Georgia and Armenia who were trying to make money by 'doing business'. Over time our respondents had tended to move out of straightforward buying and selling, and such broadening-out had been most likely when the young people had 'specialities', skills and knowledge from their education, on which businesses could be based. This applied to those who had been trained in medicine, teaching, architecture, motor repairs and other scientific and technical areas. It also applied to those who had been educated in economics and finance. But this coincidence between the young people's original specialities and their businesses was turning out to be a very fragile process. On the one hand, the insecure social and economic framework in these countries, testified by the breakdown in finance in the Russian Federation in August/September 1998, was damaging this process. On the other hand, the overlap seemed to be consolidated as individuals enrolled on further courses to upgrade or extend their skills, usually in book-keeping, accounting, marketing or management rather than technical areas. Some, who had decided that business would be their long-term occupation had also decided to become properly qualified so that they could conduct their affairs, regard themselves and be regarded by others as professional rather than amateur.

There had been a trend over time, as the young people's experience in business widened, for individuals to become increasingly committed to their business careers. As this happened they would formally quit any jobs in which they had nominally remained employed, regard business as their real and long-term profession, and make plans for the future development of their enterprises. At the time of our interviews nearly all the respondents planned to remain self-employed indefinitely. Rather than a temporary fall-back or a fast route to riches, business was coming to be regarded as a serious job, that required hard work and appropriate skills and knowledge, and step-by-step development (see Nodia 1994). Individuals were becoming more aware of the many advantages of self-employment: 'you own yourself', 'everything is up to you', 'there's more professional satisfaction than when you're just an employee'. Also, needless to say, there was the prospect of real success and riches. The careers of our respondents were mirroring the development of their countries' private sector economies in which businesses were becoming more substantial, and commerce was acting as the generator of a wider range of business activities.

Some of the young people's businesses had already become quite substantial enterprises. They had up to 94 employees and annual turnovers of up to $2,000,000. A few were still small-scale and close to our lower baseline for inclusion of $1,000 in annual turnover, but in Armenia most of the businesses had turnovers in excess of $100,000, and most of the Georgian businesses were turning over from $100,000 to $300,000 per year. All these businesses were partnerships. This was the normal way in which the young people had become involved in, and how they practised business. Individuals created enterprises with family members or friends. Sometimes they would initially do jobs for, then become partners in the enterprises. Later on, needless to say, they could become the recruiters. The number of partners in the enterprises that we studied ranged from 2 to 15. In Ukraine there were more sole proprietors, 19 out of the 50 young people, and their businesses were correspondingly smaller: most had annual turnovers of less than $40,000 and only three in excess of $80,000.

The respondents' personal incomes were not closely related to the levels of turnover and profit in their businesses. The majority were taking out just enough for decent, but not grossly extravagant, lifestyles in their countries. Most had personal incomes of $250-$600 per month. In some cases the businessmen's personal takes were higher but never above $1,000. In Armenia, the country with the lowest living standards and prices, more were taking less than $200 per month than in the other countries. The ethic governing the business careers of the young people in this study was not earn and spend, but invest, work, earn, then invest again. In Georgia there were very few respondents who had been away on holiday during the previous year. Very few in any country were going regularly to restaurants. Two-thirds in Ukraine, and rather fewer in Georgia and Armenia, had private motor cars. Their business lives were over-arched by a feeling that they needed to succeed and build-up capital as quickly as possible. As they saw their situations, a 'window of opportunity' had opened in their countries but at any time it could be slammed shut again.

Conclusion and Outlook

It is still too early to tell in which direction – economically, socially and politically – the transformation societies in these countries are moving.

But what we know from our research is that, on the one hand, it is obvious that the self-employed themselves are as active as any other parties in helping to perpetuate some of the problems about which they complain most bitterly and frequently – by avoiding taxes and paying bribes for example. They were adopting methods that enabled them to survive and sometimes flourish in post-Soviet conditions, but their ways of doing business were imposing limitations on how the enterprises could develop. Thriving in post-Soviet conditions required fast turnovers and rapid profits. Even medium term development plans, rather than just hopes, were rare. Substantial investment with the aim of long-term profit, in premises and manufacturing equipment for example, was simply too risky for the majority to contemplate.

But, on the other hand, there was a broad consensus among the young self-employed in all three countries on the main problems confronting small businesses and the changes that were needed in order to create environments favourable to businesses' growth and success. The young people wanted corrupt state officials to be replaced by 'real professionals', they wanted lower taxes on businesses and profits, and they wanted appropriate, clear and stable legal frameworks for their enterprises. In the mid-1990s legal statutes and regulations suited to private enterprise and market relationships were still being formulated (see Committee on Economic Policy and Reform of the Georgian Parliament 1996). The old state sectors were still operating in many of their old ways. In this context the young self-employed's basic problem was that could never be sure about what the law required of them. They could never be completely confident that they were not breaking some old or new rule.

Other problems varied in their intensity from country to country. Complaints about political instability were most common in Georgia. Crime and protection rackets were problems for some of the self-employed in Georgia and Ukraine, but not in Armenia where the businessmen were more likely to deplore the 'heavy' political conditions under which they operated.

Coming back to the future development of the transformation societies in general, we assume, that 'the catching-up revolution' accurately describes this development. This is the term that the German sociologist and philosopher Jürgen Habermas has used to describe the transformation societies at the beginning of the nineties:

In order for the revolution to make a return to the democratic state possible, and to catch up with the developed West, it must orient itself towards models, which, according to orthodox interpretation, were already out of date by the revolution of 1917. This may explain a feature peculiar to this revolution: the almost complete lack of innovative, forward-looking ideas (Habermas 1990, p. 181).

However, this 'catching-up revolution' in the transformation societies in CIS and CEE countries has been accompanied from the very beginning by a stubborn misunderstanding. It was and is often assumed that market economies have 'an origin' and that their development has progressed in a natural way. If the legal obstacles, which stood in the way of the free action of economic subjects, were overcome, everything would settle itself. This belief, which was often promoted by Western, especially American advisers, has proven to be false. The best or worst example of this is the liberalisation of prices by the Gaidar government in Russia in 1992 that became known as shock therapy. The failure of this brought about great disappointment amongst the people about the advantages of a bourgeois society, linked with democratic regulations and economic welfare.

A market economy can be sought and created in a political way (as for example in the three Western zones in Germany after 1945). It must then be reformed again and again, politically. Market economy is a cultural and civil achievement that must be professionally mastered by economic subjects.

The theories of civil society, which Armenia, Georgia and Ukraine are striving for (at least after their break-away from the Soviet Union in 1991/92), included the economic society from the very beginning (*cf.* Mestmaecker 1991). Market economy presupposes a very demanding legal and social environment. In the case of the transformation of a socialist planned economy, it is not only a matter of changing the legal order but it also concerns the institutions which have been created within society on the basis of civil rights connected with a legal state administration. In this respect, it is a matter of the people accepting this order, that is to say, a question of legitimisation.

This has quite considerable implications especially for groups such as the young self-employed in countries such as in Armenia, Georgia and Ukraine. The implications for the future development of these countries, whose importance cannot be exaggerated, concern how social and cultural capital can be used in order to create economic capital:

If we link the approach of the development of institutions (theory of transaction costs) with the actors' level and with that of social experience which can cover many generations, we can, along with Claus Offe, distinguish three theoretical approaches to explain different developments in CIS countries on the one hand and in CEE countries on the other, though they all started from the same line between 1989-1991 (Offe 1992, pp. 38-40):

The 'homo sovieticus' theories proceed from the fact that people in the old regime developed a belief (not founded on a legal system), which started out from (automatic) progress. Therefore they developed poor working habits like fear of innovation, lack of effort and initiative, and a tendency to gain patronage and protection as a result of submissiveness. Nowadays individuals must learn that only their own efforts count and that progress and social security arise strictly from increasing productivity at work and in other markets.

The 'homo economicus' theories proceed from the fact that aversion to hard work and exertion is a general but not culturally–conditioned phenomenon of human nature. A basic fault and serious mistake of state socialist planned economies was the absence of an effective mechanism to do away with, or to correct, unproductive workers and ineffective production.

A third theory proceeds from the 'homo hungaricus': Economic virtues like effort and inventions were actually developed under the old regime, but in very hidden, distorted ways, which were threatened by constant repression. These 'unofficial' virtues must now be recognised, generalised and rewarded through official (social as well as state) recognition.

If we apply this typology of transformation paths to our empirical results both in the three CIS countries and in the four CEE countries,[1] Offe's 'homo hungaricus' correspondents with our 'Westernised young entrepreneur', and his 'homo sovieticus' does the same with our 'post-Soviet self-employed'.

As our empirical results show that young people in the three CIS societies want the rule of law and just taxes. They want the system of corruption and state incompetence to disappear. They want organised crime to be fought. All these negative factors make them dependent on the goodwill of those who, as parasites, hinder the development of a market society. The talent of these young people can, however, only be fully developed under the normal conditions of an open society, and the parasites know this only too well.

---

[1] The last OECD study on entrepreneurship indicates striking differences in pure numbers between CEE countries and the Russian Federation (OECD 1998, pp. 269-86)

References

Bilsen, V. and Konings, J. (1996), 'Job Creation, Job Destruction and Growth of Newly Established Firms in Transition Economies: Survey Evidence from Bulgaria, Hungary and Romania', *Working Paper 59/1996*, Leuven, Institute for Central and East European Studies, Catholic University of Leuven.

Blanchflower, D. G., Decks, A. J., Garrett, M. D. and Oswald, A. J. (1987), 'Entrepreneurship and Self-Employment in Britain', Department of Economics, University of Surrey and Centre for Labour Economics, London School of Economics.

Bögenhold, D. and Stabler, U. (1991), 'The Decline and Rise of Self-employment', *Work, Employment and Society*, 5, pp. 223-39.

Bourdieu, P. (1986), 'The Forms of Capital', in J. G. Richardson (ed.), *Handbook of Theory and Research for the Sociology of Education*, New York, Greenwood Press, pp. 241-58.

Buncak, J. (ed.) (1996), *Actors and Strategies of Social Transformation and Modernisation*, Bratislava, Institute of Sociology, Slovak Academy of Sciences.

Coleman, J. S. (1988), 'Social Capital in the Creation of Human Capital', *American Journal of Sociology*, 94, pp. 95-120.

Committee of the Georgian Parliament on Economic Policy and Reform (1996), *Statute*, Tbilisi, Parliament Press.

Eberwein, W. and Tholen, J. (1997), *Market or Mafia: Russian managers on the difficult road towards an open society*, Aldershot, Ashgate.

Europa Publications (1994), *Eastern Europe and the Commonwealth of Independent States*, London.

Fischer, M. M. J. and Grigorian, S. (1993), 'Six to Eight characters in Search of Armenian Civil Society Amidst the Carnivalisation of History', in G. E. Marcus (ed.), *Perilous States*, Chicago, University of Chicago Press.

Genov, N. (ed.) (1996), *Human Development Report - Bulgaria 1996*, Sofia, United Nations Development Program.

Granovetter, M. (1992), 'Problems of Explanation in Economic Sociology', in N. Nohria and R. Eccles (eds), *Networks and Organizations: Structure, form, and action*, Boston, Harvard Business School Press, pp. 25-6).

Habermas, J. (1990), *Die Nachholende Revolution. Kleine Politische Schriften VII*, Frankfurt/M., Edition Suhrkamp.

Koridze, Z. (1995), *Sakartvelos Sazogadoeba* (Georgian Society), Tbilisi, 7 Dge.

Kusa, Z. and Tirpakova, Z. (1993), 'On Making Decision for the Career of Private Businessman', *Sociologia*, 25, pp. 73-75.

Labour Market Quarterly Report (1993), *Labour Market Trends*, August, Sheffield, Employment Department.

MacDonald, R. (1996), 'Welfare Dependency, the Enterprise Culture and Self-employed Survival', *Work, Employment and Society*, 10, pp. 431-447.

Machacek, L. (1996), *Slovak Youth Attitudes Towards the Market Challenges, 1993-1995*, Bratislava, Institute of Sociology, Slovak Academy of Sciences.

Meager, N. (1992), 'The Fall and Rise of Self-employment (again): A comment on Bögenhold and Stabler', *Work, Employment and Society*, 6, pp. 127-34.

Mestmaecker, E.-J. (1991), 'Die Wiederkehr der buergerlichen Gesellschaft und ihres Rechts', Hamburg, *Die Zeit*, 32, p. 18, 2.8.1991.

Morawska, E. (1998), 'The Malleable Homo Sovieticus: Transnational Entrepreneurs in Post Communist East Europe', Paper presented to the ISA Congress, Montreal, August, Session on Elites in the Social Transformation of Eastern Europe.

Nodia, J. (1994), *Sakartvlos Biznesmenbi* (Georgian Businessmen), Tbilisi, Samshobolo.

OECD (1998), *Fostering Entrepreneurship*, Paris, OECD.

Offe, C. (1992), 'The Politics of Social Policy in East-European Transitions. Antecedents, Agents, and Agenda of Reforms', Paper presented for the Conference at the University of Bremen, September 1992, revised for the Conference at the University of Economic Sciences, Budapest, October 1992.

Putnam, R. D. (1993), 'The Prosperous Community: Social capital and public life', *American Prospect*, 13, pp. 35-42.

Putnam, R. D. (1995), 'Bowling Alone: America's declining social capital', *Journal of Democracy*, 6, pp. 65-78.

Roberts, K. and Jung, B. (1995), *Poland's First Post-Communist Generation*, Aldershot, Avebury.

Roberts, K. and Tholen, J. (1999), 'Young Entrepreneurs in The New Market Economies', *South East Europe Review*, 2(1), pp. 157-77.

Roberts, K. and Tholen, J. (1999), 'Junge Unternehmer in den neuen Marktgesellschaften Mittel- und Osteuropas (Bulgarien, Polen, Slowakei, Ungarn) und der frueheren Sowjetunion (Armenien, Georgien, Ukraine)', in D. Boegenhold (Hg.), *Unternehmensgruendung und Dezentralitaet. Renaissance der beruflichen Selbstaendigkeit in Europa?* Wiesbaden, Publ. Westdeutscher Verlag, Opladen, pp. 257-78.

Roberts, K., Fagan, C., Tholen, J., Nemiria, G., Adibekian, A. and Tarknishvili, L. (1999), 'Employment in the Transition Countries: Evidence from Ukraine, Georgia and Armenia', in *Oesteuropaforskning, The Finnish Review of East European Studies*, 1, pp. 6-24.

Roberts, K., Tholen J., *et al.* (2000), 'The New East's New Businesses: Heart of the Labour Market Problem and/or Part of the Solution?', *Journal for East European Management Studies*, 5 (1), pp. 64-76.

Roberts, K., Tholen, J. *et al.* (2000), *Surviving Post-communism – Young People in the Former Soviet Union*, Cheltenham, Edward Elgar Publishing.

Tarkowska, J. (1994), 'Cultural Responses to Permanent Instability', in M. Kempny (ed.), *Cultural Dilemmas of Post-Communist Society*, Warsaw, IFiS Publishers.

Taylor, M. P. (1994), 'Earnings, Independence or Unemployment?', Working Paper 26, British Household Panel Survey, University of Essex.

Tholen, J. (1999), 'The Young Unemployed and the Mediterraneasation of Youth Tranisitions in (South)East-Central Europe', in *South East Europe Review*, 1(4), pp. 151-67.

Varese, F. (1994), 'Is Sicily the Future of Russia? Private protection and the rise of the Russian Mafia', *Archives of European Sociology*, 35, pp. 224-58.

Chapter 12

Social Capital and Economic Performance in Post-Communist Societies

Christian W. Haerpfer, Claire Wallace and Martin Raiser

Introduction

Social capital has received increasing attention as a crucial variable influencing economic performance (Knack and Keefer 1997; Dasgupta and Serageldin 1999). Particularly, the widely divergent and often disappointing results in the transition from a centrally planned to a market economy have been explained by variations in the stock of social capital (Nowotny 1998; Stiglitz 1999). Such efforts, however, have so far failed to take into account the differences in the definitions and concepts of social capital as they have emerged in the sociological and political literature (Tardos 1998). Moreover, for the transition economies at least, the weight ascribed to social capital in explaining the variations in economic performance stands in stark contrast to the dearth of empirical evidence that would support such conclusions.

This paper aims to make a first step towards correcting these deficiencies. We start with a brief view on the salient concepts that have become associated with the term 'social capital'. We argue that only one class of definitions used in this literature – namely definitions of what we term 'formal social capital' – will lead to non ambiguous proposals concerning the impact of social capital on the economic performance of a specific country. We then present some first and preliminary evidence on the relationship between 'formal social capital' and economic reform and economic growth. We find that, generally, the stock of social capital is low in the transition countries. The relationship between this level of social capital and economic performance is not clear, however. We find that extended trust – that is trust in persons other than relatives and close friends – is not related to growth. This distinguishes the transition countries from countries with a fully evolved market economy where this correlation does exist. Active participation in various civic groups, on the other hand, does correlate positively with growth; as does trust in public institutions.

Social capital may be created more easily in prosperous economies: it is therefore not clear what is the cause and what the effect in the link between social capital and growth. Indeed, what we find is that more rapid economic growth and higher participation in civic organisations seem to be joint results of good progress in economic and political reform and transformation.[1] Both growth and civic participation are also heavily dependent upon favourable or unfavourable initial conditions. We can, however, identify some initial conditions that seem to be closely correlated with civic participation but do *not* seem to correlate with growth. Using these initial conditions as instruments in a regression of growth against civic participation allows us to confirm the result of the simple correlation. The positive contribution of civic participation and trust in public institutions to growth is then jointly tested and supported in a regression framework, which also controls for the level of economic reform.

The paper is structured as follows. Section 1 introduces the different definitions of social capital and their implications for aggregate economic performance. Section 2 recapitulates the argument made by the existing literature that social capital is a key element in the transition and in explaining its varied outcomes. Section 3 presents the evidence on trust and civic participation in transition and some first correlations with growth. Section 4 reports some evidence on the determinants of variations in social capital in transition countries and uses this to correct for potential endogeneity problems. It also presents preliminary regression results testing jointly the effects of social capital and economic reforms. Section 5 concludes with policy implications.

Definitions of Social Capital

The theories on social capital may be broadly divided into two sub groups. Following Putnam (1993), social capital is defined as a cultural phenomenon, denoting the extent of civic mindedness of members of a society, the existence of social norms promoting collective action and the degree of trust in public institutions. According to Putnam social capital has the properties of a public good. His work on Italy further suggests that social capital is accumulated over long periods of history. According to Platteau (1994), the emergence of universalist morality in western philosophical thinking accompanies the accumulation of social capital. This permits societies to deal successfully with the problems of collective action. Similarly, Raiser (1999) argues that 'extended trust' is needed in the transition countries in order to permit the evolution of a modern and market-based division of labour. Political scientists in turn focus on the connection between social capital and the development of those political institutions that establish and

---

[1] A functioning market economy empowers the consumer; a functioning democracy the voter. Both thus establish control over the economically and politically mighty, and force the economic and political powers into a process of continuous adaptation and learning; see also M. Olson (1993).

uphold the rule of law and which thus greatly facilitate economic exchange. The empirical evidence we present below allows us to test – to some extent at least – the relationships between moral norms, collective action and trust in public institutions for the transition countries.

In contrast to the definition by Putnam, social capital in the definition of Pierre Bourdieu (1993) refers to the investment in social networks by individuals. Social capital here is a private good, which can be converted into cultural capital, real wealth or 'symbolic capital' that signals social status. An individual's stock of social capital is thus a critical component of his or her power in society. Coleman (1988), who seems to have introduced the notion of social capital, similarly emphasises the benefits of social capital to the individual or to a network of individuals. For Coleman, social capital consists of the sum of the 'relational capital' several individuals hold and is governed by norms of reciprocity which are enforced by peer pressure, gain or loss in reputation, and the like. However, social capital may have positive economic externalities at the local level, by facilitating collective action.[2] Coleman's definition thus lies somewhere between a public and a private good. For reasons explained below, it is convenient to group Bourdieu's and Coleman's definitions of social capital together, as both are based on the notion of reciprocity in social and economic relationships rather than universalistic moral norms and values.

In both these interpretations, social capital facilitates economic exchange. However, the mechanisms through which this is achieved differ fundamentally. In Putnam's model of a working democracy, there is positive feedback between individuals' sense of civic duty, their participation in social life and the efficiency of existing institutional arrangements for contract enforcement. Moral obligations are reinforced in social networks and cheating is expensive. Moreover, civic participation enhances formal rule compliance and improves the accountability of government. Social capital therefore is complementary to formal institutions in supporting a complex division of labour. We label this type of social capital formal'. The choice of terminology reflects the fact that this social capital is accessible to all, independently of personal characteristics, rather like a formal institution such as a legal right or liberty. Its effect on economic performance at the country level should be unambiguously positive.

In Bourdieu's and Coleman's view, social capital may facilitate economic transactions between individuals, but this may often happen at the expense of excluding others. Belonging to a business club, for example, might yield solid pay-offs for those with sufficient wealth and social standing to be accepted as members. But the same business clubs might play the role of a protective guild *vis à vis*

---

[2] It is intriguing to think of social capital as an asset that is accumulated the more it is used. Hence, where norms of reciprocity exist, the more I offer help to my neighbour, the more he or she will feel obliged to help me. Elster (1989) reports examples of how such a system can end up creating too much social capital, as people get burdened with offers for help from others. In one African case, a man's roof broke down from the weight of helpers wishing to demonstrate their support in repairing it.

potential new entrants. Similarly, it is not clear whether a high degree of social capital at the local level translates necessarily into a benefit for the wider society.

The real test for all dense social networks is how they adapt to new economic circumstances that would require transactions with non-members (for case studies of efficient and non-efficient adaptation see Humphrey and Schmitz 1996; see also Sedaitis 1997 for the case of Russia). Based on the relational and reciprocal aspect of most transactions conducted within these types of network, we label the Bourdieu/Coleman variety of social capital 'informal'. As explained, the effect of informal social capital on a country's overall economic performance is uncertain and could be negative.

Formal and informal social capital may co-exist, but they do not necessarily complement each other. When formal institutions are weak, informal social capital may have particular importance (Fukuyama, 1995). Over time, social relations may become increasingly formalised and dense local networks might co-exist with a high level of civic participation and well-developed formal institutions. However, reliance on informal social capital ('connections'), particularly in relationships with public officials could also undermine trust in the impartiality of formal public institutions and corrode their functions through corruption, clientelism and 'tunnelling' out of public resources for private ends. Unfortunately, the data at our disposition does not provide for very clear-cut distinctions between formal and informal social capital. But it allows us to test whether in the transition countries the two types of social capital are closely related to one another, or whether the presence of one type of social capital implies that there is less of the other type.[3]

The Role of Social Capital in Transitional Societies

The transition from central planning to a market economy and the transition from an authoritarian to a democratic regime is fundamentally a process of accelerated institutional change. Both formal and informal institutions need to adapt to the requirements of democracy and of market transactions. The resulting uncertainty places a heavy load on social arrangements. Mechanisms are thus needed to stabilise mutual expectations and to make behaviour of actual or potential counterparts more predictable (Wallace 1998).

There is large scope in transition for co-ordination of economic exchange through informal institutions and networks. These include barter arrangements, transactions in the grey and black economy and enterprise networks. All of these are based on 'informal social capital' (Kolankiewicz 1996; Rose, Mishler, and

---

[3] The question of complementarity between formal and informal social capital has a parallel in the discussion of whether relational contract enforcement and formal, written contracts are complements of substitutes. Some recent evidence for market economies suggest that important complementarities exist between the two (Poppo and Zenger 2000) although on aggregate the use of relational contracting is arguably more pervasive in less developed countries.

Haerpfer 1997). Many empirical studies have highlighted the relevance of such informal social capital in the transition process; as for instance the extent to which relationships between enterprise directors and bureaucrats as they existed under Communism have been adapted to take advantage of new economic opportunities (Stark 1997; Hayri and McDermott 1998). Yet, the use of such informal networks can imply high overall costs to the general public. Entry of potential competitors may be discouraged. State institutions may be 'captured' and subverted to serve not the public interest but private gain (Hellman *et al.* 2000a). In transition countries, the single individual might thus garner high returns from his informal social capital (Aslund, 1996). In absence of effective and countervailing public institutions, the social return on this capital could, however, become negative.

Both leading Eastern European dissidents (e.g. Vaclav Havel or Georgy Konrad) and Western social scientists have lamented the absence of a fully developed, vibrant civil society in Communist and post-Communist countries. This deficit would pose a major obstacle on the path of political and economic transition (see Smolar 1996; Rose 1993). All Communist countries had experienced a phase of stark, totalitarian rule; and even after severe repression ended with the Stalinist era, participation in public affairs remained forced and ritualistic. People therefore tended to retreat from the public sphere into privacy; into the realm of relatives and immediate friends; or into innocuous groups promoting non-controversial cultural and leisure activities. Public institutions were perceived as alien, and – in central Europe in particular – as imposed by a foreign power.

Distrust in public institutions is thus one of the most pernicious legacies of Communism (Gati 1996). Surveys that compare corruption and the rule of law in the various countries of the globe generally place the transition economies well below the advanced market economies, and in the case of the CIS member states even below developing countries with similar income levels (see Surcke 2000; Transparency International 2000). In short, Communism seems to have left as legacy the perception that while each individual might profit from informal social capital, private returns to civic participation and other forms of 'formal social capital' would be low. Despite potentially very high returns to civic mindedness and cooperation during the transition, it would not be easily established – thus providing one possible reason for the disappointing economic performance of many transition economies.

In the remainder of this paper, we investigate three sets of questions. First, how do the transition economies compare with market economies as regards the nature and the stock of social capital? Second, what is the relationship between the stock and type of formal social capital and economic performance? Third, is the level of formal social capital in each country positively or negatively associated with the level of informal social capital?

Social Capital in Transition – Preliminary Evidence

In the empirical work that follows, we benefit from the availability of data from the 1990 and 1995 World Values Survey (WVS), which included 12 and 21 transition economies respectively to construct measures of moral attitudes, trust and civic participation.[4] In this we follow Knack and Keefer (1997), who use a measure of 'trust' among anonymous individuals and the degree of participation in civic organisations as their measures of formal social capital. As measures of informal social capital we take the importance people attach to family and friends, also from the WVS.[5] We then compare the data in the WVS with survey results from the New Democracy Barometer – NDB (see Rose 1998; Rose, Mishler and Haerpfer 1997) and from EBRD's Business Environment Survey – WBES (see Hellman *et al.* 2000b). Table 12.1 summarises all indicators used, gives their definitions, and shows which concept of social capital – formal or informal – they should be attributed to.

Before going any further an important caveat on the information conveyed by different country survey data should be noted. The responses given to questions that measure trust may be influenced in important ways by cyclical swings in public morale, or by specific events in any one year. Since the resulting variations over time are unlikely to coincide across countries, substantial biases could result from comparing countries at one point in time. Equally important is the bias given to answers on issues of belief (such as trust and civic mindedness) by varying cultural traditions, or by the absence of a routine of opinion surveys. Such differences inevitably flavour the responses given and sometimes in ways that contradict the common perception of outsiders. Hungarians for instance, hold both their present political and their present economic regime in low esteem. Citizens in transition countries, worse off politically and economically, seem to have much higher esteem for their own institutions (see Rose, Mishler and Haerpfer 1997). Notwithstanding such shortcomings, opinion surveys have provided a valuable tool for comparative cross-country analysis. Bearing in mind potential country-level biases as well as the fact that we have only 21 country-level observations for the transition economies, we hope to at least uncover some first indicative trends, which might stimulate further research. The paucity of the underlying data should be borne in mind in all results that follow.

---

[4] The data were provided to the authors ahead of general publication of the WVS results. However, we only obtained country level means, rather than the individual observations themselves. This limits our study to a cross-section of 21 countries, which is obviously a poor basis for statistical inference. We also received only limited access to data for non-transition economies.

[5] This is arguably a rather weak measure of the density of social networks, as conceptualised by Coleman. As noted above, the economic significance of informal social capital is probably highest at the local level – not the national level.

Table 12.1 Formal and informal social capital, data, definitions, and sources

	Source	Definition	Type of Social Capital
Generalised trust	WVS	Percentage of respondents that say they trust other people (alternative response: can't be too careful about others)	Formal
Civic mindedness	WVS	Mean score (1=always, 10=never) of frequency of immoral actions (fare dodging, tax cheating, buying stolen goods, accepting bribes)	Formal
Altruism	WVS	Percentage of respondents who say they think about others (alternative response: only think about oneself)	Formal
Civic participation	WVS	Percentage of respondents who are active in civic organisations (alternative responses: members but inactive; not members)	Formal
Ascribed trust	WVS	Percentage of respondents who value family a lot (alternative responses: rather, not at all)	Informal
Process-based trust	WVS	Percentage of respondents who value friends a lot (alternative responses: rather, not at all)	Informal
Political interest	WVS	Percentage of respondents who frequently discuss politics (alternative response: politics not frequently discussed	Formal
Confidence in formal institutions	WVS	Mean score (1=low confidence; 4=high confidence) for each institution	Formal
Trust in institutions	NDB	Mean score (1=no trust, 7=great trust) for each institution	Formal
Confidence in legal system	BEEPS	Mean score (0=low confidence; 3=high confidence)	Formal
Quality of Investment Climate	BEEPS	Mean score of obstacles to investment (0=high obstacles; 3=low obstacles) formed over 10 dimensions, including policy instability, inflation, exchange rate, finance, taxes and regulation, infrastructure, judiciary, corruption, street crime, organised crime	Formal

The Hour-glass Society –Trust Among Anonymous Individuals

The vast World Values Survey aims to uncover differences in the social and political attitudes, as they exist between the populations of the countries covered. It was last carried out in 1995, with the inclusion of around 1500 respondents in each of 21 transition countries. The key question on trust is as follows: 'Would you agree that people can generally be trusted or would you say that you cannot be too careful about other people?' The measure of trust derived from this question is defined as the percentage of the population in one country that answered that people could generally be trusted.

Table 12.2 Extended trust in transition

	1990	1995
Transition economies	*26,4*	*23,2*
Albania		27,0
Armenia		24,7
Azerbaijan		20,5
Belarus	25,5	24,1
Bulgaria	30,4	28,6
Croatia		25,1
Czech Republic	30,2	28,5
Estonia	27,6	21,5
Georgia		23,4
Hungary	24,6	22,7
Latvia	19,0	24,7
Lithuania	30,8	21,9
FYR Macedonia		8,2
Moldova		22,2
Poland	34,5	17,9
Romania	16,1	18,7
Russia	37,5	23,9
Serbia+Montenegro		30,2
Slovak Republic	23,0	27,0
Slovenia	17,4	15,5
Ukraine		31,0
OECD	*44,5*	*43,0*
China	60,3	52,3
Turkey	10,0	5,5
T-test: Transition economies vs. OECD*	*0,00*	*0,00*
Correlation with growth:		
cumulative growth 1989-1998	*-0,15*	*-0,27*

Notes
* T-test reports P-values for difference in means; 0.00 means statistically significant at more than 1% level.
Source: World Value Survey, 1990, 1995.

Table 12.2 shows the average scores for the trust variable for all 21 transition countries in 1995 and in 1990, as well as the average for the OECD countries, for China and for Turkey. The latter two are the only developing countries that were made available to us from the data set, with China being of particular interest, as it is also a transition country.

The main finding is that in transition countries trust is generally lower than in the average OECD country; and much lower than in China; but much higher than in Turkey. Moreover, there is no indication at all from the data that in the transition countries, trust is correlated with economic performance. For instance, in 1995 the highest score for trust was achieved in the economically despondent Ukraine, whereas the second lowest score was registered for Poland, which, at that time, had already experienced two years of solid economic growth.

A high level of trust might, however, have played a role in explaining the superior economic performance of China during its transition.[6] While this remains speculation beyond the scope of this paper, it would clearly be consistent with the view that trust correlates positively with growth. It is not clear what explains Turkey's very low score, which according to Knack and Keefer's data is an outlier even among developing countries.

Note that the results are generally robust over time, as the results for the 1990 survey available for 12 transition economies show. There is a general tendency for trust to decline between the two rounds in both market and transition economies. Changes in trust between rounds have very little to do with performance during the transition either – both stagnating Russia and booming Poland see their score decline by 13.9 and 16.6 percentage points respectively; which is rather similar to the declines in trust observed in the USA and the UK.

We further check the consistency of this important result by looking at various other measures of moral attitudes or civic mindedness reported in the WVS (Table A.12.1 in the Annex). Respondents were asked to record the frequency with which they engaged activities that implied a disregard for the common good. Again, it seems that compared with citizens in the advanced and wealthy countries, citizens in the transition countries are significantly less 'civic-minded' (see also Ockenfels and Weimann 1996, but for a qualifying view see Bolle 1999). However, when asked about their attitudes towards the needs of others, citizens in the transition countries do not seem to differ that much from citizens in OECD countries. Their level of professed altruism is roughly comparable to the level of altruism in the OECD countries. On all of these counts, China shows higher scores than the transition countries to its West.

As has been mentioned, international, cross-country surveys on attitudes and opinions are plagued with numerous difficulties of interpretation. The results presented here should therefore be accepted with quite some caution. One major conclusion imposes itself nonetheless: extended trust in the sense of trust among anonymous individuals cannot be a major factor explaining the variations of

---

[6] Note that Fukuyama classifies China as a 'low trust' economy and puts much stronger emphasis on informal social capital (the extended family) in explaining its recent success.

Table 12.3 Ascribed and process-based trust in transition economies

	1995				1990			
	Reliance on family		Reliance on friends		Reliance on family		Reliance on friends	
	a lot	*rather*	*a lot*	*rather*	*a lot*	*rather*	*a lot*	*rather*
Transition economies	*86.04*	*11.91*	*35.35*	*50.17*	*79.52*	*17.21*	*27.35*	*49.09*
Albania	96.28	3.22	19.14	67.59				
Armenia	86.30	12.09	44.65	46.56				
Azerbaijan	85.13	13.26	35.27	56.73				
Belarus	84.48	13.30	31.73	50.75	76.85	19.74	36.52	43.86
Bulgaria	88.53	10.24	41.46	45.54	76.07	20.12	38.43	39.23
Croatia	85.34	12.23	48.41	43.55				
Czech Rep.	91.08	7.26	38.65	50.83	85.59	10.97	27.96	52.58
Estonia	78.13	19.61	26.89	59.27	68.54	27.15	22.81	51.10
Georgia	91.19	7.11	67.84	27.87				
Hungary	89.52	8.17	38.33	37.87	88.54	8.44	27.48	44.93
Latvia 90	68.06	25.50	24.29	57.01	72.52	23.26	16.38	52.73
Lithuania	73.97	23.22	21.89	56.02	65.31	28.79	19.01	53.08
FYR Macedonia	97.98	1.82	49.64	42.44				
Moldova	79.04	18.11	21.39	50.97				
Poland	90.15	9.50	26.11	58.49	90.59	7.91	22.76	56.20
Romania	88.83	8.90	20.76	47.45	83.21	15.23	24.70	49.03
Russia	84.06	12.65	29.35	49.78	78.94	17.68	29.24	47.59
Serbia+Montenegro	88.79	9.76	48.28	45.57				
Slovak Rep.	90.95	8.23	32.26	59.17	87.47	9.94	25.27	53.35
Slovenia	82.52	14.59	41.14	46.22	80.63	17.31	37.66	45.37
Ukraine	86.59	11.43	34.99	53.98				
China	76.67	22.06	29.91	55.95	62.19	33.00	21.55	51.96
Turkey	97.53	2.05	70.47	27.64	87.17	11.95	55.40	36.61
OECD	*85.99*	*12.12*	*56.79*	*38.69*	*84.02*	*13.48*	*47.02*	*44.74*
T-Test: TEs vs. OECD *	0.49	0.46	0.00	0.00	0.07	0.08	0.00	0.05
Correlate with Trust **								
TEs	-0.08	0.07	-0.01	0.16	-0.03	-0.01	0.00	0.11
OECD	0.16	-0.20	**0.43**	-0.30	**0.53**	**-0.56**	**0.79**	**-0.68**
All	-0.16	0.17	**0.35**	-0.22	0.22	-0.25	**0.57**	**-0.41**
All1 ***	0.01	-0.02	**0.60**	**-0.45**	**0.45**	**-0.47**	**0.81**	**-0.59**

Notes

Numbers in columns are percentage shares of respondents who considere family (friends) as very (rather) important.

* T-test reports P-value for difference in sub-group means; 0.00 means statistically significant at more than 1% level.

** Trust is measured as in table 2. All correlations significant at 5% level are shown in bold.

*** All countries without China and Turkey.

Source: World Value Survey 1990, 1995.

economic performance among the transition countries of Central/Eastern Europe and of the FSU. The evidence rather indicates that trust is generally low in the transition economies. Rose (1995) summarises the arguments why this may be so in the picture of an 'hour-glass society'. Under Communism, individuals forged strong mutual ties at the level of family and close friends, but rarely did they venture out of this well-defined circle. This part of the population formed the bottom of the hour-glass. At the top of the hour-glass were the similarly closed circles composed of the privileged, powerful and few members of the 'nomenclatura'. There was little interaction between these two levels.

Table 12.3 proceeds to check this particular argument. It reports the degree of importance individuals attach to families on one hand, and friends on the other. These are the only two indicators of informal social capital that become available through the World Value Survey. People in transition countries value families as highly as do people in wealthy countries with fully developed market economies (albeit with some notable variation across countries). However, people in transition countries seem to rely far less on friends than people in OECD countries. Moreover, in such wealthy countries reliance on friends is highly correlated with the level of trust towards outsiders. This correlation does not exist in transition countries. Social circles in transition economies would seem to be smaller and more closed than in market economies, where the positive association between informal social capital (such as networks among friends) and general moral attitudes (extended trust) is higher.

Widening the Hour-glass – Civic Participation in Transition

The World Value Survey also includes questions on the participation of individuals in civil society and on their confidence in public institutions. Participation in civil society is measured by active membership in civic organisations,[7] including the Church, sports clubs, arts associations, environmental associations, and charities. In addition, there are also questions on membership in groups that represent economic or political interests such as trade unions, political parties and professional associations. The variable used in this analysis is the share of respondents saying that they are actively involved in such organisations.

Just as in the case of extended trust, participation in civic organisations is significantly lower in the transition countries than it is in countries with fully developed market economies – at least in most cases. The difference is more pronounced in 1995 (Table 12.4) than in 1990 (Annex Table 12.2), however. In 1995, only the level of participation in political parties is comparable to the level of participation, as it exists in established democracies and market economies. Unlike in the case of extended trust, there now is a significant correlation between

---

[7] Participation in these groups can be seen as a step in the process of modernisation; as such membership enhances autonomy in two directions. It provides greater autonomy vs. primary groups like families, clans, or closely-knit local communities; but it also provides added autonomy vs the superior power of the state (Schmitter 1993).

Networks, Trust and Social Capital

Table 12.4 Civic participation, 1995

	Share of active participants in institutions, %										Type
	Church	Sports	Arts	Unions	Parties	Environment	Professional	Charity	Other	Type I *	II **
Transition economies	*5.38*	*5.25*	*3.75*	*3.75*	*2.49*	*0.90*	*2.72*	*1.45*	*2.06*	*12.08*	*9.13*
Albania	4.82	5.12	3.32	1.61	13.17	0.81	4.94	0.81	0.40	10.75	19.72
Armenia	1.45	5.05	8.15	1.25	1.15	1.15	2.35	1.60	0.35	8.10	4.75
Azerbaijan	1.50	1.55	2.10	2.80	1.80	0.25	0.85	0.25	0.05	3.30	5.44
Belarus	2.34	1.91	1.63	2.39	0.43	0.53	0.14	0.19	0.57	4.45	2.96
Bulgaria	0.84	1.68	1.68	4.94	2.24	0.19	0.56	0.75	0.47	3.26	7.74
Croatia	16.29	10.67	6.64	6.06	2.77	1.43	6.13	4.70	4.28	31.66	14.97
Czech	4.72	11.20	3.42	3.32	2.54	1.49	3.60	1.14	7.90	17.06	9.46
Estonia	2.35	5.78	5.19	1.18	0.59	0.39	1.27	0.59	1.37	8.72	3.04
Georgia	2.20	3.28	5.56	1.47	2.59	0.58	1.54	1.31	0.58	6.80	5.60
Hungary	9.40	8.31	2.15	8.00	2.62	0.62	6.00	2.46	5.54	20.17	16.62
Latvia 90	3.50	5.08	5.00	1.92	0.75	0.83	3.25	0.67	1.58	9.25	5.92
Lithuania	3.47	2.78	2.98	1.09	1.09	0.40	1.19	0.60	0.43	6.85	3.38
Macedonia	4.42	6.03	4.62	4.92	5.73	2.31	4.32	3.22	2.81	13.67	14.97
Moldova	12.50	4.17	4.78	5.89	0.91	1.32	1.73	1.52	0.00	18.19	8.54
Poland				2.08	0.52						
Romania	14.85	4.28	4.20	10.41	5.08	2.26	3.71	2.02	0.24	21.15	19.21
Russia	1.86	3.33	3.28	7.21	0.78	0.44	0.88	0.54	0.54	5.74	8.87
Serbia+Montenegro	2.31	5.59	1.97	1.97	3.29	0.46	2.96	1.84	1.25	9.74	8.23
Slovakia	9.43	7.25	2.02	2.41	2.20	1.10	3.21	1.47	6.42	18.15	7.83
Slovenia	7.27	10.26	4.49	4.59	1.30	0.80	4.88	2.89	6.29	20.42	10.77
Ukraine	2.03	1.67	1.74	3.13	0.64	0.57	0.85	0.46	0.18	4.16	4.62
OECD	*17.13*	*24.32*	*14.06*	*8.10*	*5.24*	*3.54*	*9.28*	*9.45*	*9.30*	*43.52*	*20.99*
China		10.07	5.73	5.87	6.40	2.40	2.27	2.87	12.67	12.93	14.53
Turkey	1.23	4.10	3.25	2.56	4.74	1.33	5.38	2.40	2.19	7.73	12.68
*T-test: TEs vs. OECD***	*0.03*	*0.00*	*0.00*	*0.01*	*0.06*	*0.01*	*0.01*	*0.01*	*0.00*	*0.00*	*0.01*
*Correlates****:*											
cumulative growth											
89-98	*0.35*	**0.64**	*-0.17*	*0.12*	*0.16*	*0.22*	**0.57**	*0.30*	**0.75**	**0.51**	*0.42*

Notes

* Type I is the sum of paricipants in Church, sport clubs and charity organisations.
** Type II is the sum of participants in political parties, trade unions and professonal organisations.
***T-test reports P-values for difference in means; 0.00 mean statistically significant at more than 1% level.
**** Correlations are with average growth 1989-1998 for TEs economies only.
Correlations significant at the 5% level are shown in bold.
Source: World Value Survey 1995.

participation rates in some of these civic organisatións and economic growth during the transition. Cumulative growth between 1989 and 1998 correlates positively with participation in professional associations, in sports clubs, as well as with articipation in 'other not further defined organisations' (which possibly stand as a proxy for the density of social networks as described by Coleman).

We now divide the organisations listed in Table 12.4 into three groups:

1. Organisations that relate more to the private sphere, to personal beliefs, to personal morality and to the realm of leisure. This group includes the Church, sports clubs, arts organisations and environmental organisations, and charities. For the purposes of this paper we will call this group 'Type One' organisations.

2. Organisations, which pertain more closely to the political and economic realm. The group includes political parties, trade unions, and professional groupings. For the purposes of this paper, we call this group 'Type Two' organisations.

3. For further analysis, we also form a subgroup of the 'Type One' organisations, excluding environmental and arts groups, which may be of least relevance for the formation of business ties and thus for economic performance.

We ignore the category 'other organisations' in our further analysis, as we did not know to which group it should pertain (but note that it shows the highest single correlation with economic growth).

This sub-division mirrors the sub-division into 'Putnam' and 'Olson' groups established in Knack and Keefer (1997).[8] 'Type One' groups relate directly to the idea of a vibrant civil society and thus are assumed to impact positively on growth. Expectations with regard to the economic impact of the 'Type Two' groups diverge. They could affect economic growth negatively, especially if they become associated with rent-seeking by vested interests. But, on the other hand, they are an essential element of a pluralistic society and polity. Parliamentary democracy, for instance, could not function without political parties. As a matter of fact, Knack and Keefer find that in mature market economies, participation in the 'Type Two' groups has the stronger and more significant impact on growth. This suggests that at least in mature market economies, the benefits of functioning political institutions that can resolve social conflicts overweighs the disadvantages of organised vested interests seeking rents and blocking decision making.

---

[8] Knack and Keefer (1997) use the term 'Putnam Group' for the first type of organisations; and the term 'Olson Group' for what we describe as 'Type Two' organisations. If we do not follow Knack and Keefer in using these terms, it is because we would feel uneasy about the suggestion that political parties, trade unions and professional organisations have to be identified primarily with rent seeking and mutual blockage as described by Mancur Olson. On the contrary, we see them as essential parts of a democratic and pluralistic polity. That they are not fully efficient in this function in some of the new democracies that emerged from under Communism is another issue (Przeworski 1991).

Figure 12.1 shows the three scatter plots for the three-subgroups thus defined. All three show a positive correlation with cumulative growth over the 1989-1998 period in the transition economies. These correlations are significant at the 5 per cent level. Because of its stronger correlation with economic performance, we henceforth focus on the sub-group of 'Type One' organisations (excluding arts clubs and environmental associations) in all subsequent analysis.

Correlations do not establish causality, of course. To take into account the possibility that economic growth may influence civic engagement, we repeat the exercise using civic participation in 1990. For that year, the sample of transition economies is much smaller, and the correlations of civic participation to subsequent growth are insignificant (Table A.12.2). Thus intense civic participation at the start of transition does not seem to have contributed to subsequent growth. Figure 12.2 shows the changes in 'Type One' and 'Type Two' group participation for the 8 countries for which data is available in both survey years. Slovenia, Hungary and Romania show an increase in civic participation in all three groups, Russia only in the 'Type Two' groups, and the other four countries show declines in civic participation between 1990 and 1995.

Does this evidence suggest that growth determines the extent of civic participation rather than vice versa? Not necessarily. The nature of civil organisations is unlikely to be constant during the transition.[9] At the start of transition, most organisations could have still been coloured and impregnated by the Communist legacy; while by 1995, most of such organisation would have established an autonomous identity.[10] More or less forced membership would have become supplanted by voluntary membership. We could also interpret our data as implying that an active civil society is an endogenous *outcome* of a successful transition, which in turn feeds back into higher growth rates. Indeed, in the next section, we find that high civic participation is a feature of countries with generally more favourable initial conditions and thus better overall performance during the transition.

---

[9] Indeed across the 8 countries with available data civic participation rates in 1990 and 1995 are negatively correlated.

[10] It would be interesting to check this at the level of individuals and see whether the characteristics of those actively engaged in civil society have changed. We intend to pursue this in future research.

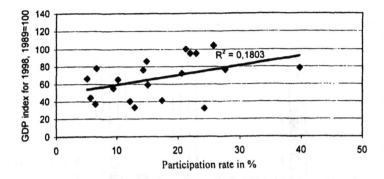

Figure 12.1a Civic participation and growth, Type I groups (large)

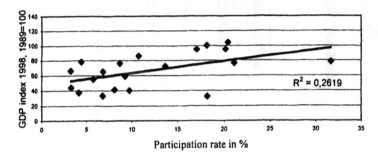

Figure 12.1b Civic participation and growth, Type I groups (small)

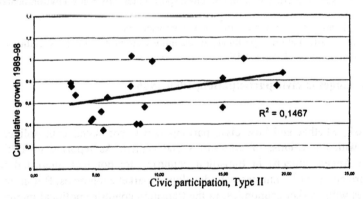

Figure 12.1c Civic participation and growth, Type II groups

Notes
Type I (large) is the sum of participation in churches, sports clubs, arts clubs, environmental associations and charities. Type I (small) excludes arts clubs and environmental associations. Type II is the sum of participation in political parties, unions and professional associations
Source: World Values Survey 1995; for growth EBRD database.

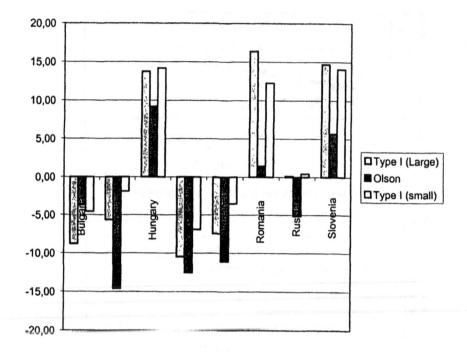

Notes
Type I (large) is the sum of participation in churches, sports clubs, arts clubs, environmental associations charities.
Type I (small) excludes arts clubs and environmental associations.
Type II is the sum of participation in political parties, unions and professional associations.
Source: World Values Survey 1990 and 1995.

Figure 12.2 Changes in civic participation, 1990-1995

We also ask, whether and how civic participation is correlated with political attitudes and with the volume of *informal* social capital. As reported in Table A.12.3 in the Annex, citizens in transition countries are not less interested in politics than are citizens of countries with developed market economies. But unlike in the countries with market economies, in the transition countries political interest does not correlate with political participation in a cross-country comparison. As noted further above, people in transition countries attach less importance to friends than do people in fully consolidated democracies and market economies (although more than people in China!). Moreover, strong reliance on friends does not lead to higher civic participation – again in contrast to market economies.

The results obtained so far show a curious disjuncture in transition economies between the cross-country pattern for civic participation and the variation of social and moral attitudes of individuals. In some ways, one might be tempted to conclude that actions speak louder than words and that the civic participation variables are simply a more reliable representation of individual attitudes and ultimately of the level of social capital than questions about trust, reliance on the family, or interest in politics. Another interpretation, however, would be that these results show the path dependence of attitudes towards everything beyond the intimate circle of relatives and close friends. These attitudes change but at a sluggish pace. Civic organisations, on the other hand, have to adapt rapidly to a changing economic and political environment. Individual attitudes and habits that define the relation to these organisations change much more slowly. This interpretation is confirmed by other experiences of transition towards democracy. In post totalitarian Germany (Conradt 1980) and Austria, or in post authoritarian Portugal, democratic institutions became established and consolidated quite quickly, whereas it took much longer – a generation at least – for the corresponding democratic attitudes to become universally shared.

Trust in State Institutions

We now turn our attention to attitudes towards the state, or trust in public institutions. While a key aspect of a functioning market economy and democracy, this might be conceived not so much as a prerequisite for the accumulation of social capital; but as its consequence. The World Values Survey asks respondents to rate their degree of confidence in a number of institutions, including government, the press, the army, the legal system, the civil service, trade unions, the enterprise sector, the church and others. Scores range from 1 to 4, with 4 representing a lot of confidence and 1 no confidence.

Table 12.5 reports average scores for confidence in various institutions and again compares the answer to those given in countries with fully developed market economies. The results show that in transition countries, trust in public institutions is *not* systematically lower than in the wealthier Western countries. But there are notable exceptions concerning some key institutions: the legal system, the police, the trade unions, commercial companies and political parties. The results are roughly similar for 1990 (Table A.12.4) and for 1995. The five first years of transition have not improved confidence in these essential institutions.

Table 12.5 Trust in formal institutions, 1995

			Legal				Confidence in institution — Police	Government	Parties	Parliament	Civil Service	Companies	Ecology mov.	Women mov.	European Union	RoL*
	Church	Army	System	Press	TV	Unions	Police									
Transition economies	*2.68*	*2.68*	*2.35*	*2.28*	*2.41*	*2.09*	*2.32*	*2.32*	*1.91*	*2.17*	*2.30*	*2.29*	*2.49*	*2.32*	*2.54*	*2.45*
Albania	2.61	2.68	2.65	1.99	2.17	1.82	2.94	2.39	2.05	2.61	1.99	2.04	1.58	2.10	3.34	2.75
Armenia	2.84	2.93	2.08	2.16	2.33	1.82	2.07	2.25	1.75	1.95	2.17	2.41	2.33	1.95	2.58	2.36
Azerbaijan	2.82	2.59	2.43	2.07	2.20	2.12	2.39	3.30	2.55	2.92	2.33	2.25	1.72	1.75	1.91	2.47
Belarus	3.00	2.95	2.45	2.31	2.42	2.33	2.21	2.49	1.77	2.05	2.48	2.75	3.00	2.84	2.77	2.54
Bulgaria	2.60	3.15	2.23	2.37	2.79	2.13	2.47	2.62	2.07	2.35	2.42	2.15	2.32	2.35	2.88	2.61
Croatia	2.66	3.02	2.54	2.08	2.07	2.05	2.69	2.53	2.05	2.37	2.32	2.13	2.55	2.07	2.18	2.75
Czech	2.11	2.33	2.09	2.34	2.45	2.27	2.36	2.11	1.87	1.91	2.24	2.24	2.54	2.26	2.39	2.26
Estonia	2.61	2.39	2.62	2.52	2.74	2.30	2.42	2.43	1.93	2.32	2.61	2.60	2.94	2.71	2.67	2.47
Georgia	3.00	2.43	2.29	2.51	2.53	1.91	2.07	2.33	2.02	2.15	2.41	2.36	2.22	2.16	2.53	2.26
Hungary	2.35	2.62	2.51	2.11	2.33	1.93	2.55	2.33	1.89	2.25	2.51	2.18	2.32	2.09	2.73	2.56
Latvia 90	2.70	2.07	2.23	2.43	2.55	2.16	2.11	2.20	1.68	1.99	2.35	2.36	2.65	2.44	2.55	2.14
Lithuania	2.82	2.36	2.10	2.73	2.80	2.20	2.01	2.31	2.01	2.17	2.36	2.26	2.59	2.38	2.50	2.16
Macedonia	2.20	2.39	2.08	2.00	2.07	1.79	2.08	1.83	1.72	1.76	1.91	2.06	2.31	2.08	2.34	2.19
Moldova	3.05	2.60	2.45	2.22	2.40	2.15	2.11	2.29	1.83	2.23	2.51	2.41	2.47	2.38	2.85	2.39
Poland	2.90	3.00	2.54	2.45	2.46	2.06	2.53	2.30	1.79	2.21	2.24	2.51	2.97	2.53	2.64	2.69
Romania	3.21	3.15	2.44	2.24	2.48	2.15	2.28	1.96	1.76	1.92	2.11	2.22	2.46	2.32	2.46	2.62
Russia	2.79	2.89	2.29	2.30	2.41	2.23	2.09	1.95	1.86	1.92	2.41	1.85	2.96	2.81	2.45	2.42
Serbia+Montenegro	2.22	2.75	2.45	2.04	2.07	2.02	2.39	2.24	1.84	2.16	2.11	2.20	2.47	2.41	1.91	2.53
Slovakia	2.67	2.75	2.32	2.37	2.48	2.21	2.29	2.31	2.00	2.10	2.29	2.17	2.49	2.41	2.54	2.45
Slovenia	2.27	2.41	2.27	2.39	2.56	2.05	2.46	2.34	1.80	2.05	2.17	2.33	2.62	2.40	2.37	2.38
Ukraine	2.85	2.79	2.34	2.33	2.41	2.20	2.17	2.29	1.85	2.18	2.32	2.53	2.70	2.64	2.64	2.43
OECD	*2.44*	*2.69*	*2.60*	*2.23*	*2.35*	*2.33*	*2.87*	*2.26*	*2.04*	*2.29*	*2.38*	*2.47*	*2.60*	*2.40*	*2.24*	*2.72*
China 90																
Turkey	2.67	3.59	2.86	2.46	2.44	2.47	2.84	2.30	1.93	2.35	2.69	2.62	3.18	2.99	2.43	3.10
T-test TEs vs OECD **	0.05	0.47	0.01	0.27	0.23	0.00	0.00	0.27	0.02	0.09	0.07	0.01	0.14	0.18	0.00	0.00
Correlate with NDB (1996)	0.88	0.79	0.30	0.22	-0.05	-0.02	0.63	0.04	0.42	0.15	-0.47	-0.77				
Correlate with BEEPS (1999)			0.30	0.37			0.50	0.73								
Correlate with BEEPS RoL ***			0.30	0.12			0.57	0.71								0.44
Correlate with cumulative growth 1989-98	-0.34	0.05	0.19				0.54	-0.14								0.33

Notes

Table reports mean scores, on a scale of 1 (low confidence) to 4 (high confidence).

* Average of scores for confidence in legal system, police and army.

** T-test reports P-values for difference in means; 0.00 mean statistically significant at more than 1% level.

*** Percentage of respondents who believe that their contract and property rights will be upheld by the courts.

Source: World Value Survey, 1995; New Democratic Barometer, 1996; Business Environment and Enterprise Performance Survey 1999.

While, on the face of this evidence, the much-lamented lack of trust in institutions seems to be specific to a few – albeit important – areas, further robustness checks on the data raise concern about the results of the World Values Survey – WVS. We compared the responses from the New Democracy Barometer NDB and the Business Environment and Enterprise Performance Survey BEEPS (implemented jointly by European Bank for Reconstruction and Development and the World Bank in 1999 – see Hellman *et al.* 2000b) with those given in the WVS. Both the NBD and the BEEPS include alternative ratings of trust in institutions by households and enterprises respectively. The NDB asks respondents to rate their trust in a given institution on a scale of 1 to 7 (with higher scores reflecting more trust). The BEEPS asks enterprises to rate the performance of various state institutions on a scale of 1 to 5.

Table 12.5 reports the correlations between the WVS and NDB and BEEPS trust scores for all those institutions where comparable questions were asked. Several correlations are negative, which raises suspicions about the usefulness of the data.[11] The strongest positive correlations can be established for the following institutions: i) political parties, ii) the police, iii) the army, iv) the Church, and v) the legal system. As it happens, with the exception of the Church and the army, these are also among the institutions where transition economies record significantly lower levels of trust than OECD countries. We henceforth focus only on trust in the legal system, the police, the army, political parties and the Church as potential determinants of performance during the transition.

In the bottom of Table 12.5, we present correlations of confidence in the five institutions highlighted above with cumulative growth in 1989-1998. Confidence in the police shows the strongest positive correlation with growth, while confidence in the Church is weakly negatively related to cumulative growth during 1989-1998. The other correlations remain statistically insignificant. Table 12.5 also presents the correlation of an aggregate 'confidence in the rule of law index' with growth. This index is constructed as the sum of confidence in the police, the legal system and the army. It is weakly correlated with growth during the 1989-1998 period.

This result is somewhat disappointing given the importance generally attributed to trust in public institutions. Indeed, when using the data from the NDB or the WBES, we get much stronger correlations. In Chart 12.3, we present a correlation of the average NDB score for trust in seven public institutions (the army, the civil servants, the courts, the government, the parliament, the political parties, and the police) against annual growth, pooled over the four years in which the NDB was implemented – 1993, 1994, 1996 and 1998. The correlation is positive and highly significant. The correlations with each of the subcomponents are also highly significant. In Chart 12.4, we correlate cumulative growth in 1989-1998 against the

---

[11] The results for confidence in 'companies' and 'trade unions' should be interpreted with caution, as the WVS asks a general question, whereas the NDB allows respondents to differentiate between private and state enterprises and old and new trade unions respectively. The highly negative correlation of WVS and NDB data applies to trust in private companies. For trust in state companies the correlation is positive, albeit low.

degree of confidence in the legal system obtained from the BEEPS – again with highly significant results.[12] Thus, while the WVS data do not yield strong conclusions about the relevance of trust in public institutions for a successful economic transition, data from other sources suggest that trust in public institutions is important.

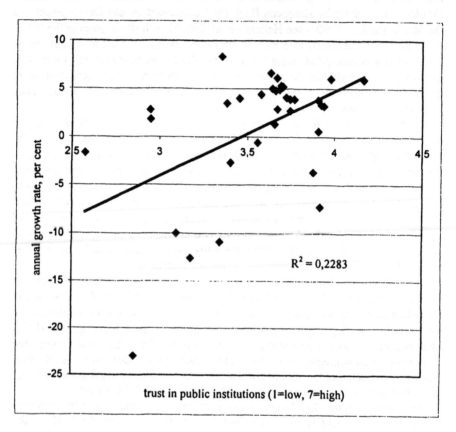

Notes
The charts represents a correlation of trust in public institutions against growth pooled over the four years: 1993, 1994, 1996 and 1998. Each dot represents one country in one of these four years.
Sources: New Democracy Barometer, 1993-1998; for growth EBRD database.

Figure 12.3 Trust in public institutions and growth, 1993-1998

---

[12] The same results can be obtained by looking only at growth in 1998 (to account for potential endogeneity problems), as well as by using an aggregate score of the quality of governance from the BEEPS rather than the single measure of confidence in the legal system.

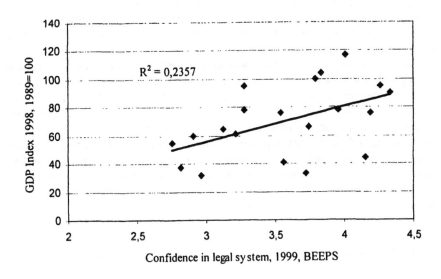

Confidence in legal system, 1999, BEEPS

Notes
Confidence in the legal system is measured on an index of 1 (low) to 5 (high). It provides the mean response to the question whether respondents trusted the legal system to enforce their contract or property rights.
Sources: Business Environment and Enterprise Performance Survey for Confidence in Legal System; EBRD database for cumulative growth.

Figure 12.4 Growth and confidence in the legal system

Civic Participation and Trust in Institutions – Making Social Capital Work

The evidence found on the positive relationship between civic participation and growth and between trust in public institutions and growth might suggest that civic participation and trust in institutions are themselves highly correlated. Indeed, at the heart of Putnam's argument about the role of civil society and of social capital for economic performance lies an argument about the impact that civil society has on the quality of government (thus the title of his famous book: *Making Democracy Work*).

Table 12.6 presents correlation coefficients between the two groups of civic organisations ('Type One' groups and 'Type Two' groups) and trust in various public institutions. The strongest positive correlation can be established between civic participation and trust in the police. Trust in the legal system and the army is also positively related to civic participation. The correlation between civic participation and trust in these three institutions is slightly higher for 'Type Two' groups than for 'Type One' groups. There thus seems to be some association between civic engagement and trust in public institutions, particularly those associated with the rule of law. But the results are too weak to draw strong conclusions.

Data from the BEEPS again show only a weak positive correlation between civic participation and confidence in the legal system. However, taking trust in public institutions in the NDB as our measure of trust in the state, we find a strong positive correlation with civic participation both for 'Type One' and 'Type Two' groups. The small sample of just 12 transition economies cautions about reading too much into these results, but they do suggest that Putnam's argument of how democracy works might find some support in the transition economies. Note that a consistency check for market economies confirms that trust in state institutions in positively associated with civic engagement in both 'Type One' and 'Type Two' groups.

Table 12.6 Trust in formal institutions and civic participation

Simple correlations	Civic Participation	
	Type I	Type II
Confidence in*		
legal system	0,21	0,30
police	0,37	0,57
army	0,06	0,22
political parties	-0,19	-0,09
church	-0,22	-0,22
WBES Confidence in legal system**	0,30	0,16
NDB avg trust***	0,84	0,74

Notes

Type I is the sum of participation in churches, sports clubs and charities.
Type II is the sum of participation in political parties, unions and professional associations

*Source: World Value Survey 1995.
**Source: Busines Environment and Enterprise Performance Survey 1999.
***Source: New Democratic Barometer Survey, 1996; average of trust in Legal system. Police, Army, Political Parties, Church.

Social Capital, Initial Conditions and Economic Reforms

What factors might explain the variation in social capital among the transition countries? And are these factors also important in explaining differences in economic performance across countries? An answer to these two questions is an important step in identifying the causal links behind the correlations established so far. They might shed some light on possible policies that might raise trust.

Initial Conditions and Social Capital

The existing literature provides some limited guidance on the possible determinants of the level of social capital in transition. Alesina and La Ferrara (2000) investigate the variation in trust among residents of the US. They find that social inequalities and ethnic heterogeneity at the local level are important determinants of trust. This is in line with the reasoning in Knack and Zak (1998) who present a model and some cross-country evidence linking trust to social distance – measured in this case by income inequality. Income inequality at the start of transition did show some variation across countries (Atkinson and Micklewright 1992), and ethnic divisions were very important in some countries but not in others. As Table 12.7 shows, *initial* income inequality is not related to civic participation five years later in 1995. By the mid-1990s, however, income inequality had started to diverge dramatically across the region and was negatively (albeit only weakly) correlated with the level of civic participation.[13] We will come back to this point in the conclusion. Ethnic heterogeneity seems to have somewhat hampered participation in the 'Type Two' civic groups and seems to have lowered trust in the legal system.

Since moral traditions and other aspects of culture are path dependent by their very nature, variations in civic participation could reflect underlying variations in historical developments (Putnam 1993; Platteau 1994). It is not evident which aspects of different historical developments should be highlighted in this respect. We focus here on religious affiliation, GDP per capita and the rate of urbanisation. The first is a proxy for cultural differences, the second two variables measure differences in economic development. The correlations in Table 12.7 show that civic participation in Type One groups and the overall investment climate rating is higher in places where the main religious affiliation is with either Protestantism or Catholicism. The level of urbanisation is negatively associated with civic participation – a finding that might support the notion of anonymity and isolation in urban agglomerations. Initial GDP per capita is not strongly correlated with either civic participation or trust in institutions.

---

[13] Income inequality rose rapidly in many transition countries, reaching an 'Latin American' level in some of the CIS countries (Nowotny 1996; Milanovic 1998).

Table 12.7 Initial conditions, social capital and growth

Simple Correlations

Initial Conditions	Type I Groups	Type II Groups	WBES investment climate	WBES legal system	Confidence in RoL (WVS)	cumulative growth 1989-1998
GINI-coefficient for income p.c., 1987-1990	0.17	0.04	-0.27	0.11	0.34	-0.35
GINI-coefficient for income p.c., mid 1990s	-0.42	-0.37	-0.27	-0.26	-0.22	**-0.60**
Ethnic heterogeneity index, mid-1990s	-0.18	**-0.49**	-0.13	-0.35	**-0.57**	**-0.50**
Religion*	0.43	-0.11	**0.71**	0.43	-0.15	**0.59**
Distance to Brussels	**-0.56**	-0.33	-0.23	-0.03	-0.16	**-0.70**
Exports to CMEA/GDP, 1990	**-0.66**	**-0.83**	0.05	-0.24	-0.34	-0.37
Natural resource endowment*	-0.35	-0.09	-0.31	-0.10	0.08	-0.25
GDP per capita, at PPP, 1990	0.30	-0.15	**0.57**	0.13	-0.32	0.47
Urbanisation rate, 1990	-0.42	**-0.60**	0.38	-0.13	-0.40	-0.06
Years under central planning	**-0.63**	**-0.56**	-0.21	-0.38	-0.23	**-0.62**
Established sovereign nation*	0.34	**0.82**	-0.03	0.27	**0.60**	**0.51**

Notes

Correlations printed in bold are significant at the 5% level.

Type I is the sum of participation in churches, sports clubs and charities

Type II is the sum of participation in political parties, unions and professional associations

* Defined as dummy variables: religion = dominant religion is western Christianity; natural resources: 2 = rich, 1 = moderate, 0 = poor

Established nation state: 2 = historical sovereign nation, 1 = autonomous part of historical nation (e.g. Czech lands, Russia), 0 = new nation state

Sources:

Data for initial conditions come from de Melo et al. (1997) for 'exports to the CMEA', 'natural resource endowment',

the 'urbanisation rate', 'years under central planning' and 'established sovereign nation'.

Data for the GINI coefficients are from Atkinson and Micklewright (1992) for 1987-1990 and from UNICEF (1999) for mid-1990s.

Ethnic heterogeneity index and the dummy for religious affiliation were calculated based on data from the Europa World Yearbook (1999).

Distance to Brussels and GDP per capita in 1990 are taken from EBRD's database, as reported in Transition Report 1999.

Variations in the size of adjustment cost following years of distortive policies under central planning might also influence the level and quality social capital in the process of economic and political transition. Where such costs are very high, people may remain tied to subsistence strategies and might tend to be politically passive rather than actively participating in the process of change. This in turn would tend to reduce the opportunity for gaining trust in others as well as gaining trust in public institutions. We propose to capture the extent of adjustment costs during transition here with the simple geographic distance to the EU (Brussels),[14] the numbers of years spent under central planning, the share of exports to the CMEA normalised by GDP, a dummy for whether a country had a prior history as a nation state and a dummy for the endowment with natural resources.[15] As Table 12.7 reveals, higher economic distortions tend to be strongly correlated with lower civic participation rates, as does abundance with natural resources. Economic distortions are, however, by and large not associated with higher or lower trust in public institutions.

Looking at the final column in Table 12.7 it becomes apparent that most of the initial conditions listed here are also significantly associated with growth performance across the transition economies. This finding confirms the view, expressed further above, that variations in economic performance and the creation of social capital are really joint products of the same underlying causes. But this fact poses a methodological problem because it does not allow us to use the correlations between initial conditions and social capital to get around the issue of causality in the relationship between social capital and growth.[16]

Luckily, two of the variables seem to be highly correlated with civic participation but not with growth rates. These are exports to the CMEA and the urbanisation rate. At least for civic participation rates, these variables would seem to provide reasonably good instruments. For trust in public institutions no valid instruments are available. We now verify the results obtained so far in a regression framework, explicitly testing to what extent endogeneity of the social capital variables biases our results, using exports to the CMEA and the urbanisation rate as instruments for civic participation.

---

[14] Countries closer to the EU from the start had better accession prospects, benefited from cross border shuttle trade and employment opportunities and had already under socialism been more exposed to western societies and their political thinking.

[15] Abundant natural resources provide a cushion during at the onset of the transition, but they might also slow or distort the transition process by providing rent seeking opportunities and diverting the government's attention away from reforms. Table 12.7 shows that, indeed, economic reliance on a few natural resources tends to lower the stock of social capital.

[16] In other words, the initial conditions variables really belong into the growth equation. They would thus be correlated with the residuals of a simple regression of growth against social capital and thus not be valid instruments.

Civic Participation, Trust in Public Institutions and Reform – Preliminary Regression Results

So far we have presented just simple correlations. But these leave open the question as to whether the various measures of social capital are jointly significant and what weight to attribute to civic participation and trust in public institutions respectively. We will now use some very simple and preliminary regression to analyse this issue. We also conduct a very basic robustness test by including economic reforms into the model. Many other potential determinants of growth in transition are not included, raising the possibility of spurious results due to model misspecification. To some extent we would argue that such problems are unavoidable when investigating transition outcomes. But the very small number of observations obliges us to limit the number of variables.

We examine a very simple model of the form:

$$\text{Growth} = a + b*\text{Civic engagement} + c*\text{Trust in Institutions} + d*\text{Reforms} + e$$

We also examine some interaction effects between all three variables. Trust in institutions is measured by the BEEPS investment climate scores. Reforms are measured as the average over the 1989-1998 period using EBRD's transition indicators. Growth is given as the logarithmic difference in income levels in between 1998 and 1989.

Table 12.8 presents the results of our various specifications. At the bottom of each column are two test-statistics, which examine whether endogeneity bias is a problem for our results. The Sargan-test for valid instruments essentially tests whether the instruments used also belong in the regression equation. As we established in the previous section, exports to the CMEA and the urbanisation rate would seem to qualify as valid instruments due to the low correlation with growth but high correlation with civic participation. The Sargan test statistic fails to reject the validity of these two instruments in all the regressions. Note that for trust in institutions no instruments could be found and results thus need to be read with caution. The Hausman test checks the assumption of exogeneity directly by comparing the OLS and the IV estimators. Again in all the regressions shown, we fail to reject OLS estimation.[17]

---

[17] Following Greene (2000, p. 385) we chose a simple F-test implementation of the Hausman test, which involves first regressing the potentially endogenous variable against the set of instruments and using the obtained fitted value as an additional regressor in the original equation. The F-test rejects the OLS specification if the fitted value is significantly different than zero. Support for the OLS model also comes from a comparison of coefficients in the two specifications: the coefficients on civic participation do not change much between the OLS and IV models.

Table 12.8 Social capital, reforms and performance: regression results

dependent variable: cumulative growth 1989-1998

	1	2	3	4	5	6	7
Constant	-1.53*** (0.41)	-1.91*** (0.30)	-0.85 (0.98)	-2.62*** (0.47)	-1.93*** (0.48)	-2.15*** (0.42)	-1.53*** (0.41)
Type I groups (Civic)	0.021** (0.007)		-.026 (0.576)		0.007 (0.007)		0.02** (0.007)
Type II groups (Civic)		0.040*** (0.011)		0.11*** (0.03)		0.029** (0.011)	
Quality of Investment Climate (Trust)	0.57* (0.27)	0.75*** (0.18)	0.095 (0.662)	1.25*** (0.34)	0.31 (0.34)	0.50 (0.29)	0.57* (0.27)
Type I*Trust			0.032 (0.038)				
Type II*Trust				-.05* (0.02)			
EBRD reform index (average 1989-1998)					0.46 (0.27)	0.35 (0.25)	
EBRD reform index (residual)							0.46 (0.27)
Adjusted R-squared	0.42	0.56	0.45	0.60	0.52	0.63	0.52
Number of observations	19	19	19	19	19	19	19
Sargan test for valid instruments (X-square)	0.08 (0.00)	0.06 (0.00)	0.09 (0.00)	0.17 (0.00)	0.004 (0.00)	0.23 (0.00)	0.23 (0.00)
Hausmann test OLS vs. IV (F-stat)	1.56 (0.23)	0.00 (0.95)	1.04 (0.32)	0.01 (0.92)	0.76 (0.40)	0.15 (0.71)	0.76 (0.39)

Notes

The regressions use simple OLS. All results were checked using Two Stage Least Squares and Exports to the CMEA and the Urbanisation Rate as instruments.

The coefficient estimates for civic participation tend to increase in the TSLS estimations but all other results remain unaffected.

* = 10% significance, ** = 5% significance, *** = 1% significance

In column 7, the residual of a regression of EBRD reform index against Type II group participation is used as a measure of reform to get rid of multicollinearity.

The Sargan test rejects the null hypothesis that the instruments do not belong into the regression on their own right for X-square values higher than a critical level.

The Hausman test accepts the null hypothesis that IV is prefered over OLS for F-values above a critical level.

Source: Own estimates.

The results in columns 1 and 2 confirm the simple correlations presented above. Over the 1989-1998 period, civic engagement is positively associated with economic growth. The value of the coefficient for 'Type One' groups is considerably lower than for 'Type Two' groups. Yet, the cross-country variance in the latter is also smaller – the value of the coefficients in both cases imply that one standard deviation in civic participation would explain around a 20 percentage point difference in cumulative growth. Moreover, the results suggest that although civic engagement may increase trust in formal institutions, it seems to have an independent positive effect on growth. One way through which civic engagement might directly benefit economic performance is by facilitating self-enforcement of market rules, without the need for recourse to third party enforcement by formal institutions.

Columns 3-4 show results of interacting civic engagement with trust in formal institutions. As mentioned, complementarity between these two variables is implied in Putnam's (1993) view of social capital. If his theory is correct, this also would imply a positive coefficient on the interaction term. Multicollinearity clouds the results in the case of 'Type One' groups, although the sign of the coefficient on the interactive term is positive. For 'Type Two' groups, we find no evidence of complementarity – in fact the interactive term is significantly negative.

In columns 5-6 of Table 12.8, we add economic reforms to the set of regressors. Economic reforms are positively correlated with each of these three variables, causing significance levels to drop relative to columns 1-4, although the total fit of the regressions improves considerably. Note, however, that for 'Type Two' groups the coefficient remains significant (column 6) and is only moderately reduced in value from the result in column 2.

One way to correct for problems of collinearity is to adopt a two-step procedure, first regressing reforms against civic participation and trust in public institutions and then using the residuals from this regression as a proxy for reforms in the performance equation. The result for 'Type One' groups appears in columns 7. Once the correction is used, the positive impact of social capital reappears, while reforms maintain a positive impact on growth. Finally, we attempted to find evidence for a positive interaction between reforms and the level of social capital but did not find convincing evidence that reforms work more effectively where civil participation or trust in the government are high.

Conclusion and Policy Implications

To recapitulate, this paper has yielded the following results. First, we established that – unlike in countries with mature market economies – differences in trust among anonymous individuals are not a good explanation for variation in economic performance of the transition countries. This, however, does not exclude the possibility that the low level of trust observed in all of these countries would impair the prospects for their long-term economic growth and would disadvantage them in this respect in comparison to other emerging markets.

Second, the evidence shows that civic participation does seem to be correlated with economic growth, although the two are probably joint products of the same underlying causes. Nonetheless, our results are robust to corrections to account for endogeneity and to the inclusion of reforms as a determinant of growth. The causal mechanism linking civic participation to growth would seem to lie in the potential of civic organisations to improve the effectiveness of markets, for instance by facilitating the transmission of information, by lowering the costs of monitoring and enforcement, and by giving voice in the political process to market participants.

Third, trust in public institutions is also positively correlated with growth. Institutions that seem to be of particular relevance during the transition are the legal system and the police, while results for political institutions are more ambiguous. Trust in the media and in the Church does not seem to be related to economic performance.

Fourth, there is some evidence that trust in public institutions is positively correlated with civic participation. Our results are thus consistent with Putnam's theory of how democracy works. Yet, both civic participation and trust in public institutions have independent positive effects on growth. Civic engagement thus benefits economic performance not just by improving the performance of the state, but also by facilitating bilateral exchange. Our results suggest therefore that Putnam and Coleman may both be right.

What implications can be drawn from this analysis for policy? As we have shown, levels of social capital achieved in the mid-1990s were significantly correlated with variables characterising the different economic and social starting points in the transition. Those countries closest geographically and historically to Western Europe seem to have had the greatest ease in developing a civil society that could support the transition process. Keeping alive the hope of 'returning to Europe' may be one way in which the outside world could help build trust and social capital in the region – particularly in South-eastern Europe. In Russia and the CIS, a careful dialogue will be needed in order to help overcome legacies of distrust. As the collection of essays in Ruffin and Waugh (1999) demonstrates there are effective ways for external donors and NGOs to support the formation of a civil society even under the more difficult circumstances of a region like Central Asia.

The negative correlation between income inequality and social capital that had evolved by the mid-1990s suggests that policies aimed a reducing high levels of income inequality could be important in a strategy of increasing trust in others and in public institutions. By the same token, governments should eschew chauvinistic tendencies within their countries, which only serve to exacerbate social divisions and thereby undermine trust. Finally, as Stiglitz (1996) and Dic Lo (1998) argue based on the success of East Asia, there are ways for governments to build trust in public institutions by offering a dialogue to members of the public and consulting over important policy changes. Low trust in public institutions is one of the predicaments politics in transition countries are faced with. But it is a predicament politics can deal with – at least in many important respects.

References

Alesina, A. and la Ferrara, E. (2000), 'The Determinants of Trust', NBER Working Paper, No 7621, March.

Aslund, A. (1996), 'Reform and Rent: Seeking in Russia's economic transformation', *Transition*, 26, January, pp. 12 – 16.

Atkinson, A. and Micklewright, J. (1992), *Economic Transformation in Eastern Europe and the Distribution of Income*, Cambridge, Cambridge University Press.

Bolle, F. (1998), 'Does Trust Pay?', European University Viadrina, Frankfurt (Oder), mimeo, August.

Bourdieu, P. (1993), 'Forms of Capital', in J. Richardson (ed.), *Handbook of Theory and Research in the Sociology of Education*, New York, Greenwood Press.

Coleman, J. (1988), 'Social Capital and the Creation of Human Capital', *American Journal of Sociology*, 94 (supplement), pp. 94-120.

Conradt, D. (1980), 'Changing German Political Culture', in G. Almond and S. Verba (eds), *The Civic Culture Re-Visited*, Boston, Little Brown, pp. 212 – 272.

Dasgupta, P. and Serageldin, I. (eds) (1999), *Social Capital. A Multifaceted Perspective*, Washington D.C., The World Bank.

Dic Lo (1995), *Economic Theory and the Transformation of the Soviet-Type System: The challenge of the late industrialisation perspective*, in Ha-Joon Chang and P. Nolan (eds), *The Transformation of the Communist Economies*, London, Macmillan.

Elster, J., Offe, C. and Preuss, K. (1998), *Institutional Design in Post-Communist Societies: Rebuilding the ship at open sea*, Cambridge, Cambridge University Press.

Fukuyama, F. (1995), *Trust. The social virtues and the creation of prosperity*, New York, Free Press.

Gati, C. (1996), 'The Mirage of Democracy', *Transition*, 22 March, pp. 6 – 12.

Greene, W. (2000), *Econometric Analysis*, Upper Saddle River, Prentice Hall.

Greif, A. (1994). 'Cultural Beliefs and the Organisation of Society: A historical and theoretical reflection on collectivist and individualist societies', *Journal of Political Economy*, 102(5), pp. 912-50.

Havel, V. (1989), *Living in Truth*, Boston, Faber and Faber.

Hayri, A. and McDermott, G. A. (1998), 'The Network Properties of Corporate Governance and Industrial Restructuring: A post-socialist lesson', *Industrial and Corporate Change* 7(1), pp. 153-193.

Hellman, J., et al. (2000a), 'Seize the State, Seize the Day: State capture, corruption and influence in transition', Washington D.C., The World Bank, mimeo, September.

Hellman, J., et al. (2000b), 'Measuring Governance and State Capture: The role of bureaucrats and firms in shaping the business environment', Washington D.C., World Bank Working Paper No. 2312.

Humphrey, J. and Schmitz, H. (1996), 'Trust and Economic Development', Brighton, Institute of Development Studies, Discussion Paper No. 355.

Knack, S. and Keefer, P. (1997), 'Does Social Capital Have an Economic Payoff? A Cross-Country Investigation', *The Quarterly Journal of Economics* Vol. CXII (December 98), pp. 1252-88.

Knack, S. and Zak, P. (1998), 'Trust and Growth', University of Maryland, mimeographed.

Kolankiewicz, G. (1996), 'Social Capital and Social Change', *British Journal of Sociology*, 47 (3), pp. 427-41.

Konrad, G. (1987), *Antipolitics*, New York, H. Holt.

Linz, J. and Stepan A. (1996), *Transition and Consolidation*, Baltimore, Johns Hopkins University Press.

Marody, M. (1997), 'Post-Transitology or is there any Life after Transition', *Polish Sociological Review* 117/1, pp. 13 – 21.

Matzner, E. (2000), *Monopolare Weltordnung*, Marburg, Metropolis.

Milanovic, B. (1998), 'Income, Inequality and Poverty during Transition from Planned to Market Economy', *World Bank Regional and Sectoral Studies*, Washington DC.

Nowotny, T. (1996), 'The Transition from Communism and the Spectre of Latin Americanisation', *East European Quarterly*, autumn 1994, pp. 69-91

Nowotny, T. (1998), *Central/Eastern Europe and Transitology*, Wien, ÖIIP.

Ockenfels, A. and Weimann, J. (1996), 'Types and Patterns: An experimental East-West comparison of co-operation and solidarity', Magdeburg, Otto-von-Guericke-Univerisity Magdeburg, Working Paper 11.

Olson, M. (1993), 'Dictatorship, Democracy and Development', *American Political Science Review*, September.

Platteau, J. P. (1994), 'Behind the Market Stage Where Real Societies Exist – Part II: Trust and generalised morality', *Journal of Development Studies* 30(4), pp. 754-817

Poppo, L. and Zenger, T. (2000), 'Substitutes or Complements? Exploring the Relationship between Formal Contracts and Relational Governance', John M. Olin School of Business, Washington University, St Louis, mimeo.

Przeworski, A. (1991), *Democracy and the Market*, New York, Cambridge University Press.

Putnam, R. D. (1993), *Making Democracy Work*, Princeton University Press.

Raiser, M. (1999), 'Trust in Transition', EBRD Working Paper, No. 39, London.

Rose R. (1995), 'Russia as an Hour-Glass Society: A constitution without citizens', *East European Constitutional Review*, 4 (3), pp. 34-42.

Rose, R. (1993), 'Rethinking Civil Society: Post-communism and the problem of trust', *Journal of Democracy* 1(1), pp. 18-29.

Rose, R. (1998), 'Getting Things Done with Social Capital: New Russia barometer VI', University of Strathclyde Studies in Public Policy, No. 303.

Rose, R., Mishler, W. and Haerpfer, C. (1997), '*Getting Real: Social capital in post-communist societies*', University of Strathclyde, Studies in Public Policy, No. 278.

Rose, R., Mishler, W. and Haerpfer, C. (1998), *Democracy and its Alternatives: Testing the Churchill hypothesis in post-communist countries*, Baltimore, Johns Hopkins University Press.

Ruffin, M. H. and Waugh, D. (eds) (1999), *Civil Society in Central Asia*, London and Seattle, Center for Civil Society International in association with University of Washington Press.

Schiff, M. (2000), 'Love thy Neighbour: Trade, migration and social capital', Development Research Group, Washington D.C., The World Bank, mimeo.

Schmitter, P. (1993), *Some Propositions about Civil Society and the Consolidation of Democracy*, Vienna, HIS.

Sedaitis, J. B. (1997), 'Network Dynamics of New Firm Foundation: Developing Russian Commodity Markets', in G. Grabher and D. Stark (eds), *Restructuring Networks in Post-Socialism: Legacies, linkages and localities*, Oxford, Oxford University Press.

Shleifer, A. (1997), 'Government in Transition', Cambridge MA, Harvard Institute for Economic Research, Discussion Paper 1783.

Smolar, A. (1996), 'Civil Society After Communism: From opposition to atomization', *Journal of Democracy* Vol. 4(1), pp. 24-38.

Stark, D. (1997), 'Recombinant Property in East European Capitalism', in G. Grabher and D. Stark (eds), *Restructuring Networks in Post-Socialism: Legacies, linkages, an localities*, Oxford, Oxford University Press.

Stiglitz, J. (1996), 'Some Lessons from the East Asian Miracle', the World Bank Research Observer, volume 2, August, pp. 151-77.

Stiglitz, J. (1999), 'Wither Reform?', Paper presented at the Annual Bank Conference on Development Economics, Washington D.C., April.

Surcke, M. (2000), 'The Quality and Size of Government in Transition Economies: Are they still different?', Hamburger Weltwirtschaftliches Archiv (HWWA), mimeo, August.

Tardos, R. (1998), 'Ways of Interpretation and the Uses of the Social Capital Concept', Paper presented at the INSA Sunbelt conference.

Wallace, C. (1998), 'Spending, Saving or Investing Social Capital: The case of shuttle traders in post-communist Central Europe', paper presented at the 5th International Conference on Social Networks, May 28-31, Spain.

Annex

Table A.12.1 Civic mindedness in transition

	Avoiding transport fare	Cheating on taxes	Buying stolen goods	Accepting bribes	Average index for 1995	Average index for 1990	Altruistic
Transition economies	*7.77*	*7.98*	*8.94*	*8.94*	*8.41*	*7.50*	*63.08*
Albania	8.85	8.68	8.58	8.58	8.67		52.99
Armenia	7.29	7.32	8.60	8.87	8.02		62.94
Azerbaijan	7.96	7.38	9.10	8.14	8.14		53.89
Belarus	6.90	7.60	9.24	8.96	8.17	8.31	73.66
Bulgaria	8.64	8.91	8.96	9.02	8.88	8.96	45.79
Croatia	6.12	7.33	8.64	8.88	7.74		70.29
Czech	7.79	8.02	8.35	8.72	8.22	2.18	69.53
Estonia	7.97	7.63	9.38	9.49	8.62	8.98	65.17
Georgia	8.10	8.09	8.71	9.09	8.50		51.75
Hungary	7.23	8.60	8.79	7.31	7.98	8.08	68.35
Latvia 90	6.87	7.42	8.83	9.01	8.04	8.81	76.86
Lithuania	7.88	7.87	9.20	9.05	8.50	8.86	77.87
Macedonia	8.60	8.65	9.37	9.58	9.05		52.63
Moldova	7.46	7.18	8.81	8.66	8.03		64.60
Poland	9.03	8.51	9.48	9.63	9.16	6.81	
Romania	8.89	8.74	9.08	9.21	8.98	8.98	61.93
Russia	6.96	7.75	9.52	9.48	8.43	8.82	76.07
Serbia+Montenegro	8.31	8.40	9.18	9.57	8.86		42.94
Slovakia	7.39	7.74	7.81	8.38	7.83	2.11	57.81
Slovenia	8.24	8.18	9.02	9.16	8.65	9.08	63.95
Ukraine	6.64	7.55	9.17	9.04	8.10		72.53
OECD	*8.74*	*8.67*	*9.34*	*9.51*	*9.07*	*8.97*	*68.74*
Turkey						9.57	
China	9.39	9.47	9.47	9.79	9.53	9.45	75.95
T-test: TEs vs. OECD *	*0.00*	*0.00*	*0.00*	*0.00*	*0.00*	*0.04*	*0.17*
Correlation with growth:							
cumulative growth 1989-98	*0.26*	*0.42*	*-0.15*	*-0.10*	*0.19*	*-0.50*	*0.15*
Correlation with Trust **							
TEs	*-0.38*	*-0.21*	*-0.41*	*-0.22*	*-0.42*	*-0.11*	*0.02*
NTEs	*-0.18*	*-0.44*	*0.06*	*-0.17*	*-0.25*	*0.46*	*-0.11*
All	*0.35*	*0.34*	*0.29*	*0.36*	*0.40*	*0.24*	*0.35*

Notes

The table reports mean scores over all respondents in each country. Respondents could choose scores between 1 (always) and 10 (never). The column 'altruistic' reports the percentage of respondents who say that they about others rather just themselves.

*T-test reports P-values for difference in means; 0.00 mean statistically significant at more than 1% level.

** Trust is measured as in Table 2.

Source: World Value Survey 1990, 1995.

Table A.12.2 Civic participation, 1990

	Share of active participants in institutions, %									Type I groups*	Type II groups**
	Church	Sports	Arts	Unions	Parties	Environment	Professional	Charity	Other		
Transition economies	*2.45*	*4.73*	*3.65*	*7.89*	*3.49*	*2.14*	*1.92*	*1.77*	*1.91*	*8.95*	*13.31*
Belarus											
Bulgaria	2.42	3.58	2.71	4.55	4.64	3.38	2.32	1.84	1.93	7.83	11.51
Czech											
Estonia	1.09	8.43	7.34	11.01	4.37	1.98	2.28	1.09	2.38	10.62	17.66
Hungary	2.60	1.70	1.90	4.60	1.20	1.30	1.60	1.70	0.80	6.01	7.41
Latvia	3.21	8.86	4.54	9.19	5.98	4.87	3.32	4.10	1.88	16.17	18.49
Lithuania	2.90	6.50	5.50	9.30	3.80	1.80	1.40	1.00	1.50	10.40	14.50
Poland											
Romania	4.35	2.72	1.45	14.14	2.18	0.91	1.45	1.81	1.81	8.88	17.77
Russia	0.97	3.06	2.60	8.62	4.54	1.43	0.87	1.27	2.35	5.30	14.02
Slovakia											
Slovenia	2.03	3.00	3.19	1.74	1.26	1.45	2.13	1.35	2.61	6.38	5.12
OECD	*7.06*	*8.71*	*5.41*	*2.69*	*4.13*	*1.77*	*3.39*	*5.07*	*3.87*	*20.36*	*10.21*
China	2.00	5.80	8.40	0.80	25.80	2.00	17.10	15.80	1.60	23.60	43.70
Turkey											
T-test: TEs vs. OECD***	0.00	0.01	0.04	0.00	0.33	0.25	0.07	0.00	0.00	0.00	0.15
Correlation with cumulative growth 1989-98	-0.02	-0.58	-0.41	-0.52	-0.83	-0.62	-0.45	-0.53	-0.51	-0.42	-0.73

Notes

* Type I is the sum of paricipants in Church, sport clubs ard charity organisations.

** Type II is the sum of participants in political parties, trace unions and professonal organisations.

***T-test reports P-values for difference in means; 0.00 mean statistically significant at more than 1% level.

Table A.12.3 Civic participation – public and private interest

	Discuss politics	*Correlation with*		Friends important	*Correlation with*	
		Putnam gr	Olson gr		Putnam gr.	Olson gr.
Transition economies	*16,16*	*0,01*	*0,05*	*35,35*	*0,03*	*-0,03*
Albania	19,63			19,14		
Armenia	22,08			44,65		
Azerbaijan	9,18			35,27		
Belarus	23,14			31,73		
Bulgaria	12,92			41,46		
Croatia	17,91			48,41		
Czech	16,73			38,65		
Estonia	15,17			26,89		
Georgia	17,90			67,84		
Hungary	17,03			38,33		
Latvia	17,60			24,29		
Lithuania	14,71			21,89		
Macedonia	15,31			49,64		
Moldova	18,01			21,39		
Poland	17,68			26,11		
Romania	16,78			20,76		
Russia	19,94			29,35		
Serbia + Montenegro	12,73			48,28		
Slovakia	13,33			32,26		
Slovenia	9,15			41,14		
Ukraine	12,51			34,99		
OECD	*15,12*	*0,48*	*0,39*	*56,79*	*0,56*	*0,75*
China	15,29			29,91		
Turkey	17,54			70,47		

Source: World Values Survey, 1995.

Table A.12.4 Trust in formal institutions, 1990

	Confidence in institutions										
	Church	Army	Legal System	Press	Unions	Police	Government	Parliament	Civil Service	Companies	European Union
Transition Economies	*2.63*	*2.46*	*2.38*	*2.41*	*2.09*	*2.21*	*1.97*	*2.47*	*2.33*	*2.18*	*2.58*
Belarus	2.64	2.77	2.11	2.15	2.04	1.99	2.00	2.18	1.94	2.29	
Bulgaria	2.03	2.84	2.43	2.27	2.16	2.45	2.09	2.48	2.14	2.22	2.48
Czech	2.24	2.27	2.40	2.39	2.06	2.21	2.44	2.43	2.22	2.06	2.80
Estonia	2.57	1.84	2.23	2.70	2.11	1.93	1.70	2.81	2.35	1.85	
Hungary	2.61	2.52	2.65	2.28	2.05	2.50		2.27	2.45	2.18	2.68
Latvia	2.71	1.83	2.27	2.68	2.00	1.92	1.73	2.97	2.26	1.68	
Lithuania	2.85	1.93	2.35	2.68	2.14	2.19	1.76	2.69	2.50	1.91	
Poland	3.33	2.78	2.48	2.49	1.91	2.08	1.41	3.02	3.07	2.95	
Romania	3.05	3.17	2.50	2.11	2.13	2.40		1.89	2.13	2.22	2.59
Russia	2.76	2.93	2.32	2.41	2.38	2.22	2.37	2.39	2.43	2.37	2.59
Slovakia	2.48	2.27	2.32	2.26	2.02	2.08	2.19	2.21	2.18	2.13	2.51
Slovenia	2.30	2.35	2.53	2.51	2.08	2.51		2.26	2.36	2.24	2.45
OECD	*2.50*	*2.46*	*2.60*	*2.29*	*2.27*	*2.82*	*2.29*	*2.36*	*2.38*	*2.45*	*2.53*
China	1.32	3.33	3.07	2.61	2.37	2.80	3.12	3.25	2.67	2.29	2.12
Turkey	2.92	3.48	2.81	2.39	2.35	2.78	2.44	2.67	2.56	2.12	2.21
*T-test TEs vs. OECD countries**	*0.16*	*0.49*	*0.00*	*0.75*	*0.00*	*0.00*	*0.11*	*0.17*	*0.32*	*0.01*	*0.22*

Notes

*T-test reports P-values for difference in means; 0.00 mean statistically significant at more than 1% level.

Source: World Value Survey 1990.

Name Index

Subject Index

For Product Safety Concerns and Information please contact our
EU representative GPSR@taylorandfrancis.com Taylor & Francis
Verlag GmbH, Kaufingerstraße 24, 80331 München, Germany